ECONOMIC
LIBERTIES
AND THE
JUDICIARY

*Copublished by the
Cato Institute*

ECONOMIC LIBERTIES AND THE JUDICIARY

Edited by
James A. Dorn
and
Henry G. Manne

George Mason University Press
Fairfax, Virginia

**Copyright © 1987 by
The Cato Institute**

George Mason University Press
4400 University Drive
Fairfax, VA 22030

Printed in the United States of America

Distributed by arrangement with
University Publishing Associates, Inc.

4720 Boston Way
Lanham, MD 20706

3 Henrietta Street
London WC2E 8LU England

Library of Congress Cataloging -in-Publication Data

Economic liberties and the judiciary.

Includes indexes.
1. Right of property-United States. 2. Judicial
process-United States. 3. Civil rights-United
States. I. Dorn, James A. II. Manne, Henry G.
KF561.E25   1987   343.73'07   87-8574
                                347.3037
ISBN 0-8026-0013-1 (alk. paper)
ISBN 0-8026-0014-X (pbk. alk. paper)

Cover design: Holly Klaine

All George Mason University Press books are produced on acid-free
paper which exceeds the minimum standards set by the National
Historical Publications and Records Commission.

To Jan Tumlir

CONTENTS

FOREWORD

THE JUDICIARY AND THE CONSTITUTION
Alex Kozinski

We are in the midst of a very important phenomenon in jurisprudence: the emergence of a new school of thought. For the first time
in a generation, legal scholars are mounting a serious challenge to
the jurisprudential approach that has dominated American legal
thinking since the New Deal. The articles in this volume are at the
forefront of this challenge, providing a reassessment of attitudes that
have long dominated constitutional law. In response, disciples of the
current doctrine have been forced to defend positions that for years
were accepted on faith. And defend they have, frequently revealing
a good deal about the premises underlying their thinking.

What many consider to be the most important response to the
challenge is Justice William Brennan's speech titled "The Constitution of the United States: Contemporary Ratification," given at
Georgetown University in 1985.[1] Justice Brennan's views of how the
Constitution should be interpreted are at the center of a very important debate over the role judges should play in constitutional adjudication. What is perhaps most fascinating about Justice Brennan's
speech is the rationale he gives for his noninterpretivist approach to
the Constitution. It provides important evidence as to the linkage
between the erosion of economic liberties and departure from other
constitutional values. If Justice Brennan's speech actually reflects
the prevailing jurisprudence—and there is every reason to believe
it does—this renders the essays in this volume timely indeed.

On reading Justice Brennan's speech, one is surprised to find a
single idea repeated again and again. This is the concept defined by

---

The author is Circuit Judge for the U.S. Court of Appeals for the Ninth Circuit in
Los Angeles. He formerly served as Chief Judge for the United States Claims Court in
Washington, D.C.
[1]William J. Brennan, Jr., "The Constitution of the United States: Contemporary Ratification." Speech at Georgetown University, Washington, D.C., 12 October 1985, p. 8.

the term "dignity." In various configurations, such as "human dignity," "fundamental dignity," or just plain "dignity," the expression appears no fewer than 35 times. According to Justice Brennan, "The Constitution is a sublime oration on the dignity of man, a bold commitment by a people to the ideal of libertarian dignity protected through law," and "a sparkling vision of the supremacy of the human dignity of every individual."[2]

Although the term "dignity" appears nowhere in the Constitution, Justice Brennan uses it to justify sweeping departures from the constitutional text. The way Justice Brennan derives the concept of human dignity and the way he applies it in interpreting the Constitution provide an illustration of how we have come so far from the text of the document in so short a time.

Justice Brennan notes that things have changed since the Constitution was drafted. At that time, freedom and dignity "found meaningful protection in the institution of real property." In those distant days, "property relationships formed the heart of litigation and of legal practice, and lawyers and judges tended to think stable property relationships the highest aim of the law."[3]

But those days are forever gone Justice Brennan assures us:

> To a growing extent economic existence now depends on less certain relationships with government—licenses, employment, contracts, subsidies, unemployment benefits, tax exemptions, welfare and the like. . . . Government participation in the economic existence of individuals is pervasive and deep. Administrative matters and other dealings with government are at the epicenter of the exploding law. We turn to government and to the law for controls which would never have been expected or tolerated before this century.

Justice Brennan recognizes the danger of allowing unbridled expansion of governmental power. He notes that "[t]he possibilities for collision between government activity and individual rights will increase as the power and authority of government itself expands, and this growth, in turn, heightens the need for constant vigilance at the collision points."[4]

For someone like me, who is firmly committed to the concept of individual freedom and highly suspicious of government power, it is difficult to disagree with Justice Brennan's conclusion, given his premises. If government is going to have free rein to meddle into

---

[2]Ibid., p. 9.
[3]Ibid.
[4]Ibid.

every aspect of our existence, I, too, favor strict controls on the way it does this.

But Justice Brennan and I part company on a very basic assumption. In his view, government control over people's lives is unavoidable: "The modern activist state is a concomitant of the complexity of modern society; it is inevitably with us."[5]

It is this aspect of Justice Brennan's analysis that is the cause for the greatest alarm, but it also provides the opportunity for the most thorough reassessment of jurisprudential attitudes toward economic regulation. Rather than accepting "the modern activist state" as a given and quibbling over how much "human dignity" we can squeeze out of the remaining portions of the Constitution, we might question whether we have not taken a wrong turn somewhere and yielded to the state too much power over our lives.

Justice Brennan is quite accurate in noting that ownership of property is an aspect of human dignity and autonomy, although he inexplicably limits the concept to real property. There can be no serious suggestion, however, that rights in real property have a different status under the Constitution than rights in personal or intellectual property. Moreover, one can dismiss as silly the anthropomorphic notion, popular among college students and law professors until recently, that property rights should be subordinated to human rights, as if property can have rights. As Wesley J. Liebeler cogently notes in his essay, the concept of property rights need not be limited to possession of tangible items, but rather can be viewed more expansively as extending generally to relationships among people. As such, the concept is applicable to control over land, goodwill, and, under some circumstances, even to communications.

For the last 50 years or so, however, courts have tended to treat certain rights differently from others. Those rights that have been classified as fundamental or human rights have been given preferred treatment. Among them are rights to speech, religion, travel, and privacy, and a variety of rights pertaining to arrest, conviction, and punishment.

Other rights, even where specifically articulated in the Constitution, have been disfavored. Government has been given a free hand to create, destroy, and adjust individual rights in the economic sphere. For example, a law forbidding Penn Central from constructing an office building over Grand Central Terminal was upheld against a taking claim,[6] and land use regulations that diminish property value

[5]Ibid., p. 10.
[6]Penn Central Transp. Co. v. New York City, 438 U.S. 104 (1978).

by 75 percent,[7] 90 percent,[8] and even 95 percent[9] have been found not to amount to takings under the Fifth Amendment. Ellen Frankel Paul points out in her essay that the public use restraint on taking private property by eminent domain has all but vanished under recent Supreme Court interpretation. Simon Rottenberg provides further examples of how property rights have been given short shrift in the courts in his discussion of judicial interference with contractually agreed upon creditor remedies.

While summarily upholding laws that drastically curtail property rights, the courts give laws infringing personal rights close and pains-taking scrutiny. The right to display obscene words on your jacket[10] or shout them at police officers[11] is constitutionally protected. A jailer who cuts a prisoner's hair too short before release commits a consti-tutional offense,[12] and male prisoners have a constitutional right not to be supervised by female prison guards when taking showers.[13]

Someone unfamiliar with the text of the Constitution reading some of these decisions would naturally assume that the Constitution is replete with references to such things as what obscene words one can display and the amenities one must provide prisoners. But one would be certain that the Constitution has little or nothing to say about property. Similarly, if one knew nothing about the Founding Fathers, one would guess that they had a deep suspicion of govern-ment when it came to personal rights but were entirely sanguine about majority rule in matters of economics.

The text of the Constitution and the historical record conclusively refute these notions. The Constitution, as amended by the Bill of Rights, shows much solicitude toward the individual. It certainly safeguards his right to speak, pray, and be secure from unwarranted government intrusion into his home. But it shows at least equal concern for the individual's right to the fruits of his endeavors: the Fifth Amendment prohibits the taking of property without due pro-cess or just compensation; even with just compensation, property may only be taken for a public purpose. Article I, section 10 forbids the states from interfering with contracts. The Third Amendment prohibits quartering of soldiers in private homes during peacetime.

---

[7]Village of Euclid v. Ambler Realty Co., 272 U.S. 365 (1926).

[8]Hadacheck v. Sebastian, 239 U.S. 394 (1915).

[9]Giuliano v. Town of Edgartown, 531 F. Supp. 1076 (D. Mass. 1982).

[10]Cohen v. California, 403 U.S. 15 (1971).

[11]Lewis v. New Orleans, 408 U.S. 913 (1972); Brown v. Oklahoma, 408 U.S. 914 (1972).

[12]Carter v. Noble, 526 F.2d 677 (5th Cir. 1976).

[13]Hudson v. Goodlander, 494 F. Supp. 890 (D.C. Md. 1980).

Bernard Siegan, in his essay, points out that "economic liberties [were] firmly rooted in the due process clause of the Fourteenth Amendment," for the purpose of protecting property rights from unrestrained state regulations.

Moreover, the entire document reflects deep concern about the excesses of governmental power and the unbridled will of the majority. The federal government is limited to functioning in certain specified areas, and its actions are constrained by internal checks and balances. The power of the states is limited by the supremacy clause; the Ninth Amendment declares that enumeration of certain rights shall not be construed to deny or disparage others retained by the people.

Nor can it be seriously disputed that the Founding Fathers were men to whom property was important and who were intensely aware of the need to safeguard property rights from majoritarian abuse. As Richard Epstein points out in his recent work on takings, the Framers were deeply influenced by natural rights thinkers such as Locke and Montesquieu. They were well aware that government, as the holder of a monopoly on the lawful use of force, can be used to siphon off the property of some for the benefit of others.[14]

The suspicion of unchecked governmental power, and the excesses to which it could lead, created a heavy presumption against laws that restricted individual rights, whether they involved liberty or property. While the courts were not always consistent, Siegan has demonstrated that for the first century and a half after ratification there was considerable judicial oversight of legislative enactments that impaired property interests.[15]

These early judicial decisions were based on principles that were antimajoritarian and antidemocratic, much as the Constitution itself. They were based also on the idea that the interests of society are best served by protecting the rights of the individual. As Justice George Sutherland stated in *Adkins v. Children's Hospital*, in the waning days of the substantive due process era, "[t]o sustain the individual freedom of action contemplated by the Constitution is not to strike down the common good but to exalt it; for surely the good of society as a whole cannot be better served than by the preservation against arbitrary restraint of the liberties of its constituent members."[16]

---

[14]Richard A. Epstein, *Takings: Private Property and the Power of Eminent Domain* (Cambridge: Harvard University Press, 1985), ch. 2.

[15]Bernard H. Siegan, *Economic Liberties and the Constitution* (Chicago: University of Chicago Press, 1980).

[16]Adkins v. Children's Hospital, 261 U.S. 525, 561 (1922), overruled in West Coast Hotel Co. v. Parrish, 300 U.S. 379 (1937).

To be sure, this view was not universally shared. And the degree of scrutiny over economic regulation has varied from time to time according to the issues presented and the composition of the Supreme Court. Yet, until this century there was a commonly shared belief that individual rights were cut from a single cloth and that whatever power government had to limit those rights applied more or less equally to all. I find significant, for example, Justice Brennan's observation that as late as 1922 the only portion of the Bill of Rights that had been held applicable to the states was the Fifth Amendment's guarantee of just compensation for official takings.[17]

This century brought a different view, leading to the deconstitutionalization of economic rights. The reason Justice Brennan gives for this is that "the modern activist state is a concomitant of the complexity of modern society."[18] The idea seems to be that things have gotten so complicated that "common law property relationships" are no longer adequate to govern the intricacies of modern life. I can see at least three problems with this view.

First, property rights, that is, the legal relationships between people pertaining to the use and enjoyment of property, become more important as resources grow scarcer and society more complex. Metes and bounds may suffice to separate adjoining farms, but city lots are measured in feet and inches; land is leased by the decade, computer time by the micro-second. Complexity calls for more certainty and precision in defining legal relationships, not less.

Second, the substitute for precisely defined property rights is an increase in the scope and power of government. As Justice Brennan recognizes, this increases "[t]he possibilities for collision between government activity and individual rights." This, in turn, "requires a much-modified view of the proper relationship of individual and state."[19] In other words, we must rewrite the Constitution to give the government wider discretion, and then rewrite it again to give people a renewed sense of dignity. The spiral is endless.

Finally, individual rights simply are not divisible or fungible. As F. A. Hayek says, "The importance of freedom . . . does not depend on the elevated character of the activities it makes possible. Freedom of action, even in humble things, is as important as freedom of thought."[20]

---

[17]Brennan, "The Constitution," p. 11.

[18]Ibid., p. 10.

[19]Ibid.

[20]F. A. Hayek, *The Constitution of Liberty* (Chicago: University of Chicago Press, 1960), p. 35.

I would be the last to denigrate the importance of freedom of speech and religion, the right to participate fully in the political process, or the right to be free from arbitrary arrest, conviction, and punishment. But it is not clear to me that these rights are any more important than rights pertaining to property. I can certainly conceive of rational people who, if pressed to a choice, would be willing to give up the right to wear a jacket with obscene words on it in order to retain the right to construct a building or run a railroad.

Economic rights are not only a crucial component of individual liberty, but an important check on governmental power. In *Capitalism and Freedom*, Milton Friedman notes as follows:

> [E]conomic arrangements are important because of their effect on the concentration or dispersion of power. The kind of economic organization that provides economic freedom directly, namely competitive capitalism, also promotes political freedom because it separates economic power from political power and in this way enables the one to offset the other.
>
> Historical evidence speaks with a single voice on the relation between political freedom and a free market. I know of no example in time or place of a society that has been marked by a large measure of political freedom, and that has not also used something comparable to a free market to organize the bulk of economic activity.[21]

To simply accept, as Justice Brennan does, that "government participation in the economic existence of individuals is pervasive and deep," and likely to get deeper still, can only lead to an erosion of constitutional values and endanger the system that served us well for most of our existence as a nation.

Just as individual rights are not divisible, so too the Constitution must be viewed as an integral whole. When a portion of it is ignored or abused, this tends to throw the entire system out of balance, with significant repercussions.

The danger signals are clear. The most important is the one so candidly articulated by Justice Brennan—the perceived need to create new constitutional rights to make up for those we lose when government intrudes into every aspect of our lives. This gives judges a roving commission continuously to rewrite the Constitution in the guise of upholding human dignity, further destabilizing the constitutional process.

There are other danger signals as well. Since the 1930s there has been a proliferation of regulatory agencies at both the state and federal levels. It sometimes seems like the only free competition left

[21]Milton Friedman, *Capitalism and Freedom* (Chicago: University of Chicago Press, 1962), p. 9.

in our economy is between government agencies as to which can grab the most power. James Miller, Robert Tollison, and Henry Manne, in their essays, articulate some of the costs of this trend: decreased regulatory efficiency, market disruptions due to lack of predictability and the loss of civil liberties.

Another sign of distress is the massive increase in litigation, what Justice Brennan calls "the exploding law."[22] An alarming proportion of our productive resources is now devoted to fighting each other and our government. It is also no accident, I think, that significant peacetime budget deficits first began appearing in the mid-1930s, about the time that judicial control over government intrusions into the economy began to disappear. Epstein points out that our Constitution reflects a general distrust of the political process. It may be that entrusting elected officials with unrestrained authority to shuttle economic resources between different individuals, regions and interest groups is a power that is not capable of containment. Much as the Framers feared, the temptation to serve the interests of faction, at the expense of the whole, may simply be too great. Perhaps, as Roger Pilon notes in his essay, by being "[u]nable to discern that due process of law is ineluctably substantive and that all the rights we have are there to be drawn from the Constitution, [the courts] have turned over to the legislature—the domain of interest and will—what was properly theirs to perform in the domain of reason."

These are difficult questions, and the answers are neither simple nor immediately apparent. My friend and esteemed colleague, Justice Brennan, has lived longer and seen far more constitutional adjudication than I have. He may be right in both his premises and his conclusions. But it is our duty not to accept without question what may be serious and irreversible changes in our system of checks and balances. It is important to challenge the assumptions of the modern activist state before we abandon ourselves and our lives to it. The New Deal, and the case law that supports it, is itself an experiment of relatively recent origin. The time has come to assess where we stand and, if necessary, to change direction, slowly and cautiously, but without fear.

The importance of a volume such as this, with its ground-breaking essays, is that it provides a forum for raising these ideas and creating what Justice Antonin Scalia calls "a constitutional ethos of economic liberty." It is difficult to imagine a work better suited to this important purpose or published in a timelier fashion.

---

[22]Brennan, "The Constitution," p. 9.

EDITORS' PREFACE

The debate over constitutional interpretation and the role of the judiciary has focused primarily on the clash between the liberals' view of judicial activism and the conservatives' stand on judicial restraint. Justice William J. Brennan Jr. has been the most outspoken proponent of judicial activism, advocating a "living constitution" and judicial policymaking to ensure social justice and equality. On the side of the conservatives, Attorney General Edwin Meese III has been joined by Chief Justice William H. Rehnquist, Associate Justice Antonin Scalia, and Judge Robert H. Bork to counter Justice Brennan and argue for a "jurisprudence of original intention."

More recently, however, a third approach to constitutional interpretation has emerged, namely, a *principled* judicial activism. Proponents of this approach, such as Richard Epstein, Stephen Macedo, and Bernard Siegan, view the Constitution not primarily as a blueprint for majoritarian democracy but as a charter for limited government and individual rights. The function of the judiciary, in their view, is to act as the "final arbiter" in protecting fundamental rights to "life, liberty, and property."[1] As a balanced approach, principled judicial activism seeks to avoid the judicial overreaching of modern liberals and the dangers to economic and noneconomic rights posed by the "New Right's jurisprudence," as Macedo has dubbed the conservative position.[2]

Principled judicial activism places individual rights and limited government at the forefront of the constitutional debate and seeks to restore property rights to the central position they held in the Founders' Constitution. Under this approach to constitutional interpretation emphasis is placed on the text and structure of the Constitution— viewed within a natural rights framework—rather than on the pref-

[1]See, in particular, Bernard Siegan, "The Supreme Court: The Final Arbiter," in *Beyond the Status Quo*, ed. David Boaz and Edward H. Crane (Washington, D.C.: Cato Institute, 1985), pp. 273–90.

[2]Stephen Macedo, *The New Right v. The Constitution* (Washington, D.C.: Cato Institute, 1986), p. 1.

erences of judges or the power of majorities. Moreover, under a principled activism the false dichotomy between economic rights and so-called fundamental rights (such as freedom of speech) would end. Both economic and noneconomic rights would be protected from legislative abuse by a vigilant judiciary. This, of course, does not mean that the Court would be allowed to interfere with the law-making process itself. The Court would not make the law; it would only review it for its consistency with the rights of persons and property—rights the Founders sought to protect under the doctrine of limited government.

The principled judicial activism proposed by Epstein, Macedo, Siegan, and others in this volume differs fundamentally from the activism proposed by modern liberals. It rejects the liberals' assumption of benevolent government and tends to see the political branches as constantly threatening property rights and individual freedom. Principled judicial activists adopt the classical libertarian position and argue that if the judiciary stands still in the face of substantial government takings—ranging from outright redistribution to indirect takings through economic regulation—no one's rights will be safe, and justice will be ill-served.

The rise of the modern redistributive state and the intensification of rent seeking can be traced to the demise of substantive due process in reviewing social and economic legislation. The late economist Jan Tumlir recognized this when he wrote: "If we are to explain the rise of rent seeking to a dominant form of democratic politics, we must focus on the change in constitutional interpretation."[3] The undermining of private property rights and freedom of contract dates to *Munn v. Illinois* (1877), and perhaps even earlier, but it was only with *Nebbia v. New York* (1934), *West Coast Hotel v. Parrish* (1937), and *United States v. Carolene Products Co.* (1938) that the Court's role in protecting property rights and economic liberties against legislative abuse effectively came to an end. Along with the Court's decision in *United States v. Butler* (1936), which removed the constraint on direct federal transfers (under Article I, section 8), these decisions permitted the emergence of the modern welfare state.[4]

Public choice theory and experience teach us to be on guard against well-meaning public officials. The lack of private property rights within the public sector generates an incentive structure that

---

[3]Jan Tumlir, *Protectionism: Trade Policy in Democratic Societies* (Washington, D.C.: American Enterprise Institute, 1985), p. 14.
[4]See James A. Dorn, "The Transfer Society," Introduction to *Cato Journal* 6 (Spring/ Summer 1986): 1–17.

is unlikely to constrain the process of redistribution and rent seeking that characterizes a majoritarian political system. The Founders recognized the "problem of the commons" and the potential for rent seeking under democratic politics. That is why they favored a *constitutional* democracy. They also believed on moral grounds that rights exist prior to government and that it is the duty of government to protect basic rights. However, the constitutional anchor to secure economic and noneconomic rights was given to the judicial branch rather than the political branches.

The Founders never intended to leave the substance of individual rights to the democratic process. The legislature, said Thomas Jefferson, "can neither pass a law that my head shall be stricken from my body without trial, nor my freehold taken from me without indemnification, and when not necessary for public use."[5] Yet, in recent Supreme Court cases such as *Hawaii Housing Authority v. Midkiff* (1984) constitutional principles were turned upside down. The Court accepted *carte blanche* the legislature's rationale for attenuating private property rights, while the express language of the Fifth and Fourteenth Amendments apparently went unnoticed. A vague "public interest" rather than the safeguarding of private rights guided the Court's decision.

The essays in this volume reconsider the case for judicial protection of economic liberties and point to the interconnectedness of all rights. The right to hold, use, and transfer property is an important component of liberty and helps protect individuals against the redistributive state. Essentially, the property right is a civil right and deserves to be respected by intelligent liberals as well as conservatives.

By challenging both the liberal and conservative approaches to constitutional interpretation, the principled judicial activism advocated by many of the authors in this volume avoids the pitfalls of both the liberals' mistaken judicial activism and the New Right's judicial restraint. The implications for economic liberties when the courts fail to protect rights to property and freedom of contract are carefully examined, as are the adverse effects of interfering with the competitive market process.

The major question addressed in this volume is whether the judiciary will restore its protection of economic liberties—as intended by the Framers—or continue to allow majoritarianism to subvert the freedom of individuals to determine the uses of their land, labor, and

[5]Letter to James Monroe, 8 January 1811. In *The Writings of Thomas Jefferson*, Library Edition, vol. 19, ed. Andrew A. Lipscomb (Washington, D.C.: The Thomas Jefferson Memorial Association, 1903), pp. 181–82.

capital and to freely carry out mutually beneficial exchanges. The central issue is, according to Gordon Crovitz of the *Wall Street Journal:* "whether the Rehnquist Court, perhaps led by Justice Antonin Scalia, will resurrect these [economic] rights or leave the task for another day and another court. . . . There is no turning back the clock to before the New Deal. But this does not mean economic rights are dead. They are still inscribed in the Constitution."[6]

Most of the articles in this volume appeared in the Winter 1985 *Cato Journal* (vol. 4, no. 3), which was based on the Cato Institute's conference "Economic Liberties and the Judiciary" (held in Washington, D.C., October 26, 1984). New material includes Judge Kozinski's Foreword, the articles by Doug Bandow and Stephen Macedo, and the comments by Charles Rowley and Nicholas Wolfson. The Introduction has been substantially revised for the book and there have been some minor revisions in Randy Barnett's article.

In preparing the volume for publication, special thanks go to Ed Crane, Roger Pilon, and Bernard Siegan for their initial encouragement and continual support. Marianne Keddington and Janet Rumbarger's assistance during the copyediting and proofreading stages is gratefully acknowledged, as is the assistance of Vernon Gras and Mark Carroll of the George Mason University Press. Thanks also go to David Lampo and Holly Klaine for their help in bringing the book to fruition. Our deepest gratitude, however, is to the Cato Institute for funding the conference upon which this volume is largely based and for the important role it has taken in generating renewed interest in the role of the judiciary and economic liberties.

[6]Gordon Crovitz, "Is the New Deal Unconstitutional?" *Wall Street Journal* (13 January 1986): 24.

1

INTRODUCTION
JUDICIAL PROTECTION OF ECONOMIC LIBERTIES
James A. Dorn

> That government can scarcely be deemed to be free, where the rights of property are left solely dependent upon the will of a legislative body, without any restraint. The fundamental maxims of a free government seem to require, that the rights of personal liberty and private property should be held sacred.
>
> —Justice Story[1]

Constitutional Principles and the Judiciary

The publication of Bernard H. Siegan's *Economic Liberties and the Constitution* in 1980 marked a resurgence of interest in the constitutional basis for judicial protection of economic liberties. Siegan explored the background of the U.S. Constitution and found overwhelming evidence that the Framers envisioned the Constitution and judiciary as safeguards against the attenuation of private property rights by the political branches. The Framers never believed that there should be unrestrained majority rule or that special interests should usurp the right to private property that lies at the heart of the Constitution, however silent the document itself may be on the precise nature of "the property right."[2]

The author is Editor of the Cato Journal *and Associate Professor of Economics at Towson State University. He is also a Research Fellow of the Institute for Humane Studies at George Mason University.*

[1]Wilkinson v. Leland, 27 U.S. (2 Pet.) 627, 657 (1829).

[2]See Siegan (1980, ch. 4, "The Judicial Obligation to Protect Economic Liberties"). In his 1985 essay "The Supreme Court: The Final Arbiter," Siegan expands on his 1980 book. He emphasizes that when judicial review is seen in its proper historical context, it becomes clear that the Framers intended the Court to protect the "liberties of the people by annulling laws that violated them, even though those liberties might not be specified" (p. 274). To do this, "the Court would have to invoke the common law" (p. 274), which "was dedicated to the rule of 'right and reason' " (p. 275). Siegan concludes that "although few liberties were enumerated in the original U.S. Constitution, a large measure of freedom was retained by the people, to be safeguarded by the judiciary" (p. 276).

According to Siegan, the Framers made no distinction between property rights and human rights or between economic liberties and other liberties. "The most important civil rights," says Siegan (1985, p. 289), "were those of life, liberty, and property." Moreover, an exhaustive review of the background materials to the Constitution indicates that "The Framers expected the federal judiciary to exercise judicial review insofar as civil liberties were concerned, primarily to secure property and other economic interests" (Siegan 1980, p. 318).

Richard Epstein's recent book, *Takings: Private Property and the Power of Eminent Domain* (1985a), lends support to Siegan's work. In particular, Epstein presents a rigorous argument for greater judicial intervention to protect economic liberties—that is, to protect against the forced takings of private property and the attenuation of freedom of contract. Like Siegan, he bases his argument for substantive economic due process on the theory of limited government embraced by the Framers and on a reading of the constitutional text within the natural rights framework of the time.

Today's legal positivism differs sharply from the Framers' natural rights conception of government and the judiciary. As the Declaration of Independence makes clear, the Founding Fathers who shaped the Constitution were classical liberals; they viewed life, liberty, *and property* as inalienable rights that preexist the written law or positive legislation. Thus, Siegan (1985, pp. 275–76) tells us: "When the Constitution was framed, the [common law] system was highly regarded as a guardian of individual rights, and many Americans equated common law with natural law. For them, the unwritten English Constitution, which consisted principally of common law rights, provided the greatest measure of human freedom."

For the classical liberal, justice was a negative concept—the absence of injustice—and injustice referred to the illegitimate use of force; namely, the use of force to take what belongs to another. The Framers used this negative concept of justice to limit the role of government and the judiciary to the protection of property rights, broadly conceived (in the Lockean tradition) as life, liberty, and property. The object of the law was not to give an exhaustive listing of what government could do, but to delimit the activities of government so that individual freedom could be maximized.

Under the negative concept of justice, there is no dichotomy between justice and individual freedom or between property rights and personal rights. Economic liberties are viewed as a fundamental component of civil liberties with equal protection under the Constitution. The "law of liberty," in F.A. Hayek's view, is incompatible with an affirmative view of justice; if the state pursues "social justice" by taking private property , it cannot at the same time protect individual freedom.[3]

Perhaps the clearest evidence to be found of the Framers' view that property preexists legislation and is an inherent right of every citizen is James Madison's essay on property.[4] According to Madison (1792, p. 174), the term "property" can be understood in both a narrow and a broad sense:

> This term [property] in its particular application means "that dominion which one man claims and exercises over the external things of the world, in exclusion of every other individual." In its larger and juster meaning, it embraces every thing to which a man may attach a value and have a right; and *which leaves to every one else the like advantage.* In the former sense, a man's land, or merchandise, or money is called his property. In the latter sense, a man has a property in his opinions and the free communication of them. He has a property of peculiar value in his religious opinions, and in the profession and practice dictated by them. He has a property very dear to him in the safety and liberty of his person. He has an equal property in the free use of his faculties, and free choice of the objects on which to employ them. In a word, as a man is said to have a right to his property, he may be equally said to have a property in his rights.[5]

Madison's acceptance of the negative concept of justice and the priority he gave to property rights over legislation or written law led him to argue for limited government (1792, p. 174):

> Government is instituted to protect property of every sort; as well that which lies in the various rights of individuals, as that which the term particularly expresses. This being the end of government, that alone is a *just* government, which *impartially* secures to every man, whatever is his *own.*

---

[3]See Hayek (1960, 1982, chaps. 5, 8–9). According to Hayek (1982, ch. 8, p. 34): "the loss of the belief in a law which serves justice [in the negative sense of this term] and not particular interests (or particular ends of government) is largely responsible for the progressive undermining of individual freedom." On the idea that the role of the judiciary is to protect property rights so that a spontaneous market order can arise, see Hayek (1982, ch. 5, especially the section entitled, "The function of the judge is confined to a spontaneous order," pp. 118–22).

[4]Madison's essay "Property" was written for the *National Gazette,* which was published by his friend Philip Freneau in Philadelphia. The original essay is unsigned but has been attributed to Madison and is contained in Volume 4 of *Letters and Other Writings of James Madison* (1865, pp. 478–80).

[5]The last sentence of this quotation can be found in the memorial room of the James Madison Library of Congress, inscribed on the wall immediately to the right of Madison's imposing figure. It is a reminder of the importance Madison placed on private property rights.

When the government goes beyond its legitimate role of protecting property rights, of protecting what is an individual's own, it becomes unjust. The focus of the Framers was on the *prevention* of injustice—the violation of property rights, broadly conceived—not on the pursuit of "social justice." Madison stated (1792, p. 174):

> That is not a just government, nor is property secure under it, where arbitrary restrictions, exemptions, and monopolies deny to part of its citizens that free use of their faculties, and free choice of their occupations, which not only constitute their property in the general sense of the word; but are the means of acquiring property strictly so called.

Further evidence that Madison held freedom of contract and other economic liberties in high esteem is provided by the following passage (1792, p. 175):

> If there be a government then which prides itself in maintaining the inviolability of property; which provides that none shall be taken *directly* even for public use without indemnification to the owner, and yet *directly* violates the property which individuals have in their opinions, their religions, their persons, and their faculties; nay more, which *indirectly* violates their property in their actual possessions, in the labor that acquires their daily subsistence, and in the hallowed remnant of time which ought to relieve their fatigues and soothe their cares, the influence will have been anticipated, that such a government is not a pattern for the United States.
>
> If the United States mean to obtain or deserve the full praise due to wise and just governments, they will equally respect the rights of property, and the property in rights.

From 1897 through 1936, the Supreme Court largely followed the Madisonian tradition and provided substantial protection for property rights and economic liberties, considering them inviolable except in rare cases. During this period, accordingly, the Court concerned itself as well with the legitimacy of legislative ends. These concerns are evident in numerous Court opinions upholding basic economic rights.

The most famous such case is probably *Lochner v. New York*, declaring unconstitutional a New York State statute that set maximum hours for bakery workers.[6] Justice Peckham's majority decision in *Lochner* reflects the principled approach to judicial review that characterized much of the substantive economic due process era: "The [legislative] act must have a . . . direct relation, as a means to an end, *and the end itself must be appropriate and legitimate,* before an act

---

[6]Lochner v. New York, 198 U.S. 45 (1905). See Siegan (1980, ch. 5) for a discussion of the history surrounding this case.

can be held to be valid which interferes with the general right of an individual to be free in his person and in his power to contract in relation to his own labor."[7]

The Demise of Economic Due Process

The demise of economic due process began in earnest in the late 1930s, as the Supreme Court decided not to give property rights and economic liberties the same protection as so-called fundamental rights and civil liberties. With this judicially created distinction in hand, argues Siegan (1985, p. 287), "legislatures have great difficulty in restraining freedom of speech or press, and almost none in curtailing freedom of enterprise."

The Court formally terminated substantive due process in reviewing economic legislation in 1937, with the decision rendered in *West Coast Hotel Co. v. Parrish*.[8] From that time forward the eyes of the judiciary have largely been closed to legislative takings, either directly via tax and transfer programs or indirectly via regulation. Likewise, the ears of the Court have largely been closed to the words of the Founders, as echoed in Justice McReynold's dissenting opinion in *Nebbia v. New York*: "The Legislature cannot lawfully destroy guaranteed rights of one man with the prime purpose of enriching another, even if for the moment, this may seem advantageous to the public."[9]

As the eyes and ears of the judiciary have turned toward the political branches in matters pertaining to economic liberties, the results have been exactly what Madison and others warned against: the politicization of economic life, great uncertainty about the law, and a system of justice based on myriad notions of social or distributive justice rather than on protection of private property and freedom of contract. The majoritarian political process, in effect, has increasingly been allowed to undermine economic liberties as special interests vie for control of private wealth in the face of judicial passivity.

The significance of the demise of economic due process for the rise of the redistributive state and rent seeking was characterized over a century ago by Frederic Bastiat (1850a, pp. 238–39) when he

---

[7]198 U.S. at 57–58, emphasis added.

[8]300 U.S. 379 (1937). See Siegan (1980, pp. 145–50) for a discussion of this case. He points out that Chief Justice Hughes, in rendering the majority opinion in *Parrish*, was not only wrong in his concept of justice—he stood "the concept of liberty on its head"— but was "wrong in his economics" as well, for the "[i]mposition of higher wages [via a minimum wage law] brings unemployment and reduces the economy's flexibility, thereby impeding economic recovery" (p. 149).

[9]291 U.S. 502, 558–59 (1934) (McReynolds, J., dissenting).

compared a legal system governed by the rule of law with one based on distributive justice:

> If you make the law the palladium of the freedom and the property rights of all citizens, and if it is nothing but the organization of their individual rights to legitimate self-defense, you will establish on a just foundation a rational, simple, economical government, understood by all, loved by all, useful to all, supported by all, entrusted with a perfectly definite and very limited responsibility, and endowed with an unshakable solidity.
>
> If, on the contrary, you make of the law an instrument of plunder for the benefit of particular individuals or classes, first everyone will try to make the law; then everyone will try to make it for his own profit. There will be tumult at the door of the legislative chamber; there will be an implacable struggle within it, intellectual confusion, the end of all morality, violence among the proponents of special interests, fierce electoral struggles, accusations, recriminations, jealousies, and inextinguishable hatreds; . . . government will be held responsible for everyone's existence and will bend under the weight of such a responsibility.

The degree to which the Court has allowed property rights and economic liberties to be eroded by the political branches is evident from even a brief review of its recent decisions.[10] Of particular importance is *Hawaii Housing Authority v. Midkiff*,[11] in which the Court upheld a Hawaii statute that permits the state to condemn private land so that the tenants who occupy the land can then purchase it, thus raising the question of whether the power of eminent domain can be exercised for private use. Although the Court sanctioned the taking of land from large landowners for resale to current leaseholders, it claims to have done so under the rubric of the public use doctrine. The fact that the Hawaiian legislature deemed it in the "public interest" to reduce the concentration of land holdings was sufficient justification in the Court's view for upholding the statute. Thus, even though the *Hawaii* decision effectively sanctioned a private taking, the decision itself was dressed in the public-use garment with its appeal to the "public interest."

In *Hawaii*, the Court merely followed the precedent set in *Berman v. Parker*,[12] where it was argued:

> We deal . . . with what traditionally has been known as the police power. An attempt to define its reach or trace its outer limits is fruitless, for each case must turn on its own facts. The definition is

---

[10]See, for example, Epstein (1984).
[11]467 U.S. 229 (1984).
[12]348 U.S. 26 (1954).

essentially the product of legislative determinations addressed to the purposes of government, purposes neither abstractly nor historically capable of complete definition. Subject to specific constitutional limitations, *when the legislature has spoken, the public interest has been declared in terms well-nigh conclusive.* In such cases the legislature, not the judiciary, is the main guardian of the public needs to be served by social legislation. . . . This principle admits of no exception merely because the power of eminent domain is involved.[13]

What the Court was actually saying in *Berman* and *Hawaii* was that the floodgates are now open; that almost any statute having a reasonable relation to the "public interest" will be sustained even if it sanctions what amounts to a private taking. As Epstein (1984) notes:

With economic liberties . . . the [C]ourt has deployed the so-called "rational basis" test to neutralize the constitutional protection of economic liberties. . . . Under present law, if any conceivable set of facts could establish a rational nexus between the means chosen and any legitimate end of government, then the rational-basis test upholds the statute. In theory, the class of legitimate ends is both capacious and undefined, while the means used need have only a remote connection to the ends chosen. In practice, every statute meets the constitutional standard, no matter how powerful the arguments arrayed against it.

The Framers' view of the judicial function as one of protecting property—understood to include both economic and personal liberties—makes it difficult to understand how the modern Court can justify its discrimination against economic liberties and its failure to safeguard private property rights.[14] The rational-basis test is certainly not a valid justification since it amounts to subjecting minorities to the will of majorities with no test to see if the resulting legislation is consistent with fundamental property rights. In *Berman* and *Hawaii*

---

[13]Id. at 32 (citations omitted), emphasis added.
[14]According to Siegan (1985, pp. 276–77): "[I]n the economic area, the Framers believed the judiciary would protect ownership and thereby help perpetuate a system based on freedom of enterprise. The Framers surely would never have accepted judicial review if they had thought it would be used to advance government authority and regulation. . . . The early courts accepted the idea that legislatures are inherently limited in power."

Hamilton's view of the judiciary lends support to Siegan's interpretation. Hamilton saw the judiciary as an instrument to limit the power of government in accordance with constitutional principles. In a republic based on a "limited Constitution," the judiciary's function, wrote Hamilton, "must be to declare all acts contrary to the manifest tenor of the Constitution void. Without this, all the reservations of particular rights or privileges would amount to nothing" (*The Federalist Papers*, no. 78, pp. 100–101, as compiled by DeKoster 1976).

(and many similar cases involving property rights and economic liberties since 1936), there is really no sound basis from a rights standpoint for saying that judicial restraint is justified. Moreover, the Court's abandonment of economic due process cannot be justified from the standpoint of economic efficiency, as Siegan and Epstein have clearly documented.[15]

When the security of property rights is undermined by a judiciary unwilling to restrain legislative activisim in the pursuit of distributive justice, individual incentives to work, save, and invest are weakened. Moreover, with a lower probability of capturing future income streams from an efficient use of one's resources, there will be less incentive to utilize what Hayek (1948, p. 81) has called "the knowledge of the particular circumstances of time and place." As such, resources are less likely to be directed to their highest-valued uses, as perceived by final consumers. The attenuation of property rights, therefore, hampers profit-seeking entrepreneurs and motivates rent-seeking.

The Court's failure to accept and enforce the theory of property rights and limited government inherent in the text and structure of the Constitution—as well as its failure to see the interconnectedness among property rights, incentives, and economic efficiency —has led to the rise of the modern redistributive state, a substantial increase in economic regulation, and the rise of vast bureaucracies often beyond the practical reach of law and judicial review.[16] These developments have imposed substantial costs on society, one of which is the ever-expanding flood of litigation that slows the wheels of economic progress.[17]

Constitutional Jurisprudence and a Logic of Rights

There are many explanations for the Court's abandonment of the constitutional principles of property and contract—principles that

---

[15]See Siegan (1980, especially ch. 13, "The Failure of Regulation") and Epstein (1985a).
[16]See Tumlir (1984, 1985, especially pp. 13–17) and Dorn (1986).
[17]Ernest Gellhorn (1984) has observed:

> The burden legal services now impose on the economy and on personal freedom is often enormous and far exceeds the out-of-pocket costs estimated at $40 billion annually. More important, it is also clear that these costs often exceed the benefits generated, that legal rules are far too complicated and intrusive, and that alternative non-litigation solutions need to be explored. . . . [T]he major source of the law explosion is the legislature, acting not in ignorance or mendacity but rather in response to public pressure for yet more rules and laws.

Without a judiciary willing to check the flood of litigation by applying substantive due process to economic and social legislation, the "law explosion" is unlikely to stop.

the Framers thought necessary for limited government. The political pressures of the New Deal era, culminating in President Roosevelt's attempt to pack the Court, are among them, of course. More fundamentally, however, the intellectual pressures created by critics from the legal realist movement, coupled with the failure of the defenders of the classical view to adequately articulate their position, helped undermine the Court's confidence in its own ability to give justified and consistent interpretations of the broad language of the Constitution.

While the Court had had a number of general insights and principles to inform its constitutional jurisprudence, it had had nothing like a well-developed theory of rights or theory of constitutional interpretation in which it could place its confidence. Absent this confidence, and under political pressure to bend to the will of the majority, the Court eventually yielded its role to the political branches. Thereafter, at least in the area of property rights and economic liberties, the legislature rather than the Court would be the principal interpreter of the Constitution. Our property rights and economic liberties would be determined by political will rather than by the moral reasoning that stood behind the. Constitution—the so-called higher law that was implicit in its broad language.[18]

In the intervening years, a number of moral and legal theorists have combined to address the intellectual deficiencies that led to the Court's loss of confidence. The work of Roger Pilon, in particular, draws some of this research together and builds upon it to show that the broad rights of the Constitution can be given a rigorous, logical justification, as against the skeptical claims of the legal realists, and can be articulated to yield a far-reaching and powerful theory of rights capable of assisting judges in their work of constitutional interpretation.[19]

In essence, Pilon shows that a rigorous approach to justifying rights requires the development of a logic of rights such that "those who deny the existence of certain rights can be shown to contradict themselves" (1979c, p. 1332). Using Alan Gewirth's "principle of generic consistency (PGC)," Pilon argues (1979c, p. 1340): "Our basic right . . . is a right to our separate lives, to the non-interference that characterizes our voluntary actions."[20]

Only a system of rights based on the claim to noninterference can generate a consistent rights structure. Positive "welfare rights" cannot

---

[18]See Corwin (1955) on the "higher law" (natural rights) background of the Constitution.
[19]See Pilon (1979a, 1979b, especially part 3, 1979c, 1981, 1982, 1983).
[20]See Gewirth (1974) for a fuller discussion of the PGC. Pilon has criticized Gewirth for overextending the PGC by trying to generate positive rights: "Gewirth has construed

9

be generated from the PGC without leading to a conflict with the negative right to noninterference. Thus, according to Pilon (1979c, p. 1341), only the following rights can be justified since they are "derived from certain necessary but normative features of human action" and do not lead to inconsistency: (1) "rights to noninterference, defined with reference to the property foundations of our action and the taking of that property"; (2) "rights to voluntary association, those associations defined by the terms agreed upon"; and (3) "rights to rectification if involuntarily involved in an association." He concludes that this system of rights is "rooted in reason, not in sentiment."[21]

Pilon's work implies, among other things, that the negative concept of justice held by the Framers when they shaped the Constitution can be justified, even if the Framers' arguments did not fully do so, whereas the affirmative concept of justice that leads to economic redistribution cannot be justified, since it is inconsistent with the negative concept. The natural rights theory that influenced the Framers generated a consistent set of rights based on the fundamental right to one's property, broadly conceived. As Pilon points out, the Framers' conclusions about rights were largely correct, but they lacked the "epistemological tools" to justify those rights. Consequently, their conclusions have not held up well against the doctrines of moral skepticism and legal positivism. What is needed, therefore, is not to reject the principles the Framers articulated but to justify them with a more rigorous defense. What must be done, says Pilon, is to base our rights on reason, not on the will of the electorate (or on popular sentiment) as expressed in legislation. Again, "the idea is to show that certain rights [those to life, liberty, and property] must be accepted as justified such that to deny that individuals have them is to contradict oneself" (Pilon 1983, p. 173).[22]

---

the normative structure of action—the front part of his argument—beyond its natural bounds: he has gone beyond the property foundations of action that alone can serve as *necessary* content for the right-claims that are inherent in human action, claims that in turn get the whole moral game off the ground" (1981, p. 12).

[21]Note the similarity between Pilon's three fundamental rights and Hume's "three fundamental laws of nature," namely: "stability of possession," "transference by consent," and "performance of promises" (cited in Hayek 1982, ch. 8, p. 40).

[22]Pilon (1981, p. 7) argues that the "Founders got it right, right as a matter of ethics." In his argument, Pilon emphasizes that to justify a right, it is not enough simply to trace it to the Constitution. In addition, one must ground it in reason. He is critical, therefore, of "constitutional positivism" (1981, pp. 6–7). Pilon's discussion of the shortcomings of classical natural law theory as a justificatory argument for basic rights is found in Pilon (1979c, pp. 1333–34, and 1983, especially pp. 172–73). In the latter reference, Pilon states: "It is one thing to develop a theory of rights that is both objectively grounded and consistent, quite another to show that that theory is *justified*. On this score, ... the Founding Fathers ... were at their weakest—not surprisingly, for the epistemological tools at their command were altogether primitive."

Hayek has reached these same conclusions, but by a somewhat different route. Instead of developing a rigorous theory of moral rights to justify the right to noninterference (that is, to property), Hayek simply assumes the legitimacy of this right. He then derives a set of auxiliary rights that are consistent with the basic property right and shows that private property and freedom of contract are necessary conditions for the emergence of a spontaneous market order.[23]

To test for consistency in the rights structure (or what Hayek calls "the rules of just conduct"), he employs a "negative test of injustice" and criticizes legal positivists for failing to realize that such a test exists. According to Hayek (1982, ch. 8, p. 54):

> What is required is merely a negative test that enables us progressively to eliminate rules which prove to be unjust, because they are not universalizable within the system of other rules whose validity is not questioned. . . . The pursuit of the ideal of justice (like the pursuit of truth) does not presuppose that it is known what justice (or truth) is, but only that we know what we regard as unjust (or untrue).[24]

The post–1936 Court appears oblivious to the long history of rights theory and to the contemporary rebirth of rights theory, both of which generate only negative justice, not the positive "social justice" embraced by modern liberalism. Similarly, the Court appears oblivious to the crucial role of private property and freedom of contract in generating a spontaneous economic order, an order in which individual plans can be coordinated and conflicting wants resolved through market exchanges rather than through coerced political processes. Indeed, the modern Court has turned the concept of justice on its head: instead of referring to the prevention of injustice (that is, the taking of property without the owners' consent) justice now refers to the pursuit of "social justice," accomplished via legislation and the use of government coercion to redistribute income and wealth. Yet, as Hayek (1982, ch. 9, p. 96) has observed: "in a society of free men whose members are allowed to use their own knowledge for their own purposes the term 'social justice' is wholly devoid of meaning."

The demise of economic due process has given rise to a judiciary that now seems all too willing to surrender property rights and economic liberties to the redistributive political state. In a strange turn

---

[23]See, in particular, Hayek (1960, 1982, vol. 2, [1966] 1967). For a detailed discussion of Hayek's theory of rights, see Dorn (1981).

[24]For a discussion of the negative character of the "rules of just conduct" and the "negative test of injustice," see Hayek (1982, ch. 8, pp. 35–48). His critique of legal positivism runs throughout this chapter.

of events, the burden of proof is now on those who have lost their property rights to show why those rights should be restored, rather than on government to show why it should have the right to interfere with economic freedom in the first place. By deferring to the legislature, the Court has created a false dichotomy between civil liberties and economic liberties, raising the former to the category of "fundamental rights" while relegating the latter to the will of the legislature and special interests. Such is the fate of those rights of property and contract that Madison and the other Framers considered inviolable and prior to any written law.

To stem the growth of the redistributive state and restore economic liberties to their original place in the Constitution, Siegan would have the Court once again apply substantive due process to economic legislation. He would require that "In matters affecting people's freedoms [including economic liberties], the scope of judicial review should be defined by its general goal of protecting and preserving liberty" (1980, p. 322). As such, there would be no dichotomy between economic freedom and other freedoms. According to Siegan (1980, pp. 324–25):

> [A] statute or ordinance should not be deemed valid if, in the absence of justification by the government under an intermediate standard of judicial scrutiny, it (a) denies an owner the use and disposition of property without just compensation, or (b) denies an individual or corporation freedom to engage in an occupation, trade, profession, or business of one's or its choosing, or (c) denies an individual or corporation freedom of contract to produce and distribute goods and services.

Siegan's test of justice for reviewing social and economic legislation would be "less exacting than strict scrutiny," but this is because he believes that "Always to subject the legislature's will to an extreme standard of justification might eliminate it as a viable branch of government" (1980, p. 324). This contention, of course, is debatable. Nevertheless, Siegan has a more justifiable approach to constitutional interpretation than that currently practiced by the Court, one that deserves serious consideration. Under Siegan's test, the burden of proof in judicial review of social and economic legislation would once again be shifted to the government, which Siegan (1980, p. 325) deems only just.[25] He concludes (1980, p. 331): "The application of judicial review to economic matters will not restore laissez-faire to our economy, but at least we should expect reduction of legislative

---

[25]See Siegan (1980, ch. 15) for an elaboration of his principled approach to judicial review.

and administrative excesses and abuses. This is an outcome not to be minimized. The rewards of liberty are vast and unpredictable."

A necessary first step in restoring economic due process is that those individuals who have been entrusted with protecting our property rights—the judiciary—reacquaint themselves with the importance of their responsibility. To do this they must acquire a better understanding of their role in the light of both prior history and current developments in rights theory and economic theory. The theory of rights shows that our constitutional rights to property and economic liberty can be morally justified, whereas economic theory shows the importance of private property for a viable system of markets and prices. If these lessons are not learned by those who declare what rights will be enforced, then the erosion of property rights in the economic sphere must ultimately lead to the erosion of rights in the noneconomic sphere as well.

If we accept the idea that the Court should exercise judicial restraint in its review of economic legislation, we face the danger that the Court will also be passive in its protection of personal freedoms. The Court must strike a principled balance between restraint and activism in all matters, but to do this it must resort to some ultimate principle of justice. The principle of justice that guided the Framers was that the right to property is fundamental and consistent with individual freedom, and that justice is best served by protecting this right. The Court's present "rule of reason"—the rational-basis test—is really a pseudo test of justice; it submits legislation neither to the moral test of the theory of rights nor to the efficiency test of the theory of economics. Instead of actively securing rights to property and contract, as envisoned by the Framers, the judiciary under the rational-basis test has yielded to majoritarianism. Consequently, justice is now viewed by the court as in *Berman* and *Hawaii:* "When the legislature has spoken, the public interest has been declared well-nigh conclusive." But as Siegan (1980, p. 325) warns: "The presumption that the state is correct in curtailing people's activities can only be accepted in societies where restraint is normal—those which, unlike ours, equate government direction and control with the public interest."

The Present State of the Debate

The Court's refusal to extend to economic rights the same protection it extends to "fundamental rights"—and the consequent attenuation of property rights by the political branches—has arisen in an intellectual climate that has lost contact with Madison's understanding of property, rights, and justice. Instead of upholding the "inviolability of property" and freedom of contract, which Madison recognized as constitutional principles, the modern Court has found it expedient to bow to Congress and the regulatory agencies in the quest for "social justice." The "Constitution of Liberty," as Hayek (1960) has called it, has steadily given way to the rule of majority power, as democratic values are allowed to override fundamental property rights.

The change in the Court's thinking about the Constitution as a charter for protecting both economic and other liberties is evidenced by the words of the new Chief Justice, William Rehnquist. According to Justice Rehnquist:

> The public perception of the nature and function of the United States Constitution as a whole has tended to become distorted. . . . The Constitution is often referred to as a "charter of liberty" or a "bulwark of individual rights against the state." The original Constitution was neither of these things. . . . [I]t was adopted not to enshrine states' rights or to guarantee individual freedom, but to create a limited national government, which was empowered to curtail both states' rights and individual freedom.[26]

The Chief Justice, therefore, sees no grounds "for elevating the doctrine of freedom of contract into a constitutional principle."[27]

Underlying Rehnquist's jurisprudential attitude is the same moral skepticism and deference to majoritarianism that characterize other conservatives on the bench who favor judicial restraint in reviewing social and economic legislation. Judge Robert Bork (1984, p. 8), for example, argues:

> Our constitutional liberties arose out of historical experience and out of political, moral, and religious *sentiment* [emphasis added]. They do not rest upon any general theory. Attempts to frame a theory that removes from democratic control [popular sovereignty] areas of life the framers intended to leave there can only succeed if abstractions are regarded as overriding the constitutional text and structure, judicial precedent [as in *Berman* and *Hawaii*?], and the history that gives our rights life, rootedness, and meaning. It is no small matter to discredit the foundations upon which our constitutional freedoms have always been sustained and substitute as a bulwark only abstractions of moral philosophy.[28]

---

[26]William H. Rehnquist, quoted in Saperstein and Lardner (1986, p. A8).

[27]Rehnquist, quoted in Lardner (1986, p. A14).

[28]According to Bork (1984, p. 7): "the attempt to define individual liberties by abstract reasoning, though intended to broaden liberties, is actually likely to make them more vulnerable." This is true, however, if and only if one pursues a positive theory of justice, which creates "rights" that cannot be justified in any rational sense. If one sticks instead

14

In contrast, the liberal element of the judiciary, as represented by Justice William Brennan Jr., for example, has favored an open-ended, noninterpretivist approach to the Constitution—engaging in policy-making to create rights according to judicial preferences. This type of judicial activism, which Meese (1985, p. 14) has described as "one which anchors the Constitution only in the consciences of jurists," has led to a substantial degree of judicial overreaching.

The failure of both conservatives and liberals to offer a principled approach to judicial review—one that is consistent with the Framers' view of justice as the protection of both persons and property—has been addressed by Siegan, Epstein, Macedo, Pilon, and others in this volume. These contrasting views of the judicial function in a constitutional democracy, together with the implications of the demise of substantive economic due process for individual freedom and the smooth operation of a market economy, set the stage for a useful and important debate on economic liberties and the judiciary. Whether the courts should become more active in protecting property rights, including freedom of contract, is essentially a question of whether the role of the judiciary is to protect property rights or to defer to Congress and the regulatory agencies, allowing them to redistribute property according to whatever forces are driving them at the time. It is a question of whether the Framers sought to create a limited government or a redistributive state. The evidence from the text and structure of the Constitution, as well as from its natural rights background, clearly supports an active, protective judiciary, not a redistributive state.[29]

The debate over the role of the judiciary in protecting economic liberties can thus be reduced to a debate over three jurisprudential positions: a jurisprudence of judicial restraint, in which the protection of property rights is left to the political branches (what might be called the "jurisprudence of the New Right"); a "negative jurisprudence," which views the judiciary as an institution to safeguard property rights (what might be called a "principled judicial activ-

---

to Madison's negative concept of justice and to the rational theory of rights that stands implicitly behind the Constitution, far from making our liberties vulnerable, one enhances them.

Bork appears to be an unquestioning constitutional positivist when he argues: "In a constitutional democracy the moral content of law must be given by the morality of the framer or the legislator, never by the morality of the judge" (p. 11). Although there is some truth in this statement, it is also true, as Pilon (1981) has shown, that one must go beyond the written constitution if one is to justify that constitution and the rights it sets forth, and for this we need a substantive theory of moral or natural rights.

[29]See especially Epstein (1985a), Macedo (1986), and Siegan (1980).

ism"); and an "affirmative jurisprudence," which views the judiciary as a mechanism for creating new rights—such as "welfare rights"— that are inconsistent with our rights to property and freedom of contract (what might be called "misguided judicial activism").[30]

The failure of the Court over the last 50 years to afford property rights and economic liberties the same protection as other civil rights and liberties—judicial restraint—and the willingness of the Court to create positive rights where such rights clash with rights to property and contract—misguided judicial activism—have paved the way for a general reappraisal of the role of the judiciary as it affects both economic and noneconomic liberties. Jurisprudence has once again become fashionable as constitutional law searches for a firm theoretical base, which, according to Epstein (1985b), is to be found in "a sound and neutral theory of interpretation"—one that is consistent with "the constitutional means selected by the [F]ramers to ensure a just and stable society." A "sound theory of original intention," argues Epstein, "makes it indefensible to assume that modern zoning, landmark preservation and rent-control statutes, or collective bargaining and minimum-wage laws are beyond constitutional review simply because none was heard of in 1791." The Constitution is a charter of rights resting on the Framers' acceptance of "a political theory of limited government," notes Epstein, and "[i]t is the disregard of that substantive principle that discredits Justice Brennan's brand of judicial activism."

The question of whether the judiciary should extend the same scrutiny to cases involving economic liberties as it has to personal freedoms (such as speech, press, and assembly) is a question, therefore, of whether the Court will actively uphold constitutional protections for persons and property or whether it will remain passive and defer to the will of the political branches, or even create new rights by engaging in misguided activism. In this sense, the debate over the judiciary and the Constitution with respect to the protection of economic liberties is a debate over whether the Constitution will survive as a charter for limited government and individual freedom or whether majoritarianism and rent seeking will further erode both economic and personal freedoms.

[30]Epstein (1985b, and this volume, ch. 3) provides a strong attack on judicial restraint as it affects economic liberties; Macedo (1986, and this volume, ch. 5) discusses the jurisprudence of the New Right and contrasts it to a principled judicial activism; Siegan (1980, ch. 14) distinguishes negative and affirmative jurisprudence; Pilon (1981) contrasts judicial passivism, judicial negativism, and judicial activism; and Bandow (this volume, ch. 11) separates principled activism from misguided judicial activism—or from what Rottenberg (this volume, ch. 15) calls "mistaken judicial activism."

In order to better understand the judicial change of events since 1936, and return the judiciary to its original role, the following questions need to be addressed:

- What forces led the judiciary to alter its course in protecting property rights and economic liberties?
- Are there fundamental principles to guide the judiciary in its review of economic legislation, or must the courts defer to the legislature in this area?
- What is the legitimate role of the judiciary, and of government and law generally, in a free society?
- How does the existing incentive structure confronting judges affect their behavior?
- What are the implications of the demise of substantive due process in economic matters for the maintenance of a spontaneous market order?
- Do judges understand the relationship between economic freedom and personal/political freedom, and the consequences for the latter when private property rights and freedom of contract are attenuated?

These questions—which were conveniently ignored in the recent confirmation hearings for William Rehnquist and Antonin Scalia—deserve serious thought and discussion, especially as we celebrate the Constitution's bicentennial.

The articles in the present volume discuss in much greater detail many of the ideas presented in this Introduction and provide valuable contributions to the debate over the role of the judiciary in protecting economic liberties, as well as to the broader field of constitutional economics.

In the Scalia-Epstein exchange, Justice Scalia defends the reluctance of the Court to return to substantive due process in reviewing economic regulation. He does not disagree with basic constitutional principles of property and freedom of contract, but thinks that in today's environment—with the cries for social justice and affirmative jurisprudence—the judiciary would not be able to limit itself to the protection of property rights and economic liberties in their traditional form. Instead, the Court would face the danger of creating rights where none should be created. To avoid committing this type of error, Scalia favors judicial restraint in reviewing social and economic regulation. In his view, what needs to be accomplished before the Court can actively review economic legislation is to create "a constitutional ethos of economic liberty." Once such a climate is created, the Court will be able to protect the rights of property and contract. Until then, it does no good to try to constitutionalize these rights.

Richard Epstein recognizes the same problems that Scalia sees in today's judicial system but strongly disagrees with Scalia's defense of the Court's post–1936 termination of economic due process. He thinks that the present Court has gone much too far in the direction of judicial restraint in its review of economic legislation, with the result that legislative abuse of property rights and economic liberties has substantially increased. Scalia pays too much attention, Epstein argues, to avoiding the error of striking down economic legislation that should be sustained. In doing so, however, he increases the risk that the Court will fail to review statutes that conflict with the basic economic rights the Framers meant to be protected by the judiciary. The goal of judicial review, says Epstein, should be to minimize the sum of both types of error, which can be done only by adhering to constitutional principles. By taking a principled approach to judicial review, therefore, the Court can strike the proper balance between activism and restraint. If it does not, it will further erode our rights to property and contract.

Peter Aranson examines judicial control of the political branches. He argues that the Court, in its review of socioeconomic legislation, must recognize the scope for legislative abuse. In his view, judges should acquire a better understanding of economic principles, but economic analysis is not sufficient to protect economic liberties and may even be harmful. Instead, legislative abuse is best constrained by the development of constitutional doctrine in line with the intent of the Framers to protect property rights against the redistributive state. If the Court were to protect our rights to property and contract, it would help to promote a sound economy as well.

Stephen Macedo provides a careful analysis of the "jurisprudence of the New Right." He criticizes the moral skepticism and majoritarianism of the New Right's "Jurisprudence of Original Intent" and proposes a "principled judicial activism." The New Right's constitutional vision is deeply flawed, says Macedo, because it searches the historical record for specific intentions and in doing so misunderstands the broad moral purposes that the Framers actually enshrined in the Constitution. The New Right also fails to understand that democratic institutions are but one feature of a Constitution dedicated to limited government and the protection of a broad array of rights, both economic and personal. By placing democracy above what the Framers saw as fundamental rights to life, liberty, and property, the New Right's jurisprudence undermines the Constitution as a charter of freedom, endangering the nation's moral and social fabric.

Bernard Siegan continues the theme of his earlier work on economic liberties and the Constitution. Here, however, he focuses on the Fourteenth Amendment, demonstrating that the due process clause, authored by Rep. John Bingham, was intended not only to secure the civil liberties of the recently freed slaves but to protect broadly our property rights and economic liberties from incursions by the states. In light of recent debates over federalism and the meaning of the Tenth Amendment, Siegan's paper is a particularly important contribution.

Wesley J. Liebeler leads off the second section of the book by taking a property rights approach to adjudication. Drawing on the work of Ronald Coase and Harold Demsetz, he suggests that such an approach can help in determining standards for judicial review of social and economic regulation. According to Liebeler, economic regulation should be applied only in cases involving significant third-party effects. In such cases, the assignment of rights should proceed as if private transaction costs were zero; the adjudication process, therefore, should approximate the market process. Resource efficiency would then result and the final rights configuration—arrived at via voluntary exchange—would be consistent with constitutional principles. The property rights approach, says Liebeler, can prove beneficial because judges will always have to compare costs and benefits at some level of the adjudication process.

Roger Pilon's paper contributes to our understanding of the predicament of the post–1936 Court. Without a well-developed theory of moral and constitutional rights, and believing that democratic theory serves to justify more than in fact it does, the Court "abandoned reason to will," allowing the legislature, which is driven always by a shifting political climate, to determine what property and economic rights we have and to redetermine those rights as conditions change. Those who believe that democratic processes are sufficient to determine and justify our rights, including many of today's conservative critics of the Court, have simply not looked closely at democratic theory, Pilon argues. If they would scrutinize that theory, they would see that democratic processes justify very little. In particular, our rights, as the authors of the Declaration of Independence made clear, preexist government; it is not by democratic will that they are justified but by principles of reason—the same principles of reason that the Court must invoke when it reviews legislation to see whether rights are violated by that legislation. By undercutting democratic theory's overextended claims to establishing legitimacy, Pilon shows that "due process of law" is inescapably substantive. If judges are to properly perform their judicial review, therefore, they must look, in interpreting the broad language of the Constitution, to the substantive, rational theory of rights that tells us more precisely just what our rights are. Pilon concludes that judges must know their philosophy as well as their law.

Randy Barnett adds a new term to the legal lexicon: "judicial pragmactivism." He defines this as "the jurisprudential mean that lies somewhere between the extremes of judicial activism and passivism." The characteristic feature of judicial pragmactivism is that it is a principled approach to the choice between the legislature and the judiciary. Whether the judiciary should strike down a statute or whether it should defer to the legislative will is determined by the principles judicial pragmactivists use to evaluate the consequences of these two alternatives. Barnett offers three examples of possible principles: economic efficiency, wealth equalization, and safeguarding individual rights. Depending on which principle is adopted, a pragmactivist may be classified as an "efficiency pragmactivist," an "equal-wealth pragmactivist," or a "rights pragmactivist." For the efficiency pragmactivist, the choice between the judiciary and the legislature will rest on the expected efficiency of the statute; for the equal-wealth pragmactivist, it will depend on whether the statute is expected to create greater wealth equalization; and for the rights pragmactivist, the choice will depend on whether the statute protects or impairs individual rights. Barnett concludes that for the rights pragmactivist, "judicial activism in pursuit of liberty is no vice; judicial restraint in pursuit of justice is no virtue."

Mario J. Rizzo examines the decline of the rule of law in the modern administrative state and explains how a rules-based approach under the common law is policy-neutral compared with a "balancing" approach, based on the subjective evaluation of costs and benefits. He therefore favors a strict liability rule over the use of a negligence standard in tort law. For Rizzo, as for Hayek, the proper function of a legal system is to provide a basis for the emergence of a spontaneous market order, not to balance the interests of conflicting parties by way of cost-benefit analysis. In a world of ignorance and diffused knowledge, the superiority of the principled approach of the common law is evident to Rizzo. A return to a policy-neutral common-law approach to judicial decision making, argues Rizzo, would restore the spontaneous market order, which has been seriously hampered both by the onslaught of the administrative state and by a judiciary that has lost sight of the principle of spontaneous order. Before such a change can be made, however, it is essential that both economists and lawyers acquire the proper understanding of this important principle.

Doug Bandow examines the conservative judicial agenda and (like Epstein, Macedo, and Siegan) finds it seriously flawed. Conservatives such as Edwin Meese dislike the modern liberal view of the judiciary as a policymaking branch of government and, instead, favor judicial restraint in all policy areas. The danger of such judicial passivity, says Bandow, is that it will eliminate effective judicial review and place constitutionally guaranteed rights of person and property at the mercy of competing political factions. It was exactly this crass majoritarianism that the Framers warned against and sought to limit by constitutional government—using the judiciary to hold the political branches in check. In place of the conservative reform agenda, which emphasizes a legal philosophy of judicial restraint and seeks to pressure activist judges, Bandow would restore the Constitution's intended judicial balance by opposing both judicial restraint and "misguided judicial activism." In their place, he would substitute a principled activism to protect both economic and other rights.

In the book's final section, the authors consider various economic issues in the courts and the implications for both justice and economic efficiency. The article by OMB Director James C. Miller III, and those by Professor Tollison, Dean Manne, and Professor Rottenberg all deal with the problems inherent in overregulation of economic affairs and a judiciary that is unwilling to protect property rights and economic liberties. Property rights theory and public choice theory have revealed the problems plaguing economic regulation and the proclivity of government failure in this area. In particular, incentives facing bureaucrats are different from those facing private owners. Individuals within government cannot sell shares of stock in their organizations or capture take-home profit for efficient behavior; thus, they are apt to have a weaker incentive to promote wealth-increasing activities than under conditions of private ownership.

James C. Miller draws on the principles of property rights theory and public choice to conclude that in setting standards for business practices, self-regulation and voluntary standards are superior to government regulation. Private parties will have a stronger incentive to monitor business practices that increase profits and lower costs than would some government agency. The function of government and the Federal Trade Commission here should be to minimize regulation and make sure that self-regulation is not used to restrain trade by keeping valuable information from rivals.

Robert Tollison criticizes the public interest theory of antitrust and uses public choice theory to derive implications for the administration of antitrust laws. In considering antitrust policy, says Tollison, one must look at the constraints facing self-interested policymakers. He is not convinced that "better people make better government." Unless underlying institutions and incentive structures change, we should not expect any significant increase in governmental efficiency to come from putting "better" people in government. Thus Tollison wants to formulate a positive theory of antitrust policy using the public choice framework. If we are to arrive at sensible policy decisions in antitrust, we must carefully examine the behavior of decision makers—in this case enforcement officials—as well as judges and others involved in the antitrust process.

Henry Manne examines the Securities and Exchange Commission's regulation of insider trading and provides a number of arguments against such regulation. The SEC, even though it has the best of intentions, has not been very effective in developing law in this area, says Manne. Moreover, such regulations can pose a threat to civil liberties. Manne views insider trading as a "victimless crime" for which no government policing is warranted. In a competitive securities market, argues Manne, government regulation of insider trading can be expected to result in inefficient use of information and rent-seeking activity. He therefore favors deregulating the SEC's insider-trading program to foster both economic efficiency and personal freedom.

Simon Rottenberg uses the law of creditor remedies to demonstrate that often when judges try to do good they end up doing harm because of faulty economic reasoning. He examines alternative rules for creditor-remedy law from a property rights perspective and uses a price-theoretic methodology to derive the implications of alternative remedies for economic behavior. He concludes that economic efficiency is best served when the judge's role is limited to the enforcement of contracts and the protection of private property rights. When judges fail in this role and interfere with consensual-contractual terms, they upset normal expectations and impose additional costs on the trading parties. Judges, therefore, need to understand the impact of alternative creditor remedies on incentives and individual behavior. If they do not, they will err by intervening when, in fact, the existing consensual arrangement is superior to the judge-enforced terms. This is a case of what Rottenberg calls "mistaken judicial activism." We can minimize this, says Rottenberg, by allowing market participants to determine the terms of contract and the optimal creditor remedies.

In the volume's final article, Ellen Frankel Paul illustrates how the Court, by its decisions in *Berman* and *Hawaii*, has all but ended the public-use constraint on governmental takings. She finds the Court's interpretations of the Fifth and Fourteenth Amendments incorrect and inconsistent with the originally intended right to private property. Moreover, the Court's economic logic in *Hawaii* cannot be supported. Judicial deference to the legislature's quest for popular support has led to the erosion of individual property rights and promises to further erode these rights in the future. Once a precedent for arbitrary redistribution of property is set, there is little protection in the present judicial system—based on the rational-basis test—for limiting legislative abuse. Thus, Professor Paul sees little hope for restoring private property rights unless there is a significant change in judicial thinking, a change that upholds basic constitutional principles.

The Return to Principle and Reason

The papers in this volume raise many important questions, but perhaps the most important is this: If the judiciary fails to protect our property rights and economic liberties, can we realistically expect these civil liberties to be protected by the political branches? We may hope with Justice Scalia that "logic will out," but can we afford to wait for a "constitutional ethos of economic liberty" to develop in the electorate? Moreover, is it realistic to wait once we recognize, as did the Framers, that the incentives that drive the legislature argue against the appearance of such an ethos in that branch? Is it not the Court's duty to uphold constitutional principles, including the right to property? Finally, if the Court does not fulfill this obligation, is it not also failing to safeguard what Madison (1792, p. 174) called a person's "property in his rights"?

In his speech to the Virginia state convention, Madison ([1829] 1865, pp. 51–52) reiterated his adherence to a government limited to the protection of the rights of persons and property and warned of the danger majoritarianism posed for these rights:

> It is sufficiently obvious, that persons and property are the two great subjects on which Governments are to act; and that the rights of persons, and the rights of property, are the objects, for the protection of which Government was instituted. These rights cannot well be separated. The personal right to acquire property, which is a natural right, gives to property, when acquired, a right to protection, as a social right. The essence of Government is power; and power, lodged as it must be in human hands, will ever be liable to abuse. . . . In Republics, the great danger is, that the majority may not sufficiently

respect the rights of the minority. . . . The only effectual safeguard to the rights of the minority must be laid in such a basis and structure of the Government itself as may afford, in a certain degree, directly or indirectly, a defensive authority in behalf of a minority having right on its side.

The structure of government favored by Madison, of course, was a constitutional democracy within which the natural right to property was to be ultimately protected against majoritarian impulses by a strong judicial branch. Madison ([1834] 1865, pp. 349–50) thought that all three branches of government should "be guided by the text of the Constitution" but that special status should be reserved for the judiciary "as the surest expositor of the Constitution."

If the judiciary becomes passive in protecting rights of persons and property, or if it becomes an active instrument of the political branches for implementing distributive justice, judges become agents—even if by default—for the redistributive state. The resulting rent seeking and socialization of wealth that occurs when judges fail to actively protect property rights, in effect, transforms the judiciary into an agent for socialism. In the redistributive state—the antithesis of a constitutional regime—the role of the judiciary is turned upside down; judges, in essence, become pseudo judges. Instead of providing for the stability of rights to property and freedom of contract, conservative passivist judges and liberal activist judges undermine these rights and, in the process, undermine the basis for a free-market order.[31]

If judges defer to the popular will and to the special interests that invariably determine that will—that is, if judges do not perform their proper function—then some portion of popular sentiment rather than reason will determine our "rights." This, of course, creates the pos-

---

[31]Hayek (1982, ch. 5, p. 121) notes:

[A] socialist judge would really be a contradiction in terms; for his persuasion must prevent him from applying only those general principles which underlie a spontaneous order of actions, and lead him to take into account considerations that have nothing to do with the justice of individual conduct. He may, of course, be a socialist privately, and keep his socialism out of the considerations which determine his decisions. But he could not act as a judge on socialist principles. . . . [T]his has long been concealed by the belief that instead of acting on principles of just individual conduct he might be guided by what is called 'social justice', a phrase which describes precisely that aiming at particular results for particular persons or groups which is impossible within a spontaneous order.

Hayek's socialist label would obviously apply to activist liberal judges favoring "welfare rights" and other redistributive measures. But it could also be applied, indirectly, to conservative judges favoring judicial restraint in the protection of property rights, since such restraint is likely to encourage further socialization of property by the political branches.

sibility for numerous redistributive schemes that jeopardize individual rights. Justice Scalia seems willing to accept this risk because he believes that without broad public sentiment for protection of property rights, an activist Court may pose a greater threat to economic liberties than the present passivist Court. Yet, by leaving the determination of economic rights to the democratic process, he increases the likelihood of a further attenuation of property rights, as Epstein notes.

The Framers understood the threat unlimited democracy would pose for individual liberty and thought it judicious to have the Court act as the final guardian for both personal and economic rights, that is, for what Pilon calls our "private sovereignty." The Court's function, then, is not to wait for a post-constitutional "social consensus" to develop with respect to protection of property, but to guard the rights of property and contract that were enshrined in the Founders' Constitution and Bill of Rights. Insofar as the judiciary fails in this task, it will generate expectations on the part of special interest groups that almost any attenuation of property rights will be permitted if it passes the legislative muster.

A return to principle and reason, or to what Bastiat called "the law of justice," in reviewing economic and social legislation would restore the stability necessary for a spontaneous market order.[32] Restoring substantive economic due process, however, requires (1) that judges understand the role of private property rights and freedom of contract in providing incentives for efficient economic performance, and (2) that they come to appreciate the logic of rights and thus the moral argument for private ownership and freedom of exchange.

The developments in property rights theory and the theory of public choice offer considerable hope on the first front, while the development of a rational foundation for the theory of rights offers considerable encouragement on the second front. In generating a "constitutional ethos" that upholds the right to property, it is also important to revive the arguments made by Madison and his intellectual forebears, particularly John Locke, as well as 19th-century writers such as Bastiat.[33] Our intellectual heritage is an essential element in creating a solid framework for economic liberties.

---

[32]Bastiat (1850b, p. 94) summed up the relationship between a just legal order and a stable economic order as follows:

Law is justice. And it is under the law of justice, under the rule of right, under the influence of liberty, security, stability, and responsibility, that every man will attain to the full worth and dignity of his being, and that mankind will achieve, in a calm and orderly way—slowly, no doubt, but surely—the progress to which it is destined.

[33]Epstein (1985a) takes a Lockean approach to deriving his theory of constitutional

If the courts fail to understand the nature of a spontaneous market order and the essential function of private property in creating such an order, or if they fail to recognize the logic of moral rights implicit in the Constitution and its mandate for limited government and private enterprise, they are unlikely to provide adequate protection for property rights and economic liberties. In this sense, Justice Scalia's call for a "constitutional ethos of economic liberty" must be taken seriously, as Judge Kozinski notes in his Foreword.

The essays in this volume help lay the intellectual groundwork for a return to principle and reason in the treatment of economic liberties. They also call attention to the fact that before popular sentiment for traditional economic rights can be created (assuming as Scalia does that such sentiment has been lost), the judiciary itself must stand firm in the protection of property and contract. Judicial scapegoating will only confuse the public and misplace the locus of responsibility for safeguarding those rights to life, liberty, and property that the Framers regarded as inviolable. Only if the judiciary protects the rights of persons and property against crass majoritarianism and bureaucratic imperialism will the Constitution survive as a charter of freedom and a balwark against the redistributive state.

References

Bastiat, Frederic (1848). "Property and Law." In *Selected Essays on Political Economy*, pp. 97–115. Translated by Seymour Cain. Edited by George B. de Huszar. Irvington-on-Hudson, N.Y.: Foundation for Economic Education, 1964.

Bastiat, Frederic (1850a). "Plunder and Law." In *Selected Essays*, pp. 229–39.

Bastiat, Frederic (1850b). "The Law." In *Selected Essays*, pp. 51–96.

Bork, Robert H. "Tradition and Morality in Constitutional Law." The Francis Boyer Lectures on Public Policy. Washington, D.C.: American Enterprise Institute, 1984.

Corwin, Edward S. *The "Higher Law" Background of American Constitutional Law*. Ithaca, N.Y.: Cornell University Press, 1955.

Dorn, James A. "Law and Liberty: A Comparison of Hayek and Bastiat." *Journal of Libertarian Studies* 5 (Fall 1981): 375–97.

Dorn, James A. "Economic Liberties and the Judiciary." Introduction. *Cato Journal* 4 (Winter 1985): 661–87.

Dorn, James A. "The Transfer Society." Introduction. *Cato Journal* 6 (Spring/Summer 1986): 1–17.

---

interpretation based on eminent domain. Bastiat (1848, 1850a, 1850b) offers a fairly sophisticated version of natural rights theory for limited government (see Dorn 1981, 1985, pp. 667–69, 1986).

Epstein, Richard A. "Asleep at a Constitutional Switch." *Wall Street Journal* (9 August 1984): 28.

Epstein, Richard A. *Takings: Private Property and the Power of Eminent Domain.* Cambridge, Mass.: Harvard University Press, 1985a.

Epstein, Richard A. "Needed: Activist Judges for Economic Rights." *Wall Street Journal* (14 November 1985b): 32.

The Federalist Papers: A Contemporary Selection. Abridged and edited by Lester DeKoster. Grand Rapids, Mich.: Wm. B. Eerdmans Publishing Co., 1976.

Gellhorn, Ernest. "Too Much Law, Too Many Lawyers, Not Enough Justice." *Wall Street Journal* (7 June 1984): 28.

Gewirth, Alan. "The 'Is-Ought' Problem Resolved." *Proceedings and Addresses of the American Philosophical Association* 47 (1974): 34–61.

Hayek, Friedrich A. *Individualism and Economic Order.* South Bend, Ind.: Gateway Editions, Ltd., 1948.

Hayek, F[riedrich] A. *The Constitution of Liberty.* Chicago: University of Chicago Press, 1960.

Hayek, F[riedrich] A. "The Principles of a Liberal Social Order." 1966. Reprinted in *Studies in Philosophy, Politics, and Economics,* ch. 11. Chicago: University of Chicago Press, 1967.

Hayek, F[riedrich] A. *Law, Legislation and Liberty.* Reprint (3 vols. in 1). London: Routledge & Kegan Paul, 1982. [Vol. 1, *Rules and Order* (chaps. 1–6); Vol. 2, *The Mirage of Social Justice* (chaps. 7–11); Vol. 3, *The Political Order of a Free People* (chaps. 12–18).]

Lardner, George Jr. "'50s Memos Illustrate Rehnquist Consistency." *Washington Post* (20 July 1986): A1, A14.

Macedo, Stephen. *The New Right v. The Constitution.* Washington, D.C.: Cato Institute, 1986.

[Madison, James.] "Property." *National Gazette* 1, no. 44 (29 March 1792): 174–75. Reprinted in *Letters and Other Writings of James Madison.* Vol. 4, pp. 478–80. Philadelphia: J.B. Lippincott & Co., 1865.

Madison, James. "Notes on Suffrage." 1829. Reprinted in *Letters and Other Writings of James Madison.* Vol. 4, pp. 21–30. Philadelphia: J.B. Lippincott & Co., 1865. (These notes were dated 1829 in the volume, but the title states that Madison wrote them "at different periods after his retirement from public life.")

Madison, James. "Speech in the Virginia State Convention of 1829–'30, on the Question of the Ratio of Representation in the Two Branches of the Legislature." 2 December 1829. Reprinted in *Letters and Other Writings of James Madison.* Vol. 4, pp. 51–55. Philadelphia: J.B. Lippincott & Co., 1865.

Meese, Edwin III. Address before the D.C. Chapter of the Federalist Society Lawyers Division, Washington, D.C., 15 November 1985.

Pilon, Roger. "Ordering Rights Consistently: Or What We Do and Do Not Have Rights To." *Georgia Law Review* 13 (Summer 1979a): 1171–96.

Pilon, Roger. "Corporations and Rights: On Treating Corporate People Justly." *Georgia Law Review* 13 (Summer 1979b): 1245–1370.

Pilon, Roger. "On Moral and Legal Justification." *Southwestern University Law Review* 11(1979c): 1327–44.

Pilon, Roger. "On the Foundations of Justice." *Intercollegiate Review* 17 (Fall/Winter 1981): 3–14.

Pilon, Roger. "Capitalism and Rights: An Essay Toward Fine Tuning the Moral Foundations of the Free Society." *Journal of Business Ethics* 1 (February 1982): 29–42.

Pilon, Roger. "Property Rights, Takings, and a Free Society." *Harvard Journal of Law and Public Policy* 6 (Summer 1983): 165–95.

Saperstein, Saundra, and Lardner, George Jr. "Rehnquist: Nixon's Long Shot For a 'Law and Order' Court." *Washington Post* (7 July 1986): A1, A8.

Siegan, Bernard H. *Economic Liberties and the Constitution*. Chicago: University of Chicago Press, 1980.

Siegan, Bernard [H.] "The Supreme Court: The Final Arbiter." In *Beyond the Status Quo: Policy Proposals for America*, pp. 273–90. Edited by David Boaz and Edward H. Crane. Washington, D.C.: Cato Institute, 1985.

Tumlir, Jan. "Economic Policy as a Constitutional Problem." Fifteenth Wincott Memorial Lecture. Occasional Paper 70. London: Institute of Economic Affairs, 1984.

Tumlir, Jan. *Protectionism: Trade Policy in Democratic Societies*. Washington, D.C.: American Enterprise Institute, 1985.

PART I

INTERPRETING THE CONSTITUTION: THEORY AND PRACTICE

2

ECONOMIC AFFAIRS AS HUMAN AFFAIRS

Antonin Scalia

The title of this article—Economic Affairs as Human Affairs—is derived from a phrase I recall from the earliest days of my political awareness. Dwight Eisenhower used to insist, with demonstrably successful effect, that he was "a conservative in economic affairs, but a liberal in human affairs." I am sure he meant it to connote nothing more profound than that he represented the best of both Republican and Democratic tradition. But still, that seemed to me a peculiar way to put it—contrasting economic affairs with human affairs as though economics is a science developed for the benefit of dogs or trees; something that has nothing to do with human beings, with their welfare, aspirations, or freedoms.

That, of course, is a pernicious notion, though it represents a turn of mind that characterizes much American political thought. It leads to the conclusion that economic rights and liberties are qualitatively distinct from, and fundamentally inferior to, other noble human values called civil rights, about which we should be more generous. Unless one is a thoroughgoing materialist, there is some appeal to this. Surely the freedom to dispose of one's property as one pleases, for example, is not as high an aspiration as the freedom to think or write or worship as one's conscience dictates. On closer analysis, however, it seems to me that the difference between economic freedoms and what are generally called civil rights turns out to be a difference of degree rather than of kind. Few of us, I suspect, would have much difficulty choosing between the right to own property and the right to receive a Miranda warning.

In any case, in the real world a stark dichotomy between economic freedoms and civil rights does not exist. Human liberties of various

The author is Associate Justice of the United States Supreme Court. This paper is an edited version of the author's remarks delivered at the Cato Institute's conference "Economic Liberties and the Judiciary," Washington, D.C., 26 October 1984, at which time he served as Circuit Judge for the U.S. Court of Appeals, D.C. Circuit.

types are dependent on one another, and it may well be that the most humble of them is indispensable to the others—the firmament, so to speak, upon which the high spires of the most exalted freedoms ultimately rest. I know no society, today or in any era of history, in which high degrees of intellectual and political freedom have flourished side by side with a high degree of state control over the relevant citizen's economic life. The free market, which presupposes relatively broad economic freedom, has historically been the cradle of broad political freedom, and in modern times the demise of economic freedom has been the grave of political freedom as well. The same phenomenon is observable in the small scales of our private lives. As a practical matter, he who controls my economic destiny controls much more of my life as well. Most salaried professionals do not consider themselves "free" to go about wearing sandals and nehru jackets, or to write letters on any subjects they please to the *New York Times.*

My concern in this essay, however, is not economic liberty in general, but economic liberty and the judiciary. One must approach this topic with the realization that the courts are (in most contexts, at least) hardly disparaging of economic rights and liberties. Although most of the cases you read of in the newspaper may involve busing, or homosexual rights, or the supervision of school districts and mental institutions, the vast bulk of the courts' civil business consists of the vindication of economic rights between private individuals and against the government. Indeed, even the vast bulk of noncriminal "civil rights" cases are really cases involving economic disputes. The legal basis for the plaintiff's claim may be sex discrimination, but what she is really complaining about is that someone did her out of a job. Even the particular court on which I sit, which because of its location probably gets an inordinately large share of civil cases *not* involving economic rights, still finds that the majority of its business consists of enforcing economic rights against the government—the right to conduct business in an unregulated fashion where Congress has authorized no regulation, or the right to receive a fair return upon capital invested in a rate-regulated business. Indeed, some of the economic interests protected by my court are quite rarefied, such as a business's right to remain free of economic competition from a government licensee whose license is defective in a respect having nothing to do with the plaintiff's interests—for example, one radio station's challenge to the license of a competing station on the basis that the latter will produce electronic interference with a third station.

Fundamental or rarefied, the point is that we, the judiciary, do a lot of protecting of economic rights and liberties. The problem that some see is that this protection in the federal courts runs only by and large against the executive branch and not against the Congress. We will ensure that the executive does not impose any constraints upon economic activity which Congress has not authorized; and that where constraints *are* authorized the executive follows statutorily prescribed procedures and that the executive (and, much more rarely, Congress in its prescriptions) follows constitutionally required procedures. But we will never (well, hardly ever) decree that the substance of the congressionally authorized constraint is unlawful. That is to say, we do not provide a *constitutionalized* protection except insofar as matters of process, as opposed to substantive economic rights, are concerned.

There are those who urge reversal of this practice. The main vehicle available—and the only one I address specifically here—is the due process clause of the Fifth and Fourteenth Amendments, which provides that no person shall be deprived of "life, liberty, or property, without due process of law." Although one might suppose that a reference to "process" places limitations only upon the *manner* in which a thing may be done, and not upon the *doing* of it, since at least the late 1800s the federal courts have in fact interpreted these clauses to prohibit the *substance* of certain governmental action, no matter what fair and legitimate procedures attend that substance. Thus, there has come to develop a judicial vocabulary which refers (seemingly redundantly) to "procedural due process" on the one hand, and (seemingly paradoxically) to "substantive due process" on the other hand. Until the mid-1930s, substantive due process rights were extended not merely to what we would now term "civil rights"— for example, the freedom to teach one's child a foreign language if one wishes—but also to a broad range of economic rights—for example, the right to work twelve hours a day if one wishes. Since that time, application of the concept has been consistently expanded in the civil rights field (*Roe v. Wade* is the most controversial recent extension) but entirely eliminated in the field of economic rights. Some urge that it should be resuscitated.

I pause to note at this point, lest I either be credited with what is good in the present system or blamed for what is bad, that it is not up to me. (I did not have to make that disclaimer a few years ago, when I was a law professor.) The Supreme Court decisions rejecting substantive due process in the economic field are clear, unequivocal and current, and as an appellate judge I try to do what I'm told. But

I will go beyond that disclaimer and say that in my view the position the Supreme Court has arrived at is good—or at least that the suggestion that it change its position is even worse.

As should be apparent from what I said above, my position is not based on the proposition that economic rights are unimportant. Nor do I necessarily quarrel with the specific nature of the particular economic rights that the most sagacious of the proponents of substantive due process would bring within the protection of the Constitution; were I a legislator, I might well vote for them. Rather, my skepticism arises from misgivings about, first, the effect of such expansion on the behavior of courts in other areas quite separate from economic liberty, and second, the ability of the courts to limit their constitutionalizing to those elements of economic liberty that are sensible. I will say a few words about each.

First, the effect of constitutionalizing substantive economic guarantees on the behavior of the courts in other areas: There is an inevitable connection between judges' ability and willingness to craft substantive due process guarantees in the economic field and their ability and willingness to do it elsewhere. Many believe—and among those many are some of the same people who urge an expansion of economic due process rights—that our system already suffers from relatively recent constitutionalizing, and thus judicializing, of social judgments that ought better be left to the democratic process. The courts, they feel, have come to be regarded as an alternate legislature, whose charge differs from that of the ordinary legislature in the respect that while the latter may enact into law good ideas, the former may enact into law only *unquestionably* good ideas, which, since they *are* so unquestionably good, *must* be part of the Constitution. I would not adopt such an extravagant description of the problem. But I do believe that every era raises its own peculiar threat to constitutional democracy, and that the attitude of mind thus caricatured represents the distinctive threat of our times. And I therefore believe that whatever reinforces rather than challenges that attitude is to that extent undesirable. It seems to me that the reversal of a half-century of judicial restraint in the economic realm comes within that category. In the long run, and perhaps even in the short run, the reinforcement of mistaken and unconstitutional perceptions of the role of the courts in our system far outweighs whatever evils may have accrued from undue judicial abstention in the economic field.

The response to my concern, I suppose, is that the connection I assert between judicial intervention in the economic realm and in other realms can simply not be shown to exist. We have substantive due process aplenty in the field of civil liberties, even while it has been obliterated in the economic field. My rejoinder is simply an abiding faith that logic will out. Litigants before me often characterize the argument that if the court does w (which is desirable) then it must logically do x, y, and z (which are undesirable) as a "parade of horribles"; but in my years at the law I have too often seen the end of the parade come by. There really is an inevitable tug of logical consistency upon human affairs, and especially upon judicial affairs— indeed, that is the only thing that makes the system work. So I must believe that as bad as some feel judicial "activism" has gotten without substantive due process in the economic field, *absent* that memento of judicial humility it might have gotten even worse. And I have little hope that judicial and lawyerly attitudes can be coaxed back to a more restricted view of the courts' role in a democratic society at the same time that we are charging forward on an entirely new front.

Though it is something of an oversimplification, I do not think it unfair to say that this issue presents the moment of truth for many conservatives who have been criticizing the courts in recent years. They must decide whether they really believe, as they have been saying, that the courts are doing too much, or whether they are actually nursing only the less principled grievance that the courts have not been doing what *they* want.

The second reason for my skepticism is the absence of any reason to believe that the courts would limit their constitutionalizing of economic rights to those rights that are sensible. In this regard some conservatives seem to make the same mistake they so persuasively argue the society makes whenever it unthinkingly calls in government regulation to remedy a "market failure." It is first necessary to make sure, they have persuaded us, that the cure is not worse than the disease—that the phenomenon of "government failure," attributable to the fact that the government, like the market, happens to be composed of self-interested human beings, will not leave the last state of the problem worse than the first. It strikes me as peculiar that these same rational free-market proponents will unthinkingly call in the courts as a *deus ex machina* to solve what they perceive as the problems of democratic inadequacy in the field of economic rights. Is there much reason to believe that the courts, if they undertook the task, would do a good job? If economic sophistication is the touchstone, it suffices to observe that these are the folks who developed three-quarters of a century of counterproductive law under the Sherman Act. But perhaps what counts is not economic sophistication, but rather a favoritism—not shared by the political branches of government—toward the institution of property and its protection. I have no doubt that judges once met this qualification. When Madison described them as a "natural aristocracy," I am sure he had in mind an aristocracy of property as well as of manners. But with the proliferation and consequent bureaucratization of the courts, the relative modesty of judicial salaries, and above all the development of lawyers (and hence of judges) through a system of generally available university education which, in this country as in others, more often nurtures collectivist than capitalist philosophy, one would be foolish to look for Daddy Warbucks on the bench.

But, the proponents of constitutionalized economic rights will object, we do not propose an open-ended, unlimited charter to the courts to create economic rights, but would tie the content of those rights to the text of the Constitution and, where the text is itself somewhat open-ended (the due process clause, for example), to established (if recently forgotten) constitutional traditions. As a theoretical matter, that could be done—though it is infinitely more difficult today than it was fifty years ago. Because of the courts' long retirement from the field of constitutional economics, and because of judicial and legislative developments in other fields, the social consensus as to what are the limited, "core" economic rights does not exist today as it perhaps once did. But even if it is theoretically possible for the courts to mark out limits to their intervention, it is hard to be confident that they would do so. We may find ourselves burdened with judicially prescribed economic liberties that are worse than the pre-existing economic bondage. What would you think, for example, of a substantive-due-process, constitutionally guaranteed, economic right of every worker to "just and favourable remuneration ensuring for himself and his family an existence worthy of human dignity?" Many think this a precept of natural law; why not of the Constitution? A sort of constitutionally prescribed (and thus judicially determined) minimum wage. Lest it be thought fanciful, I have taken the formulation of this right verbatim from Article 23 of the United Nations' Universal Declaration of Human Rights.

Finally, let me suggest that the call for creating (or, if you prefer, "reestablishing") economic constitutional guarantees mistakes the nature and effect of the constitutionalizing process. To some degree, a constitutional guarantee is like a commercial loan: you can only get it if, at the time, you don't really need it. The most important, enduring, and stable portions of the Constitution represent such a deep social consensus that one suspects that if they were entirely eliminated, very little would change. And the converse is also true. A guarantee may appear in the words of the Constitution, but when the society ceases to possess an abiding belief in it, it has no living effect. Consider the fate of the principle expressed in the Tenth Amendment that the federal government is a government of limited powers. I do not suggest that constitutionalization has no effect in helping the society to preserve allegiance to its fundamental principles. That is the whole purpose of a constitution. But the allegiance comes first and the preservation afterwards.

Most of the constitutionalizing of civil rights that the courts have effected in recent years has been at the margins of well-established and deeply held social beliefs. Even *Brown v. Board of Education*, as significant a step as it might have seemed, was only an elaboration of the consequences of the nation's deep belief in the equality of all persons before the law. Where the Court has tried to go further than that (the unsuccessful attempt to eliminate the death penalty, to take one of the currently less controversial examples), the results have been precarious. Unless I have been on the bench so long that I no longer have any feel for popular sentiment, I do not detect the sort of national commitment to most of the economic liberties generally discussed that would enable even an activist court to constitutionalize them. That lack of sentiment may be regrettable, but to seek to develop it by enshrining the unaccepted principles in the Constitution is to place the cart before the horse.

If you are interested in economic liberties, then, the first step is to recall the society to that belief in their importance which (I have no doubt) the founders of the republic shared. That may be no simple task, because the roots of the problem extend as deeply into modern theology as into modern social thought. I remember a conversation with Irving Kristol some years ago, in which he expressed gratitude that his half of the Judeo-Christian heritage had never thought it a sin to be rich. In fact my half never thought it so either. Voluntary poverty, like voluntary celibacy, was a counsel of perfection—but it was not thought that either wealth or marriage was inherently evil, or a condition that the just society should seek to stamp out. But that subtle distinction has assuredly been forgotten, and we live in an age in which many Christians are predisposed to believe that John D. Rockefeller, for all his piety (he founded the University of Chicago as a Baptist institution), is likely to be damned and Ché Guevara, for all his nonbelief, is likely to be among the elect. This suggests that the task of creating what I might call a constitutional ethos of economic liberty is no easy one. But it is the first task.

3

JUDICIAL REVIEW: RECKONING ON TWO KINDS OF ERROR

Richard A. Epstein

Antonin Scalia has explained why he believes courts should refrain from intervening to protect what are generally described as economic liberties—chiefly, the right to own and use property and the right to dispose of both property and labor by contract. In so doing, he has recounted at length all the errors and confusions that beset courts when they try to vindicate these basic economic rights by constitutional means.

There are powerful reasons why judges may do badly in this endeavor. They are isolated, and they tend to be drawn from political or social elites. Their competence on economic matters is often limited. When they pass on complex legislation, they often misunderstand its purpose and effect. By any standard, the error rate of their decisions has been high. I cannot challenge his conclusions simply by saying that he underestimates the sterling performance of his colleagues on the bench. If the only issue were judicial competence, Scalia's conclusion would swiftly follow: Since courts cannot master economic matters, they should adopt a form of judicial laissez faire that keeps judges' hands off the economic system.

As stated, Scalia's plea for judicial restraint is not a defense of legal anarchy. Instead, it accepts government control over economic affairs, but guarantees that this control will be exercised by the legislative and executive branches of government (as well as the administrative agencies they have created). By necessity, only political checks are available to ensure that national policy does not stray too far from the social consensus.

Scalia's position represents the mainstream of American constitutional theory today. My purpose is to take issue with the conventional

---

The author is James Parker Hall Professor of Law at the University of Chicago. This paper is an edited version of the author's remarks delivered at the Cato Institute's conference "Economic Liberties and the Judiciary," Washington, D.C., 26 October 1984.

wisdom. I hope to persuade Scalia to take upon himself, and to pursue energetically, the tasks that our Constitution assigns to him and to other federal judges. Note that in urging this course I speak as an academic who would impose on sitting judges duties more extensive than they are often willing to assume.

In my view, Scalia has addressed only one side of a two-sided problem. He has pointed out the weaknesses of judicial action. But he has not paid sufficient attention to the errors and dangers in unchanneled legislative behavior. The only way to reach a balanced, informed judgment on the intrinsic desirability of judicial control of economic liberties is to consider the *relative* shortcomings of the two institutions—judicial and legislative—that compete for the crown of final authority. The constitutionality of legislation restricting economic liberties cannot be decided solely by appealing to an initial presumption in favor of judicial restraint. Instead, the imperfections of the judicial system must be matched with the imperfections of the political branches of government.

What are the problems with legislation? When we put someone in charge of the collective purse or the police force, we in effect give him a spigot that allows him to tap into other people's property, money, and liberty. The legislator that casts a vote on an appropriations bill is spending not only his own wealth, but everyone else's. When the power of coalition, the power of factions, the power of artifice and strategy come into play, it often turns out that legislatures reach results that (in the long as well as the short run) are far from the social optimum.

To take the limiting case, suppose a group of people have a profound and anxious debate, and then decide, by a bare majority, that the prevailing distribution of wealth is wrong. So the 51 percent decide to condemn, without payment, all the property of the 49 percent. Strict majoritarian principles would allow them to get away with that. But Scalia and others would say, "It cannot be done because the eminent domain clause in our Constitution provides that when government takes private property for public use, it must pay." The winners in a legislative battle may not confiscate the property of the losers.

Now, note the slippery slope. We have identified a form of legislative failure, along with a constitutional provision that seems to respond to that kind of failure. The first step down the slope is the announcement that a particular piece of legislation, even if it reflects the consensus of the population at large, is not going to work. And once we take that step, where in principle do we stop? Suppose we change the dynamics of coalition building, so that it takes 80 percent of the population to confiscate the wealth of the other 20 percent. Does this broader consensus mean that the program is acceptable and can proceed? Or are the perils of faction not indeed, in many ways, even greater in the second case than they were before, since the minority is now more isolated and less able to defend itself in the legislative forum?

Once one starts down the slippery slope, one cannot stop, at least without a theory. Intellectually, we must conclude that much of the impetus behind legislative behavior is to induce forced exchanges—to take from some people more than they get in exchange, in order to provide benefits to those who happen to control the political levers. To some extent this is unavoidable, since we need a system of collective controls in order to operate the police, the courts, the national defense, and so on. And opportunities for abuse in government operations are inseparable from that collective need.

The theory of constitutionalism, as I understand it, tries to find a way to minimize the sum of the abuses that stem from legislative greed on the one hand, and judicial incompetence on the other. There is, by and large, no third alternative to this sorry state of affairs. What I fear is wrong with Scalia's statement of the argument is this: By focusing exclusively on the defects he finds in the judicial part of the process, he tends to ignore the powerful defects that pervade the legislative part of the process. Our Constitution reflects a general distrust toward the political process of government—a high degree of risk aversion. That is why it wisely spreads the powers of government among different institutions through a system of checks and balances. To provide no (or at least no effective) check on the legislature's power to regulate economic liberties is to concentrate power in ways that are inconsistent with the need to diversify risk. To allow courts to strike down legislation, but never to pass it, helps to control political abuse without undermining the distinctive features of the separate branches of government. Once we realize that all human institutions (being peopled by people) are prey to error, the only thing we can hope to do is to minimize those errors so that the productive activities of society can go forward as little hampered as possible.

Thus far I have been discussing general political theory: How is it that one would want to organize a constitution? But we do not have to talk about constitutions in the round and in the abstract. We have an actual constitution, and since it is a written one, we can check to see how it handles the particular problem of protecting economic liberties.

To listen to my colleague—and to the many other advocates of judicial restraint—one would almost think that the Constitution contained only the following kinds of provisions: those organizing a judiciary, a legislature, and an executive; and those providing for separation of powers, checks and balances, and so on. All those devices—efforts to divide and conquer the governing power—are efforts to limit the abuses of factions. But they are not the only provisions our Constitution contains. It also contains many broad and powerful clauses designed to limit the jurisdiction of both federal and state governments. The commerce clause, at least in its original conception, comes to mind. Other clauses are designed to limit what the states and the federal government can do within the scope of their admitted powers. These include the eminent domain clause (which always bound the federal government and since the Civil War amendments has bound the states as well), the contracts clause, the privileges and immunities clause found both in the original Constitution and the Fourteenth Amendment, the equal protection clause, and due process.

These provisions are not curlicues on the margins of the document; they are not without force or consequence. They are provisions designed to preserve definite boundaries between public and private ordering. Take the question of minimum wages. The principle of freedom of contract—that parties should be free to set wage terms as they see fit—is, given the contracts clause, on a collision course with that sort of legislative regulation of the economy. So it is with the eminent domain question discussed above. Many of the particular provisions of the Constitution are designed to deal with the very kinds of questions that political theory indicates to be sources of our enormous uneasiness and distrust of the legislative process.

The next question is, how have these constitutional provisions been interpreted in actual practice? A key element is the "rational basis" test, which holds that so long as there is some "plausible" or "conceivable" justification for the challenged legislation, it is invulnerable to constitutional attack. Under the guise of this test, judges have decided that the last thing they will do is look hard and analytically at any political institution, at any legislative action, that regulates economic affairs. It turns out that Scalia's position, already stated even more forcefully by the Supreme Court itself, completely abandons the idea that serious intellectual discussion can yield right and wrong answers on matters of political organization and constitutional interpretation. Courts simply give up before they try, and embrace an appalling sort of ethical noncognitivism. Anything legislatures do is as good as anything else they might have done; we cannot decide what is right or wrong, so it is up to Congress and the states to determine the limitations of their own power—which, of course, totally subverts the original constitutional arrangement of limited government.

Part of the explanation for the judiciary's poor performance now becomes clear. When courts do not try, they cannot succeed. When they use transparent arguments to justify dubious legislation, they cannot raise the level of debate. When courts (following the lead of the Supreme Court) hold that the state has the right to say X, when they know X is wrong, they fritter away their own political authority on an indefensible cause.

But can matters ever be this clear? In some instances it has seemed that no conceivable interpretation of the constitutional text could generate or justify the results that the Supreme Court has been prepared to reach. Take its decision in *Hawaii Housing Authority v. Midkiff* (1984). There is a good reason why the constitutional clause restricting the seizure of property by eminent domain contains a provision specifying that the seizure must be for public use. The last thing one needs a government for is to arrange a set of coerced transfers between A and B when voluntary markets can arrange the same transfers without the abuses of faction. For the most part, this means that when we want the government to take property, we want it to do so in order to generate a public good, some nonexclusive benefit, that a private market cannot generate. Legislation (like that challenged in *Hawaii*) that simply takes land and transfers it from landlords to tenants, or the reverse, constitutes the paradigmatic transaction that the eminent domain clause was designed to prohibit. So when the Court sustained the Hawaiian statute, it declared the central wrong to be perfectly legal. The justices stood the Constitution on its head. They said, in effect, that although the eminent domain clause must have been put there for some purpose, we cannot figure out what that purpose might be, so we might as well read it out of the document and act as if it had never existed.

The courts have shown the same pattern of behavior in other cases. For example, it seems clear today that they will no longer construe the police power to protect private contracts of any sort—even when those contracts complied with all applicable rules at the time of their formation. What does a clause that prohibits impairing the obligation of contracts mean? Today, it turns out (with only minor exaggeration) that a legislature can simply decide to nullify contractual provisions on the grounds that this legally imposed breach of contract makes one of the contracting parties better off than it was before. If that is the only test, then every contract is vulnerable to judicial nullification.

This judicial deference in the protection of economic rights has enormous costs. The moment courts allow all private rights to become unstable and subject to collective (legislative) determination, all of the general productive activities of society will have to take on a new form. People will no longer be able to plan private arrangements secure in the knowledge of their social protection. Instead, they will take the same attitude toward domestic investment that they take toward foreign investment. Assuming that their enterprise will be confiscated within a certain number of years, domestic investors will make only those investments with a high rate of return and short payout period, so that when they see confiscation coming, they will be able to run. To be sure, the probability of expropriation is greater in many foreign contracts than it is in the United States. But given our record of price controls and selective industry regulation, it is clear that the once great protections we enjoyed have been compromised, and for no desirable social goal.

I submit that this is not what we want legislatures to do. It is wrongheaded to argue that, because an auditor cannot hope to correct every abuse in the Defense Department's procurement policies, he should therefore refuse to go after the $5,000 coffee pot—or that because a judge cannot hope to correct every infringement of economic liberties, he should therefore refuse to go after large-lot zoning restrictions. There are many blatantly inappropriate statutes that cry out for a quick and easy kill. Striking them down puts no particular strain on the judiciary. To invalidate a statute, a judge need not make complex factual determinations or continually supervise large branches of the federal government. He need not take over school boards, try to run prisons or mental hospitals, or demand that Congress appropriate funds. He need only say that, in certain circumstances, the government cannot do something—period—while in other circumstances, it can, but must pay those people on whom it imposes a disproportionate burden.

Government exists, after all, because the market's ability to organize forced exchanges is limited. We need to collect taxes, to impose regulations, to assign rights and liabilities through a centralized process, but only for limited public purposes. Our guiding principle should derive from our Lockean tradition—a tradition that speaks about justice and natural rights, a tradition that understands the importance of the autonomy of the person, and respects it in religion, in speech, and in ordinary day-to-day affairs. When government wishes to encroach on those rights in order to discharge its collective functions, it must give all the individuals on whom it imposes its obligations a fair equivalent in exchange. It may be that it is not always possible to measure that equivalence. Possibly we cannot achieve the goal of full compensation and simultaneously provide the collective goods. I am prepared to debate at great length where the proper margins are with respect to the application of this general principle. What I am not prepared to say is that we can organize our society on the belief that the question I just posed is not worth asking. Consequently, when the government announces that it has provided a comparable benefit, courts should not take its word on faith, when everything in the record points indubitably to the opposite conclusion.

When one compares the original Constitution with the present state of judicial interpretation, the real issue becomes not how to protect the status quo, but what kinds of incremental adjustments should be made in order to shift the balance back toward the original design. On this question, we can say two things. First, at the very least, we do not want to remove what feeble protection still remains for economic liberties. Any further judicial abdication in this area will only invite further legislative intrigue and more irresponsible legislation. Yet recent Supreme Court decisions have tended to invite just that. Second, since courts are bound to some extent by a larger social reality, we cannot pretend that the New Deal never happened. Rather, we must strive to regain sight of the proper objectives of constitutional government and the proper distribution of powers between the legislatures and the courts, so as to come up with the kinds of incremental adjustments that might help us to restore the proper constitutional balance.

Judicial restraint is fine when it keeps courts from intervening in areas where they have no business intervening. But the world always has two kinds of errors: the error of commission (type I) and the error of omission (type II). In the context of our discussion, type I error refers to the probability of judicial intervention to protect economic rights when such intervention is not justified by constitutional provisions. And type II error refers to the probability of forgoing judicial intervention to protect economic liberties when such intervention is justified. This second type of error—the failure to intervene when there is strong textual authority and constitutional theory—cannot be ignored.

What Scalia has, in effect, argued for is to minimize type I error. We run our system by being most afraid of intervention where it is not appropriate. My view is that we should minimize both types of error. One only has to read the opinions of the Supreme Court on economic liberties and property rights to realize that these opinions are intellectually incoherent and that some movement in the direction of judicial activism is clearly indicated. The only sensible disagreement is over the nature, the intensity, and the duration of the shift.

At this point, the division of power within the legal system is not in an advantageous equilibrium. If the judiciary continues on the path of self-restraint with respect to economic liberties, we will continue to suffer social and institutional losses that could have been reduced by the prudent judicial control that would result from taking the constitutional protections of economic liberties at their face value.

4

JUDICIAL CONTROL OF THE POLITICAL BRANCHES: PUBLIC PURPOSE AND PUBLIC LAW

Peter H. Aranson

I. Introduction

The Supreme Court of the United States long has enjoyed a history of economic error,[1] especially in its reviews of actions taken by the political branches of government. In defense of the Court, we must acknowledge that neither the Constitution nor its own pronouncements delegates to the judiciary a "roving commission" to decide cases on economic grounds. Nor is it apparent that we would prefer such a delegation.[2] The Court, for that matter, seldom indicates any concern at all for the economic content of its cases and decisions, and economic sophistication certainly is not one of its stated goals. Nevertheless, the conclusion that the Court often is incapable of "doing" economics correctly finds supporting evidence in cases decided wrongly (from an economist's perspective) even during the reign of substantive due process, when it is alleged to have specifically accepted the economist's garb,[3] as well as in more recent

---

The author is Professor of Economics at Emory University. He wishes to thank George E. Butler and Jonathan R. Macey for their helpful comments in preparing this paper for publication. He also acknowledges his intellectual debt to Richard A. Epstein and thanks him for discussing his interpretation of Home Building & Loan Association v. Blaisdell *with the author.*

[1]See, for example, Slaughter House Cases, 83 U.S. (16 Wall.) 36 (1873) (refusing to overturn an 1869 Louisiana law granting a monopoly in slaughterhouses and stockyards, because the state's police power here could find no limitation *inter alia* on privileges and immunities or equal protection grounds).

[2]See, for example, Richard A. Epstein, "Taxation, Regulation, and Confiscation," *Osgood Hall Law Journal* 20 (September 1982): 433–53, and James M. Buchanan, "Good Economics—Bad Law," *Virginia Law Review* 60 (March 1974): 483–92.

[3]See, for example, Muller v. Oregon, 208 U.S. 412 (1908) (upholding state statute setting a ten-hour maximum work day for women employed in laundries). For a brief discussion of the economic error involved, see Richard A. Posner, *Economic Analysis of Law*, 2d ed. (Boston: Little, Brown, & Co., 1977), p. 502. See also Bunting v. Oregon, 243 U.S. 426 (1917) (upholding statute limiting manufacturing employees' work day to 10 hours).

cases that it decided at least partially or implicitly on economic grounds.[4] More often than not the Court's announced rationale for its economic decisions overtly concerns issues of law and the plain (or ambiguous) language of statutes, rather than the economic preferences or conclusions of the justices. So, for example, in *Barron v. Baltimore*,[5] on economic grounds the Court could well have awarded Barron damages for the injury to his wharf brought about by the city's rechanneling of streams. It declined to do so, because it could find no power to do so: There did not yet exist a Fourteenth Amendment, applying the Bill of Rights and the Fifth Amendment's takings clause to the states.[6]

Today, the Court specifically rejects many invitations to apply economic analysis to the cases brought before it. Instead, it grants to federal, state, and sometimes local legislatures the nearly unassailable rights to define their goals and to fashion legislation to achieve them.[7] Even so, many legal writers recently have urged the courts to

---

But see Adkins v. Children's Hospital, 261 U.S. 525 (1923) (holding District of Columbia minimum wage law unconstitutional under due process clause of the Fifth Amendment); Morehead v. New York *ex. rel.* Tipaldo, 298 U.S. 587 (1936) (holding New York act setting minimum wage for women repugnant to the due process clause of Fourteenth Amendment); New State Ice Co. v. Liebmann, 285 U.S. 262 (1932) (invalidating Oklahoma entry restriction on ice manufacturers); and Adams v. Tanner, 244 U.S. 590 (1917) (holding unconstitutional a statute outlawing employment agencies that collect fees from workers).

[4]See, for example, Penn Central Transportation Co. v. City of New York, 438 U.S. 104 (1978) (upholding as not a taking application of New York City act to limit use of air rights over Grand Central Terminal), discussed at text accompanying infra notes 75–82; Monsanto Company v. Spray-Rite Service Corporation, 104 S. Ct. 1464 (1984); Hawaii Housing Authority v. Midkiff, 467 U.S. 229 (1984), discussed at text accompanying infra notes 29–40; and Block v. Community Nutrition Institute, 104 S. Ct. 2450 (1984).

[5]7 Pet. 343, 8 L. Ed. 672 (1833).

[6]Chicago, B. & Q. R.R. v. Chicago, 166 U.S. 226 (1897).

[7]See, for example, Nebbia v. New York, 291 U.S. 502 (1934). The Court there held:
> So far as the requirement of due process is concerned, and in the absence of other constitutional restriction, a state is free to adopt whatever economic policy may reasonably be deemed to promote public welfare, and to enforce that policy by legislation adapted to its purpose. The courts are without authority either to declare such policy, or, when it is declared by the legislative arm, to override it. If the laws passed are seen to have a reasonable relation to a proper legislative purpose, and are neither arbitrary nor discriminatory, the requirements of due process are satisfied, and judicial determination to that effect renders a court functus officio.   [Id. at 537]

The most broad ranging application and extension of this doctrine in recent years is Hawaii Housing Authority v. Midkiff, 467 U.S. 229 (1984), discussed at text accompanying infra notes 29–40. Existing judicial limitations on legislative action are discussed at text accompanying infra notes 55–6, 71–3, 119–31, 141–44, 155–56, and 165–72.

(re)apply doctrines that strongly resemble the substantive due process requirements more or less consistently rejected since *Nebbia*.[8]

This essay's central themes are that judges as economists—Posnerian judges, if you will—can provide at best only a feeble protection for economic liberties as constitutional rights; that this casting of the judge's role as economist would be constitutionally, philosophically, and even economically unacceptable; and that judges should interpret broadly and comprehensively the plain language of the Constitution to protect existing economic rights. They should be less concerned with promulgating economically preferable results. Protecting such rights, we hasten to add, will nearly always promote the economically "correct" results. But courts must find doctrinal, not economic, bases for containing the growing mischief of the political branches.

Getting to these conclusions is not difficult, but it requires an argument in several parts. Section II begins this task by examining briefly the Supreme Court's stated reasons for eschewing the activity of economic analysis and by reviewing one theory of the Court's reluctance to constrain the political branches.[9] Section III discusses some recent Supreme Court decisions, to illustrate the Court's inadequate hold on economic principles, brought about by error itself as well as by a reluctance to apply economic analysis. Section IV brings the argument full circle by showing the inadequacy of economic analysis as a protector of economic rights as well as the inherent threat that such an analysis can pose to those rights, especially if carried on at higher appellate levels. Section V outlines a strategy

---

[8]See, for example, Bernard H. Siegan, *Economic Liberties and the Constitution* (Chicago: University of Chicago Press, 1980) (arguing that Congress intended the Fourteenth Amendment to require judicial scrutiny, on economic due-process grounds, of economic legislation); Epstein, "Taxation" (arguing for a test of "*disproportionate impact* of a tax or regulation [to serve] . . . as an indirect measure of the adequacy of compensation," p. 438); Richard A. Epstein, "Toward a Revitalization of the Contract Clause," *University of Chicago Law Review* 51 (Summer 1984): 703–51; and Jerry L. Mashaw, "Constitutional Deregulation: Notes Toward a Public-Public Law," *Tulane Law Review* 54 (June 1980): 849–76, who argues:

> The Constitution presumes that private activities will be constrained only to promote public purposes. The recognition, first, that there is a wide range of such purposes, and second, that democratic, collective choice may pursue any or all of them in a complex and eclectic body of regulatory statutes, in no way reduces the force of the basic principle. The citizen has a constitutional right to demand that public law be public-regarding. Otherwise, his private harm is constitutionally inexplicable.   [Mashaw, p. 849]

[9]William M. Landes and Richard A. Posner, "The Independent Judiciary in an Interest-Group Perspective," *Journal of Law and Economics* 18 (December 1975): 875–901.

for leading the Court to an assertion of those rights within a constitutional framework.

II. The Court's Reluctance to Apply Economic Judgments

It is useful at the outset to review the Court's stated reasons for its reluctance to review statute law on economic grounds, if only to form the factual predicate for constitutional judgments. Then, we examine one economic theory proffered to explain this reluctance. The Court's reasons and the theoretical explanation are not competing views, in that the Court's reasons provide a legal rationalization for the economic theory's predictions. An acknowledgment of the theory's implications nevertheless remains central to an understanding of how and why the Court might become the guardian of economic rights.

The Court's Rationale

During its 1977 Term, the Supreme Court decided the case of *Moorman Mfg. Co. v. Bair.*[10] *Moorman* involved a challenge to Iowa's method of apportioning the income of interstate corporations in calculating the Iowa corporate income tax. At the time *Moorman* was decided, 43 states and the District of Columbia used a three-factor apportionment, which calculated the ratios of sales, property, and payroll in the taxing state to the corporation's total national sales, property, and payroll, usually giving equal weight to each ratio, and multiplying the resulting fraction (divided by three) times total national profit, to arrive at a tax base.[11] Iowa, by contrast, used a single-factor tax based on sales, although it did allow taxpayers to petition for a different formula if the single-factor formula subjected the firm "to taxation on a greater portion of its net income than is 'reasonably attributable' to business within the state . . . ."[12]

Considering the existential datum that nearly all other states used a three-factor formula, Iowa's single-factor tax, based solely on sales, would discriminate against certain foreign (out-of-state) corporations. Firm A might do all of its manufacturing, warehousing, and managing

---

[10]437 U.S. 267 (1978).

[11]Id. at 283 n.1 (Powell, J., dissenting). The footnote points out that West Virginia uses a two-factor formula. Colorado uses a two-factor apportionment, and Missouri uses a single-factor apportionment based on sales, but each of these states allows these formulae as alternatives to the three-factor apportionment. The rest of the states had no corporate income tax.

[12]Id. at 270.

in Illinois, but sell its product exclusively in Iowa, through traveling salesmen living beyond Iowa's boundaries. Such a firm would have its full income taxed as if it had originated in Iowa. Firm B, completely domiciled in Iowa, but selling exclusively in Illinois, would pay no Iowa corporate income tax at all. Moorman Mfg. Company, an Illinois corporation doing some of its business in Iowa, not unlike firm A, brought suit in Iowa's courts, claiming that Iowa's application of the single-factor formula to calculate its tax base constituted "extraterritorial taxation" in violation of the due process clause of the Constitution,[13] and that the resulting tax liability of profits to more than 100 percent of the net-income base also worked a violation of the commerce clause,[14] because firms could only escape this "double taxation" by locating their entire operations in Iowa.[15]

The unusual aspect of *Moorman* is that a group of distinguished economists of every political stripe submitted a brief *amicus curiae*, urging the Court to overturn Iowa's single-factor formula.[16] The brief pointed out, on purely theoretical but altogether compelling grounds, that Iowa's formula *perforce* had to burden interstate commerce, relative to a taxing scheme that used a three-factor attribution. In truth, the brief was more an exercise in accounting than in economics, and the conclusions stated therein equally well supported the charge of extraterritoriality.

The Court, per Justice Stevens, gave short shrift to this argument, principally on the ground that no empirical evidence was before it:

> Appellant does not suggest that it has shown that a significant portion of the income attributed to Iowa in fact was generated by its Illinois operations; the record does not contain any separate accounting analysis showing what portion of appellant's profits was attributable to sales, to manufacturing, or to any other phase of the company's operations. But appellant contends that we should proceed on the assumption that at least some portion of the income from Iowa sales was generated by Illinois activity.[17]

And then the economists were dismissed: "Whatever merit such an assumption might have from the standpoint of economic theory or legislative policy, it cannot support a claim in this litigation that Iowa in fact taxed profits not attributable to activities within the

[13]Id. at 272–73.

[14]Id. at 276.

[15]This relocation strategy would eliminate Illinois taxes. The firm could only avoid Iowa taxes by selling no goods in Iowa. The trial court found for Moorman, and the Supreme Court of Iowa reversed, 254 N.W. 2d 737 (1977).

[16]Brief *amicus curiae*, Moorman Mfg. Co. v. Bair, 437 U.S. 267 (1978).

[17]Moorman Mfg. Co. v. Bair, 437 U.S. at 272.

State . . . ."[18] Justice Stevens went on to argue that Illinois operations might show a loss, leaving Iowa profits to subsidize those operations.[19] But all of Moorman's manufacturing for the Iowa market was done in Illinois.[20] And even though the firm had over 500 salesmen and six warehouses in Iowa,[21] nevertheless the firm's percentage of total income attributable to Iowa was about 50 percent higher under the single-factor formula than under the three-factor calculation.[22] In short, Justice Stevens's hypothetical rebutter does not appear to be logically possible.

The Court rejected Moorman's due process claim largely on precedential grounds.[23] Then, it turned to the commerce clause challenge. Again rejecting the claim as "speculative" because of a lack of evidence, the Court went on to consider the wisdom of judicial action in this and similar cases. "If the Constitution were read to mandate such precision [invalidating overlapping taxes] in interstate taxation, the consequences would extend far beyond this particular case. For some risk of duplicative taxation exists whenever the States . . . do not follow identical rules. Accepting appellant's view of the Constitution, therefore, would require extensive judicial lawmaking."[24] Or would it? Only Iowa, West Virginia, Missouri, and Colorado might have been affected,[25] but then only if their taxes were challenged. More important still, the Court here conveniently glosses over any distinction between judicial lawmaking and judicial *constraints* on lawmaking. Moorman's claim was eminently sensible on both due process and commerce clause grounds, and the Court might at least have remanded for a consideration of factual questions, even though the economists' brief logically showed violations whose proof required no evidence. But the Court balanced Moorman's constitutional rights

[18]Id.

[19]Id.

[20]Id. at 269.

[21]Id.

[22]Id. at 271.

[23]Id. at 274–75.

[24]Id. at 278.

[25]The Court points out that it might find uniformity problems with other kinds of taxes. See Id. at 279. Certainly, this possibility, as well as the likelihood that various taxes may have interactive effects, might imply that I have read Justice Stevens's opinion at text accompanying supra note 24 too broadly. But the Court's practice is to consider various taxes separately and require facial equality for each tax. See Armco, Inc. v. Hardesty, 104 S. Ct. 2620 (1984). Furthermore, as Justice Powell, joined by Justice Blackman, argued in dissent, we must not forget that Iowa's tax was a clear commerce clause violation, because, *inter alia*, a firm could only avoid the tax by locating in Iowa. Id. at 288–90 (Powell, J., dissenting).

against an implied judicial economy and deference to the political branches, to Moorman's detriment and in derogation of the rights that it had asserted.

There was also a commonly expressed sense of relative "fitness" to decide acknowledged in *Moorman*. "Although the adoption of a uniform code would undeniably advance the policies that underlie the Commerce Clause, it would require a policy decision based on political and economic considerations that vary from state to state."[26] Again, a constitutionally based assertion of judicial constraint on legislation becomes equivalent to "a policy decision." But the Court would have none of either (as if its failure to uphold Moorman's challenge was not itself a policy decision). It expressed a concern lest its constitutionalizing of this problem by adopting the majority formula would divest any states that the change disadvantaged of their right to political representation in the decision-making process. The judicially promulgated uniform rule, that is, "could not reflect the national interest, because the interests of those States whose policies are subordinated in the quest for uniformity would be excluded from the calculation."[27] Justice Stevens's decision similarly hardened the economic consequences of Moorman's disenfranchisement in Iowa.

The Court referred the matter to Congress, as the more suitable body for deciding such questions:

> While the freedom of the States to formulate independent policy in this area may have to yield to an overriding national interest in uniformity, the content of any uniform rules to which they must subscribe should be determined only after due consideration is given to the interests of all affected States. It is clear that the legislative power granted to Congress by the Commerce Clause of the Constitution would amply justify rules for the division of income. It is to that body, and not this Court, that the Constitution has committed such policy decisions.[28]

Congress has consistently declined such invitations, and its majoritarian but pluralistic "group-veto" nature makes the premise of giving "due consideration . . . to the interests of all affected states" at least doubtful. Nevertheless, in *Moorman* we find spread out before us many of the Court's stated reasons for refusing to provide a judicial

[26]Id.

[27]Id. at 279–80 (footnote omitted). Of course, the Court here overlooks the possibility of granting intervenor status to such states. We cannot say whether the Court would accept this possibility as a surrogate for the constitutional basis of representation as mandated for the House and Senate.

[28]Id. at 280.

protection of constitutional rights: a wrong that exists allegedly only in theory; the need for judicial economy and the repugnance of so-called judicial lawmaking; and finally, the claimed superior fitness of Congress to create "policy" compared implicitly with the Court's "inferior" ability to protect rights.

This acquiescence in legislative determinations reaches its breathtaking but (by its own reasoning) logical conclusion in The 1983 Term, when a unanimous Court decided *Hawaii Housing Authority v. Midkiff.*[29] *Hawaii* involved a challenge to a statute that empowered the state to transfer land ownership in fee simple from large landowners to residents on the land who held ground leases. The court of appeals[30] had reversed a federal district court's[31] holding that the act did not violate the "public use" provision of the Fifth Amendment, as applied to the states by the Fourteenth Amendment. The Supreme Court reversed, thus upholding the Hawaii statute.

Justice O'Connor's decision for the Court sustained the act by observing, first, that the subject matter of the legislation is well within the scope of the police power, and indeed the act's subject matter need only invoke "a conceivable public purpose"[32] to escape constitutional infirmity. In this instance, that power was not unlike an attempt at "land reform" carried out by a banana republic[33]:

[29]467 U.S. 229 (Justice Marshall took no part in the decision).
[30]702 F.2d 788 (1983).
[31]483 F. Supp. 62 (Haw. 1979).
[32]467 U.S. at 241.
[33]The dissent in the court of appeals cited at length from a commentary on the act, urging just such a parallel:

> One factor that argues in favor of the Act and may be considered by the Court, if only subconsciously, is the current political reality that in much of the world, land reform is essential if democratic forms of government are to emerge or to prevail. In both Asia and Latin America it is taken for granted that a redistribution of the land must be accomplished as a vital first step in carrying out reforms that will allow democratic governments to be established and survive. Land reform is necessary for the economic, political, and social health and stability of many of these nations.
>
> It would be anomalous and somewhat hypocritical if the United States Government were to insist that land reform be undertaken in other countries when its own Constitution prevented similar reforms in the American States.

James P. Conahan, "Hawaii's Land Reform Act: Is It Constitutional?" *Hawaii Bar Journal* 6 (July 1969), p. 53 (cited in Midkiff v. Tom, 702 F.2d 788, 808 (1983) (Ferguson, C. J., dissenting)).

Such land reform seems desirable neither for Hawaii nor for Third World nations. The breakup of large land holdings subverts the ability of these nations to exploit scale economies in agriculture and to spread risk through crop and locational diversification. The urging of these policies by the United States similarly may elicit small sympathy among those who regard the preservation, not redistribution, of rights as the most important goal for enhancing political stability and advancing human rights.

The people of Hawaii have attempted, much as the settlers of the original 13 Colonies did, to reduce the perceived social and economic evils of a land oligopoly traceable to their monarchs. The land oligopoly has, according to the Hawaii legislature, created artificial deterrents to the normal functioning of the State's residential land market and *forced* thousands of individual homeowners to lease, rather than buy, the land underneath their homes. Regulating oligopoly and the evils associated with it is a classic example of a State's police powers. . . . We cannot disapprove of Hawaii's exercise of this power.[34]

The factual and theoretical predicates required to base the use of the police power on a finding of oligopoly were at best questionable. The Court points out that "[i]n the mid-1960's, after extensive hearings, the Hawaii Legislature discovered that, while the State and Federal Governments owned almost 49% of the State's land, another 47% was in the hands of only 72 private landowners. . . . The legislature further found that 18 landholders with tracts of 21,000 acres or more, owned more than 40% of this land and that on Oahu, the most urbanized of the islands, 22 landowners owned 72.5% of the fee simple titles."[35]

To begin with, this concentration of landholding was potentially subject to dilution by federal and state land sales (provided that the lands held by governments were habitable), as governments were the single largest landholders. Second, much of Hawaii's land is allocated to large agricultural units, which exploit scale economies.

---

[34]Hawaii Housing Authority v. Midkiff, 467 U.S. at 241–42 (emphasis added) (note and citation omitted). In a footnote Justice O'Connor cites early Virginia and Pennsylvania statutes, as well as two 19th-century cases, to the effect that "After the American Revolution, the colonists in several states took steps to eradicate the feudal incidents with which large proprietors had encumbered land in the colonies." Id. at 241 n.5.

My examination of these cases and of one of the two statutes (the other is unavailable to me at this writing) suggests that Justice O'Connor's reading is inapposite. The Virginia Act of May 1779, 10 *Hening's Statutes at Large* 64, ch. 13, ¶ 6 (1822), extinguishes the British Crown's rights to royalties paid on former royal mines. Wilson v. Iseminger, 185 U.S. 55 (1902), sustains a state statute of repose that extinguished quit rents that attached to sales of title in fee simple, provided that 20 years had elapsed without payment, acknowledgment, or demand of the rent. Those due the rent had three years from the Act's passage to perfect their claims. Stewart v. Gorter, 70 Md. 242, 16 A. 644 (Md. 1889), perhaps the closest of these cases to Justice O'Connor's view, upheld a Baltimore ordinance providing for the termination of leases running for more than 15 years, on six months notice, if the landlord pays the remaining rent to the tenant, discounted at 6 percent. The ordinance's apparent purpose was to increase alienability of property (including leaseholds), through indirect derogation of long-term leases. Citation of this case, whose decision rested on other, technical grounds, hardly puts into evidence a powerful precedent upon which the Court might rely in *Hawaii*.

[35]Hawaii Housing Authority v. Midkiff, 467 U.S. at 232 (citations omitted).

If land leased for residences indeed earned supracompetitive returns, then converting agricultural land to residential use would reduce the 47 percent statistic. Third, much of the remaining land is not yet appropriate for residential use, but its conversion to residential use again would reduce the 47 percent statistic. Fourth, even "47% [of the land] owned by 72 private landowners" or "18 landowners with tracts of 21,000 acres or more owning 40% of this land" or "22 land-owners [owning] 72.5% of the fee simple titles" do not in economic theory or practice an oligopoly make. And, even if it did so, there is no evidence on the record of price coordination, raising the possi-bility that some or all of the landowners might be receiving at any given time less than the so-called fair market value for their ground leases.

This absence of convincing economic evidence also goes to the question of the means that the Hawaii legislature chose to overcome this probably nonexistent problem. Justice O'Connor wrote: "Nor can we condemn as irrational the Act's approach to correcting the land oligopoly problem. The Act presumes that when a sufficiently large number of persons declare that they are willing but unable to buy lots at fair prices the land market is malfunctioning."[36] The Court does not concern itself with the landowner's unwillingness to sell "at fair prices."[37] More to the point, the Court refused, in now familiar language, to review the legislature's chosen means to arrest the sup-posed effects of this fictitious oligopoly, even if those means were found to be mistaken:

---

[36]Id. at 242.

[37]The Court does advert to the tax consequences of selling willingly versus those of a "forced sale," Id. at 233, thereby raising the possibility that the Hawaii legislature had done the large landowners a favor. But the very existence of appellee's claim seriously diminishes the force of this argument. The challenged taking also occurred against the background of an estate held in perpetual trust. This feature of *Hawaii* is not compelling, however. Presumably, not all land was so held, and even if it were so, the trustees, when confronted with offers in excess of their reservation prices, could have brought actions to set aside the perpetuity on public-policy grounds. Any court sensibly could have preferred this approach to the unwarranted expansion of the power of eminent domain that *Hawaii* occasioned. For a similar application of this reasoning to the Court's abrogation of the contracts clause in Home Building and Loan Assoc. v. Blaisdell, 290 U.S. 398 (1934), see Epstein, "Contract Clause," pp. 735–38, and text accompanying infra notes 244–56.

Here again, the determination of a dangerous level of market concentration is at issue. George J. Stigler, *The Organization of Industry* (Chicago: University of Chicago Press, 1968), p. 39, puts that level at the four largest sellers controlling 70 to 80 percent of the market share. Frederic M. Scherer, *Industrial Market Structure & Economic Performance*, 2d ed. (Chicago: Rand McNally, 1970), p. 185, puts it at the four largest sellers controlling 40 percent. The land owners in *Hawaii* fall far below either of these thresholds.

Of course, this Act, like any other, may not be successful in achieving its intended goals. But "whether *in fact* the provision will accomplish its objectives is not the question: the [constitutional requirement] is satisfied if . . . the . . . [state] legislature *rationally could have believed* that the [Act] would promote its objective.". . . When the legislature's purpose is legitimate and its means are not irrational, our cases make clear that empirical debates over the wisdom of takings—no less than debates over the wisdom of other kinds of socioeconomic legislation—are not to be carried out in the federal courts. Redistribution of fees simple to correct deficiencies in the market determined by the state legislature to be attributable to land oligopoly is a rational exercise of the eminent domain power.[38]

The decision in *Hawaii* rested principally on the meaning of "public use" in the Fifth Amendment's command, "nor shall private property be taken for public use, without just compensation." The court of appeals had held that, "[w]hen we strip away the statutory rationalizations contained in the Hawaii Land Reform Act, we see a naked attempt on the part of the state of Hawaii to take the private property of A and transfer it to B solely for *B's* private use."[39] Later, we reflect on the court of appeals's and the Supreme Court's conflicting interpretations of "public use," the Supreme Court holding here and in earlier cases that the words mean "public *purpose.*"[40] Here we emphasize merely that the Court exhibited its usual reluctance to inquire fully into whether the so-called public purpose was indeed

---

[38]Hawaii Housing Authority v. Midkiff, 467 U.S. at 242–43 (citing Western & Southern Life Ins. Co. v. State Bd. of Equalization, 451 U.S 648, 671–72 (1981); Minnesota v. Clover Leaf Creamery Co., 449 U.S. 456, 466 (1981); and Vance v. Bradley, 440 U.S. 93, 112 (1979)) (emphasis in original).

Such a broad reading of state legislative power seems fully consistent with the Court's pre-*Lochner*-era cases, in which the *possibility* of damage to the public alone will suffice to legitimate state action. Considering the cartel alleged to operate among Chicago grain warehouses, the Court, per Chief Justice Waite, wrote toward the end of the 19th century:

For our purposes we must assume that if a state of facts could exist that would justify such legislation [regulating rates], it actually did exist when the statute now under consideration was passed. For us the question is one of power, not of expediency. If no state of circumstances could exist to justify such a statute, then we must declare this one void, because in excess of the legislative power of the State. But if it could, we must presume it did. Of the propriety of legislative interference within the scope of legislative power, the Legislature is the exclusive judge.

[Munn v. Illinois, 94 U.S. 113, 132–33 (1877)]

[39]Midkiff v. Tom, 702 F.2d at 798 (1983).

[40]See infra note 262. See also Hawaii Housing Authority v. Midkiff, 467 U.S. at 239–44, and Berman v. Parker, 348 U.S. 26 (1954) (sustaining District of Columbia's condemnation of land to redevelop slums, where land might eventually be sold to private interests).

"public." An important preexisting right being in the balance, the Court's political manners would seem to have overcome its constitutional obligation.

A Theory of Judicial Acquiescence

The Supreme Court's acquiescence in legislative actions—its failure either to correct economic error or to constrain legislatures that ignore rights of property and contract—would not seem so serious were the errors not so great and, more importantly, were the rights not so fundamental.[41] In *Hawaii*, for example, the Court refused to interpret "public use" narrowly and simultaneously refused to consider the economic question: Is the stated public purpose actually public *qua* welfare regarding? Therefore, under its broad reading of "use" as "purpose," its stated reluctance to second-guess the legislature on the economic question of the Hawaii act's economic incidents was dispositive and, we might add, conclusory. While there is no reason to believe that judges are better at doing economics than are legislators (although I think that they are so), they *are* charged with interpreting the Constitution, *inter alia*, to protect individual rights. Why do they commonly fail to constrain (putatively incorrect) legislative "economic" judgments that diminish those rights by imposing their own constitutional judgments that might restore those rights?

Landes and Posner[42] provide an ingenious theoretical explanation for the judiciary's reluctance to constrain the legislature in terms of the legislature's own (economic) evaluation of policy alternatives. The explanation's central focus is the now developing and increasingly robust economic theory of legislation, sometimes called the "interest-group" theory of legislation, which we discuss at greater length in Section V.[43] This theory of legislation holds that lawmakers and bureaucrats design statutes and regulations to benefit private, divisible groups in the population, commonly called interest groups, and that the costs of these statutes and regulations ordinarily (but not always) fall on the population in general. That is, the legislature stands as a market place in which political entrepreneurs create private, divisible benefits (allowing them to be residuals claimants) at collective cost.[44]

[41]See, for example, Judge Alarcon's opinion in Midkiff v. Tom, 702 F.2d at 790–93.

[42]Landes and Posner, "Independent Judiciary."

[43]See text accompanying infra notes 193–210.

[44]In ordinary spending programs, such as porkbarrel legislation, costs are almost always collective and diffuse, although their incidents may on occasion be concentrated. Concentrated costs sometimes occur in state taxation of out-of-state corporations, in tax

Landes and Posner's important insight into this process is to recognize that legislators might enact such programs to last for a single
legislative period, for several periods, or in perpetuity. Once the
proposition is so stated, it becomes apparent that a benefit that flows
over several periods should be superior, in both the legislator's and
the beneficiary's judgment, to one that lasts for fewer periods or for
just a single legislative session. The transaction costs of enactment
may be lower for the more nearly permanent program, as compared
with the continual transaction costs of reenactment, and the net present value of the associated income stream is certainly greater. Indeed,
by enacting a full-blown "entitlement" program to run in perpetuity,
the legislator immediately can capture his share of the program's
residual value (rent), even if he intends to leave the legislature at the
end of the present session.

Two institutional forces threaten this arrangement. The first is the
deliberations of the legislature itself in future periods. Next year's
Congress could threaten rescission unless its members are paid an
amount equal to the program's current surplus value to the recipients.
Such a threat would reduce both the interest group's initial willingness to seek such programs and the amount that it would pay for
them, thus diminishing the enacting politician's share of the benefits.
Legislatures in general, and the Congress in particular, solve this
internal, multi-period prisoners' dilemma by adopting procedural
rules that raise the cost of both the original and the potentially can-
celling legislation. These rules include the filibuster and the enhanced
capacity of legislative committees and subcommittees to kill both
new bargains and abrogations of old ones. Landes and Posner argue
that while both the enactment of new programs and the overturning
of old ones grow more expensive (and therefore less likely) under
these rules, nevertheless the legislator's net benefits from the operation of these rules are positive.[45]

The second threat to this arrangement is the judiciary, and particularly a judiciary that is not politically "independent." By an

---

exportation generally, and in some regulatory programs, although the theoretical structure of interest-group analysis can accommodate the concentration of costs. See infra
note 199.

[45]"[U]nder plausible assumptions the increase in the value of legislation will exceed
the increase in its cost, since a modest increase in the cost of enacting legislation could
multiply many-fold the length of the period in which the legislation was expected to
remain in force." Landes and Posner, "Independent Judiciary," p. 879.

Similarly, "it is in large measure the constitutional structure envisioned by the
framers [for example, bicameralism and the presidential veto] that . . . makes it very
difficult to dismantle large government programs once they are in place. This fact,
however, does not so much reflect shortcomings of the framers' scheme [to limit government in favor of economic rights] as its abandonment by subsequent legislatures."
Epstein, "Contract Clause," p. 714, n.32.

independent judiciary Landes and Posner mean "one that does not make decisions on the sorts of political factors (for example, the electoral strength of the people affected by the decision) that would influence and in most cases control the decision were it made by a legislative body, such as the U.S. Congress."[46] Were the Supreme Court not independent, for example, then a legislator who sought abrogation of a prior bargain in the face of high legislative transaction costs might turn to the Court to achieve his purpose. If the Court were to become an agent of the current legislature, it doubtless could abrogate the acts of an earlier legislature at a lower cost than could the current legislature, which is constrained by its own rules. Hence, the legislature "buys" protection from the judiciary by making the Court independent, through such provisions as life tenure. The Court reciprocates by not second-guessing the legislature's political judgments, on economic or political grounds.

The history of the judiciary, especially in its response to occasional threats to its independence such as Roosevelt's plan to pack the Court, shows that it has indeed adapted its approach to examining legislation, to preserve its own independence by not challenging too often the legislature's economic—political—decisions.

> The Supreme Court's activity is thus notable, not for what it does, but for what it does not do: namely, interfere with the private-interest bargains struck in the legislature. One can even sense in the Court's decisions the operation of implicit rules requiring the preservation of prior legislation. The Supreme Court goes beyond not tampering with prior enactments to finding ways to enhance their survival. For example, in statutory interpretation, the Court often examines the original congressional hearings and speeches, to discern the intent of the originating legislators. While this activity sometimes results in peculiar readings of the legislative record, nevertheless, statutory construction is a common judicial practice. Indeed, even when the Court confronts an otherwise unconstitutional statute, it usually tries to narrow the scope of the statute or otherwise interpret its terms so that it will pass constitutional muster, to preserve as much of the original bargain's intent as possible.[47]

As we have seen in our brief review of *Moorman* and *Hawaii*, as well as in our references to other cases, the political forces that

---

[46]Landes and Posner, "Independent Judiciary," p. 875.

[47]Peter H. Aranson and Peter C. Ordeshook, "Public Interest, Private Interest, and the Democratic Polity," in *The Democratic State*, ed. Roger Benjamin and Steven L. Elkin (Lawrence: The University Press of Kansas, forthcoming 1985). For examples of the Court's reading of otherwise unconstitutional statutes to make them constitutional, see National Cable Television Assoc. v. United States, 415 U.S. 336 (1974), and Kent v. Dulles, 357 U.S. 116 (1958).

Landes and Posner identify result in two strong tendencies of judicial review. First, the Court evaluates legislation on dimensions orthogonal to those economic—political—dimensions that legislators themselves might invoke. For example, the Court will assess an act's constitutionality but not its economic fitness. To do otherwise the Court would have to challenge the legislature in territory that the elected body sees as its own monopoly. Second, even in the application of constitutional standards, the Court ordinarily will be especially forgiving of legislative error. As in *Hawaii,* for example, the Court will allow the legislature largely to decide for itself what a "public use" (*qua* "public purpose") might be. The result is the derogation of individual economic rights and the concomitant expansive acquisition of legislative ones.

This explanation of Supreme Court acquiescence in legislative activity may appear to be counterfactual. First, many of the Court's decisions uphold the actions of *state* legislatures, and not those of the Congress. Why does the Court fail to apply more stringent standards to the state bodies, which, after all, do not directly control any facet of Supreme Court independence? We could argue that the Court's application of judicial-review precedents to the federal legislature's challenged activities provides a decisional penumbra for its judgments about the state legislature's challenged activities. And indeed, this argument seems at least partly reasonable. But we need not rely on it. The Court's institutional memory is certainly long enough to recall the passage of the Eleventh Amendment, eliminating its power to hear "any suit in law or equity, commenced or prosecuted against one of the United States by Citizens of another State, or by Citizens or Subjects of any foreign State," in the wake of its decision in *Chisholm v. Georgia,*[48] which held that a South Carolina resident could sue the state of Georgia. National politics in the United States enjoys a profoundly local base, and the Congress would doubtless respond quickly today to a perceived serious judicial threat, based on the Court's competing economic judgments, to the states' abilities to make economic policy.

Second, one might argue, contrary to Landes and Posner's explanation, that during its period of applying substantive due process, the Court did confront legislatures with the economic errors of their ways. While there may be some truth to this claim, it does not mate-

---

[48] 2 Dall. 419 (1793). The Court has restored much of its power to hear such suits if, for example, the state originates them (see Cohens v. Virginia, 6 Wheat. 264, 411–12 (1821)), or if a state official's actions impair constitutionally protected rights (see Osborne v. Bank of the United States, 9 Wheat. 738, 858–59 (1824)).

rially diminish the explanation's power. First, this claim goes more to the effect of the Court's rulings, and less to express language about economics. True, the *Lochner*-era Court did dwell at length on the right of contract as expressed in substantive due process reasoning, but its language sustained this right on perceived *constitutional*, not *economic*, grounds[49]; it also sustained a good many state statutes limiting the right to contract.[50] Second, one does not have a sense that these cases were decided against a background of national consensus on the issues raised, one way or the other. Some state legislatures appeared to embrace economic regulatory legislation more quickly than did others, even before the New Deal. But the Court's decisions in cases such as *New State Ice Co. v. Liebmann*[51] might well have served the interests of those same legislatures, whose members passed economic legislation under severe political pressure and against their better judgment. Third, the Court did sustain in this period several broad congressional delegations of legislative power to federal regulatory agencies, in which its own traditional *dicta*, whose application might have limited such delegations, were raised and set down again, to no effect.[52]

A third attack on the Landes-Posner theory might point to the Court's famous 1930s delegation-doctrine cases themselves, as instances in which the theory finds clear contradiction in the judicial nullifications of acts of Congress.[53] But even here the matter is not so obvious. Two of the three cases, *Panama Refining* and *Schechter*, struck at the broadly applicable National Industrial Recovery Act (NIRA), a statute crafted in haste, involving most of the economy. NIRA's enactment had not been preceded by the usual focus of interest-group and congressional bargaining that ordinarily presages a political exchange in the market place for public policy. Instead, NIRA was a broad-based omnibus statute providing for self-regulation, from which the members of Congress collected no appar-

---

[49]The Court relied on due process considerations in the *Lochner* era, because early on it had ruled out the use of the contracts clause of the Constitution to limit prospective impairments of the obligation of contract, as found in most regulations, in Ogden v. Saunders, 25 U.S. (12 Wheat.) 213 (1827). For a careful and trenchant criticism of this decision and its consequences, see Epstein, "Contract Clause," pp. 723–30, and text accompanying infra notes 58–62.

[50]See, for example, cases cited supra note 3.

[51]285 U.S. 262 (1932).

[52]See New York Cent. Sec. Co. v. United States, 287 U.S. 12 (1932); Radio Comm'n v. Nelson Bros. Co., 289 U.S. 266 (1933); and FTC v. R. F. Keppel & Bros., 291 U.S. 304 (1934).

[53]Panama Refining Co. v. Ryan, 293 U.S. 388 (1935); A.L.A. Schechter Poultry Corp. v. United States, 295 U.S. 495 (1935); and Carter v. Carter Coal Co., 298 U.S. 239 (1936).

ent rents. Indeed, by the time *Schechter* reached the Court, NIRA was in deep administrative and political trouble, and the Court's overturning of the statute saved both Congress and the Roosevelt administration from serious embarrassment.[54]

The *Schechter*-era cases might also reflect the Court's limitations in reading public and legislative opinion. While this *ad hoc* explanation seems less than satisfactory, the Court's rapid turnabout in reaction to its decision in *Schechter* gives it a paradoxical plausibility. The Court's more recent decision in *Chadha*,[55] overturning the legislative veto, is more problematic to explain within the Landes and Posner theory. Yet *Chadha*, like *Schechter*, was aimed at no particular regulatory device, thus raising the cost of aggregating the interests of legislative opponents, because of high transaction costs and free-rider problems.[56] At least in terms of transitional gains and losses, *Chadha* threatened all members of Congress and their regulatory-client constituents. Hence, no one had an incentive to do anything about it.

III. Recent Cases

Besides *Moorman* and *Hawaii,* recent Supreme Court decisions provide a rich menu of disputes in which the Court faced economic issues. We can usefully categorize our discussion of a sample of these cases according to whether the Court did or did not apply economic analysis as its principal vehicle for decision, and according to whether or not the Court's reasoning and result reached a correct economic conclusion.[57] Our purpose here is not to construct a catalogue of

[54]See Ellis W. Hawley, *The New Deal and the Problem of Monopoly* (Princeton, N.J.: Princeton University Press, 1966), pt. 1.

[55]I.N.S. v. Chadha, 103 S. Ct. 2764 (1983).

[56]See infra note 198.

[57]There is considerable hubris in any judgment that the Court got its economics right or wrong. Indeed, in a few instances we must stand mute, because the matter is indeterminate. See the discussion of Arizona v. Maricopa County Medical Society, 102 S. Ct. 2466 (1962), at text accompanying infra notes 101–18. The kind of error present also differs in various contexts. Sometimes the Court simply gets it wrong, as in its analysis of oligopoly in *Hawaii*, discussed at text accompanying supra notes 29–41. In other cases the Court reaches a result that a careful economic analysis might have precluded, as in its finding of unequal treatment in Arizona Governing Committee for Tax Deferred Annuity & Deferred Compensation Plans v. Norris, 103 S. Ct. 3492 (1983), discussed at text accompanying infra notes 141–44. In still other cases the Court's opinion, read as economic analysis, is simply incoherent, as in its "diminution-in-use" test applied in Penn Central Transportation Co. v. New York City, 438 U.S. 104 (1978), discussed at text accompanying infra notes 75–82. The particular economic problem or error in each case should be apparent from its context. I plead guilty to any and all charges of hubris but regard them as an acceptable cost of getting on with the discussion.

errors. Instead, we wish merely to lay the groundwork for assessing the Court's capacity for economic judgments.

Economic Grounds, Correct Results

Even during the years that substantive due process partly dominated the Supreme Court's decisions about economic legislation, the Court seldom if ever based its opinions on strictly economic judgments. Its decisions often adverted, instead, to individual rights of contract.[58] In *Lochner*,[59] for example, the Court in 1905 overturned the conviction of a bakery owner who allowed an employee to work more than 60 hours per week, in violation of a New York labor law. The Court, per Justice Peckham, held the law to be unconstitutional, because "[t]he general rights to make a contract in relation to his business is part of the liberty of the individual protected by the Fourteenth Amendment of the Federal Constitution."[60] While the Court did look to the condition of bakers, it could find no reason to limit the "protected" worker's right of contract. Such laws as New York's, the Court held, "are meddlesome interferences with the rights of the individual, and they are not saved from condemnation by the claim that they are passed in the exercise of the police power . . . , unless there be some fair ground, reasonable in and of itself, to say that there is material danger to the public health or to the health of the employees, if the hours of labor are not curtailed."[61] While the Court did search for such "material danger[s]," its point of departure was grounded on a constitutional right, not on economic analysis *per se*.[62]

The Court today seldom applies economics clearly and cleanly to arrive at its decisions. More often, economic analysis provides a factual predicate to fill in the details of a legal test. In one recent case, however, the Court did approach the application of such an analysis and appears to have done so correctly. That case, *Kassel v.*

---

[58]See supra note 49.

[59]Lochner v. New York, 198 U.S. 45 (1905).

[60]Id. at 53.

[61]Id. at 61.

[62]To the extent that the Court's decision rested on a constitutional basis, Justice Holmes was mistaken in chiding the *Lochner* Court that "[t]he 14th Amendment does not enact Mr. Herbert Spencer's Social Statics." Id. at 75 (Holmes, J., dissenting). The Court, at least in terms of its own language, intended no such result, any more than the *Hawaii* Court intended to enact a socialist theory of property. The Court in *Lochner* enunciated a constitutional theory of government, and not "a particular economic theory." Id. Nor did the Court in *Lochner* subvert the police power, as most of the New York law regulating bakeries stood unchallenged. See Epstein, "Contract Clause," pp. 732–34.

Consolidated Freightways Corp.,[63] involved a challenge to an Iowa statute limiting the length of trucks operating in Iowa. All other western and midwestern states imposed a 65-foot limit on "double" trailors, while Iowa imposed a 60-foot limit. The Court repeated *dicta* concerning its customary deference to state legislatures. "[I]f safety justifications are not illusory, the Court will not second-guess legislative judgment about their importance in comparison with related burdens on interstate commerce."[64] But the presumption of validity can just go so far, for "the incantation of a purpose to promote public health or safety does not insulate a state law from Commerce Clause attack. Regulations designed for that salutary purpose nevertheless may further the purpose so marginally, and interfere with commerce so substantially, as to be invalid under the Commerce Clause."[65] The Court agreed with the court of appeals in finding that Iowa would benefit from its limit principally because other states would carry the rerouted traffic. A state, said the Court, "cannot constitutionally promote its own parochial interests by requiring safe vehicles to detour around it."[66] The Court, accordingly, overturned the Iowa statute.

Economists long have understood that regulation is a form of taxation.[67] And on this reading the tax sustained in *Moorman* seems indistinguishable from the regulation overturned in *Consolidated Freightways.* Here, though, the Court found the "exportation" of damage to other states to be far more explicit than the implied loss to Illinois in *Moorman.* In that case either a defense of rights or a correct economic analysis might have led the Court to overturn Iowa's single-factor tax. In *Consolidated Freightways* the Court only incidentally considered the loss to truckers,[68] but its economic reasoning turned instead on the issue of the damage to, and the rights of, other states. Hence, its reliance on an economic approach sustained a view of rights that the state otherwise might have truncated. In any case, the decisions in *Moorman* and *Consolidated Freightways,* from the perspective of economic analysis, seem plainly inconsistent.

---

[63]450 U.S. 662 (1981). The case is analyzed in Charles E. McLure, Jr., "Incidence Analysis and the Supreme Court: An Examination of Four Cases from the 1980 Term," *Supreme Court Economic Review* 1 (1982): 69, 93–6.

[64]Kassel v. Consolidated Freightways Corp., 450 U.S. at 667.

[65]Id. at 670.

[66]Id. at 678.

[67]See, for example, Richard A. Posner, "Taxation by Regulation," *Bell Journal of Economics & Management Science* 2 (Spring 1971): 22–50.

[68]Kassel v. Consolidated Freightways Corp., 450 U.S. at 674.

Consolidated Freightways appears uncommon, however, because it extends the Court beyond the boundaries that it has set for itself in similar cases. In *Moorman,* for example, the Court would not look behind the words of a facially neutral state statute to find a discriminatory intent. This reluctance reached an absurd conclusion in *Commonwealth Edison Co. v. Montana,*[69] in which the Court turned aside a commerce clause challenge to a sudden seven-fold increase in Montana's severance tax on coal, most of which was either exported to consumers living elsewhere or borne by mine owners and power-company shareholders, again living outside of Montana. But in recent cases, such as *Armco, Inc. v. Hardesty,*[70] *Bacchus Imports, Ltd. v. Dias,*[71] *Westinghouse Electric Corp. v. Tully,*[72] and *Maryland v. Louisiana,*[73] the Court has struck down facially discriminatory taxes, even where there might have been offsetting taxes on domestic firms (as in *Armco*).

Economic Grounds, Incorrect Results

Cases such as *Consolidated Freightways,* in which the Court "correctly" applied economic analysis to reach its decision, seem scarce in the last several terms. Cases such as *Hawaii,* in which the Court failed entirely to reflect prevailing economic wisdom, seem far more common. And it should come as no surprise that it is precisely in the area of takings in general, and "taking by regulation" in particular, that the Court's grasp of economics seems most flawed.[74] In *Penn Central Transportation Co. v. New York City,*[75] for example, the Court heard a challenge to an application of the city's preservation law, forbidding Penn Central from using its air rights to construct a building over Grand Central Terminal. The Court, per Justice Brennan, applied, *inter alia,* a "diminution-in-value" test, which relies not on how much value a regulation has taken, but on how much value remains after the uncompensated loss: " '[T]aking' jurisprudence" said the Court, "does not divide a single parcel into discrete segments and attempt to determine whether rights in a particular

---

[69]453 U.S 609 (1981). The case is discussed in McLure, "Incidence Analysis," pp. 84–89, and the decision is criticized in Epstein, "Taxation," pp. 445–49.
[70]104 S. Ct. 2620 (1984).
[71]104 S. Ct. 3049 (1984).
[72]104 S. Ct. 1856 (1984).
[73]451 U.S. 725 (1981).
[74]See, for example, James E. Krier, "The Regulation Machine," *Supreme Court Economic Review* 1 (1982): 1–37, for a cogent review of many of the recent takings cases.
[75]438 U.S. 104 (1978).

segment have been entirely abrogated."[76] Instead, each property interest represents a bundle of rights, and government may remove an indeterminate number of "sticks" in the bundle as long as what remains provides a "reasonable return" on investment. The Court repeated this logic in *Agins v. City of Tiburon*,[77] a facial challenge to a zoning ordinance that limited construction on a five-acre tract of land to single-family dwellings at low density. There the Court said that the regulation was not a taking, because the owners continued to enjoy an "economically viable use"[78] of their property. And again in *Hodel v. Indiana*,[79] the Court sustained on similar grounds the federal Surface Mining Control and Reclamation Act against another facial challenge:

> [T]he prime farmland provisions do not prohibit surface mining; they merely regulate the condition under which the activity may be conducted. The prime farmland provisions say nothing about alternative uses to which farmland may be put since they come into play only when an operator seeks to conduct mining operations on his land. We therefore conclude that these provisions do not, on their face, deprive a property owner of economically beneficial use of his property.[80]

This "economically viable use" or "beneficial use" theory, derived from Michelman's famous essay on just compensation.[81] On its face the theory is incoherent as economics. No matter how complete or incomplete it might be, loss of value is loss of value, and if the loss is a consequence of governmental action, then there is at least a rebuttable presumption that a taking has occurred. The Court's use of the terms "reasonable expectation" and "distinct investment-backed expectations" in *Penn Central*[82] cannot save it from embarrassment. The kind of information required to make judgments about what is "reasonable" and about what the original expectations might have been simply does not exist in any palpable form. In these cases the Court should have been as wary of substituting its judgment for that of the market place as it has been of substituting its judgment for that of the legislature.

[76] Id. at 130–31.
[77] 447 U.S. 255 (1980).
[78] Id. at 260.
[79] 452 U.S. 314 (1981).
[80] Id. at 335 (footnote omitted).
[81] Frank I. Michelman, "Property, Utility, and Fairness: Comments on the Ethical Foundations of 'Just Compensation' Law," *Harvard Law Review* 80 (April 1967): 1165–1258. The argument is reviewed in Krier, "Regulation Machine," pp. 6–8.
[82] 438 U.S. at 124–25, 127, 130 n.27.

Two final cases in this category—economic grounds, incorrect results—go to the heart of two of the Court's central problems with economics. The first of these, *Texaco, Inc. v. Short*,[83] involved a challenge to a 1971 Indiana statute that automatically transferred mineral rights that had not been exercised for 20 years or more to the owners of the corresponding surface rights under which they lay. The act provided for a two-year grace period, but it only required notice to the original owners *after* reversion, and it treated owners of 10 or more such bundles of mineral rights in a single county more leniently than it treated those who owned fewer than 10 bundles.

Texaco asserted that the act was unconstitutional. First, the absence of prior notice denied it due process of law.[84] Second, the act constituted a taking without just compensation.[85] Third, the act violated the contracts clause of the Constitution.[86] Fourth, the act's unequal treatment, based on the number of bundles owned, violated the equal protection clause of the Fourteenth Amendment.[87] And finally, the act was not rationally related to the state's goals, thus violating Texaco's asserted right of substantive due process.[88] The Court rejected all of these claims, and in my view the Court's response was mistaken on all five of them. Here, though, I want to concentrate on the "rational-relation" test.

The Court accepted the opinion of the Indiana Supreme Court, that dormancy of mineral interests "is mischievous and contrary to the economic interests and welfare of the public," because "[t]he existence of stale and abandoned interests creates uncertainties in titles and constitutes an impediment to the development of the mineral interests . . . and to the development of the surface rights as well."[89]

The highest economic use of mineral rights, unlike surface rights, however, may be to keep them in inventory (until prices rise or technology improves):

---

[83]454 U.S. 516 (1982). The case is brilliantly analyzed in David D. Haddock and Thomas D. Hall, "The Impact of Making Rights Inalienable: *Merrion v. Jicarilla Apache Tribe, Texaco, Inc. v. Short, Fidelity Federal Savings & Loan Ass'n v. de la Cuesta*, and *Ridgway v. Ridgway*," *Supreme Court Economic Review* 2 (1983): 1–41. My discussion follows theirs closely.

[84]Texaco, Inc. v. Short, 454 U.S. at 530.

[85]Id.

[86]Id.

[87]Id. at 538–40.

[88]Id. at 525–30.

[89]Id. at 523 (quoting 406 N.E.2d at 627).

> Most mineral rights are . . . held in inventory. That is, at any moment there is active exploitation of minerals only under a tiny percentage of the total land area of the world, all of the rest being held on the chance that minerals will someday become exploitable through a price increase of that mineral or through innovation of lower-cost production techniques, or that known deposits of exploitable quality will become even more valuable in the future.[90]

The common statute of repose or rule of adverse position thus seems far more appropriate for surface rights (when it is appropriate at all) than for mineral rights:

> The active-use *versus* inventory proportions are reversed for surface rights. Most surface rights are actively used for some purpose at any moment. Even that land awaiting imminent conversion to a higher use is often employed in some easily preemptible activity. Consequently, owners or heirs of surface rights periodically take note of their ownership, because of regular rental payments, recurring taxes, and the like. Such reminders encourage them to reevaluate the use to which they are putting that asset, with uses being allocated as conditions change.[91]

It is contrary to a public policy aimed at efficient extraction rates to enact adverse possession laws that, in the view that the Indiana Supreme Court urged, would treat surface and mineral rights alike, inasmuch as these laws may encourage too rapid extraction and less efficient use as inventory. After all, if state legislators can go as far as they did in *Short*, might they not go further, to confiscate other inventoried mineral rights on "public policy" grounds? To the extent that owners worry about such possibilities, in the wake of *Short*, they may hasten extraction rates. Indeed, future state enactments of the *Short* variety might actually require inefficient extraction rates. But "rapid extraction is substantially more costly than extraction at a more deliberate rate, in part because some of the minerals actually become lost in isolated underground pockets if extraction is too rapid."[92] Similarly, because of common-pool problems, "there is an incentive to consolidate mineral holdings into relatively large units before minerals exploration occurs, thus reducing the bargaining costs incurred when negotiating for extraction at the proper rate after mineral discoveries become known."[93] But the act reimposes the

[90]Haddock and Hall, "Making Rights Inalienable," p. 21.
[91]Ibid.
[92]Ibid., p. 20 (footnote omitted).
[93]Ibid.

"bargaining costs associated with the consolidation . . . , all to no socially valuable purpose."[94]

Haddock and Hall suggest two reasons why the Indiana legislature went wrong. First, surface-rights owners, compared to mineral-rights owners, are proportionately more likely to be Indiana residents. Hence, the act resembles a tax whose incidence falls disproportionately on those without political representation in Indiana.[95] Second, politicians, whose future incumbency is uncertain, may have a higher discount rate, preferring more tax revenues now to a greater amount later, than is efficient for the state or nation.[96]

But the social costs of the Indiana act are greater still. These include the effects of reduced interstate diversification of mineral-rights holdings, increased resources wasted in monitoring state legislatures, and the costs of the "redundant consolidations"[97] mentioned earlier. Surely, the Court's economic probing in *Short* might have been deeper, and that result might have occurred if the Court was less generous on constitutional grounds in the deference that it gave to the Indiana legislature. For that matter, the same outcome would have followed from the Court's noneconomic but principled sustaining of Texaco's constitutional rights.

Two of the Court's problems with economics, which Easterbrook identifies,[98] but about which he is far more optimistic than are we,[99] concern its handling of private-interest legislation and its resolution of *ex ante* versus *ex post* analysis. *Short* clearly indicates that the Indiana legislature was responding to private demands for a redistribution of rights from mineral-interest owners to surface-rights owners. The Court simply has no way to limit such expropriations, given both its deference to legislative bodies and its consistent gutting of the contracts clause and of other constitutional provisions controlling the actions of state governments.[100] Similarly, it has not come to grips with the notion that *ex post* redistributions have *ex ante* consequences of the sort found in our analysis of *Short*. The decision in *Short* thus changes potential mineral-interest owners' and state legislators' incentives, *ex ante*, in wholly undesirable ways.

---

[94]Ibid., p. 21.
[95]Ibid., p. 23.
[96]Ibid., p. 21.
[97]Ibid., p. 24.
[98]Frank H. Easterbrook, "Foreword: The Court and the Economic System," *Harvard Law Review* 98 (November 1984): 4–60.
[99]See text accompanying infra notes 173–82 and 212–30.
[100]See Epstein, "Taxation," and "Contract Clause."

The final case in this category is *Arizona v. Maricopa County Medical Society*,[101] in which the Court decided, for the first time, that horizontal *maximum*-price agreements are *per se* violations of the Sherman Act. The Court focused, *inter alia*, on the claim that such a "restraint . . . may discourage entry into the market and may deter experimentation and new developments by individual [medical] entrepreneurs."[102] This claim implied that the Maricopa County Medical Society might have set maximum prices low enough to eliminate potential competition from HMOs. Thus, the Court really applied a *per se* rule to a potential act of predatory pricing, but without any evidence that predation had actually occurred.

The Court invoked its usual reasons for finding a practice to be a *per se* violation of the Sherman Act:

> The costs of judging business practices under the rule of reason . . . have been reduced by the recognition of *per se* rules. Once experience with a particular kind of restraint enables the Court to predict with confidence that the rule of reason will condemn it, it has applied a conclusive presumption that the restraint is unreasonable. As in every rule of general application, the match between the presumed and the actual is imperfect. For the sake of business certainty and litigation efficiency, we have tolerated the invalidation of some agreements that a full-blown inquiry might have proved to be reasonable.[103]

But in *Maricopa* the Court could predict nothing "with confidence," for no court had made any inquiry at all. Indeed, the United States Court of Appeals for the Ninth Circuit had upheld the application of the rule of reason, pointing out that the "record reveals nothing about the actual competitive effects of the challenged arrangement. . . . In truth, we know very little about the impact of this and many other arrangements within the health care industry."[104] Hence, the application of a *per se* rule without a judicial inquiry into the effects of the maximum-price agreement would "substitute an unsupported belief for proper proof."[105] With this proposition the dissenters in the Supreme Court agreed:

> Before characterizing an arrangement as a *per se* price fixing agreement meriting condemnation, a court should determine whether it is a "naked restrain[t] of trade with no purpose except stiffling of competition." . . .

---

[101]102 S. Ct. 2466 (1982).

[102]Id. at 2475.

[103]Id. at 2473 (footnotes omitted).

[104]Arizona v. Maricopa County Medical Soc'y, 643 F.2d 553, 556 (9th Cir. 1980).

[105]Id. at 557.

... the fact that a foundation sponsored health insurance plan *literally* involves the setting of ceiling prices among competing physicians does not, of itself, justify condemning the plan as *per se* illegal. . . . [T]he *per se* label should not be assigned without carefully considering substantial benefits and procompetitive justifications. This is especially true when the agreement under attack is novel, as in this case.[106]

The *Maricopa* decision seems especially troubling in light of the history of American antitrust law. When Congress passed the Sherman Act in 1890, it created an overly broad statute that declared illegal "[e]very contract, combination in the form of trust or otherwise, or conspiracy, in restraint of trade or commerce among the several States, or with foreign nations. . . ."[107] It takes little imagination to understand that *any* contract between buyer and seller is a restraint of trade, the buyer binding a part of his budget to the seller, and the seller binding a part of his output to the buyer, each to that extent to the exclusion of all others.[108] To leaven this overly broad statute, the Court has often applied a "rule of reason" to various restraints and practices, which rule requires that courts "consider the facts peculiar to the business to which the restraint is applied; its condition before and after the restraint was imposed, the nature of the restraint and its effect, actual or probable."[109] The development of economic theory since 1890, and especially in the last 20 years, commends this practice. Activities such as alleged predatory pricing,[110] vertical integration,[111] retail price-maintenance agreements,[112]

---

[106]102 S. Ct. at 2482-83 (Powell, J., dissenting) (quoting United States v. Topco Assocs., Inc., 405 U.S. 596, 608 (1972), quoting in turn White Motor Co. v. United States, 372 U.S. 253, 263 (1963)) (italics original).

[107]15 U.S.C. § 1 (1976).

[108]As Justice Brandeis noted, "[e]very agreement concerning trade, every regulation of trade, restrains. To bind, to restrain, is of their very essence." Chicago Bd. of Trade v. United States, 246 U.S. 231, 238 (1918).

[109]Id. at 238.

[110]John S. McGee, "Predatory Price Cutting: The Standard Oil (N.J.) Case," *Journal of Law & Economics* 1 (October 1958): 137–69.

[111]Ronald H. Coase, "The Nature of the Firm," *Economica* 4 (November 1937): 386–404, and Benjamin Klein, Robert G. Crawford, and Armen A. Alchian, "Vertical Integration, Appropriable Rents, and the Competitive Contracting Process," *Journal of Law & Economics* 21 (October 1978): 297–326.

[112]Lester Telser, "Why Should Manufacturers Want Fair Trade?" *Journal of Law & Economics* 3 (October 1960): 86–105. The argument is cogently explained in Howard P. Marvel, "Hybrid Trade Restraints: The Legal Limit of Government's Helping Hand," *Supreme Court Economic Review* 2 (1983): 168–77 (reviewing Rice v. Norman Williams Co., 102 S. Ct. 3294 (1982)).

and base-point pricing,[113] when considered in the light of recent economic analysis, turn out to be improbable (predatory pricing), benign (base-point pricing), or actually beneficial (vertical integration and retail price-maintenance agreements).

The Court in *Maricopa* departed from its usual practices in at least two ways. First, it adopted a *per se* rule of illegality with no inquiry at any judicial level about the maximum-price agreement. Second, while the Court did not explicitly call the maximum-price agreement an instance of predation, its reasoning implicitly embraced that view. But predatory-pricing cases had never contemplated *ex ante*, prophylactic prohibition under a *per se* rule, although that is exactly what the Court invoked in *Maricopa*.[114] Thus, *Maricopa* abandons a judicial approach—the rule of reason—designed to tame what would otherwise be an unreasonably broad statute, arguably to the detriment of both sellers and the citizenry.

Economists and other scholars have disagreed over whether the horizontal maximum-price agreement declared illegal in *Maricopa* is actually beneficial or harmful. Easterbrook,[115] for example, suggests that such agreements and their publication might inform consumers about lower-price alternatives. Hall[116] argues that the arrangement is economically efficient. And Leffler,[117] using a model similar to but more complex than Hall's, argues that HMOs might suffer. It was doubtless this confusing economic picture that led both the district court and the court of appeals to deny summary judgment under a *per se* rule and to require instead that the case be tried under a rule of reason. The Supreme Court was seriously in error when it decided otherwise, as the underlying theory of predation itself is fundamentally flawed.[118] But for our purposes the problem lies elsewhere. Economic complexity appears to have led the Court to declare a practice illegal *per se*, to the derogation of the right of physicians to contract with each other to lower prices. Their rights have fallen

---

[113]David D. Haddock, "Base-Point Pricing: Competitive v. Collusive Theories," *American Economic Review* 72 (June 1982): 289–306.

[114]The Court also suggested that the maximum-price agreement might become a minimum-price agreement, promoting uniform pricing as well, but again there was no proof on the record. See Arizona v. Maricopa Medical Society, 102 S. Ct. at 2475.

[115]Frank H. Easterbrook, "Maximum Price Fixing," *University of Chicago Law Review* 48 (Fall 1981): 886–910.

[116]Comment, "Physician Maximum Price Agreements: *Arizona v. Maricopa County Medical Society*," *Emory Law Journal* 31 (Fall 1982): 913–71.

[117]Keith B. Leffler, "*Arizona v. Maricopa County Medical Society*: Maximum-Price Agreements in Markets with Insured Buyers," *Supreme Court Economic Review* 2 (1983): 187–211.

[118]See, for example, McGee, "Predatory Price Cutting."

away in the face of a theoretically unlikely charge that, in any case, remains unproved.

Noneconomic Grounds, Correct Results

The third set of cases involves decisions that the Supreme Court decided on noneconomic grounds but which it could have decided equally well on the basis of consistent economic analysis. These cases, nevertheless, are marked by occasional analysis in *dicta*, which often seems inadequate. The first of these is *Fidelity Federal Savings & Loan Ass'n v. de la Cuesta*,[119] which concerned a challenge to the application by a California court of appeals of the Supreme Court of California's decision in *Wellenkamp v. Bank of America*,[120] which in turn nullified the right of banks in California to enforce due-on-sale clauses in home-mortgage contracts. In *Wellenkamp*, the California court granted the plaintiff injunctive relief against the bank's foreclosure on her property, when she refused to agree to accept escalation of the interest rate on a mortgage that she had assumed from the sellers. The Court held that the due-on-sale clause violated a California statute, enacted a century earlier, which said that "[c]onditions restraining alienation, when repugnant to the interest created are void."[121] The California Court of Appeals for the Fourth Appellate District's decision[122] in *Fidelity Federal* applied the *Wellenkamp* doctrine against a challenge of federal preemption, which the lower court had agreed to,[123] because of a 1976 Federal Home Loan Bank Board regulation granting federally chartered savings and loan associations the right to place and enforce due-on-sale clauses in mortgage contracts.[124] The Supreme Court of California refused to review the appeals court's decision.

Considering the competitive nature of mortgage banking, a correct economic analysis of due-on-sale clauses would ask whether a bank will shoulder the risk that interest rates might rise when it had agreed to mortgage contracts assumable at the original contract's interest rate, or whether the mortgagor will accept the risk that the higher rate might impose a lower market price for his property. (A complete analysis would also consider the effect of interest rate declines.)

---

[119]102 S. Ct. 3014 (1982). The case is discussed cogently in Haddock and Hall, "Making Rights Inalienable," pp. 25–30.

[120]21 Cal. 3d 943, 582 P.2d 970, 148 Cal. Rptr. 379 (1978).

[121]Cal. Civ. Code § 711 (West 1982).

[122]102 S. Ct. at 3020.

[123]Id.

[124]12 C.F.R. §§ 545.8-3(f) (1982).

Absent substantial market failure, competition among banks and mortgagors should be sufficient to insure that the contracting parties "got it right." Hence, the judicial (or, implicitly, legislative) nullification of the due-on-sale clause could only benefit present home sellers (and some buyers, depending upon the economic incidence of nullification), to the detriment of future mortgagors. Thus, on economic grounds we can approve of the Supreme Court's decision to overturn the California court's ruling.

The Court based its decision on a narrow reading of federal preemption, and it would have been untoward for it to have done otherwise. Congress then quickly removed any doubt about the matter by extending to all banks, not just to those that are federally chartered, the right to incorporate due-on-sale clauses in mortgage contracts.[125] But it is useful to consider how the Court might have treated *Fidelity Federal* in the absence of the preempting federal banking regulation or congressional action. Surely, the same Court that decided *Hawaii* could not find in its own arsenal grounds to argue with a California legislature or court that identified a significant public danger in inflated housing costs and rising interest rates. After all, an imaginary threat to ownership is common to both the California and Hawaii situations. Nor should we conclude that the banks would be entitled to compensation for their lost income in *Wellenkamp's* present and prospective judicial impairment of the obligation of contract.[126] After all, the banks would continue, in the words of *Penn Central,* to receive a "reasonable return" on their mortgages. Three courts interpreted the preemption question in *Fidelity Federal* in three different ways. But it would have been comforting to know that, reflecting a constitutionally based set of principles laid down by the Supreme Court, even the California courts would have regarded

---

[125]Garn-St. Germaine Depository Institution Act of 1982, Pub. L. No. 97-320, 96 Stat. 1469 (codified as amended in scattered sections of 12 U.S.C.).

[126]It is generally agreed that the contracts clause does not apply to decisions by state courts about the law of contracts. See Epstein, "Contract Clause," pp. 747–50. There are limits to this rule, however. See Gelpcke v. Dubuque, 68 U.S. (1 Wall.) 175 (1864). To the extent that the California courts relied on an old and otherwise innocuous state statute to void due-on-sale clauses, however, it is at least arguable that the federal courts might have vacated the judgment below. Judicial common law activity in contract cases, moreover, is largely prospective, filling in details when contracts stand mute about particular rights and obligations. The overriding intent of this kind of judicial activity is to reduce both uncertainty and transaction costs, for the benefit of future contracting parties. The decisions of the California courts in both *Wellenkamp* and *de la Cuesta* seem plainly at odds with this intent. And in these cases, as in so many others, California courts have transcended a judicial role and taken on the mantle of legislatures.

the de la Cuestas' suit as a frivolous attempt at a private, uncompensated taking, and would have treated it accordingly.

The second case involving noneconomic grounds but economically correct results is *Edgar v. Mite Corp.*,[127] in which the Supreme Court struck down the Illinois Business Take-Over Act. That act, passed in 1977, set up substantial barriers, far beyond those contemplated in the federal Williams Act, to corporate takeovers. The Court, per Justice White, decided that the Williams Act preempted the Illinois act and as well, the state statute placed an unacceptable burden on interstate commerce. We could certainly analyze *Edgar v. Mite* in the category of "economic grounds, correct results," because Justice White's opinion relies heavily on recent developments in the law and economics of corporate governance.[128] Indeed, considerations of efficiency in the market for corporate ownership and control tipped the balance against the interests of Illinois in Justice White's application of the commerce clause.[129] Similarly, the judicially recognized belief in a congressional "balance" struck between the interests of present shareholders and future owners provided support for the majority's claim that the Williams Act preempted the Illinois statute.[130]

The problem with *Edgar v. Mite*, as Jarrell[131] has carefully argued, is that the Williams Act is fully subject to all of the criticisms that Justice White's opinion aims at the Illinois act. Any hindrance of corporate takeovers, save those involving common law fraud, renders the market for corporate control less efficient and thereby *ex ante* reduces all investors' returns. If Justice White is correct about the Illinois act's economic mischief, then he can only argue that the Williams Act works a slightly reduced degree of mischief.

Noneconomic Grounds, Incorrect Results

The final group of cases involves decisions in which, from an economic perspective, the Supreme Court came to incorrect results

---

[127]102 S. Ct. 2629 (1982).

[128]See, for example, Id. at 2642 (citing Frank H. Easterbrook and Daniel R. Fischel. "The Proper Role of a Target's Management in Responding to a Tender Offer," *Harvard Law Review* 94 (April 1981): 1161–1203, and Daniel R. Fischel, "Efficient Capital Market Theory, The Market for Corporate Control, and the Regulation of Cash Tender Offers," *Texas Law Review* 57 (December 1978): 1–46).

[129]102 S. Ct. at 2640.

[130]Id. at 2629–35.

[131]Greg A. Jarrell, "State Anti-Takeover Laws and the Efficient Allocation of Corporate Control: An Economic Analysis of *Edgar v. Mite Corp.*," *Supreme Court Economic Review* 2 (1983): 111–29. Jarrell adds that Justice White emphasizes the "inefficient-management" explanation for takeovers but pays no attention to "synergy"-related explanations. Ibid., pp. 121–23.

but on noneconomic grounds. In terms of the deference paid to state legislatures, *Hawaii* and *Moorman* fall easily into this category, although in the first the Court uttered economic heresy and in the second it specifically rejected compelling economic reasoning. Three other cases, however, help to document how legal opinion with neither constitutional principle nor economic reasoning as guides often can lead the Court astray.

The first case, *Ridgway v. Ridgway*,[132] involves a dispute over the proceeds of a deceased serviceman's GI insurance. Sgt. Ridgway, as part of a divorce decree, had agreed to designate his ex-wife as the policy's beneficiary, in trust for their minor children, or to replace the GI insurance with a comparable private policy. Sgt. Ridgway subsequently remarried, designated his new wife as the policy's beneficiary, and then died one year later, without replacing the original policy. The Supreme Judicial Court of Maine turned aside a lower-court ruling against the first wife, based on federal-preemption grounds.[133] The United States Supreme Court then reversed the Maine court, relying on a reading of the Serviceman's Group Life Insurance Act of 1965,[134] which provided that servicemen could redesignate beneficiaries at will, and that the policy's proceeds "shall not be liable to attachment, levy, or seizure by or under any legal or equitable process whatever, either before or after receipt by the beneficiary."[135]

The Court's supremacy clause argument rested partly on public-policy grounds. In a related case, the Court had earlier decided that "insurance, payable to the relative of his choice, might well directly enhance the morale of the serviceman."[136] And so it might, although the application in *Ridgway* seems strained. By a correct reading of the underlying economics, however, the Court might have found the application of its supremacy clause argument contrary to public policy and certainly contrary to the spirit, and even, by implication, the letter of the 1965 act. The obvious difficulty that the Court's opinion in *Ridgway* poses is that it makes inalienable the serviceman's property interest in his GI insurance policy's proceeds. He can no longer enter a contract that designates the policy's beneficiary, because after *Ridgway* such a designation provision would be unenforceable. The

[132]454 U.S. 46 (1981). For a discussion of *Ridgway*, see Haddock and Hall, "Making Rights Inalienable," pp. 4–7. My discussion follows theirs at several points.

[133]Ridgway v. Prudential Ins. Co., 419 A.2d 1030 (Me. 1980).

[134]38 U.S.C. § 770(a) (1976).

[135]Id. at § 770(g).

[136]Wissner v. Wissner, 338 U.S. 655, 660–61 (1950).

serviceman's choice set is thus restricted, and he may have to turn to a less preferred alternative, such as a contractual hostage, if the Court will allow it, to satisfy his opposite number in any negotiations. In sum, the Court's opinion in *Ridgway* has reduced the value of GI insurance for all servicemen covered under these policies.[137]

The same reasoning applies to the Court's opinion in *Merrion v. Jicarilla Apache Tribe*.[138] In *Jicarilla*, several companies had been operating under long-term mineral leases on tribal lands. The leases contemplated rents and royalties on oil and natural gas extracted following exploration. But in 1976 the tribe decided to impose an *ad valorem* tax in addition to the royalties previously agreed upon. Noting the special circumstances and sovereignty of Indian tribes, the Court sustained the tax against commerce clause, federal preemption, and breach of contract challenges.

Jicarilla resembles *Ridgway*, but with an important twist. The resemblance is clear. After *Jicarilla*, no oil company can make a contract with an Indian tribe whose sovereignty is recognized by law, without the possibility of subsequent confiscatory tribal taxation. The tribes therefore have lost some of their ability to sell—alienate— mineral rights, to their substantial detriment. Hence, the Court's opinion(s) in *Jicarilla (Ridgway)* have harmed precisely those persons that federal Indian (servicemen's) law sought to protect. Now the tribe may have to go to the less preferred and more risky alternative of extracting minerals itself, of foregoing exploration and possible extraction altogether, or, as in *Ridgway*, of developing a contractual hostage, if the Court determines that its form of sovereignty so allows.

The twist in *Jicarilla* seems equally clear.[139] Payments for mineral rights can take two forms: a rent on the use of the land and a royalty on the amount or the value of the minerals extracted. To the extent that the contract calls for a royalty, the tribe carries some of the risk that exploration will prove fruitless. Before *Jicarilla*, these contract terms emerged from the parties' information, bargaining, and market conditions. After *Jicarilla*, however, the tribes can charge one price (a rent) for exploration, and if it is successful, charge yet another price

---

[137]Whether or not Ridgway's first wife would have an action against his estate under contract law is problematical. Future similarly situated plaintiffs probably have beer. put on notice that they could not sustain such an action.

[138]455 U.S. 130 (1982). The case is carefully analyzed in Haddock and Hall, "Making Rights Inalienable," pp. 7–18.

[139]The following argument relies on Haddock and Hall, pp. 8–9.

(a royalty) for extraction in an apparently lawful exercise of post-contractural opportunistic behavior.[140]

The final opinion in this category, *Arizona Governing Committee for Tax Deferred Annuity & Deferred Compensation Plans v. Norris*,[141] was the most startling and widespread in its implications. In *Norris*, the Court held as illegal, under Title VII of the Civil Rights Act of 1964 as amended,[142] the practice of providing lower monthly annuity payments to women than to men. Title VII reads in pertinent part, that it is unlawful "to discriminate against any individual with respect to his compensation, terms, conditions, or privileges of employment, because of such individual's race, color, religion, sex or national origin."[143]

The practice complained of is simple enough to understand. Suppose that an employer pays a man and woman equal salaries over equal periods of employment and sets aside or contributes equal percentages of their wages into earmarked retirement funds. Both employees retire at age 65, and the funds provide each with a monthly annuity calculated to pay out the full value of the earmarked amount, net of administrative costs and related fees, over each employee's actuarially calculated remaining life. Since women, on average, live longer that do men, the woman's monthly payments are commensurately smaller than the man's payments.

The Court required little effort to place such annuities in the category of "compensation, terms, conditions, or privileges of employment," and to regard the apparent inequality as discrimination. But the inequality was far more apparent than real. Considered *ex post*, as the Court had done, the monthly payments are unequal. Considered *ex ante*, as a proper economic analysis (and the market) would do, during the period of employment, the net present value of the income streams from the man's and woman's annuities are exactly equal. "Inequality" must reside somewhere in this calculus, no matter which payment method is chosen, and the Court plainly chose the wrong place. One result of the *Norris* decision is that the Court worked a serious inequality as between men and women. A second result is that the Court has created an implicit wealth transfer from women who remain at home and rely on their husbands' pensions to those who enter the job market and rely on their own

---

[140]For a discussion of post-contractual opportunistic behavior in the context of decisions to integrate vertically, see Klein, Crawford, and Alchian, "Vertical Integration."

[141]103 S. Ct. 3492 (1983).

[142]42 U.S.C. § 2000e *et seq.*

[143]Id. at §§ 2000e-2(a)(1).

pensions. A third result of *Norris* will be some decoupling of employee remuneration and the purchase of annuities. A fourth result will be a serious distortion of economic decision making and a reduction in welfare.[144] Nothing in Title VII specifically compelled such a result. We may nevertheless explain it as the Court's misguided attempt to expand on congressional intent in a "good cause." The decision betrays the Court's inconsistency, however, as in cases such as *Norris* it appears to accept the role of legislature, but only because, in its view, the legislature itself has pointed the way.

IV. Judges as Economists Reconsidered

One simple response to this litany of economic error might hold that judges should learn more about and apply economic analysis to the cases and controversies that they must decide. In certain areas of law, such as antitrust and the traditional common law areas—property, contracts, and torts—this response has much to recommend it, and indeed it holds good where the courts must answer explicit economic questions. In these same areas there is at least an argument, yet one that we later question, that the Supreme Court is showing a growing sophistication.[145] But in the area of constitutional law generally, as well as in common law cases that rise to the level of constitutional disputes, this response may be seriously ill-founded.

I hasten to add, beyond the confines of a mere footnote, that my dissatisfaction with the explicit judicial application of economics to the law of the Constitution does not grow out of a dissatisfaction with the economic analysis of law as an academic discipline. That discipline, like all other academic pursuits, comes in all shapes and sizes. Similarly, the discipline's practitioners, like its critics, have provided works that range from the profound[146] to the frivolous.[147] The academic exercise of law and economics views judges and litigants,

---

[144]For a careful analysis of the annuity-equality problem, see George J. Benston, "The Economics of Gender Discrimination in Employee Fringe Benefits: *Manhart* Revisited," *University of Chicago Law Review* 49 (Spring 1982): 489–542.

[145]See Easterbrook, "Court and Economic System," and text accompanying infra notes 173–82 and 212–30.

[146]See, for example, Buchanan, "Good Economics."

[147]See, for example, Mark G. Kelman, "Misunderstanding Social Life: A Critique of the Core Premises of 'Law and Economics,' " *Journal of Legal Education* 33 (June 1983): 274–84. Kelman's errors probably reflect at least in part a reaction to Posner's procrustean bed of wealth maximizing. See, for example, Richard A. Posner, "Utilitarianism, Economics, and Legal Theory," *Journal of Legal Studies* 8 (January 1979): 103–40, and Posner, "The Ethical and Political Basis of the Efficiency Norm in Common Law Adjudication," *Hofstra Law Review* 8 (Spring 1980): 487–507.

producers and consumers, and governors and the governed, as *objects* of study, not as those whom we might approach as supplicants, and whom we are driven to advise because we share "the fire of truth."[148] Our experience with both courts and legislatures suggests a different approach.

The Problem of Welfare and Rights

The first problem with asking judges to become the ultimate social controllers in pursuit of social efficiency—wealth maximizing—seems apparent in the manner that the proposition is thus stated. As a normative model for judges to follow explicitly, wealth maximizing incorporates the notion that all of the wealth in society, and correspondingly all of the rights of property and contract, are available for contraction, expansion, and redistribution, at the expense of their owners or of others.[149] Sometimes these reallocations will come with compensation, as in *Hawaii,* and sometimes without compensation, as in *Penn Central* and as in the vast array of other takings by regulation.

The philosophical basis for such a view of rearrangeable rights would place the courts, as agencies of the state, above the ultimate source of consent. It would create a hubris that knows no bounds. And it seems contrary to any notion of ordered liberty. Courts that adopt this view would become indistinguishable in their purpose from super regulatory agencies and legislatures, charged with promoting the general welfare, and with all of the property and rights in the hands of the citizens available for confiscation and redistribution. If we assert for the judiciary the efficiency goal and nothing more, then we must assert as well the means for its accomplishment. Our assessment of this view of law found its best summary in the words of an otherwise very staid and dispassionate colleague of mine

---

[148]See Edmund W. Kitch, ed., "The Fire of Truth: A Remembrance of Law and Economics at Chicago, 1932–1970," *Journal of Law & Economics* 26 (April 1983): 163–234.

[149]As Epstein notes,

> Into this picture of uncontested hegemony I should like to inject a note of doubt. It must be asked by what warrant, by what title, does the public policy analyst proceed on the implicit assumption that all entitlements lie within the public domain? At the very least the question deserves some sort of an answer because of the way in which the study of law and economics—even that of the conservative stripe—cuts against the ideals of limited government, individual liberty and private property, which, especially in the American context, have deep and powerful roots of their own.
>
> [Epstein, "Taxation," p. 433]

who, after reading Judge Posner's *Economic Analysis of Law*,[150] offered the opinion that Posner is a socialist.

This interpretation of Posnerian law and economics doubtless holds the elements of a caricature, but it is a caricature by invitation. This interpretation doubtless also will convey the impression of a no-nothing intellectual atavism, not the least because all law incorporates some capacity for redistribution. But such redistribution is "less bad" if it is an incidental by-product of preserving rights, rather than the explicit judicial tool of wealth maximizing.[151] Here, judicial motive and form become central, because they condition the citizen's expectations of how secure his rights of property, contract, and person might remain under the alternatives.

Judges as Legislators

The most apparent counterclaim to the assertion that the wealth-maximizing jurist is a less than desirable normative model grows out of recent literature on the common law.[152] The model of common law adjudication developed in this literature is ingenious and, I believe, correct, even in its utter simplicity. Rubin's model examines the contesting parties' incentives to sue or settle out of court. If the judicial precedent governing the dispute is efficient (for example, it places liability in a tort case on the least-cost accident avoider), then the parties have an incentive to settle rather than sue. But if the precedent is inefficient, then thay have an incentive to go to trial. The only assumption about judges' decisions in this model is that they tend to follow precedent. The end result is that efficient precedents tend to remain unchallenged, while the parties continually litigate cases governed by an inefficient precedent until some court overturns the inefficient rule. The theory's predictions are most robust if both parties have a continuing future interest in the precedent and if there are few serious free-rider problems in aggregating the interests of all potential future litigants.

The notion that Supreme Court justices or appellate court judges should decide cases and set precedents so as to maximize wealth rests on two critical assumptions. The first is that judges should be conscious (and educated) about what they are doing. The second is that they should do it at a constitutional level. The problem with the

---

[150]Posner, *Economic Analysis of Law*.

[151]See supra note 126.

[152]See, for example, Paul H. Rubin, "Why Is the Common Law Efficient?" *Journal of Legal Studies* 6 (January 1977): 51–63, and George Priest, "The Common Law Process and the Selection of Efficient Rules," *Journal of Legal Studies* 6 (January 1977): 65–82.

first assumption is that it would have courts act consciously and explicitly as super legislatures. Indeed, the judicial model implicit in this view is precisely the Supreme Court's own caricatured model of the legislature, expressed in cases such as *Nebbia, Hawaii,* and *Moorman,* but absent any degree of representativeness.

Such a comparison immediately raises the question of whether a court seized by this view of its role would act any differently than do present legislatures. Even though the Supreme Court, in the deference that it grants to the political branches, has explicitly eschewed such a role, we might consider what would happen if it specifically embraced it. Present models of legislatures, which Section V[153] reviews, indicate that legislators face powerful incentives to produce private benefits for private, divisible groups in the population, all at collective costs that probably exceed the groups' benefits (to the extent that such costs and benefits remain comparable). A court that decided explicitly to maximize wealth would to that extent cast off precedent and ignore preexisting rights, because these could only impair its operation. The broad-based collection of the citizenry would face severe free-rider problems in assembling its interests to provide a defense against the inevitable interest-group assault on its welfare through judicial territory. The only litigants that would tend to remain, and whose welfare would have standing in fact, would be the interest groups themselves, as banks would battle brokers, truckers would assault railroads, small towns would attack airlines, in a process now carried on in the legislatures and regulatory agencies.[154] What surprises us about this proposed model (but really should not) is that it predicts an outcome that strongly resembles the present order. The Court today, by becoming *functus officio,* tends merely to recapitulate the legislature's process and determinations.

But there is more. On a few occasions the Court does find grounds for reversing legislative determinations. As mentioned earlier,[155] for example, in *Maryland v. Louisiana, Armco, Bacchus,* and *Tully* the Court read the explicit language of state tax statutes to discriminate impermissibly against out-of-state corporations. But it did so on principled, constitutional grounds, not on economic ones. Indeed, in *Armco* it might have found on economic grounds that a different state tax on local firms offset (or was larger than) the tax on foreign companies. And in decisions such as *Chadha,* the Court has taken a dim

---

[153]See text accompanying infra notes 193–210.

[154]See Peter H. Aranson, Ernest Gellhorn, and Glen O. Robinson, "A Theory of Legislative Delegation," *Cornell Law Review* 68 (November 1982): 1–67.

[155]See supra note 7 and text accompanying supra notes 69–73.

view of congressional attempts to circumvent what it held to be constitutionally mandated legislative processes.

Suppose that, in each of these and similar (or even different) cases, the Court came to similar results on the merits but based its opinions on explicit economic grounds, not on principled constitutional ones. Now it says to Congress: "We have argued and bargained among ourselves, and our opinion is different—and controlling." How would Congresss respond? Recall that Landes and Posner's model[156] asserts that the judiciary maintains its "independence" by not becoming an auxiliary legislature. By implication, the Court can more easily "get away" with opposing legislative determinations occasionally on grounds orthogonal to those engaged by the political branches. Could it do so if it merely recapitulated the legislative process, and particularly the political considerations inherent in that process? I think not. The Court's appellate jurisdiction is a gift from Congress, and it is subject to rescission. Hence, the result of explicit judicial legislation, on economic or other nonconstitutional grounds, well might be the negation of any control that the judiciary now imposes on the political branches through constitutional argument.

Judges as Planners

Conscious and explicit judicial decision making on wealth-maximizing grounds might create other mischief as well, although here the analysis becomes far more speculative. Let us draw an analogy from actors in a competitive market place to the participants in a common law process. Firms as price takers face horizontal demand schedules and in long-run equilibrium set output and scale where marginal cost equals marginal revenue (price) and where long-run average total cost is minimized. None of this occurs, nor need it occur, as the result of conscious calculation.[157] Indeed, the Austrian economists teach us that it cannot be planned or perhaps even be done consciously.[158] The firm, that is, by using a heuristic or even by acting randomly, either adopts the "correct" output and technology or tends to go out of business or be subject to takeover by more "efficient" owners and management teams. The traditional judgment of welfare economics is that the resulting resource allocation is

---

[156]See "Independent Judiciary" and text accompanying supra notes 41–56.

[157]See Armen A. Alchian, "Uncertainty, Evolution, and Economic Theory," *Journal of Political Economy* 58 (June 1950): 211–21.

[158]See, for example, Friedrich A. Hayek, "The Use of Knowledge in Society," *American Economic Review* 35 (September 1945): 519–30. Here, I extend an Austrian argument from a foundation of neoclassical economic equilibrium. Austrians justifiably might protest.

efficient, even though none of the parties—buyers and sellers—specifically intended it to be so.

By analogy, the participants in common law adjudication each face a set of incentives and operate under a set of heuristics designated as rules of legal procedure, standing, jurisdiction, and the like. The judge applies these rules and (usually) a precedent to arrive at a decision. Again, if we credit much of the recent literature in law and economics, the resulting resource allocation is efficient. The central question is: "What would happen in each setting if the actors sought to promote economically efficient results, instead of seeking to apply their respective heuristics (or even random decision making, as the case might be)?"

The question is at least partly fanciful, because the analogy breaks down at certain critical points. The firm's manager, for example, need not know the nature of each buyer's preferences, because price provides an adequate summary. The judge, by contrast, "knows" only the preferences of the instant litigants and the datum that they have not come to a settlement. Similarly, this market, by definition, is devoid of external effects, while these same effects often form the core of efficiency judgments about common law rules, especially at the appellate level, where judges "sell" not merely decisions on the merits but also precedents governing the disposition of future disputes.

But substantial similarities between the two situations remain. Neither the manager nor the judge has sufficient information to make adequate globally efficient welfare judgments in the face of geographically different conditions. Neither has an incentive to collect, nor could each collect, Pareto-relevant information about widespread external effects, because the manager "knows" only price and the judge "knows" only the litigants' interests and arguments. Most important, the analogy breaks down when the judge's decision loses its "competitive" nature and governs a widespread territory of many litigants with diverse preferences operating under different conditions. And this is precisely the point at which the second critical assumption of the notion that Supreme Court justices or appellate court judges should decide cases and set precedents so as to maximize wealth comes into play—the notion that judges should do this at a constitutional level.

The model of the Posnerian judge is highly seductive, not the least because it works, and sometimes such judges are even conscious about what they are doing. But the model applies best to a local judge applying common law, whose lesser lack of the *correct* information can do little mischief, rather than to a national judge applying constitutional law, whose lack of information may be far more profound, and thus cause far greater harm. Consider, for example, a simple problem in landlord-tenant (and tort) law: Who should be liable for injury caused a third party by negligence on the leased property, the landlord or the tenant? For many years the common law placed liability on the tenant, and then it changed to the landlord. Goetz[159] provides an interesting explanation for this change. In earlier years leased residences were principally single-family dwellings with long periods of tenancy. The tenant was in the best position to know about dangerous conditions. More recently, renters tend increasingly to occupy multiple-family apartment units, and especially those with short-term leases and common areas. Information asymmetries between the landlord and tenant and free-rider problems among tenants, with some exceptions, would place liability at reduced relative cost on landlords.

At lower judicial levels judges at common law might distinguish cases involving large apartment complexes with high tenant turnover from those involving single-family dwellings leased for long periods of tenancy. The judge would have the best grasp of local conditions, and in the absence of specific contractual provisions, we would approve of his acting "like an economist" to find the least-cost accident avoider. At the national level, however, matters are different. First, the judge is not likely to understand local conditions. Second, he may have to worry, more than would the local judge, about legislative opposition. Third, the problem of asymmetric interests may grow larger at the national than at the local level. Recall that in the Rubin model, both parties must have a continuing interest in precedent, and both parties must be reasonable proxies for all other potentially similarly situated persons. But to the extent that the litigation rises to the federal appellate level, one or the other of these assumptions seems likely not to apply. Large housing corporations that own and operate apartment complexes, for example, may be better able to internalize some of the collective benefits of litigation than are individual tenants, leading the tenants to underinvest in litigation, with the consequent adoption of an inefficient precedent.[160]

---

[159]Charles J. Goetz, "Wherefore the Landlord-Tenant Law 'Revolution?' Some Comments," *Cornell Law Review* 69 (March 1984): 592–603.

[160]Both parties—landlords and tenants—lose if the precedent is inefficient. Because of free-rider problems, the tenant will take a less than efficient amount of care (reflecting free-rider problems) if the landlord is not held liable, but simultaneously he might have to invest more than the landlord would have to pay in pursuit of an efficient level of precautionary measures (if he alone bears the entire cost of an efficient level of care), because the landlord can identify and repair hazards at a lower cost. The tenant, if he alone pays for an efficient level of accident avoidance, will also be willing only to pay

Left to their own devices, federal appellate judges will have only what the litigants and intervenors tell them and their own ideological predilections to rely on in deciding such cases. They certainly could not (and might be unwilling to) rely on their knowledge of local conditions. In *Javins v. First National Realty Corporation*,[161] for example, Judge J. Skelly Wright held that tenants who had not paid their rent could not face eviction where the landlord had failed to meet an implied warrant of habitability, based on the standards found in the local housing code, which warrant he created out of whole cloth. Judge Wright's later justification for this and similar decisions contains most of the elements leading to a failure to get the economics right:

> I was . . . influenced by the fact that, during the nationwide racial turmoil of the sixties and the unrest caused by the injustices of racially selective service in Vietnam, most of the tenants in Washington, D.C. slums were poor and black and most of the landlords were rich and white. There is no doubt in my mind that these conditions played a subconscious role in influencing my landlord and tenant decisions.
>
> I came to Washington in April 1962 after being born and raised in New Orleans, Louisiana for 51 years. I had never been exposed, either as a judge or as a lawyer, to the local practice of law which, of course, included landlord and tenant cases. I was Assistant U.S. Attorney, U.S. Attorney, and then U.S. District Court judge in New Orleans before I joined the U.S. Court of Appeals in Washington. It was my first exposure to landlord and tenant cases, the U.S. Court of Appeals here being a writ court to the local court system at the time. I didn't like what I saw, and I did what I could do to ameliorate, if not eliminate, the injustice involved in the way many of the poor were required to live in the nation's capital.
>
> I offer no apology for not following more closely the legal precedents which had cooperated in creating the conditions that I found unjust.[162]

---

a lower rent than if the landlord were liable. If the landlord is liable, then he will pass along some of the expected cost of liability to the tenant, but the cost will be lower than the tenant (efficiently) would bear if he were liable. All of this is merely an application of the Coase Theorem. See Ronald H. Coase, "The Problem of Social Cost," *Journal of Law & Economics* 3 (October 1960): 1–44.

[161]428 F.2d 1071 (D.C. Cir.), *cert. denied*, 400 U.S. 925 (1970).

[162]Letter to Professor Edward H. Rabin from Judge J. Skelly Wright, in Edward H. Rabin, "The Revolution in Residential Landlord-Tenant Law: Causes and Consequences," *Cornell Law Review* 69 (March 1984): 549.

The *Javins* opinion may seem inappropriate to cite here, in the light of the previous hypothetical, which found large rental firms to be better able to represent—aggregate—all other similar firms' interest in precedent. Here, the tenants have "won," or so they might believe. The actual interests aggregated were those of the so-called public interest groups. First National Realty Corporation was represented by Mr. Herman

The problem with Judge Wright's decision in *Javins* and in his other landmark landlord-tenant cases[163] is a failure to understand the underlying economic nature of contracts. Unless a lease contract so specified, there was no implied warrant of "habitability,"[164] of the sort that he contemplated, in the common law. Thus, the tenants in *Javins* and in similar cases had agreed to live in the affected residences. Requiring landlords to do "more" would simultaneously require tenants to pay more and to face a reduced availability of housing stock. The reduction in available and affordable housing following *Javins* and its terms' enactment in several state codes therefore should occasion no surprise. Nor is Judge Wright's reliance on ideology and ignoring of economic reality an astonishing development. He enjoyed neither the information nor the perspective necessary to get it right. Landlords' rights and tenants' welfare (and contract rights) suffered as a consequence.

V. Constitutional Principles and Economic Rights

The preceding discussion of judges as economists would appear to close off one possible avenue of improving judicial control of the political branches. First, the notion of judges as economists seems philosophically objectionable, because it eviscerates any notion of the judiciary as a protector of rights. Second, if judges acted as legislators, their actions would incorporate in the judiciary all of the failures of legislatures, threaten judges' independence, and obliterate any reasonable control that judges now exercise. Finally, the idea of judges as planners—Posnerian judges—might be an acceptable normative model for local, common law adjudication, but certainly not for federal appellate-level disputes involving constitutional questions, in which the judges may tend to substitute their personal

---

Miller, of Washington, D.C. Ms. Javins was represented by Mr. Edmund E. Fleming, of Boston. In addition, briefs *amicus curiae*, urging reversal in Ms. Javins's favor, were filed by the Washington Planning and Housing Association, the Neighborhood Legal Services Program (with Patricia M. Wald on brief), and the National Housing Law Project. The financial supporters of these groups (probably including the federal government) had aggregated *their* ideological interests.

[163]See, for example, Edwards v. Habib, 397 F.2d 687 (D.C. Cir. 1968), *cert. denied*, 393 U.S. 1016 (1969) (barring failure to renew lease in retaliation for tenant's complaining to housing authority over code violations), and Robinson v. Diamond Housing Corp., 463 F.2d 853 (D.C. Cir. 1972) (barring failure to renew lease in retaliation for tenant's abatement of rent for code violation and requiring landlord to keep property on market, repair it, and bear burden of proof that any subsequent lease nonrenewal is not retaliatory).

[164]Judge Wright's implied warrant of habitability goes far beyond requiring the provision of barely suitable housing to requiring that all appliances, outlets, and so forth actually "work" up to the specifications of the operant housing code.

ideologies in the absence of information and a roughly symmetric interest of the litigants. Furthermore, the activities of common law judges, unlike those of federal jurists, as in *Javins,* or of state appellate court judges, as in *Wellenkamp,* would seem to promote contract and property rights, not to subvert them. In sum, almost by the default of the other branches, the judiciary becomes a source of control of those branches, but there is not yet available a set of robust rules, doctrines, or even attitudes, that courts might apply to accomplish this task.

Citizens' Welfare in the Political Branches

Any attempt to use the judiciary to control the apparent failures of federal, state, and local political branches to advance, rather than to diminish the interests of the citizenry must first confront the existential fact that the Supreme Court gives scant recognition that such failures exist. In the view of the Court, the public interest is what the legislature says it is, and the appropriate means for pursuing that interest ordinarily are the means that the legislature has embraced. The Court's very peculiar applications of specious economic reasoning, more often than not, are but frail attempts to give color to patently welfare-diminishing and rights-derogating legislative actions.

The rare exceptions to this generalization indicate the very restrained lengths to which the Court is willing to go to repair legislative damage. Some of these exceptions entail attempts to perfect the basis of representation itself. In cases such as *City of Port Arthur, Texas v. United States,*[165] *Anderson v. Celebrezze,*[166] and *Karcher v. Daggett,*[167] the Court has sought recently to protect citizens from racial discrimination, statutory handicapping of minority candidates, and congressional-district numerical inequality and gerrymandering, respectively. At best, the Court's decisions aimed at providing for "fair" and "equal" political representation serve only to give legitimacy to the welfare-diminishing decisions of legislatures. But the Court's reading of other recent cases, such as *Brown v. Thompson*[168] and *Ball v. James,*[169] also suggests limits as to how far the Court is willing to go to insure numerical equality. Certainly, it is fair to say that the Court has no *a priori* theoretical basis for asserting the existence of *any* connection between voting inequality and unequal treatment in public policy. And recent advances in public choice can

---

[165] 103 S. Ct. 530 (1982).
[166] 103 S. Ct. 1564 (1983).
[167] 103 S. Ct. 2653 (1983).
[168] 103 S. Ct. 2690 (1983).
[169] 451 U.S. 355 (1981).

offer the Court no guidance, because no empirical or theoretical basis for claiming that such a connection prevails appears to exist.[170]

A second set of cases, namely those involving alleged commerce clause violations, would appear to have the Court claiming that foreign corporations suffer from an absence of representation in the offending states' legislatures. And indeed, we may read the Court's opinions to that effect in cases such as *Maryland v. Louisiana, Armco, Bacchus,* and *Tully,* in which state legislatures have adopted facially discriminatory taxation. But if this claim about the absence of representation holds true, it certainly cannot explain the Court's decisions in cases such as *Moorman, Commonwealth Edison,* and *Western & Southwestern Life Ins. Co. v. State Board of Equalization,*[171] where the discrimination, while not facial, seems just as palpable. Nor is there any evidence that the Court has achieved any great degree of sophistication about tax "exportation."[172]

Finally, Easterbrook,[173] in a highly creative essay, recently has argued that the Court has grown more sophisticated, *inter alia,* about the economic theory of politics, which we shall discuss here as the interest-group theory of representative democracy. In his view of recent cases, the Court limits the extent of damage that such political decision making creates by applying literally the maxim: "Statutes in derogation of the common law are to be strictly construed."[174] In other words, if an interest group does not specifically secure a right in the legislative arena, then the Court should not supply it. These interest-group promoting cases are to be distinguished from those (perhaps, mistakenly, such as *Norris*) in which the general welfare is engaged as motive: "Remedial statutes are to be liberally construed."[175]

The problem with Easterbrook's optimistic claim is that it may be counterfactual. For example, in *Silkwood v. Kerr-McGee Corp.,*[176]

---

[170]See William H. Riker, "Democracy and Representation: A Reconciliation of *Ball v. James* and *Reynolds v. Sims,*" *Supreme Court Economic Review* 1 (1982): 31–68, and Peter H. Aranson, "Political Inequality: An Economic Approach," in *Political Equilibrium: A Delicate Balance,* ed. Peter C. Ordeshook and Kenneth A. Shepsle (Boston: Martinus Nijhoff, 1982), pp. 133–50.

[171]451 U.S 648 (1981). *Western & Southwestern* concerned a retaliatory tax that California levied against insurance companies domiciled in other states that taxed California firms more than California taxed the relevant out-of-state firms. The court upheld the tax, which appears difficult to classify as to its facial neutrality. The effect of the tax is to punish other states' firms because their states did not adopt California's tax rate.

[172]See generally McLure, "Incidence Analysis."

[173]Easterbrook, "Court and Economic System," pp. 42–58.

[174]Ibid., p. 15.

[175]Ibid., p. 14.

[176]104 S. Ct. 615 (1984).

the Court turned aside a federal-preemption challenge to a state court's award of punitive damages against a utility company generating electricity in nuclear power plants. In Easterbrook's view, the Court was correct in not granting the utility a federal-preemption based exemption from state tort law that it could not find explicitly in congressional actions in favor of the nuclear-energy "cartel." If the Court had read the statute as based on the public interest, then it might have granted such an exemption. While I agree with Easterbrook's analysis of *Silkwood* on the merits, I cannot agree with him (or disagree, for that matter) on the majority's putative motives. The decision looks too much like a "deep-pockets" reaction to the facts, especially in view of its punitive-damage aspects.[177]

The other cases that Easterbrook points to in support of his argument for increased judicial sophistication about interest-group legislation seem equally ambiguous, and perhaps more so. In *Local No. 82, Furniture and Piano Moving, Furniture Store Drivers v. Crowley*,[178] the Court held against aggrieved union members, who had brought a private action in federal court against their union, which, the Supreme Court so held, had violated their rights to a fair election as guaranteed under Section I of the Labor Management Reporting and Disclosure Act. The Court found that Section IV of the Act gave sole power for an action against the union to the secretary of labor, if the election had already begun, and the secretary's actions may occur only after the election. Easterbrook[179] reads the statute as providing for this result in the legislative bargain. Justice Stevens,[180] I believe correctly, did not. In any case, no reading of the statutory history or of the opinion in *Local No. 82* provides evidence that either Easterbrook or the Court understood the underlying interest-group conflict.[181] Readings of other cases that Easterbrook treats in a similar

---

[177]Easterbrook argues against just such reactions in "Court and Economic System," pp. 19–33. Similarly, Easterbrook here repeats the oft-committed error of asserting that federal "public interest" statutes require preemption. This claim, which the Court often has embraced, is a *non sequitur* whose implication we can show to be false. In environmental regulation, for example, federal statutes often fail to "internalize" Pareto-relevant externalities, creating situations that further litigation might ameliorate. The Court apparently found otherwise in City of Milwaukee v. Illinois, 451 U.S. 304 (1981) and in Middlesex County Sewerage Authority v. National Sea Clammers Assoc., 101 S. Ct. 2615 (1981).

[178]104 S. Ct. 2557 (1984).

[179]Easterbrook, "Court and Economic System," pp. 48–49.

[180]104 S. Ct. at 2572 (Stevens, J., dissenting).

[181]On the interest group's preference for ambiguity in legislative delegations to bureaus and departments, see Aranson, Gellhorn, and Robinson, "Legislative Delegation." The act in question, the Landrum-Griffin Act, was a blatantly anti-union statute.

manner, such as *Block v. Community Nutrition Institute*,[182] show his reasoning to be equally inapposite.

Can we rise above the tautology that the public interest is what the legislature says it is? I believe that we can, although we cannot, as Easterbrook would wish, use the Court's language and reasoning. More important still, we must interpret the words and reasons that we substitute for the Court's merely as tools of criticisms, to get us out of the *cul de sac* in which the Court and its apologists have placed us. Our goal here is to sever the Court from the myth of legislative infallibility. It need not adopt our words and phrases, but it must acknowledge the existence of political failure and its incorrigibility through judicial monitoring of the equality of representation alone. Once the Court has done so, it can reflect, as shall we, on appropriate *judicial* means for confining the untoward effects of that failure.

Because the Court provides no standards of success or failure, we shall, again as a critical tool, propose our own: the economic theory of welfare.[183] In this theory competitive markets, in the absence of Pareto-relevant external costs or benefits, or market power, reach allocatively efficient results. Several problems may intervene, however, to prevent decision makers in such markets from achieving a theoretically desirable result. All of these problems reflect a failure to include a relevant cost or benefit in the decision maker's economic calculation, given the prior structure of rights. That is, because of some transaction cost or inability to exclude, say, it is impossible or too costly to make an efficient market in the associated good or service.

The first problem concerns the provision of public goods, such as national defense and public peace. The theory holds that he who provides a public good, because beneficiaries are not excludable, cannot capture the benefits of his actions. Free-rider problems abound, and a suboptimal (or no) supply of the public good may result. The potential existence of a public good, of course, is not a sufficient condition for governmental action. The cost of even "optimal" supply may exceed the benefit, or the extent of the public-good problem may not be Pareto-relevant.[184] Nor does the presence of significant potential external benefits compel a particular manner of political

---

[182]104 S. Ct. 2450 (1984). See Easterbrook, "Court and Economic System," pp. 49–50.

[183]This discussion follows that of Aranson and Ordeshook, "Public Interest."

[184]See, for example, Edwin G. West, "The Political Economy of American Public School Legislation," *Journal of Law & Economics* 10 (October 1967): 101–28, and West, "An Economic Analysis of the Law and Politics of Non-Public School 'Aid,' " *Journal of Law & Economics* 19 (April 1976): 79–101.

response[185] or jurisdiction.[186] Many public-goods problems can also find a market solution, sometimes with but a modest readjustment of property rights.[187]

The second problem is that of public "bads," external diseconomies such as air and water pollution. This problem is the same in structure as that of public goods. People find it individually beneficial to use the ambient air or a water source as a "sink," but they pay neither for this benefit nor for the damage that their actions impose on others. Again, the presence of a potentially reversible public-bads problem does not by itself compel a governmental solution, a particular kind of solution, or an appropriate jurisdiction.

The third problem, that of property rights, is in truth a public goods-public bads problem, but we commonly associate it with common pool-inefficient usage patterns, such as occur with the too rapid extraction of petroleum[188] or crowding in the radio-frequency spectrum.[189] Inefficient usage, brought about by uncoordinated action or the inappropriate definition of property rights, constitutes the public bad. The application of appropriate rules or rights raises the value of the common resource to all users.

The fourth problem, redistribution, is hotly contested, but it exhibits an undeniable public-goods aspect. Persons A and B, being wealthy altruists, both gain welfare from increases in poor man C's consumption. Thus stated, the free-rider problem of A and B seems apparent.[190]

The final problem relates to the presence of monopoly and various sources of market power. As noted earlier,[191] most of the alleged problems of market power, such as vertical integration and resale

[185]See, for example, Ronald H. Coase, "The Lighthouse in Economics," *Journal of Law & Economics* 17 (October 1974): 357–76.

[186]See, for example, Peter H. Aranson, "Pollution Control: The Case for Competition," in *Instead of Regulation: Alternatives to Federal Regulatory Agencies*, ed. Robert W. Poole, Jr. (Lexington, Mass.: D.C. Heath, 1982), pp. 339–93, and Charles M. Tiebout, "A Pure Theory of Local Expenditures," *Journal of Political Economy* 64 (October 1956): 416–24.

[187]See, for example, Marvel, "Hybrid Trade Restraints"; Stephen F. Williams, "Free Trade in Water Resources: *Sporhase v. Nebraska* ex rel. *Douglas*," *Supreme Court Economic Review* 2 (1983): 89–110; and Coase, "Lighthouse in Economics."

[188]See generally James C. Cox, R. Mark Isaac, and Vernon L. Smith, "OCS Leasing and Auctions: Incentives and the Performance of Alternative Bidding Institutions," *Supreme Court Economic Review* 2 (1983): 43–87; Haddock and Hall, "Making Rights Inalienable"; and text accompanying supra notes 91–4.

[189]See, for example, Ronald H. Coase, "The Federal Communications Commission," *Journal of Law & Economics* 2 (October 1959): 1–40.

[190]See, for example, Harold D. Hochman and James D. Rogers, "Pareto Optimal Redistribution," *American Economic Review* 59 (September 1969): 542–57.

[191]See text accompanying supra notes 110–13.

price-maintenance agreements, turn out to be beneficial practices. But a core of problems remain, concerning such matters as natural monopolies. In these situations there is too little surplus, because of restricted output and price set above average total cost. Again, however, the existence of a monopoly problem does not compel a particular political solution.[192]

Because the market is said to fail under all five problems to produce theoretically preferred results, scholars sometimes argue for a governmental solution—a redistribution of rights and resources to increase welfare. For example, "[g]overnmental provision of public goods is required precisely because each individual in uncoordinated [sic] pursuit of his self interest must act in a manner designed to frustrate the provision of these items."[193]

The intellectual dismemberment of this claim has held a central place in the development of public-choice theory over the last two decades. Our review of this theory is necessarily brief, but it begins with two central observations. First, the claim asserts the costless and error-free operation of a series of political and economic connections: (1) the citizenry costlessly and effortlessly aggregates and expresses its preferences over various public policies to "solve" the five problems just listed and so informs election candidates of its wishes; (2) these candidates reflect the electorate's revealed preferences and, if they win, enter office to carry them out; (3) the legislative process (and elected chief-executive decision making) responds to the instructed delegates' wishes, which results in the enactment of a set of laws reflecting citizens' preferences; (4) bureaucrats likewise act as a set of perfect agents in carrying out legislative intent; and (5) the judiciary reinforces this process and does not impermissibly violate citizens' preferences.[194] Second, the claim asserts that the same conditions of utility interdependencies—free riders, public goods, and the like—do not infect the political process.

Both assertions are demonstrably false, for one (or both) of two reasons. First, the aggregation of preferences in the electorate and

---

[192]See, for example, Harold Demsetz, "Why Regulate Utilities?" *Journal of Law & Economics* 11 (April 1968): 347–59, and George J. Stigler and Claire Freidland, "What Can Regulators Regulate? The Case of Electricity," *Journal of Law & Economics* 5 (October 1962): 1–16.

[193]William J. Baumol, *Welfare Economics and the Theory of the State*, 2d rev. ed. (Cambridge: Harvard University Press, 1965), p. 21.

[194]For a detailed discussion of these connections, see Aranson, Gellhorn, and Robinson, "Legislative Delegation," pp. 30–36.

in the legislature is subject to global intransitivities.[195] As a consequence, there may be no public-policy platform in the electorate or motion in the legislature that can defeat or tie all other platforms or motions. For example, proposal x might defeat y, while y defeats z, and z defeats x. The resulting electoral or legislative outcome then occurs by accident or by agenda control or as the result of sophisticated voting,[196] but it has no necessary connection to a "welfare"-regarding "public interest."[197]

Because electoral or legislative voting equilibria may be absent, and the resulting social choice may be unstable, neither we nor the Court can say anything about the desirability of the public policies that majority-rule institutions eventually choose. Citizens' or legislators' preferences do not map unambiguously into desirable social choices. But this suspension of judgment does not prevail concerning the second reason for claiming that public policies are most unlikely to be welfare-regarding, namely, that the political process itself is crenelated with—indeed driven by—the same public goods-public bads problems that are said to afflict the market.

First, consider the electorate, and assume that a group within it is organized to pursue the public supply of a (not necessarily public) good or service, at collective cost. By virtue of its organization, the group can monitor, reward, sanction, and inform its own members, election candidates, and legislators far better than can any unorganized subset of the rest of the electorate, or the entire unorganized electorate itself, for that matter.[198] In any public policy decision,

[195]See, for example, *Political Equilibrium: A Delicate Balance*, ed. Peter C. Ordeshook and Kenneth A. Shepsle; William H. Riker, "Implications from the Disequilibrium of Majority Rule for the Study of Institutions," *American Political Science Review* 74 (June 1980): 349–66; Charles R. Plott, "Axiomatic Social Choice Theory: An Interpretation and Overview," *American Journal of Political Science* 20 (May 1976): 511–96; and Kenneth J. Arrow, *Social Choice and Individual Values*, 2d ed. (New York: Wiley, 1963).

[196]See, for example, Richard D. McKelvey, "Intransitivities in Multidimensional Voting Models and Some Implications for Agenda Control," *Journal of Economic Theory* 12 (June 1976): 472–82; Riker, "Disequilibrium of Majority Rule"; Riker, "The Paradox of Voting and Congressional Rules for Voting on Amendments," *American Political Science Review* 52 (June 1958): 349–66.

[197]Easterbrook has also demonstrated that the problem of intransitive social choice may limit the Supreme Court's ability to develop consistent doctrine over a line of related cases. See Frank H. Easterbrook, "Ways of Criticizing the Court," *Harvard Law Review* 95 (February 1982): 802–32.

[198]Olson points out that members of such groups often face free-rider problems in establishing and maintaining these organizations. See Mancur Olson, *The Logic of Collective Action: Public Goods and the Theory of Groups*, rev. ed. (New York: Schocken, 1971). Ordeshook and I show, however, that elected officeholders pass laws to overcome these problems, such as statutes mandating union membership, when they calculate that it is in their interest to do so. See Aranson and Ordeshook, "Public Interest."

therefore, candidates and officeholders will be disproportionately more responsive to the preferences of group members, if only because the transaction costs in the public policy market place will be lower with them than with members of the general electorate.

But what kinds of public policies do such groups demand? Our models show very generally that when faced with a budget constraint, these groups will pursue the political production of private, divisible benefits, to be provided at collective cost, rather than the political production of public goods.[199] Furthermore, the tendency is for such groups to purchase cost-benefit efficient goods and services in the private sector, while spreading the costs of inefficient goods and services by demanding their public-sector supply; in a dynamic view, political service thus becomes an inferior good.[200] In sum, all interest groups are locked in an n-person prisoners' dilemma, which is exactly analogous to the situation of private-sector persons and firms that create a public bad by "overgrazing the budgetary commons."[201]

Second, consider the legislature. The structure of elected legislatures and the incentives of their members are perfectly consistent with those of interest groups. Groups in a legislator's constituency—perhaps the entire constituency itself in the case of porkbarrel legislation—will not reward the legislator for helping citizens in other districts, nor will they credit his claim that he was influential in shaping beneficial legislation aimed at producing appropriate levels of broadly national public goods or suppressing public bads.[202] Instead,

---

[199]Peter H. Aranson and Peter C. Ordeshook, " A Prolegomenon to a Theory of the Failure of Representative Democracy," in *American Re-evolution: Papers and Proceedings*, ed. Richard D. Auster and Barbara Sears (Tucson: University of Arizona Department of Economics, 1977), pp. 23–46.

Costs also may fall on concentrated groups, as sometimes occurs with state taxation of out-of-state firms. See text accompanying supra notes 69–72. The problem in such circumstances is not that interests are diffuse but that representation is absent. I address the regulatory problem of concentrated costs at text accompanying infra notes 206–7.

[200]Peter H. Aranson and Peter C. Ordeshook, "Alternative Theories of the Growth of Government and Their Implications for Constitutional Tax and Spending Limits," in *Tax and Expenditure Limitations*, ed. Helen F. Ladd and T. Nicholas Tideman (Washington, D.C.: Urban Institute Press, 1981), pp. 143–76.

[201]Kenneth A. Shepsle, "Overgrazing the Budgetary Commons: Incentive-Compatible Solutions to the Problem of Deficits," in *The Economic Consequences of Public Deficits*, ed. Lawrence Mayer (Boston: Martinus Nijhoff, 1983), pp. 211–19.

There is no apparent easy way out of the resulting prisoners' dilemma. Any group or coalition of groups that might oppose this process would, in effect, be supplying a public good to all other groups, which is a result that these models do not predict. The same problem afflicts the legislature.

[202]See, for example, Morris P. Fiorina, *Congress: Keystone of the Washington Establishment* (New Haven, Conn.: Yale University Press, 1977) and David R. Mayhew, *Congress: The Electoral Connection* (New Haven, Conn.: Yale University Press, 1974).

constituents reward legislators for providing them with private, divisible benefits, supplied at collective cost. Indeed, by the very nature of the nondivisibility of public goods, legislators who produce them could not assure themselves of rewards from any beneficiaries. A market in public policy, like any other market, requires divisibility for its operation.

Third, consider the bureaucracy, and particularly the problem of regulation. How we interpret the bureaucracy's actions will depend on whether we adopt the monopoly-bureau view,[203] the alternative view that the bureaucracy is a reasonably perfect agent of the legislature,[204] or the view that it is something in between these two polar interpretations.[205] Under the first view, that of the monopoly bureau, we merely (but sometimes in a complicated manner) add another interest group, the bureau itself, as a demander of private benefits at collective cost. Under the second view, that of the bureau as disciplined agent of the legislature, we merely conclude that the bureau reinforces electoral- and legislative-process tendencies to produce private benefits at collective cost. The compromise view, of course, does not suddenly raise the bureaucracy to the level of a promoter of welfare-regarding public policies.

Scholars have exerted considerable effort to studying the problem of bureaucracy as regulator.[206] The principal conclusion of their research is that regulation often provides a means for creating private benefits for the regulated industry but at collective cost for consumers, usually in the form of reduced services and higher prices than would prevail

[203]William A. Niskanen, *Bureaucracy and Representative Government* (Chicago: Aldine Atherton, 1971).

[204]Barry R. Weingast and Mark J. Moran, "Bureaucratic Discretion or Congressional Control? Regulatory Policymaking by the Federal Trade Commission," *Journal of Political Economy* 91 (October 1983): 765–800; Weingast, "Regulation, Reregulation, and Deregulation: The Political Foundations of Agency Clientele Relations," *Law & Contemporary Problems* 44 (Winter 1981): 147–77; Moran and Weingast, "Congress as the Source of Regulatory Decisions: The Case of the Federal Trade Commission," *American Economic Review Papers & Proceedings* 72 (May 1982): 109–13; Weingast, "The Congressional-Bureaucratic System: A Principal-Agent Perspective (With Applications to the SEC)" *Public Choice* 44 (1984): 147–91.

[205]Cotton M. Lindsay, "A Theory of Government Enterprise," *Journal of Political Economy* 84 (October 1976): 1061–77.

[206]See, for example, Posner, "Taxation by Regulation"; Posner, "Theories of Economic Regulation," *Bell Journal of Economics & Management Science* 5 (Autumn 1974): 335–58; George J. Stigler, "The Theory of Economic Regulation," *Bell Journal of Economics & Management Science* 2 (Spring 1971): 3–21; Sam Peltzman, "Toward a More General Theory of Regulation," *Journal of Law & Economics* 19 (August 1976): 211–40; Peter H. Aranson and Peter C. Ordeshook, "Regulation, Redistribution, and Public Choice," *Public Choice* 37 (1981): 69–100; and references cited supra notes 203–205.

in an unregulated market. But one additional aspect of regulation concerns the legislative delegation of legislative authority to regulatory agencies, with the open-ended mandate to act "in the public interest, safety, and convenience." Delegation occurs when two or more industries or sectors of a single industry compete in Congress for economically beneficial legislation. Not wishing to alienate either group, the members of Congress create a public-policy "lottery" by delegating the matter to an agency.[207] Whichever group wins the subsequent regulatory battle, the resulting incidence of benefits is private, and of costs, both private (for the losing group) and collective (for the consumers of services).

Fourth, concerning the electoral process, we might hypothesize that the *national* election of a chief executive *qua* chief legislator might tame the process among interest groups, legislatures, and bureaus, just described. But our models of electoral processes with private-benefit provision as issues cannot sustain this belief. Instead, under the not unreasonable assumptions of incremental decision making about which groups' claims to satisfy or reject, and information asymmetries if benefits are concentrated while costs are diffuse, more private-benefit programs are added than are deleted. At the legislative level, with interest groups and constituencies as the fundamental households, the same electoral process merely reinforces interest-group and legislative proclivities to demand and supply private, divisible benefits at collective cost.[208]

Finally, concerning the courts, we have already reviewed Landes and Posner's explanation of the judiciary's place in the production and maintenance of interest-group based public policies.[209] Except where legislatures run up against the barriers of an explicit *constitutional* (noneconomic) issue, as in *Chadha;* or are overtly and facially discriminating in interstate taxation, as in *Maryland v. Louisiana, Bacchus, Armco,* or *Tully;* or (sometimes) fail to constitute their memberships on one-man, one-vote apportionments, as in *Karcher;* the Supreme Court is unlikely to do anything except stand aside, or perhaps even refine the underlying private-interest legislative bargain.[210]

---

[207]See Aranson, Gellhorn, and Robinson, "Legislative Delegation," and Morris P. Fiorina, "Legislative Choice of Regulatory Forms: Legal Process or Administrative Process?" *Public Choice* 39 (1982): 33–66.

[208]See, for example, Aranson and Ordeshook, "Public Interest," and "Growth of Government."

[209]See Landes and Posner, "Independent Judiciary," and text accompanying supra notes 41–56.

[210]See text accompanying and cases cited supra notes 155–56 and 165–72.

Constitutional Approaches

The preceding discussion compels the depressing conclusions that the political branches are incompetent and incoherent: they cannot enact welfare-regarding policies; those policies that they do enact promote inefficient private benefits at collective cost; and electorates and legislatures experience a profound absence of electoral and public-policy equilibria—majority rule by itself reveals nothing. In the face of these failures, more often than not the judiciary defers to the political branches. Nor is there convincing evidence that the judiciary enjoys the kind of economic expertise or incentives to do otherwise.

It is not surprising that several authors have already documented the judiciary's part in this pattern of institutional failure and have sought various approaches to escape the resulting dilemmas.[211] A review of some of this literature, beginning with Easterbrook, can aid in separating promising from unproductive approaches.

Easterbrook[212] identifies three areas in which the Supreme Court has failed in the past to exploit the benefits of economic reasoning. These areas concern the use of *ex ante* versus *ex post* analysis, the invoking of marginal versus average effects, and the appreciation that the political branches respond to interest-group demands, not to more nearly diffuse demands for welfare-regarding policies. But Easterbrook then draws samples of cases from the 1953, 1963, and 1983 Terms of the Court to support the proposition that the Court's (at least implicit) use of economic reasoning is actually improving in all three areas.

The first of these areas, *ex ante* versus *ex post* analysis, concerns several cases in which the Court might have, and sometimes did, come to grips with the problem of choosing *ex post* to "divide the stakes" in a lawsuit strictly regarding the conflict between plaintiff and defendant or choosing instead to look prospectively at the effects of the incentives that its decision might create *ex ante*. In his most convincing argument, Easterbrook reviews recent cases in patents and copyrights—intellectual property generally—to show that the Court indeed is at least tending to balance *ex ante* and *ex post* considerations, thus in turn tending "to get it right" where the legislature

---

[211]See, for example, Cass R. Sunstein, "Naked Preferences and the Constitution," *Columbia Law Review* 84 (November 1984): 1689–1732; Easterbrook, "Court and Economic System"; Epstein, "Taxation" and "Contract Clause"; Aranson, Gellhorn, and Robinson, "Legislative Delegation"; and Mashaw, "Public-Public Law."
[212]"Court and Economic System."

(did not or) stood mute.[213] But intellectual-property questions literally cry out for such an approach (although its results are hardly dispositive). Other cases, especially in the face of contrary legislative action, do not do so with such force. Hence, it seems difficult to square Easterbrook's claim of increasing judicial sophistication about *ex post* versus *ex ante* judgments in the light of such recent decisions as *Jicarilla, Hawaii, Norris, Penn Central, Ridgway,* and *Short.*

A more difficult claim for Easterbrook to establish is that the Court has tended increasingly to examine effects at the margin rather than changes in the litigants' average positions.[214] Surely, the intellectual-property cases of the 1983 Term may partake of some implied marginal analysis, because the Court, in the face of rapid technological change and given its penchant for balancing, really has no other analytical course open to it. But Easterbrook also suggests that the commerce clause cases of that term, such as *Bacchus* and *Tully,* involving state taxation of out-of-state firms, invoke the same marginal, instead of average, considerations. We think not. While the Court in *Bacchus* and *Tully* does look to the direction of change on market conditions at the margin, what distinguishes these decisions from those in *Commonwealth Edison* and *Moorman* is that they involve facially discriminatory taxation. The Court's *dicta* in *Bacchus* and *Tully* may weakly suggest a growing sophistication in its use of marginal analysis, as does its decision in *Consolidated Freightways.* But until the Court is willing to apply the tests it laid down in *Complete Auto Transit, Inc. v. Brady*[215] or similar but far more robust ones to facially nondiscriminatory state taxation, Easterbrook's claim of growing judicial sophistication enjoys merely intellectual force absent any public-policy consequences.

Easterbrook's final claim, which we dismissed earlier,[216] is that the Court appears to be acting with an increased awareness of the interest-group basis of legislation. Here again, however, as in *Bacchus* and *Tully,* the Court's increased awareness seems to make no

---

[213]Ibid., pp. 19–33. See particularly the analysis of Sony Corp. of America v. Universal City Studios, Inc., 104 S. Ct. 774 (1984).

[214]Easterbrook, "Court and Economic System," pp. 33–42.

[215]430 U.S. 274 (1977). I do not recommend this course. I merely suggest that the application of the *Brady* rule would indicate that the Court's new-found economic analysis would then have some actual force. The test contemplates that a state tax can pass commerce clause muster if it "is applied to an activity with a substantial nexus with the taxing State, is fairly apportioned, does not discriminate against interstate commerce, and is fairly related to the services provided by the State." Id. at 279. The Court showed in *Commonwealth Edison* that it is unwilling to apply this test seriously. See the discussion in Epstein, "Contract Clause," pp. 447–49.

[216]See text accompanying supra notes 173–82.

difference. Easterbrook, for example, contrasts the Court's 1943 decision in *Parker v. Brown*[217] with its 1984 decision in *Hoover v. Ronwin*.[218] In *Parker* the Court upheld against an antitrust attack a state of California program aimed at cartelizing the raisin market. In *Hoover* the Court upheld against a similar attack a state system of "curving" bar examination scores to limit the number of lawyers practicing in Arizona. Easterbrook argues that "[t]he Court's analysis [in *Hoover*] revealed that the transition from the public-interest vision of *Parker* to a private-interest perception of regulation is complete. . . . In *Parker* the Court thought it pertinent that the state's plan rectified market failures. All pretense that regulation is ordinarily beneficent now has vanished."[219] But so what? As Easterbrook himself points out, "[t]he majority [in *Hoover*] observed repeatedly that it did not need to endorse the wisdom of Arizona's choices."[220] Nor would it examine the wisdom of Hawaii's choices in *Hawaii v. Midkiff*. The apparent perception of legislative failure overtly counts for nothing in this realpolitik application of *Parker*-doctrine, state-action immunity from antitrust laws. *Hoover* not so much heartens us as it further hardens us to the force of the Landes/Posner argument concerning the judiciary's "independence." Still, if Easterbrook is right in this matter (although I believe that he is not), then the Court may be one step closer to finding other, and even doctrinal grounds, for overturning the political branches' private-interest apple cart.

The larger problem with Easterbrook's optimistic analysis and sometimes strained reading of cases is not that he is wrong, but that he would set the Court on a tack that we have dismissed earlier as inappropriate.[221] Whatever merit there may be in increased judicial sophistication, the political and jurisprudential reality is that economic analysis may be inapposite and even inappropriate for constitutional argument.[222] Our cases show that this road leads nowhere except to the eventual dismemberment of constitutional protection.

---

[217]317 U.S. 341 (1943).

[218]104 S. Ct. 1989 (1984).

[219]Easterbrook, "Court and Economic System," pp. 53–4.

[220]Ibid. (citing 104 S. Ct. at 1995, 1999 n.28, 2000 n.31).

[221]See text accompanying supra notes 145–64.

[222]This essay concentrates on cases specifically involving economic problems. But the Court recently has applied economic-like reasoning to cases involving, say, the exclusionary rule. Easterbrook points out that "[e]xclusionary rule cases, once addressed in terms of 'judicial integrity' or the moral standing of the police, are today treated as occasions for the assessment of the marginal deterrent effects of excluding particular categories of evidence." Easterbrook, "Court and Economic System," p. 59, n.157 (citing, *inter alia*, I.N.S. v. Lopez-Mendoza, 104 S. Ct. 3479, 3486–90 (1984), and United

We can sharpen our criticism of Easterbrook's approach by once again juxtaposing common law adjudication with constitutional argument. While most of the cases that Easterbrook considers do not rise to an explicitly constitutional level, enough of the cases considered here earlier do so. And it is in this connection that we might wonder whether we would want the Court to frame constitutional argument in, say, *ex post* versus *ex ante* terms. I think not. The Constitution does not concern the kinds of balancing of judgments that Easterbrook and its own opinions[223] find so appealing. The Constitution sets out a variety of limitations on federal, state, and local legislatures.[224] It provides for the rescission of these limitations through a difficult amendment procedure, and not through the changing whims of legislatures and courts. In this sense, when a constitutional problem comes to the Court, it asks not for a balancing of *ex post* and *ex ante* considerations, or even for attention to *ex ante* considerations alone. Instead, it asks the Court to apply the Constitution.[225] Such a doctrinal approach even may enjoy utilitarian or economic support, which would deny, on Easterbrook's own grounds, judicial attempts to find ways around the express language of the Constitution.[226]

Nor can we find in Easterbrook's analysis any real hope for desirable change. Certainly, in the three areas that he describes there may be a growing sophistication on the Court. But to what end? He argues, for example, that "judges have not been charged with imposing their substantive views on the economic system,"[227] and that their "claim to authority rests on a plausible demonstration that they are faithfully executing decisions made by others."[228] Does that mean decisions

---

States v. Leon, 104 S. Ct. 3405, 3418–22 (1984)).

While many conservatives have applauded this judicial retreat from earlier, more principled applications of the exclusionary rule, I am reluctant to do so. The Court has gutted, on "pragmatic" grounds, constitutional constraints on economic legislation, for example in its reading of the contracts and taking clauses. This regrettable retreat from constitutional argument in economic affairs should not occasion a similar withdrawal from protecting the rights of those who confront the state agents who enjoy the most palpable monopoly on the use of force. This is not to say that the Court in recent civil liberties cases reached the wrong result on the merits. But its use of pragmatic tests in the face of constitutional guarantees seems highly questionable.

[223]See for example, Complete Auto Transit, Inc. v. Brady, 430 U.S. 274 (1977) and text accompanying supra note 215.

[224]See text accompanying infra notes 227–30.

[225]I am grateful to George Butler for pointing out this conflict to me.

[226]See, for example, James M. Buchanan and Gordon Tullock, *The Calculus of Consent: Logical Foundations of Constitutional Democracy* (Ann Arbor: University of Michigan Press, 1962).

[227]Easterbrook, "Court and Economic System," p. 60.

[228]Ibid.

made by the framers? Probably not, for Easterbrook concludes by arguing that "[t]he consequence of honest and capable discharge of that function may be more rent-seeking legislation, or it may be more general-interest legislation. An increase in economic astuteness among judges facilitates both kinds of legislation. Which occurs is not the judges' affair."[229] Still, there is much to applaud in Easterbrook's essay. It urges the Court to think about what he claims that it is doing. But it must fashion principled constitutional doctrine to go in this direction, and Easterbrook even reminds the Court of some doctrine that is available for this purpose.[230]

Sunstein[231] takes a more focused approach to the problem of judicial control of the political branches than does Easterbrook, in that Sunstein is interested in the problem of private-interest legislative redistributions *per se,* and not in the additional problems of *ex ante* versus *ex post* and marginalist versus average reasoning. Sunstein's discussion, nevertheless, covers quite as wide a collection of cases and subject matter as does Easterbrook's.

Sunstein argues that several clauses in the Constitution—the dormant commerce clause, the privileges and immunities clause, the due process clause, the contracts clause, and the eminent domain (takings) clause—all "are united by a common theme and focused on a single underlying evil: the distribution of resources or opportunities to one group rather than another solely on the ground that those favored have exercised the raw political power to obtain what they want."[232] Sunstein calls "this underlying evil a naked preference"[233] and juxtaposes it to "[t]he notion that government actions must be responsive to something other than private pressure [which] is associated with the idea that politics is 'not the reconciling but the transcending of the different interests of the society in a search for a single common good.' "[234] Divorced from the mystical idea of transcendence or disembodied interest, Sunstein's distinction coincides perfectly with the notion of private-interest versus welfare-regarding legislation, reviewed earlier.[235] And as Easterbrook, Epstein, and

---

[229]Ibid.

[230]For example, "[s]tatutes in derogation of the common law are to be strictly construed. . . ." Easterbrook, "Court and Economic System," p. 15.

[231]"Naked Preferences."

[232]Ibid., p. 1689.

[233]Ibid.

[234]Ibid., p. 1691 (quoting Gordon S. Wood, *The Creation of the American Republic, 1776–1787* (New York: Norton, 1972), p. 58).

[235]See text accompanying supra notes 183–210.

others have noted, this distinction coincides with the framers' concerns about the real world of politics:

> The prohibition of naked preferences captures a significant theme in the original intent. It is closely related to the central constitutional concern of ensuring against capture of government power by faction [citing the *Federalist* nos. 10, 51 (J. Madison)]. The framers' hostility toward naked preferences was rooted in the fear that government power would be usurped solely to distribute wealth or opportunities to one group or person at the expense of another. The constitutional requirement that something other than a naked preference be shown to justify differential treatment provides a means, admittedly imperfect, of ensuring that government action results from a legitimate effort to promote the public good rather than from a factional takeover.[236]

This interpretation of a wide variety of constitutional provisions appears in Sunstein's essay as "the best candidate for a unitary conception of the sorts of government action that the Constitution prohibits."[237] And it comes brutally close to turning the judiciary to substantive tasks:

> The prohibition of naked preferences, enforced as it is by the courts, stands as a repudiation of theories positing that the judicial role is only to police the process of representation to ensure that all affected interest groups may participate. It presupposes that courts will serve as critics of the pluralist vision, not as adherents striving only to "clear the channels" in preparation for the ensuing political struggle. In this respect, the prohibition of naked preferences reflects a distinctly substantive value and cannot easily be captured in procedural terms. Moreover, it reflects an attractive conception of politics, one that does not understand the political process as simply another sort of market.[238]

Again, Sunstein overdraws the normative model of politics disembodied from individual preferences, but the error is excusable in his pursuit of a potentially useful distinction between politics as it is and politics as the Court ought to constrain it. Sunstein's analysis, however, suffers from the same problem that afflicts Easterbrook's essay. As we travel with him through a discussion of how the Court might use, and indeed has used, the various clauses of the Constitution to suppress the legislative satisfaction of "naked preferences," we can find mostly what we find in our earlier review of cases: judicial surrender and deference, with only occasional impositions of control.

---

[236]Sunstein, "Naked Preferences," p. 1690 (citations and footnotes omitted).

[237]Ibid., p. 1693 (citation and footnote omitted).

[238]Ibid., pp. 1692–93 (citations and footnotes omitted).

Sunstein may be right, "that the prohibition of naked preferences serves as the most promising candidate for a unitary theory of the Constitution."[239] But in light of decisions such as *Hawaii, Penn Central, Hoover,* and many others, it is not yet a theory that the Court appears willing to embrace.

Finally, we come to Epstein's analysis of the contracts clause.[240] He, like Sunstein, finds behind the clause prohibiting states from impairing the obligation of contracts a general belief shared with Madison, that interest-group politics lead to mischievous results:

> This central problem of governance is very old, but in recent years it has been captured in the language of economics: any grant of legislative power will invite "rent-seeking" behavior; each group will try to use that legislative power to expropriate the wealth of its rivals. . . .
>
> . . . The framers were concerned that legislative deals would often be tainted by interest-group politics, and occasionally by outright bribery, and that preoccupation with redistributive matters would divert individuals from productive activities. They sought to control those abuses by adopting a scheme of limited government.[241]

Epstein views constitutional control of the political branches as invoking a variety of instruments. The Constitution imposes on the federal government several procedural burdens, such as bicameralism and the presidential veto, reflecting a belief "that, generally, the error costs from too much legislation exceed the error costs from too little."[242] But control of state-legislative mischief, absent control of state-government procedures themselves, must reach to the substance of state enactments. "The control of abuse in state government had to take a different tack. Since state legislative processes were beyond federal control, the Constitution had to place substantive limitations upon state legislative power."[243]

The contract clause provides one such substantive limit, but as Epstein carefully shows, it is a limit that the Supreme Court has voided almost in its entirety. In this regard Epstein's important contribution consists not merely in detailing the history of the clause's judicial abrogation and in arguing forcefully for its revitalization, but

---

[239]Ibid., p. 1732.

[240]Epstein, "Contract Clause."

[241]Ibid., pp. 713, 715.

[242]Ibid., p. 715. But substantive limitations remain, such as the uniformity clause, which the Court inartfully managed to circumvent in United States v. Ptasynski, 103 S. Ct. 2239 (1983) (upholding as not a violation of the uniformity clause the windfall profits tax on oil, exempting oil extracted from northern Alaska).

[243]Epstein, "Contract Clause," p. 716.

also in identifying the central places where the Court goes astray. His analysis of *Home Building and Loan Association v. Blaisdell*[244] provides a good example.

In *Blaisdell*, the Court heard a contract clause challenge to a Minnesota Depression-era statute that for a time deferred mortgage payments while outlawing foreclosure sales. The opinion of Chief Justice Hughes, turning that challenge aside, entirely supplanted any contract clause limitations on state actions by replacing them with a police-power interpretation of the problem. Justice Hughes's language is both sweeping and dangerous:

> It is no answer to say that this public need was not apprehended a century ago, or to insist that what the provision of the Constitution meant to the vision of that day it must mean to the vision of our time. If by the statement that what the Constitution meant at the time of its adoption it means today, it is intended to say that the great clauses of the Constitution must be confined to the interpretation which the framers, with the conditions and outlook of their time, would have placed upon them, that statement carries its own refutation. It was to guard against such a narrow conception that Chief Justice Marshall uttered the memorable warning—"We must never forget that it is a *constitution* that we are expounding"—"a constitution intended to endure for ages to come, and consequently, to be adapted to the various *crises* of human affairs."[245]

Justice Hughes's claim here is thrice wrong. First, there is agreement all around that the practice of relieving debtors through state statutes was precisely the action that the framers had in mind when crafting the contract clause.[246] There was nothing new in *Blaisdell* on this count, considered separately. Second, as Epstein points out, Hughes's use of Marshall's decision in *McCulloch*, is ill considered.[247] Marshall's words in *McCulloch* argued for giving "full force"[248] to the necessary and proper clause of Article I. In *Ogden v. Saunders*,[249] however, Chief Justice Marshall had given a similar full-force argument in support of a broad reading of the contract clause. In sum, it is the *Constitution*, in Marshall's view, that should receive a broad and expansive reading, not the power of government, as Hughes

---

[244]290 U.S 398 (1934).

[245]Id. at 442–43 (citations omitted) (quoting McCulloch v. Maryland, 17 U.S. (4 Wheat.) 316, 407, 415 (1819)).

[246]See, for example, Benjamin F. Wright, *The Contract Clause of the Constitution* (Cambridge: Harvard University Press, 1938), pp. 4–5.

[247]Epstein, "Contract Clause," p. 736.

[248]Ibid.

[249]25 U.S. (12 Wheat.) 213, 332 (1827) (Marshall, C.J., dissenting).

would have us believe. Third, and most generally, Hughes's words turn the judicial interpretation of the Constitution into "situation ethics," thus subverting the idea of a constitution itself. As Epstein comments:

> The operative assumption seems to be that questions of constitutional law are to be answered according to whether or not we like the Constitution as it was originally drafted. If we do not, we are then free to introduce into the document those provisions that we think more congenial to our time. . . . By this standard a court can invest itself with the power of a standing constitutional convention. The importance of a fixed constitutional framework and stable institutional arrangements is necessarily lost once the framework that was designed to place a limit upon politics becomes the central subject of the politics it was designed to limit.[250]

What else might the Court have done with *Blaisdell?* The answer is far from clear. Epstein argues that "Hughes's error lay in insisting that a change in social conditions required a change in the meaning of a text."[251] Instead, the Court should have "take[n] into account the vast social dislocations of the Depression without abandoning a principled account of the police power limitation. Such an argument would attempt to show how a change in social and economic conditions could give rise to a novel application of a settled legal principle whose meaning remained wholly unchanged."[252] But even so, "[i]t is at this level that *Blaisdell* is an extraordinarily difficult case."[253]

If the debtors in *Blaisdell* merely had sought relief from a bad bargain, then the Court should have upheld their obligations. If, instead, as Epstein argues, the federal government's deflationary policies had made fulfillment of the debtors' obligations impossible, then that may have been a different matter, depending on whether mortgagee or mortgagor could better foresee or insure against the federal government's actions.[254] "On this analysis, the result in *Blaisdell* clearly serves the ends of the police power limitation. The statute tends to restore the original contractual balance that had been undone by [federal] government action."[255] This reasoning does not necessarily commend either the state's chosen means or the Court's result

[250]Epstein, "Contract Clause," p. 736. See also text accompanying supra notes 223–26.
[251]Epstein, "Contract Clause," p. 736.
[252]Ibid., pp. 736–37.
[253]Ibid., p. 737.
[254]See, for example, Richard A. Posner and Andrew M. Rosenfield, "Impossibility and Related Doctrines in Contract Law: An Economic Analysis," *Journal of Legal Studies* 6 (January 1977): 83–118.
[255]Epstein, "Contract Clause," p. 737.

on the merits in *Blaisdell*, for appraisals of these matters would take us far afield of our original direction. Perhaps in some circumstances the federal government's mistakes, on frustration grounds, can serve to discharge or delay debtors from fulfilling their contractual obligations. Perhaps not. But that was not the question that Justice Hughes asked or answered. Instead, he destroyed the contract clause:

> However, these questions [about frustration and discharge] may be resolved, they highlight the fact that the *Blaisdell* case was extremely difficult not because of anachronistic constitutional doctrine but because of the intrinsic complexity of the world.
>
> Justice Hughes, however, rather than confronting the difficulty of the facts, chose to manipulate the doctrine. The subsequent history of the police power limitation on the contract clause reflects the costs of that choice. Had Hughes written the right kind of opinion, *Blaisdell* would have reflected an inevitable struggle with an intractable set of facts, but the opinion would have announced no broad interpretive principle. The police power exception would not have been transformed into an open invitation to private rent seeking. Instead, *Blaisdell* trumpeted a false liberation from the constitutional text that has paved the way for massive government intervention that undermines the security of private transactions. Today the police power exception has come to eviscerate the contracts clause.[256]

A Summing Up

There is enough in our preceding recital of cases and of recent public choice research, along with our review of Easterbrook's, Sunstein's, and Epstein's essays, to suggest the broad outlines of further judicial approaches to the judicial control of the political branches. First, the Court must come to recognize, to a greater extent than it does today, that the legislature is the most dangerous branch of government. The evidence for this proposition comes from three sources. The first is the Constitution itself and its procedural and substantive checks on federal and state governments. Sunstein is correct in asserting that the relevant clauses all point to a distrust of legislatures as satisfiers of naked preferences. The second source is the development of public choice theory and its very exciting appearance in the legal literature.[257] Legal scholars are showing an

---

[256]Ibid., p. 738.

[257]Besides the works of Sunstein, "Naked Preferences," Easterbrook, "Court and Economic System," Epstein, "Taxation" and "Contract Clause," Mashaw, "Public-Public Law," and Aranson, Gellhorn, and Robinson, "Legislative Delegation," we also find applications of this analysis to particular cases in various issues of *The Journal of Law & Economics*, *The Journal of Legal Studies*, and *The Supreme Court Economic Review*, as well as in more traditional legal literature. See for example, Jonathan R. Macey, "Special Interest Group Legislation and the Judicial Function: The Dilemma of Glass-Steagall," *Emory Law Journal* 33 (Winter 1984): 1–40.

increasing sophistication about the manner in which the political system works, and the members of the judiciary will doubtless not be far behind. In this claim we might agree with Easterbrook, although his view seems overly optimistic as a reflection of present Supreme Court developments. The third source is the content of the Court's own cases. Many of the Court's decisions, as our review indicates, grow out of overt expropriations and redistributions, all to no public purpose. The paean to imaginary public-interest motives found in *Parker v. Brown* might reflect the optimism and enthusiasm about government that marked an earlier age, naive as they may have been. As extended in recent cases such as *Hawaii*, however, the same justification is an embarrassment that will wither respect for the Court as an institution.

Second, the judiciary, and particularly the Supreme Court, should not follow the mistaken path of trying to substitute its own educated economic judgments for the legislature's political ones. There is scant evidence that the Court enjoys a comparative advantage in such a contest. The very content of law and economics itself, furthermore, suggests that this strategy faces severe limitations. The use of such a strategy might invite specific legislative retaliation. Instead, it is precisely the notion that the Court has embraced, that the legislature is omnipotent in its redistributionist activities, that seems the greatest evil. This notion should now become a candidate for serious judicial rethinking.

Careful doctrinal development, of the sort that Epstein urges, remains the single most promising approach for the Court to follow. At the national level a redeployment of the delegation doctrine,[258] an insistence on following the constitutional requirements of legislative procedure,[259] and the application of the plain language of provisions such as the uniformity clause[260] would move the Court in the correct direction, as would its refusal to extend private-interest legislative bargains beyond a strict construal of their statutory terms.[261] In its review of state legislation, the Court would do well to apply analysis such as Epstein's to refresh the various clauses that Sunstein identifies, to limit the unprincipled redistributionist tendencies of state governments.[262] In all matters doctrine, not a pragmatic sanction,

---

[258]Aranson, Gellhorn, and Robinson, "Legislative Delegation."

[259]The *Chadha* decision is in this spirit. See I.N.S. v. Chadha, 103 S. Ct. 2764 (1983).

[260]A reversal of United States v. Ptasynski, 103 S. Ct. 2239 (1983), would thus be in order.

[261]See supra note 230.

[262]Public "use," for example, cannot mean public "purpose" under robust constitutional interpretation. A fully compensated taking of private land to build a flood-control dam is one thing. A taking of A's land and its transfer to B, as in *Hawaii*, is quite another.

must come first, for "it *is* a constitution that we are expounding." Economic analysis "merely" indicates the presence of uncompensated damage or undeserved protection or the extent to which the political branches have breached the walls that the framers so wisely provided.

5

MAJORITY POWER, MORAL SKEPTICISM, AND THE NEW RIGHT'S CONSTITUTION

Stephen Macedo

> The strength of the Courts of law has always been the greatest security that can be offered to personal independence; but this is more especially the case in democratic ages. Private rights and interests are in constant danger if the judicial power does not grow more extensive and stronger to keep pace with equality of conditions.
>
> —Alexis de Tocqueville[1]

The New Right's Constitutional Vision

In the field of constitutional law, partisans of the New Right advocate a new majoritarianism and a fundamental narrowing of judicial protections for individual rights. The New Right's constitutional vision, if accepted by the nation's courts, would represent a decisive shift of power to legislative majorities and a basic revision of the nature of citizenship in America. A careful examination of the jurisprudence of the New Right is, therefore, in order.

The partisans of the New Right portray their constitutional vision as the culmination of hallowed tradition: they claim to be the ideological heirs of the Founding Fathers and the standard-bearers of the "historical constitution." But the New Right's claim to the Founders' legacy is dubious, its allegiance to the Constitution largely rhetorical, and its stature in relation to the great tradition of American constitutional thought unimpressive. What is striking, in fact, is how far the New Right has departed from the ideas of the Founders, the majestic phrases of the Constitution, and what is best in the American political tradition.

The author is Assistant Professor of Government at Harvard University. He acknowledges the support of the Cato Institute and thanks David Boaz, Edward Crane, Sotirios A. Barber, and Walter F. Murphy for their helpful comments on earlier drafts. The usual caveat applies. A more detailed discussion of the major themes of this article can be found in the author's monograph The New Right v. the Constitution *(Washington, D.C.: Cato Institute, 1986).*

[1]Alexis de Tocqueville, *Democracy in America*, vol. 2 (New York: Vintage, 1961), p. 343.

No brief work could encompass all the constitutional arguments of everyone associated with the New Right. The discussion in this article, therefore, focuses on a set of claims advanced by prominent New Right scholars and politicians—claims that together constitute the most distinctive and important features of the New Right's jurisprudence. For the sake of simplicity and clarity, the discussion concentrates on the jurisprudence of Judge Robert H. Bork, who has articulated the New Right's most important claims boldly and without inhibition. Bork's assault on the active judicial protection of individual rights draws on the most formidable and oft-used weapons in the conservative armory.

First, partisans of the New Right profess a reverence for the "historical Constitution" and argue that judges should intervene in the workings of the political process only where it can be shown that the Framers of the Constitution clearly intended it. "The [F]ramers' intentions with respect to freedoms," says Bork, "are the sole legitimate premise from which constitutional analysis may proceed."[2] Bork is particularly skeptical about the broad rights to privacy and free speech that liberal judges have claimed to discover in the Constitution.

Second, to circumscribe judicial power, conservatives charge that democracy is the basic constitutional value: "The original Constitution was devoted primarily to the mechanisms of democratic choice. . . . The makers of our Constitution . . . provided wide powers to representative assemblies and ruled only a few subjects off limits by the Constitution."[3] Giving majorities the power to pass laws defining how everyone should live is, says Bork, the "major freedom, of our kind of society." And Assistant Attorney General William Bradford Reynolds adds, "It was well understood at the American Founding that all governmental power derived from the people. Nothing other than popular sovereignty could comport . . . with the principles of the Revolution."[4] In construing individual rights broadly, say the partisans of the New Right, willful judges usurp matters that are properly legislative.

Third, the New Right claims that "abstract philosophical principles," which are often invoked to support rights claims, should have no authority in politics. For the conservatives, authority resides in

---

[2]Robert H. Bork, *Tradition and Morality in Constitutional Law*, Francis Boyer Lectures on Public Policy (Washington, D.C.: American Enterprise Institute, 1975), p. 10.

[3]Ibid., p. 9

[4]William Bradford Reynolds, "Reviewing the American Constitutional Heritage," *Harvard Journal of Law and Public Policy* 8 (1985): 226.

the text of the Constitution interpreted in light of the specific historical intentions of the Framers, in democratic principles, and in the "common sense" of the people. Bork, moved by a deep moral skepticism, claims that moral ideas reflect only arbitrary, subjective preferences. Therefore, such "philosophical abstractions" as individual rights should be banished from our political discourse: they dress up and obscure the mere preferences of intellectuals, which deserve no special weight. Political majorities have, according to Bork, the right to define and "suppress" moral harms even if doing so thwarts what some people take to be individual rights or liberty.[5]

All three components of the constitutional vision of the New Right, it is argued here, are faulty. References to original intentions do not settle hard constitutional issues. The Constitution does not set up a basically democratic scheme of government but rather a limited constitutional democracy. The New Right's moral skepticism is wholly unconvincing and deeply at odds with the constitutional text and our political traditions. In sum, it will be argued that the New Right misunderstands the intentions of the Founders, misreads the text of the Constitution, and adopts an unreasoned moral skepticism radically at odds with American traditions.

The Empty Vessel of Original Intent

Invocation of the intent of the Framers has long been a crucial element in the conservative attack on an active judiciary. Bork is unequivocal: "The [F]ramers' intentions with respect to freedoms are the sole legitimate premise from which constitutional analysis may proceed."[6] Activist judges, say conservatives, willfully ignore the intentions of the Framers, insert their own preferences into the Constitution, and in doing so perpetrate "limited coups d'etat."[7]

The invocation of the Framers' intentions has great political appeal. Attorney General Edwin Meese has now made it the centerpiece of the Reagan administration's jurisprudence:

> It has been and will continue to be the policy of this administration to press for a Jurisprudence of Original Intention. In the cases we file and those we join as *amicus*, we will endeavor to resurrect the original meaning of constitutional provisions and statutes as the only reliable guide for judgment.[8]

[5]Bork, *Tradition*, p. 3
[6]Ibid., p. 10.
[7]Robert H. Bork, "Neutral Principles and Some First Amendment Problems," *Indiana Law Journal* 47 (1971): 6.
[8]Edwin Meese III, address before the American Bar Association, Washington, D.C.: 9 July 1985. Copies may be obtained from the U.S. Department of Justice.

If every phrase in the Constitution were as easy to interpret as "neither shall any Person be eligible to that Office [the presidency] who shall not have attained the Age of thirty five Years," enforcing its provisions would be an almost mechanical process. But even the First Amendment, whose words appear to speak plainly ("Congress shall make no law . . . abridging freedom of speech, or of the press"), raises extremely difficult problems of interpretation. There are some clear cases: for example, while citizens have a constitutionally protected right to criticize the government (though even that was not always so, witness the Alien and Sedition laws), they do not have a right to publicize the sailing times of troop ships during wartime. But between the easy cases lie many hard ones. Can people advocate forcible overthrow of the government? Can scholars publish and professors teach doctrines that public authorities consider dangerous to the established order?

Of course, the First Amendment does not specify that only political speech is to be protected; it says simply "speech." But what does "speech" include? Words that offend or libel? Words that some find obscene? Printed material that a majority of the community considers pornographic? Is corporate advertising a form of speech? In deciding these hard cases, judges have to articulate the basic principles and fundamental values that give substance and specificity to broad constitutional guarantees like the First Amendment.

Although the First Amendment raises a host of difficult issues, it is relatively straightforward compared with the truly majestic generalities that must also be interpreted and applied by judges. Witness the expansive phrases of the Fourteenth Amendment:

> No State shall make or enforce any law which shall abridge the privileges or immunities of citizens of the United States; nor shall any State deprive any person of life, liberty, or property, without due process of law; nor deny to any person within its jurisdiction the equal protection of the laws.

It is no easy matter to decide what these important phrases require. The Constitution's overall structure, the relation of its parts, the nature of the institutions it establishes, and our political traditions provide some assistance. Since 1925, the Supreme Court has given substance to the Fourteenth Amendment by incorporating into its general phrases the more specific guarantees contained in the first eight amendments of the Bill of Rights. In this way the Court has sought, in Justice Cardozo's words, those principles "of justice so rooted in the traditions and conscience of our people as to be ranked as fundamental."[9]

[9]Palko v. Connecticut, 302 U.S. 319 (1937).

As difficult to interpret as the Fourteenth Amendment is, other parts of the Constitution have been deemed so obscure as to wholly defy judicial interpretation. Consider the Ninth Amendment: "The enumeration in the Constitution of certain rights shall not be construed to deny or disparage others retained by the people." But which other rights do citizens retain under the Constitution? The Ninth Amendment sets a moral question for constitutional interpreters: What rights do people have and retain under the Constitution? It is disappointing, but perhaps not surprising, that Supreme Court justices and other constitutional interpreters have typically fled from the hard moral judgments called for by the Ninth Amendment.

A justice might doubt that the Ninth Amendment has been taken seriously enough; he might suspect that people have fundamental rights that are being ignored. But how does he decide what these rights are? Besides considering text, structure, and precedent, a justice considering what rights Americans have may turn to our political traditions and to moral philosophy.

Partisans of the New Right call for a simpler process of constitutional interpretation. They insist, as Richard Nixon once did, that Supreme Court justices should be "strict constructionist": they must be prepared to enforce the law as it is and not "twist or bend" it to suit their own personal political convictions.[10] As Bork puts it, "the judge must stick close to the text and the history."[11] When considering the meaning of the "majestic generalities" of the Constitution, judges should confine themselves to applying only the specific historical intentions of the Framers, say the conservatives; only those individual freedoms clearly specified and intended should be protected.

Here, it is worth considering in some detail the hurdles which must be cleared by the Jurisprudence of Original Intent—hurdles that are sidestepped by Bork and Meese.

First of all, whose intent is to count as original and authoritative? Who were "the Framers," and how are we to make sense of the idea that this large and disparate group had a unified "intent"? Should the intentions of all the delegates to the Philadelphia convention be counted equally, or should the intentions of those who took a leading role in drafting the text count for more? Given the rather spotty records, one would need to rely on the intent of the leading advocates, but clearly, men such as Alexander Hamilton and James Madison were proponents of particular and, as it turned out later, different

---

[10]Richard Nixon, quoted in Ronald Dworkin, *Taking Rights Seriously* (Cambridge: Harvard University Press, 1977), p. 131.

[11]Bork, "Neutral Principles," p. 8.

theories of the Constitution. And why count the intentions of the Philadelphia delegates but ignore the intentions of participants in state ratifying conventions? Ratification gave the Constitution the force of fundamental law. In short, simply deciding whose intent counts will require an elaborate theory and considerable historical research.[12]

The second problem is to decide what counts as evidence of intent? Should we count unpublished correspondence and manuscripts? No official record of the closed proceedings in Philadelphia was ever published, an incomprehensible oversight if it had been expected that future interpreters would be guided by the Framers' intentions. James Madison's unofficial account of the convention, reconstructed from his notes, was published posthumously in 1840, after everyone who had attended the convention was dead.[13] Meese, however, in defending his Jurisprudence of Original Intent, claims, "The disputes and compromises of the Constitutional Convention were carefully recorded. The minutes of the Convention are a matter of public record."[14]

Even if we were to accept Madison's account of the convention as authoritative and complete, we would still need to confront the fact that public statements often do not reflect actual intentions. How would we distinguish between genuine evidence of intent and the delegates' posturings, rationalizations, and statements for public or scholarly or historical consumption? Should we count the Framers' expectations as to how particular provisions would be interpreted, or their hopes?[15] And what of the intentions of those legislators who did not speak?

It is with good reason that constitutional scholar Walter F. Murphy concludes: "The difficulties that confront any painstakingly thorough and intellectually scrupulous researcher who tries to establish legislative intent are typically insuperable."[16] At the very least, it would take an extremely elaborate theory, a series of difficult judgments,

---

[12]For further discussion of these problems, see Walter F. Murphy, "Constitutional Interpretation: The Art of the Historian, Magician, or Statesman?" *Yale Law Journal* 87 (1978): 1752–71.

[13]See Winton U. Solberg, *The Federal Convention and the Formation of the Union of American States* (Indianapolis: Bobbs-Merrill Co., 1976), pp. 67–70.

[14]Edwin Meese III, address before the District of Columbia chapter of the Federalist Society Lawyers Division, 15 November 1985.

[15]See Ronald Dworkin's important discussion of the problems of Original Intent in "The Forum of Principle," *New York University Law Review* 56 (1981), reprinted in Dworkin, *A Matter of Principle* (Cambridge: Harvard University Press, 1985).

[16] Murphy, "Constitutional Interpretation," p. 1761.

and a wealth of historical research to hack through the great tangle of problems surrounding the Jurisprudence of Original Intent. What began as a flight from hard judgments, therefore, ends in a series of nearly impossible judgments and insuperable obstacles.

But let us suppose that the first two hurdles have, against all odds, been cleared: we have decided whose intentions are to count and what is to count as evidence of intent. But after all this labor we find that the intentions of those involved in the long and arduous process of proposing and ratifying a constitutional amendment are complex and conflicting. We find that vague and general language cloaks disagreement and constitutes a delegation to future interpreters.

Conservative proponents of the Jurisprudence of Original Intent ignore the crucial distinction between language that is ambiguous, admitting of different but specific meanings, and language that is vague or general. As John Hart Ely argues, "The choice of a general term should, in the absence of contrary evidence, be assumed to have been conscious."[17] Meese implies that we should accept the Constitution's general phrases as written and interpret them as such, but he fails to understand that this undermines his own reliance on specific historical intentions: "Those who framed the Constitution chose their words carefully; they debated at great length the most minute points. The language they chose meant something."[18]

The Framers of the Constitution were perfectly capable of being specific when they wanted to be: they said, for example, that the President must "have attained the age of thirty five years," not "the President must be mature." Surely there is no reason to suppose, as do the conservatives, that judges are obliged to read the Framers' sweeping phrases narrowly, in light of specific unstated intentions, given that more specific phrases could have been chosen but were not. To rely on specific but unstated intentions is to ignore the obvious generality and sweep of the language actually chosen.

The Fourteenth Amendment, for instance, requires that no state shall "deny to any person within its jurisdiction the equal protection of the laws." Should judges be confined to the specific examples of unequal protection that the "framers" of that amendment might have had in mind? That is, if many of those responsible for the Fourteenth Amendment foresaw that it would put an end to racial discrimination in common law but not segregated schooling, are judges bound by that concrete "intention" to allow segregated schooling? Judges could,

[17]John Hart Ely, *Democracy and Distrust* (Cambridge: Harvard University Press, 1981), pp. 198–99.
[18]Meese, ABA address, p. 16.

instead, seek and apply the best understanding of the principles and values that give substance to the sweeping phrase "the equal protection of the laws." The "best" meaning here would be the one that makes equal protection the most worthy value or goal in light of other ultimate purposes, ends, and values in the Constitution.

There is one final disability that plagues the Jurisprudence of Original Intent—a disability that would alone prove fatal even to a theory healthy in other respects. Conservatives such as Bork and Raoul Berger simply assume that the Constitution "was written against a background of interpretive presuppositions," and, in particular, that the Framers intended future interpreters to carry out their "original" intentions.[19] But if the conservatives are wrong about this particular intention, which we might call the original "interpretive intent," then the Jurisprudence of Original Intent self-destructs.

The fatal evidence has now been provided. In his painstaking and impressive study of the historical record, H. Jefferson Powell concludes that "there is no indication that they [the Philadelphia Framers] expected or intended future interpreters to resort to any extra-constitutional intentions revealed in the convention's secretly conducted debates."[20]

During the debates in the states over the ratification of the Constitution, the Framers had ample opportunity to affirm the controlling authority of their intentions, if they had so wished. But to the contrary, James Madison and Alexander Hamilton, who were most prominent in framing and securing the ratification of the Constitution, positively opposed reliance on the intentions of the Framers. They stressed that fallibility and tentativeness were inescapable features of human expression. Constitutional meaning would have to be elucidated and extended by judges in the course of adjudication through reasoned, legal deliberation, not by historical research. As Hamilton put it, "The rules of legal interpretation are rules of common sense, adopted by the courts in the construction of the laws. . . . In relation to such a subject [a constitution], the natural and obvious sense of its provisions, apart from any technical rules, is the true criterion of construction."[21]

Madison emphasized that the judiciary would play a necessary part in fleshing out the meaning of the law of the land, which included the Constitution:

[19]Raoul Berger, *Government by Judiciary: The Transformation of the Fourteenth Amendment* (Cambridge: Harvard University Press, 1977), pp. 365–66, quoted in H. Jefferson Powell, "The Original Understanding of Original Intent," *Harvard Law Review* 98 (1985): 886.

[20]Powell, "Original Understanding," p. 903.

[21]Alexander Hamilton, *Federalist*, no. 83.

> All new laws, though penned with the greatest technical skill, and
> passed on the fullest and most mature deliberation, are considered
> as more or less obscure and equivocal, until their meaning be liq-
> uidated and ascertained by a series of particular discussions and
> adjudications.[22]

Some years after the ratification of the Constitution, when debating
the constitutionality of the national bank bill, Hamilton explicitly
rejected the relevance of historical evidence of the Framers' intentions:

> Whatever may have been the intention of the framers of a consti-
> tution, or of a law, that intention is to be sought for in the instrument
> itself, according to the usual and established rules of construction.
> Nothing is more common than for laws to express and effect, more
> of less than was intended.[23]

We have no reason to believe that the Founders intended us to be
guided by their specific intentions rather than by the general purposes set out in the Constitution itself. The Constitution declares
itself to be supreme, and the preamble lays out its objects and purposes in broad terms, including "Justice" and "the Blessings of Liberty for ourselves and our Posterity." As intelligent statesmen, the
Framers recognized that the Constitution is not a contract or a statute
but a majestic charter for government, intended to govern for ages to
come and to apply to both unforeseen and unforeseeable circumstances. The notion that specific but unstated intentions ought to
supplant the interpreter's best understanding of the general words
and structure of the document represents a devaluation of the status
of the Constitution itself. It is in light of the aspiration to justice and
liberty, and the other objects and ends stated and implied in the
Constitution, that the founding document and its problematic pas-
sages should be interpreted.

What accounts for the allure of the Jurisprudence of Original Intent?
For judges seeking to avoid difficult questions of political morality,
resort to the Framers' intentions appears, at first, to be an avenue of
escape. And for those seeking to constrain the discretion and political
influence of judges, Original Intent appears to be a useful straitjacket.
Original Intent, however, can be neither an escape nor a straitjacket,
for there is no simple canonical intent locked in the historical record
waiting to be uncovered and deferred to. Nor can conscientious

---

[22]James Madison, *Federalist*, no. 37.
[23]Alexander Hamilton, "Opinion on the Constitutionality of an Act to Establish a Bank"
(1791), reprinted in *Papers of Alexander Hamilton*, vol. 8, ed. H. Syrett (New York:
Columbia University Press, 1965), p. 111; quoted in Powell, "Original Understanding,"
p. 815.

interpreters avoid making difficult judgments of political morality, for the Constitution itself will not allow it. Judges who wish to live up to their oath to support the Constitution cannot flee from the difficult political judgments with which the founding document confronts them. And those who invoke, against a robust judiciary, the founding document and the intent of its Framers have understood neither.

In any case, the conservative invocation of Original Intent has less to do with reverence for the ideas of the Founders than with a political preference for majority power over individual rights and liberty. Underlying the New Right's jurisprudence is a majoritarian impulse that, far from being in accord with the intentions of the Framers, is deeply at odds both with the text and structure of the Constitution and the project of constitutionalism itself.

The Majoritarian Myth

The real basis of the New Right's jurisprudence is not reverence for historical or original intentions, as is evident from the fact that conservatives are selective rather than consistent in their invocation of Original Intent. If the conservatives were really interested in honoring historical intentions they would not simply assert, with Bork, that "the [F]ramers' intentions with respect to freedoms are the sole legitimate premise" for "constitutional analysis."[24] Rather, consistent and conscientious proponents of Original Intent would interpret not only freedoms in light of specific intentions but also government powers.

What the New Right position really comes down to is the Jurisprudence of Selective Intent: judges are referred to original intentions only when it serves a deeper political commitment, that of construing government powers and the powers of majorities broadly and individual rights narrowly. This preference for political power over individual rights controls the conservatives' use of the idea of Original Intent and thereby forms the real basis of their theory of the Constitution. The New Right's commitment to majoritarianism is deeply opposed to the only intentions that really count: those embodied in the text of the Constitution itself.

Innumerable analyses of the Constitution begin with the assumption that America is basically a democratic polity. As Alexander Bickel put it, "Judicial review is a deviant institution in the American

---

[24]Bork, *Tradition*, p. 10.

democracy."[25] Judges are unelected and are responsible to no constituency, and their power is most controversial when the courts review the acts of elected legislators for conformity with the Constitution. Given the assumption that America is basically a majoritarian democratic polity, judicial review stands out as an anomaly, and the imposition of limits on the review power of judges appears as an imperative. As Bork puts it, "The makers of our Constitution . . . provided wide powers to representative assemblies and ruled only a few subjects off limits by the Constitution.[26] And Justice Antonin Scalia, Reagan's most recent Supreme Court appointee, advocates a "restricted view of the courts' role in a democratic society."[27]

Bork depicts judicial deference to legislatures as an avoidance of value choice:

> The choice of "fundamental values" by the Court cannot be justified. Where constitutional materials do not clearly specify the value to be preferred, there is no principled way to prefer any claimed human value to any other. The judge must stick close to the text and history, and their fair implications, and not construct any new rights.[28]

Judicial deference, however, is not an avoidance of choice. Rather, it is a choice of majority power over individual liberty and a presumption against constitutional rights. This choice of political values is as "fundamental" and important as any choice can be, and it needs to be defended or abandoned, not hidden under the guise of skepticism, deference, and neutrality.

The majoritarian rendering of the Constitution is a crucial underpinning of the selective invocation of Original Intent and of the New Right's attack on the judiciary. But this conservative strategy for defining individual rights narrowly and government powers broadly rests on a nonexistent foundation: the Constitution is not basically a simple democratic or majoritarian document.

Direct democracy and majoritarianism were decisively rejected by the Framers, and the system of government established by the Constitution embodies this rejection.[29] Senators were originally chosen by state legislators, and it was only in 1913, with the passage of the

---

[25]Alexander Bickel, *The Least Dangerous Branch* (Indianapolis: Bobbs-Merrill, 1962), p. 18.

[26]Bork, *Tradition*, p. 9.

[27]Antonin Scalia, "Economic Affairs as Human Affairs," this volume, p. 35.

[28]Bork, "Neutral Principles," p. 8. On Bork's opposition to the "method of moral philosophy," see Bork, "Commentary: The Impossibility of Finding Welfare Rights in the Constitution," *Washington University Law Quarterly* (1979): 695–97.

[29]See the *Federalist*, especially nos. 10 and 49.

Seventeenth Amendment, that they became popularly elected; even so, each state continues to have two senators regardless of population. State legislatures were given the power to choose presidential electors, and less-populous states continue to be overrepresented in the electoral college. Staggered elections, long terms for senators and the President, the system of separated powers, and the embrace by one national government of a large or "extended" republic were all designed by the Framers to make it difficult for a national majority to gain effective control of the government. It was thereby hoped that ample room would be left for deliberation, statesmanship, and the rule of justice. On the "input" side, therefore, democracy is tempered and compromised by many checks and balances, including the power of the courts.

As for the courts, the Constitution extends the judicial power "to all Cases, in Law and Equity, arising under this Constitution."[30] Judges take an oath to support the Constitution, and in declaring itself supreme, the Constitution then adds that judges should take special notice: "This Constitution, and the Laws of the United States which shall be made in Pursuance thereof . . . shall be the supreme Law of the Land; and the judges in every State shall be bound thereby."[31]

In the first Congress Madison proposed and led the passage of the Bill of Rights, explaining that once passed and "incorporated into the Constitution, independent tribunals of justice will consider themselves in a peculiar manner the guardians of those rights." The courts, Madison continued, will be an "impenetrable bulwark against every assumption of power in the legislative or executive" branches.[32]

The *Federalist*, no. 78, is Hamilton's extended defense of an independent, active judiciary. He defined limited government as one that protects individual rights through the courts even against "legislative invasions . . . instigated by the major voice of the community," and declared:

> The courts were designed to be an intermediate body between the people and the legislature, in order, among other things, to keep the latter within the limits of their assigned authority. The interpretation of the laws is the proper and peculiar province of the courts. A constitution is, in fact, and must be regarded by judges as, a

[30]U.S. Constitution, Article III, sec. 2.

[31]Ibid., Article VI.

[32]James Madison, quoted in Robert Rutland, "How the Constitution Secures Rights: A Look at the Seminal Years," in *How Does the Constitution Secure Rights?* ed. Robert Goldwin and William Schambra (Washington, D.C.: American Enterprise Institute, 1985).

fundamental law. . . . [T]he constitution ought to be preferred to the statute. . . . This independence of judges is equally requisite to guard the constitution and rights of individuals from the effects of those ill-humors which the arts of designing men, or the influence of particular conjunctures, sometimes disseminates among the people themselves . . . to occasion dangerous innovations in the government, and serious oppressions of the minor party in the community. . . . It would require an uncommon portion of fortitude in the judges to do their duty as faithful guardians of the Constitution, where legislative invasions of it had been instigated by the major voice of the community.[33]

Thus, Hamilton defended the "permanent tenure of judicial offices" so as to make the courts "bulwarks of a limited constitution against legislative encroachments."

The Framers of the Constitution took pains to check popular will and not simply to empower it. They agreed with Madison that "the invasion of private rights is chiefly to be apprehended, not from acts of Government contrary to the sense of its constituents, but from acts in which the Government is the mere instrument of the major number of constituents."[34]

So much for the claims of democracy on the "input" side. On the "output" side the Constitution imposes a number of limitations on the ends the federal government may pursue. The Constitution explicitly denies Congress the power to suspend habeas corpus in peacetime, to pass bills of attainder or ex post facto laws, or to undertake certain other actions.[35] It also denies to the states the power to conduct their own foreign policies, grant titles of nobility, emit bills of credit, make paper money legal tender, pass bills of attainder and ex post facto laws, or impair the obligation of contracts.

The Constitution's specific prohibitions may seem rather thin. Indeed, one of the chief complaints of those who opposed ratification of the Constitution was the absence of a bill of rights limiting the power of the national government in the name of fundamental rights and liberties. This absence, however, was not the consequence of any skepticism on the part of the Framers about the existence of broad natural rights.

As Hamilton explained in the *Federalist*, no. 84, the enumeration of rights in a Constitution could, paradoxically, be harmful to rights

[33]Alexander Hamilton, *Federalist*, no. 78.

[34]James Madison, letter to Thomas Jefferson (1788), quoted in Walter F. Murphy, "The Art of Constitutional Interpretation," in *Essays on the Constitution of the United States*, ed. M. Judd Harmon (Port Washington, N.Y.: Kennikat, 1978), pp. 130–59. I have benefited greatly from Murphy's essay.

[35]See U.S. Constitution, Article I, sec. 9.

themselves. The Founders distrusted the "aphorisms" that tended to be embodied in bills of rights and, more important, they positively opposed the natural implication of an enumeration of rights. To specify the rights to be protected against oppressive majorities might imply, wrongly, that these rights are exceptions to a general grant of government powers.[36]

A government of enumerated powers need not specify the rights to be protected against the power of majorities. "The Constitution is itself," as Hamilton put it in the *Federalist*, no. 84, "in every rational sense, and to every useful purpose, A BILL OF RIGHTS." When conservatives like Bork treat rights as islands surrounded by a sea of government powers, they precisely reverse the view of the Founders as enshrined in the Constitution, wherein government powers are limited and specified and rendered as islands surrounded by a sea of individual rights.

To help quiet the fears of the Anti-Federalists, the proponents of the Constitution did eventually propose a Bill of Rights in the first Congress. But the logic of limited government was not overturned. Madison embedded this logic in the Bill of Rights itself. Thus, to the first eight amendments, which specify various liberties to be protected against government, were added the Ninth Amendment, which explicitly denies that popular rights can be limited to those enumerated in the Constitution, and the Tenth Amendment, which reserves all powers not delegated to the federal government to the states and the people.

Constitutional interpreters should not be so preoccupied with the Bill of Rights as to neglect the power-limiting logic of the Constitution itself. Whereas the President is granted "The Executive Power," and the courts "The Judicial Power," the Congress is conspicuously given only "all legislative powers *herein granted*" (emphasis added). Legislative powers are specifically enumerated and not general.

Just how narrowly the specific grants of legislative powers should be read is a hard question of constitutional interpretation, a harder question than the conservatives admit. Article 1, section 8, of the Constitution enumerates Congress's powers. The first eight powers concern commerce broadly: the power to tax, to borrow money on credit, regulate commerce, establish uniform rules for naturalization and bankruptcy, to "coin money," punish counterfeiting, establish post offices, and grant exclusive patents. The other powers granted to Congress provide for the establishment of lower courts, the gov-

[36]See the discussion in Herbert Storing, "The Constitution and the Bill of Rights," in Harmon, *Essays*, pp. 32–48.

erning of the District of Columbia, and, most important, for national security. At the end of section 8 stands the "necessary and proper" clause: Congress may "make all laws which shall be necessary and proper for carrying into Execution the foregoing Powers, and all other Powers vested by this Constitution in the Government of the United States."

The "necessary and proper" clause certainly allows Congress to do many things incidentally required to carry out the enumerated powers. The question of just how much "elasticity" the "necessary and proper" clause imparts to the enumerated powers is beyond the scope of this discussion.[37] Nevertheless, it is possible here to compare the Constitution's restrictive language on Congress's powers with its expansive language on individual liberties, both economic and personal, in the Bill of Rights.

The Constitution lends explicit support to the values of economic freedom, private security, property rights, and liberty of contract. Article I, section 10, prohibits any state "Law impairing the Obligation of Contracts." The Third Amendment protects the sanctity of the home against the quartering of troops, and the Fourth Amendment protects "The right of the people to be secure in their persons, houses, papers, and effects, against unreasonable searches and seizures." Personal security and privacy are thus clearly linked with property ownership. The Fifth Amendment brings "life, liberty and property" under the protection of "due process of law," and this guarantee is explicitly extended to the states by the Fourteenth Amendment. The Fifth Amendment also requires that private property may be taken only for public use and with "just compensation."

There is, of course, considerable textual support in the Constitution for other, noneconomic liberties, including religious freedom and freedom of speech, of the press, and of assembly. The founding document also protects the many privileges and immunities associated with the rule of law and with fair proceedings in criminal cases, in the Fifth, Sixth, Seventh, and Eighth Amendments. The Ninth Amendment, as noted, explicitly warns against construing the "enumeration" of "certain rights" to "deny or disparage others retained by the people." And the Tenth Amendment emphasizes that the powers of the federal government are limited to those "delegated" to it (though, of course, not necessarily to those expressly or explicitly

---

[37]This issue hinges on John Marshall's landmark opinion in McCulloch v. Maryland, 4 Wheaton 316 (1819), which I discuss in Macedo, *The New Right v. the Constitution* (Washington, D.C.: Cato Institute, 1986).

enumerated). The Bill of Rights closes with the reminder that powers not delegated are "reserved to the States respectively, or the people."

The Constitution is basically concerned not simply with empowering the people's representatives to govern, but with checking and limiting the powers of legislative majorities in a host of important ways, both procedurally and substantively (or on both the "input" and the "output" sides). There is no presumption in the Constitution in favor of legislatures and against judges, or in favor of majority power and against individual rights and liberties. Judicial review is not an anomalous blotch on a democratic scheme of government. Contrary to what the conservatives hold, judicial review is an integral part of a scheme of constitutionally limited government.

How best to reconcile the elasticity of the "necessary and proper" clause with the Constitution's commitment to a broad expanse of individual rights is a hard question to be confronted by judges in adjudicating cases, and also by legislators and other political actors. Conscientious interpreters must undertake the difficult, but far from impossible, task of drawing lines between the powers of the national government and the rights of individuals, and between the powers of the national government and the reserved powers of the states. What must be utterly unacceptable is a jurisprudence that ignores broad individual rights so well anchored in the Constitution.

Morality and Constitutional Law

Bork insists, uncontroversially, that judicial decisions must rest on "reasoned opinions," that is, a "legitimate" court must have "a valid theory, derived from the Constitution" to justify its actions.[38] Bork's view of what constitutes a constitutional principle is, however, extremely narrow: valid constitutional principles are drawn only from the text interpreted in light of specific historical intentions. On Bork's reading, therefore, the equal protection clause of the Fourteenth Amendment has only two requirements: "formal procedural equality," as the bare text clearly requires, and no government discrimination along racial lines, because a concern with race is revealed by the history of the Fourteenth Amendment.

Cut loose from plain text and historical intentions, there is, for Bork, "no principled way of saying which . . . inequalities are permissible."[39] Beyond text and intention are "matters of morality," which "belong . . . to the political community."[40] Political morality

[38]Bork, "Neutral Principles," p. 3.
[39]Ibid., p. 11.
[40]Ibid., p. 12.

is of no help in deciding constitutional questions because, says Bork, any system of "moral and ethical values ... has no objective or intrinsic validity of its own." There is, in effect, no right and wrong because all that can be said about morality is "men can and do differ."[41] As if to make moral skepticism or subjectivism official U.S. government policy, Attorney General Meese approvingly quotes Bork's aphorism: "The judge who looks outside the Constitution always looks inside himself and nowhere else.[42]

Bork's skepticism turns to cynicism when he reduces all moral pleas to claims for "gratification": "Every clash between a minority claiming freedom and a majority claiming power to regulate involves a choice between the gratifications of two groups.[43] When examining *Griswold* v. *Connecticut*, a case in which married couples asserted, as a matter of constitutional and political morality, the right to use contraceptives in the privacy of their own home, Bork sees no serious moral problem but only a question of "sexual gratification." Since there is no principled way, according to Bork, to discriminate between kinds of "gratification," the majority should have its way.[44]

William Rehnquist, now Chief Justice and generally considered the intellectual leader of the conservative bloc on the Supreme Court, shares Bork's moral skepticism: "Many of us necessarily feel strongly and deeply about our own moral judgments, but they remain only personal moral judgments until in some way given the sanction of law."[45] What Rehnquist, like Bork, gives us is moral skepticism in the service of majoritarianism.

The New Right's attitude to rights claims appears to have the advantage of a tough-minded, down-to-earth realism. Bork makes much of preferring the "common sense of the people" to the "theorists of moral abstraction," to "intellectuals," and to "what-have-you philosophy."[46] But the appearance of realism is spurious, for Americans could not make sense of their traditions, practices, and habitual ways of thinking, acting, and judging, or of the Constitution, if they accepted the New Right's radical moral skepticism. Indeed, one could not even make sense of the New Right's apparently principled preference for democracy on the basis of sheer skepticism. (After all,

---

[41]Ibid., p. 10.

[42]Meese, Federalist Society address, p. 11.

[43]Bork, "Neutral Principles," p. 9.

[44]Ibid., p. 11; and see Griswold v. Connecticut, 381 U.S. 479 (1965).

[45]William H. Rehnquist, "The Notion of a Living Constitution," *Texas Law Review* 54 (1976): 704.

[46]Bork, *Tradition*, pp. 7–11.

why should we, except on the basis of some principle of moral equality, prefer the gratifications of the majority to a minority?)

The apparent lesson of the New Right's derision of rights and moral reflection is that moral claims can be ignored because they are no more than the way that "intellectuals" dress up their preferences and gratifications. By reducing rights claims to demands for "gratification," New Right theorists destroy the distinction between moral reasons and mere arbitrary preferences. And as Sotirios Barber points out, to insist that a community's authoritative ethical values need express no more than the merely subjective preferences of the majority is to put forward "a sophisticated version of the maxim that might makes right."[47]

Fortunately, despite its apparent tough-mindedness, the New Right's conception of morality is so counterintuitive that hardly anyone would accept it. Who really believes that moral claims express only desires for "gratification," as Bork asserts? To accept Bork's position one would have to believe that there is no moral difference between the "gratification" of a murderer and the "gratification" of his potential victim who wishes to live. According to Bork, "Anything some people want has, to that degree, social value."[48] But what of the desires of the rapist, the thief, and the arsonist? Do these desires have social value? And do they fail to win moral approval and become lawful only because they are the desires of minorities?

Contrary to Bork, the truth is that we can and do distinguish between mere gratifications and genuine moral claims all the time. We say with moral confidence that the gratifications of those who enjoy murdering, raping, stealing, burning other people's homes, or violating rights in other ways, count for nothing. We believe in fundamental rights, to freedom of conscience and of speech, to life and to at least some forms of privacy, on the basis of moral reason and not on the basis of absurd calculations about net gratifications.

In telling the majority, those with the strength of numbers, that morality may be ignored (because moral reasons are mere preferences) the New Right calls upon what is worst, not what is best, in the public. The Framers recognized this stance; indeed they feared it. They feared the untutored, unrefined "prejudices" of the people,

---

[47]Sotirios Barber, "Judge Bork's Constitution," in *Courts, Judges, and Politics*, 3rd ed., ed. Walter F. Murphy and C. Herman Pritchett (New York: Random House, forthcoming), pp. 691–95. Barber also has pointed out to the present author that Bork's position is essentially that of Thrasymachus, in Plato's *Republic*, who argued against Socrates that justice is no more than the interest of the stronger.

[48]Bork, "Neutral Principles," p. 29.

and they regarded those who would flatter and enflame these prejudices as demagogues.

The Framers feared the "passions" of the people, and argued that "the reason, alone, of the public . . . ought to control and regulate the government."[49] They rejected the idea that popular government was necessarily good government and sought to ensure that political power would be in the hands of the wisest members of the community: "The republican principle demands that the deliberate sense of the community should govern."[50] And, unlike the New Right, the Framers were neither moral skeptics nor derisive of abstract ideas.[51] For what else but abstract ideas are the "self-evident" truths of the Declaration of Independence? What else but philosophical principles are "unalienable Rights" that belong naturally to all men? And how else, except as the assertion of an abstract moral claim, can one understand the Framers' assertion that "Justice is the end of government"?[52] Thomas Paine expressed the faith of his generation when he claimed, "The Independence of America was accompanied by a Revolution in the principles and practices of Governments. . . . Government founded on a moral theory . . . on the indefeasible hereditary Rights of Man, is now revolving from West to East."[53]

The main sources of the political ideas of the founding generation were the legal authorities Edward Coke and William Blackstone and the great classical liberal political theorist John Locke.[54] All three

[49]*Federalist*, no. 49.

[50]*Federalist*, no. 71.

[51]My reliance on certain arguments of the Framers here and elsewhere may seem inconsistent with my criticism of the New Right's reliance on the "intentions of the Framers." One might argue, of course, that moral rights ought to be taken seriously out of respect for the intentions of the Framers, but I have already displayed the fatal weaknesses of the resort to Original Intent. There are, however, different ways of using historical sources.

My position is that the invocation of historical sources ought to rest on critical judgments of political morality. My purpose is to rely on the Framers, and other sources in our history, where they are consistent with our best understanding of political morality. Historical sources have no automatic authority, but, other things being equal, it is reasonable to prefer political arrangements rooted in a community's past. What we must try to do is distill a worthy tradition from our checkered history, and this involves the exercise of critical judgments of political morality, judgments of precisely the sort about which the New Right is so skeptical.

[52]*Federalist*, no. 51.

[53]Thomas Paine, quoted in Thomas Pangle, "Patriotism American Style," *National Review* (29 November 1985): 30–34.

[54]On the influence of Locke, see Bernard Bailyn, *The Ideological Origins of the American Revolution* (Cambridge: Harvard University Press, 1982), especially pp. 27–28. On Locke and Coke, see Edward S. Corwin, *The "Higher Law" Background of American Constitutionalism* (Ithaca, N.Y.: Cornell University Press, 1979). On Blackstone's

accepted the political centrality of "natural law" morality. Coke and Locke, in particular, continually stressed that moral standards defining individual rights were binding on all political actors, including popular majorities, legislatures, and judges.

John Locke, the political thinker who exercised the greatest influence on the republic's founding generation, argued that men gave up none of their natural rights when entering political society; they gave to government only the power to better "preserve" their natural rights to "liberty and property."[55] Thomas Jefferson echoed Lockean theory when, in 1816, he asserted:

> Our legislators are not sufficiently apprised of the rightful limits of their power; that their true office is to declare and enforce only our natural right and duties, and to take none of them from us. . . . When the laws have declared and enforced all this, they have fulfilled their functions; and the idea is quite unfounded that on entering society we give up any natural right.[56]

Not all the Founders adhered strictly, even in theory, to Lockeanism, and none of them acted from considerations of political morality alone. Prudence, together with forms of political wisdom beyond moral theorizing, come into play in any successful act of statecraft. These facts notwithstanding, it is safe to say that the Founders did not doubt the existence of moral rights that bind popular governments. The Constitution itself, moreover, does not claim to confer rights, but only "secures" them. And the Ninth Amendment explicitly calls upon constitutional interpreters not to "deny or disparage" the existence of rights not stated explicitly in the Constitution. By implication, then, the Constitution calls upon all citizens and officials to reflect upon the rights that people have even in the absence of explicit political acknowledgment. The Ninth Amendment calls upon conscientious interpreters to reflect upon our rights and so to engage in moral theory.

The Supreme Court has often heeded the Constitution's call to moral thinking. In *Ogden* v. *Saunders*, John Marshall invoked the "abstract philosophy" of natural rights: "Individuals do not derive from government their right to contract, but bring that right with

---

teaching on "natural law" and its influence on the Founders, see W. A. Mell, "James Wilson, Alexander Hamilton, and William Blackstone" (Ph.D. diss., University of Oregon, 1976; University Microfilms, Ann Arbor, Mich., 1980).

[55] John Locke, *Two Treatises on Government*, Second Treatise, ed. Peter Laslett (New York: New American Library, 1965), par. 131, pp. 398–99.

[56] Thomas Jefferson, as quoted in Murphy, "Art of Constitutional Interpretation," p. 140.

them into society. . . . [E]very man retains [the right] to acquire property, to dispose of that property according to his own judgment, and to pledge himself for a future act."[57]

And not only the courts have invoked morality. In the Gettysburg Address, Abraham Lincoln described the central proposition of the Declaration of Independence, to which the nation was dedicated at its birth, as "an abstract truth applicable to all men and all times." Lincoln, unlike Bork, held that right and wrong depend on standards of judgment independent of mere opinion.[58] After the Civil War, the development of the doctrine of "substantive due process" carried forward the "higher law" tradition in the form of judicially protected economic liberties.[59]

There is clearly a close fit among the three elements of the New Right's jurisprudence. The resort to historical intentions to construe rights narrowly is supported by the preference for majority power over individual liberty, and that in turn is supported by moral skepticism. And yet at each level, the New Right's position is diametrically opposed to the ideas of the Framers, the text of the Constitution, and the best arguments we have been able to muster. Having proceeded thus far in the task of clearing the ground, it is now worthwhile to consider briefly the possible form of a principled judicial activism.

A Principled Judicial Activism

A principled jurisprudence would draw on all the sources available and relevant to the task of constitutional interpretation. First and foremost among these sources are the text and structure of the Constitution and the nature of the institutions it establishes. However, both the text, especially the preamble and the Ninth Amendment, and our tradition direct us beyond the rights explicitly stated in the document, so it is not possible to dispense with an understanding of morality. For the conscientious interpreter, moral theory is an aid to, not a substitute for, interpretation of the text.

Bork is on firm ground when he charges that modern courts, in defining values sufficiently "fundamental" to warrant judicial protection, have unreasonably neglected some rights, especially eco-

[57]Ogden v. Saunders, 2 Wheaton 213 (1827).
[58]See Henry V. Jaffa, *Crisis of the House Divided* (Seattle: University of Washington Press, 1973), chap. 14; and Gary J. Jacobsohn's excellent "Abraham Lincoln 'On this Question of Judicial Authority': The Theory of Constitutional Aspiration," *Western Political Quarterly* 36, no. 1 (1983): 52–70.
[59]For a discussion of the relevant case law and related issues, see Bernard Siegan, *Economic Liberties and the Constitution* (Chicago: University of Chicago Press, 1980).

nomic ones. In this way, the Court has indeed been "political"; it has erected a constitutional "double standard" by giving a high place to "personal rights" while neglecting economic rights at least as well founded in the Constitution.

The jurisprudence of the modern Court was born under the shadow of the era of "substantive due process," a doctrine now identified most closely with the case of *Lochner v. New York*.[60] In *Lochner,* the Court struck down a New York statute limiting the working hours of bakery employees as an abridgment of "liberty of contract." The modern Court has not abandoned the idea that the Fourteenth Amendment, which says, "No state shall . . . deprive any person of life, liberty, or property without due process of law," implies that there are substantive limits on the ways in which the state can interfere with private relations. The Court has simply shifted its inquiries away from the economic sphere. When it comes to state economic regulation, the Court requires nothing more than the merest "rationality" to justify restrictions on individual liberty. In instances when legislators have not put forward a rational basis for restrictions on economic liberty, the Court has simply hypothesized its own rationale, as in *Williamson v. Lee Optical* and *Ferguson v. Skrupka.*[61]

The modern Court has largely abandoned the protection of substantive economic values, but it has not abandoned fundamental values altogether. The Court closely scrutinizes legislation touching on a list of "preferred freedoms," such as the right to freedom of speech, of religion, and of the press, and more recently the right to privacy and the equal protection of the laws.

Griswold v. Connecticut, which Bork derides as an arbitrary judicial creation of a new right, struck down a Connecticut statute that made it illegal for married couples to use contraceptives.[62] The Court based its decision on an implicit constitutional right to zones of privacy, which emanate from, or form "penumbras" around, the specific guarantees of the Bill of Rights. As Justice Douglas argued, these implicit, penumbral rights, including one protecting the privacy of the marriage relationship, help give life and substance to express guarantees. Justice Goldberg, concurring, emphasized the importance of taking the Ninth Amendment seriously.

Most commentators on the left applaud the Court's shift from protecting economic values to protecting noneconomic ones such as privacy. Conservatives like Bork, on the other hand, see the new

[60]198 U.S. 45 (1905).
[61]348 U.S. 343 (1955) and 372 U.S. 726 (1963), respectively.
[62]381 U.S. 479 (1965).

132

jurisprudence as no better than the old. Conservatives want the Court to abandon the protection of "fundamental" interests or "substantive" values other than those explicitly stated in the constitutional text and originally intended by the Framers.

Both the new "activist" jurisprudence and the old are flawed. In both cases the choice of values to be protected is partial, unprincipled, and, therefore, political. The modern Court can and should be criticized for the narrowly political way it has defined those "fundamental" values and "preferred" freedoms worthy of judicial protection. Such flaws, however, cannot be corrected by abandoning the active judicial defense of liberty and rights. A principled activism is supported by the Constitution's text, by the ideas of the Framers, and by our political traditions. The proper course is for conscientious interpreters of the Constitution to correct, not abandon, judicial activism.

While the Court of the *Lochner* era may justly be accused of inadequate concern for noneconomic freedoms, even the crustiest of the "Old Men" on the Court recognized the close relation between economic and other personal liberties, and thus pointed the way toward a principled synthesis. In *Meyer v. Nebraska*, the Court overturned the conviction of a German-language teacher under a statute prohibiting the teaching of foreign languages to young children.[63] Justice McReynolds articulated a broad conception of the liberty protected by the Fourteenth Amendment:

> Without doubt, it denotes not merely freedom from bodily restraint, but also the right of the individual to contract, to engage in any of the common occupations of life, to acquire useful knowledge, to marry, establish a home and bring up children, to worship God according to the dictates of his conscience, and generally to enjoy those privileges long recognized at common law as essential to the orderly pursuit of happiness by free men.[64]

Justice McReynolds correctly linked the autonomy and intellectual freedom of parents and students with the "economic" right of language teachers to pursue their calling.[65]

Constitutional commentators on and off the bench are coming to see that what is needed is a jurisprudence that recognizes the constitutional status of both economic and other important liberties. As Justice Stewart pointed out in *Lynch v. Household Finance Corporation*:

---

[63] 262 U.S. 390 (1923).
[64] Id. at 399.
[65] See also Pierce v. Society of Sisters, 268 U.S. 510 (1925).

[T]he dichotomy between personal liberties and property rights is a false one. Property does not have rights. People have rights. The right to enjoy property without unlawful deprivation, no less than the right to speak out or the right to travel, is, in truth, a "personal" right. . . . [A] fundamental interdependence exists between the personal right to liberty and the personal right in property. Neither could have meaning without the other. That rights in property are basic civil rights has long been recognized.[66]

A recent Michigan case highlights the deep interdependence of property rights and such noneconomic values as self-determination and community. *Poletown Neighborhood Council v. City of Detroit* arose over the taking by eminent domain of an entire Detroit neighborhood that the General Motors Corporation wanted to raze for the construction of an automobile plant.[67] The Michigan Supreme Court refused to step in and protect the property owners in this ethnic working-class neighborhood despite state and federal constitutional requirements that land be taken only for "public use." Construing government powers broadly and individual rights narrowly, as Bork recommends, the Michigan Supreme Court said the Constitution would be satisfied because the seizure and transfer to General Motors would provide a "public benefit." However, if property rights are to count for so little in the face of a government pursuing policy ends, then families, communities, and the other traditional groups of which the New Right is so solicitous are all rendered insecure and vulnerable to political vagaries and the passions of the moment.

The New Right's reply to the proposal for a principled activism—that is, for the judicial protection of a broad sphere of individual liberties, both economic and personal—would undoubtedly be that such an approach merely combines two types of judicial activism, both of which should be rejected in favor of judicial restraint. The conservative response does avoid a constitutional double standard, but only at the expense of a total blindness to the constitutional status of individual liberty.

Conclusion

A principled judicial activism would give democracy its due place in constitutional interpretation but would protect against untrammeled majoritarianism. Judicial activism should not be confused with judicial supremacy. Principled activism in no way implies that the Supreme Court is the final interpreter of the Constitution (except for

[66]405 U.S. 538, 552 (1972).
[67]410 Mich. 616, 304 N.W. 2d 455 (1981).

the parties to the cases that come before it, and for inferior courts) or that Supreme Court interpretations of the Constitution are binding on Congress, the President, or the citizenry. The Constitution itself is supreme, and the members of each of the three coordinate branches of the federal government (and their counterparts in state governments) are sworn to uphold the Constitution in performing their official functions.[68]

The issues discussed here are constitutional in the broadest sense, affecting not only the determination of court cases but also the shape of our polity and our lives as citizens. In this sense, constitutional interpretation cannot help but be political, and politics, at least at its best, cannot dispense with serious constitutional debate. Therefore, the debate over the meaning of the Constitution is one that should involve the whole citizenry.

In the recent hearings leading up to the confirmations of Chief Justice Rehnquist and Associate Justice Scalia, the Senate, quite properly, went to great lengths to assure itself of the personal integrity and intellectual acumen of the two nominees. But in confining itself to considerations of integrity and intelligence, the Senate missed a valuable opportunity to weigh the substance of the jurisprudence of the New Right. (The neglect of jurisprudential substance was reflected in the fact that all 33 of the senators who voted against Rehnquist later voted for Scalia, despite the similarity of their jurisprudential views.) And by failing to critically weigh the defensibility of the constitutional theories of Rehnquist and Scalia, the Senate shirked its own responsibility to interpret and apply the Constitution in performing its duties.

The supremacy of the Constitution embodies our ultimate commitment to moral standards. The supremacy of the Constitution stands for the supremacy of a moral vision because the founding document embodies not simply the will of some authoritative group but a commitment to justice and individual rights. The New Right, by continually emphasizing that judges owe their allegiance to the will of the Framers (in the form of specific intentions) or the will of the majority, would deny a genuine moral status to the Constitution. And in the place of rights, justice, and morality, the New Right would enshrine the gratifications and preferences of the greatest number. This moral skepticism cheapens the currency of our political discourse and undermines the possibility of a genuine moral community in America.

[68]See John Agresto, *The Supreme Court and Constitutional Democracy* (Ithaca: Cornell University Press, 1984).

The Constitution is best read as embodying a morality of broad liberties, both economic and personal. The society constituted by these fundamental values would reckon tolerance, openness to change and diversity, and reflectiveness among its public virtues. This public morality is "liberal" in the true, broad sense of that term and is uniquely suited to a vast heterogeneous republic such as the United States. We can neither hope nor expect that one vision of the good life will ever secure the allegiance of both Jerry Falwell and Jane Fonda, of urban yuppies and suburban families, of Midwest farmers and Vietnamese immigrants. To grant supreme political status to majoritarianism—that is, to the preferences of the greatest number— rather than to impersonal moral norms protecting the liberty of all, would invite oppression and social conflict.

Rejecting the constitutional vision of the New Right should not be confused with a wholesale rejection of conservative sentiments or of patriotism. Only a blind conservatism is without reasons for valuing what it seeks to preserve. Only an unreflective and uncritical patriotism ("my country right or wrong") forgets that it is in aspiring to worthy principles and ideals that a country, its government, and its constitution become worthy of allegiance, loyalty, and self-sacrifice. Instead of the unreflective and spurious traditionalism of the New Right, we would do far better to aspire to Lincoln's eulogistic remembrance of Henry Clay, who, said Lincoln, "loved his country partly because it was his own country, but mostly because it was a free country; and he burned with a zeal for its advancement . . . because he saw in such, the advancement . . . of human liberty, human right, and human nature."[69]

[69]Quoted in Pangle, "Patriotism," p. 30.

6

ECONOMIC LIBERTIES AND THE CONSTITUTION: PROTECTION AT THE STATE LEVEL

Bernard H. Siegan

I. Introduction

In terms of protecting personal liberty, no provision of the Constitution is more important than the second sentence of the Fourteenth Amendment's Section 1, which states:

> No State shall make or enforce any law which shall abridge the privileges or immunities of citizens of the United States; nor shall any State deprive any person of life, liberty, or property, without due process of law; nor deny to any person within its jurisdiction the equal protection of the laws.[1]

The importance of this sentence derives from the fact that there are few other provisions in the Constitution that protect citizens or other persons against violation of their rights by the states. The Bill of Rights, for example, applies only to the federal government.[2] Were there no Fourteenth Amendment, such commonly accepted liberties as those of speech, press, religion, and property might not be guaranteed against infringement by the states. Because most efforts to limit individual or corporate activity occur at the state or local levels, Section 1 of the Fourteenth Amendment likely is involved in more litigation than any other provision of the Constitution.

The author of the above-quoted provision was Rep. John Bingham of Ohio (described by Justice Black as "the Madison of the first section of the Fourteenth Amendment"[3]), who explained to his colleagues in the debates on the framing of the amendment that it protected from abridgment or denial by a state "the privileges and

---

The author is Distinguished Professor of Law and Director of Law and Economic Studies at the University of San Diego.

[1]U.S. Constitution.

[2]Barron v. Baltimore, 32 U.S. (7 Pet.) 243 (1833).

[3]Adamson v. California, 332 U.S. 46, 74 (1947) (Black, J., dissenting).

immunities of all of the citizens of the Republic and the inborn rights of every person within its jurisdiction."[4] For Bingham, privileges and immunities encompassed all fundamental rights protected by the Constitution, and he used "inborn" as a synonym for natural rights. No speaker in the debates challenged this interpretation, which is consistent with the explanation presented by both the Senate and House managers of the joint congressional resolution proposing the amendment.[5]

History and background support Bingham's interpretation. The provision under discussion was designed to accord maximum protections for liberty at the state level. Each of its three clauses— privileges and immunities, due process, and equal protection—was directed toward this end, and collectively they constitute a formidable barrier against state excesses and oppression.

Although this general commitment is quite plain, it does not reveal what activity is safeguarded and to what extent. This inquiry may not be readily resolved for many areas, but it can be satisfied for the liberties about which this article is concerned, those relating to property and economics. In the civil area these were liberties of the highest concern to the people responsible for drafting the Fourteenth Amendment's Section 1. This concern is evident in the statute and commentaries that are most important for understanding it; the Civil Rights Act of 1866;[6] Justice Bushrod Washington's famous definition of privileges and immunities in *Corfield v. Coryell;*[7] and the commentaries of William Blackstone and James Kent. All of these emphasize the importance of property in a free society and of the liberties— such as the right of contract—required to make it meaningful. There should be little doubt that people supportive of the doctrines expounded or contained in these background materials would strive to secure economic freedoms in the Fourteenth Amendment.

Section II of this paper briefly summarizes the background materials that helped shape the Fourteenth Amendment. Section III considers the importance of due process in protecting economic liberties. Section IV discusses the antislavery, corporate, and judicial advocates of substantive due process, and Section V presents some concluding remarks. The reader should be aware that although it protects many liberties, the U.S. Supreme Court has not enforced economic rights since 1936.

[4]*Congressional Globe*, 39th Cong., 1st Sess. 2542 (1866).
[5]Ibid., pp. 2459 and 2764.
[6]Act of 9 April 1866, ch. 31, 14 Stat. 27.
[7]6 F. Cas. 546 (C.C.E.D. Pa. 1823) (No. 3, 230).

II. The Fourteenth Amendment: Background

Civil Rights Act of 1866

There is little disagreement that Section 1 of the Fourteenth Amendment established the principles of the Civil Rights Act of 1866 in the Constitution so that they could not be repealed by a subsequent Congress. Section 1 of this act states:

> That all persons born in the United States, and not subject to any foreign Power, excluding Indians not taxed, are hereby declared to be citizens of the United States; and such citizens of every race and color, without regard to any previous condition of slavery or involuntary servitude, except as a punishment for a crime, whereof the party shall have been duly convicted, shall have the same right in every State and Territory to make and enforce contracts, to sue, to be sued, be parties and give evidence, to inherit, purchase, lease, sell, hold, and convey real and personal property, and to be entitled to full and equal benefit of all laws and proceedings for the security of person and property as is enjoyed by white citizens, and shall be subject to like punishment, pains and penalties and to none other, any law, statute, ordinance, regulation or custom to the contrary notwithstanding.

Thus the act protected against discriminatory treatment the rights of most U.S. citizens "to make and enforce contracts . . . [and] to inherit, purchase, lease, sell, hold and convey real and personal property."

The congressional debates evidence the existence of dual goals for the civil rights legislation: to secure an equality of rights for blacks as well as for most other citizens. While primarily directed to protect the emancipated blacks against discrimination, the act applied to most citizens and all of the states. Sen. Lyman Trumbull, author of the original bill and chairman of the Senate judiciary committee, viewed the bill as generally affecting state legislation. In his introductory statements Trumbull cited a note to Blackstone's *Commentaries* that liberty required an equality of the laws: "In this definition of civil liberty, it ought to be understood, or rather expressed, that the restraints introduced by the law should be equal to all, or as much so as the nature of things will admit."[8] Trumbull subsequently denied charges that the bill benefited black men exclusively:

> [It] applies to white men as well as black men. It declares that all persons in the United States shall be entitled to the same civil rights, the right to the fruit of their own labor, the right to make contracts, the right to buy and sell, and enjoy liberty and happiness. . . .[9]

[8]*Congressional Globe* (1866), p. 474.
[9]Ibid., p. 599.

The only object "is to secure equal rights to all citizens of the country."[10]

Trumbull expressed essentially the same views in his speech urging the Senate to override President Andrew Johnson's veto of the bill (which Congress did). Again he emphasized the bill's racial objectives and acknowledged its applicability to the rest of the population. The following passage from his speech suggests the bill would impose a reasonableness standard on state legislation:

> The bill neither confers nor abridges the rights of any one, but simply declares that in civil rights there shall be an equality among all classes of citizens, and that all alike shall be subject to the same punishment. Each State, so that it does not abridge the great fundamental rights belonging, under the Constitution, to all citizens, may grant or withhold such civil rights as it pleases; all that is required is that, in this respect, its laws shall be impartial.[11]

In his introductory statement, Rep. James Wilson, chairman of the House judiciary committee and the House floor manager for the bill, asserted that "the entire structure of this bill rests on the discrimination relative to civil rights and immunities made by the states" on account of race, color, or previous condition of servitude.[12] It was necessary, however, to enact the statute "to protect our citizens, from the highest to the lowest, from the whitest to the blackest, in the enjoyment of the great fundamental rights which belong to all men."[13]

This broad approach to civil rights was consistent with abolitionist doctrine that emphasized legal equality generally and not just with respect to race. The abolitionists maintained that "slaves and free Negroes . . . must receive legal protection in their fundamental rights, along with all other human beings."[14] They had long comprehended the moral and practical problems of isolating their pleas for legal equality to one area. Because the result would be to limit the powers of government, this perspective was highly acceptable in the generally laissez-faire climate of the Republican party—the party of the antislavery movement that in 1866 held a huge majority in the Congress. The explanations of the civil rights bill by both Trumbull and Wilson reflected these important philosophical concerns and appealed to the vast majority of their party who shared them.

---

[10]Ibid.

[11]Ibid., p. 1760.

[12]Ibid., p. 1118.

[13]Ibid.

[14]Jacobus TenBroek, *Equal Under Law* (London: Collier Books, Collier-Macmillan, Ltd., 2d printing, 1969), p. 118.

Freedmen's Bureau Bill

The 1866 Congress also passed the Freedmen's Bureau bill,[15] intended to protect for a limited period, the rights of emancipated slaves in the formerly rebellious states then controlled by the Union forces. Trumbull introduced this bill on the same day he presented the civil rights bill. President Johnson successfully vetoed it, but Congress subsequently passed a modified version, which survived against another veto. Section 7 of the Freedmen's Bureau bill protected blacks, mulattoes, and some others against deprivation of the same rights enumerated in Section 1 of the Civil Rights Act, again evidencing Congress' high priority for property and economic freedoms.

Washington's Definition of Privileges and Immunities

Justice Washington's definition of privileges and immunities (as contained in Art. 4, Sec. 1 of the Constitution) was frequently cited in the debates on both the Civil Rights Act and the Fourteenth Amendment. According to Washington, in *Corfield v. Coryell*, the privileges and immunities belonging to citizens of all free governments include:

> [T]he enjoyment of life and liberty, with the right to acquire and possess property of every kind, [and with respect to citizens of one state] the right . . . to pass through, or to reside in, any other state for purposes of trade, agriculture, professional pursuits [and] to take, hold and dispose of property, either real or personal.[16]

Washington did not specifically refer to them, but contracts would be comprehended under the property rights he did mention. Contracts are a form of property in that they are an asset or acquisition (Blackstone's term) that can be purchased, held, and sold. They are requisite likewise for the acquisition, use, and transfer of real and personal property.

Commentaries of Blackstone and Kent

It is evident from the debates on the Freedman's Bureau bill, the Civil Rights bill, and the Fourteenth Amendment that the foremost legal authorities for the Congress of 1866 were William Blackstone and James Kent, whose commentaries on the protection of life, liberty, and property were quoted. Both of these commentators had

---

[15]*Congressional Globe* (1866), app., pp. 209–10.
[16]6 F. Cas. 546 (1823) at 551–52.

declared that the three "absolute rights" of individuals were those of personal security, personal liberty, and personal property. For Blackstone, the right of property meant the "free use, enjoyment, and disposal [by the owner] of all his acquisitions, without any control or diminution, save only by the laws of the land."[17] Kent wrote that "the right to acquire and enjoy property [is] natural, inherent, and unalienable."[18]

III. Economic Liberties and Due Process

The legitimacy of economic due process—that is, application of the due process clause to invalidate economic regulation—should be considered in light of this background. Because it incorporates the Civil Rights Act's principles, resolution of this issue should not differ under the Fourteenth Amendment's Section 1 from what it would under the 1866 statute.

Securing Freedom of Contract

Consider in this regard the most controversial of the economic due process cases, *Lochner v. New York*, which was decided by the United States Supreme Court in 1905.[19] *Lochner* involved the question whether New York's statute limiting working hours in bakeries and confectioneries to 10 hours per day or 60 hours per week violated the due process clause of the Fourteenth Amendment. The Civil Rights Act used the terminology "to make and enforce contracts" without qualification, which would therefore comprehend the employment contracts involved in *Lochner*. Moreover, the 1866 Congress had drafted the act to protect, among other things, the right of emancipated blacks to contract freely for the purchase and sales of goods and services. The legislators had sought to eliminate state laws that regulated the terms of employment for blacks because these laws discriminated against them. Such specific purposes became general ones applicable to other individuals and groups both under the language of the act and the Fourteenth Amendment.

---

[17]William Blackstone, *Commentaries on the Laws of England: A Facsimile of the First Edition of 1725–1769*, vol. 1 (Chicago: University of Chicago Press, 1979), pp. 134–35.
[18]James Kent, *Commentaries on American Law*, vol. 2, reprint of the 1827 edition (New York: Da Capo Press, 1971), p. 1.
[19]198 U.S. 45 (1905). An extensive analysis of the background of the Lochner decision is given in Bernard H. Siegan, "Rehabilitating Lochner," which will appear in *University of San Diego Law Review* 22, no. 2 (March 1985). See also Siegan, *Economic Liberties and the Constitution* (Chicago and London: University of Chicago Press, 1980), pp. 113–20.

Mr. Lochner complained that he and other bakery employers were the only ones denied the right to contract freely with their employees about working hours. Were the statute in *Lochner* confined to black employers, there is little question it would invite inquiry under the act. The same would be true, of course, were only black workers affected. Under the act, the state would have the burden to justify different treatment for the black employers or black workers. Being a legal equality law, the state would have the same obligation under it were a group of white persons similarly restricted, as occurred under the *Lochner* statute.

The constitutional outcome should not differ even if it is assumed that the Civil Rights Act was confined solely to racial discrimination, as some contend it was. The liberties enumerated in the statute were of most concern to the 1866 Congress or they would not have been named in both the Civil Rights bill and the Freedmen's Bureau bill. It would be most unlikely that Congress would have secured them under the statutes but not under the Constitution. It would be very odd indeed if Congress did not intend to safeguard liberty of contract under Section 1 of the Fourteenth Amendment.

Lochner was an interpretation of the due process clause. The charge that *Lochner* was a lawless construction of that clause is in part grounded on the theory that due process in the 1860s related only to procedure and not to substance. However, there is no indication in the relevant debates that Bingham and his fellow Republicans so confined it. Bingham's perspective was much different; for him and his colleagues, particularly the many Republicans active or involved in the antislavery movements, due process meant essentially protection against all government oppression, which could take many forms.

Bingham on the Inviolability of Property Rights

According to Bingham, the due process guarantee of the Fifth Amendment secures natural rights for all persons, requires equal treatment by the law, and comprehends the highest priority for ownership. Note in the quotes that follow his statement that no one shall be deprived of property "against his consent," a stronger affirmation of property rights than contemplated in the Fifth Amendment, which contains no such qualification. Consider some of Bingham's opinions on these subjects:

> [N]atural or inherent rights, which belong to all men irrespective of all conventional regulations, are by this constitution guaranteed by the broad and comprehensive word "person," as contradistinguished from the limited term citizen—as in the fifth article of

amendments, guarding those sacred rights which are as universal and indestructible as the human race, that "no person shall be deprived of life, liberty or property but by due process of law, nor shall private property be taken without just compensation."[20]

. . . .

Who . . . will be bold enough to deny that all persons are equally entitled to the enjoyment of the rights of life and liberty and property; and that no one should be deprived of life or liberty, but as punishment for crime; nor of his property, against his consent and without due compensation?[21]

. . . .

It must be apparent that the absolute equality of all, and the equal protection of each, are principles of our Constitution, which ought to be observed and enforced in the organization and admission of new States. The Constitution provides, as we have seen, that *no person* shall be deprived of life, liberty, or property, without due process of law. It makes no distinction either on account of complexion or birth—it secures these rights to all persons within its exclusive jurisdiction. This is equality. It protects not only life and liberty, but also property, the product of labor. It contemplates that no man shall be wrongfully deprived of the fruit of his toil any more than of his life. . . .[22]

The foregoing are excerpts from speeches that Bingham delivered in 1857 and 1859. The due process guarantee was no less important to him in 1866. Delivered in his oratorical style, the following passage from a speech urging adoption of an early version of Section 1 of the Fourteenth Amendment reveals Bingham's commitment to a natural rights perspective holding due process to embody the highest reaches of justice:

Your Constitution provides that no man, no matter what his color, no matter beneath what sky he may have been born, no matter in what disastrous conflict or by what tyrannical hand his liberty may have been cloven down, no matter how poor, no matter how friendless, no matter how ignorant, shall be deprived of life or liberty or property without due process of law—law in its highest sense, that law which is the perfection of human reason, and which is impartial, equal, exact justice; that justice that requires that every man shall have his right; that justice which is the highest duty of nations as it is the imperishable attribute of God of nations.[23]

[20]*Congressional Globe*, 35th Cong., 2d Sess. 983 (1859).
[21]Ibid., p. 985.
[22]*Congressional Globe*, 34th Cong., 3d Sess., app. 140 (1857).
[23]*Congressional Globe* (1866), p. 1094.

IV. Advocates of Substantive Due Process

Antislavery Advocates

While they may not have expressed themselves so passionately, most Republican congressmen, with their antislavery backgrounds, held views similar to Bingham's. Interestingly, Rep. Wilson (chairman of the House judiciary committee) asserted that the Civil Rights Act merely applied the protections of the Fifth Amendment's due process clause to the states.[24]

Due process was an often-used term before, during, and after the Civil War. Both sides of the slavery controversy employed it to further their own causes. Proslavery forces contended that slaves were property and therefore owners were protected against loss without due process. In contrast, beginning in the mid-1830s, antislavery activists thought of the due process guarantee as "constitutionalizing" their natural rights beliefs in the sanctity of life, liberty, and property. They repudiated any notion that a person could be someone else's property; people possessed property in their own selves and the due process clause obligated the national government to secure it in the territories.

The due process concept was a major verbal weapon for the abolitionists. Howard Jay Graham (the respected Fourteenth Amendment scholar) observed that due process "was snatched up, bandied about, 'corrupted and corroded', if you please, for more than thirty years prior to 1866. For every black letter usage in court, there were perhaps hundreds or thousands in the press, red schoolhouse, and on the stump. Zealots, reformers and politicians—not jurists—blazed the paths of substantive due process."[25]

Thus the political parties committed to eradicating slavery used the term "due process" to advance this position. In 1843 the Liberty Party platform declared that the Fifth Amendment's due process clause legally secured the inalienable rights referred to in the Declaration of Independence.[26] The 1848 and 1852 platforms of the Free Soil Party contended that the clause served both as a restraint on the federal government and as an obligation on the government to enforce the inalienable rights set forth in the Declaration.[27] More significantly, according to the 1856 and 1860 platforms of the Republican

---

[24]Ibid., p. 1294.

[25]Howard Jay Graham, *Everyman's Constitution* (Madison, Wisc.: State Historical Society of Wisconsin, 1968), p. 250.

[26]tenBroek, *Equal Under Law*, p. 139.

[27]Ibid., pp. 140–41, n. 3 and n. 4.

party, the clause denied Congress the power to allow slavery to exist in any territory in the Union: "[I]t becomes our duty to maintain [the due process provision] by legislation against all attempts to violate it."[28] Some of those involved in the drafting or consideration of the Republican platforms would probably later, as members of Congress or in other political roles, be responsible for framing or adopting the Fourteenth Amendment. In the 1856 political campaign, "due process of law" was a leading catch phrase of Republican orators.[29]

Corporate Advocates

Due process advocacy was not confined to the antislavery movement. At the time the Fourteenth Amendment was being framed, insurance and other corporations submitted large numbers of petitions to Congress that were permeated with due process of law reasoning, urging federal relief from state legislation depriving them of property and economic freedoms.[30] Commentators have noted the commonality of interests between corporate and civil rights groups: Each group thought it would benefit from the imposition of due process, just compensation, and privileges and immunities restraints on the states.[31] Both accordingly lobbied for these positions. The abolition of slavery eliminated the argument over ownership of the person, and all sides could thereafter promote personal freedom under the same reasoning.

Judicial Advocates

This layman's perception of due process was reflected to a considerable degree in the courts. While the contours of due process are never precise, it was a definable legal concept in 1866, and to this extent the framers of the Fourteenth Amendment spoke with clarity, obviating the need to inquire into their intentions. By then it was accepted that due process required certain processes and procedures in civil and criminal law. In this respect due process was a substantive restraint on state legislatures, forbidding them from passing these kinds of oppressive laws. There was also considerable precedent that due process of law went much further and that it protected ownership. In 1857 Chief Justice Taney invoked substantive due process as one basis for his decision in the *Dred Scott* case. Taney held that Congress had no power to prohibit slavery in specified areas because

[28]Ibid., p. 141, n. 5 and n. 6.
[29]Graham, *Everyman's Constitution*, p. 80.
[30]Ibid., pp. 83–88.
[31]Ibid., p. 81.

the "powers over person and property . . . are not granted to Congress, but are in express terms denied, and they are forbidden to exercise them." Taney explained this "express" limitation as follows:

> And an act of Congress which deprives a citizen of the United States of his liberty or property, merely because he came himself or brought his property into a particular Territory of the United States, and who has committed no offense against the laws, could hardly be dignified with the name of due process of law.[32]

Substantive due process was a very viable concept among Supreme Court justices at the time the Fourteenth Amendment was framed and ratified. In a federal circuit court case in 1865, Supreme Court Justice Grier held that a Pennsylvania statute repealing a railroad corporation charter violated the due course of law provision of the state constitution.[33] The first high court ruling on due process after framing of the amendment was *Hepburn v. Griswold*, delivered February 7, 1870[34] by a court then consisting of seven members, all appointed prior to Congress' action. For the majority of four, Chief Justice Chase held (among other matters) that holders of promissory contracts entered into prior to the effective date of the Legal Tender Act of 1862 were deprived by that act of the right to receive payment in gold or silver coin in violation of the Fifth Amendment's due process guarantee. Justice Grier was then no longer a member of the Court, but had been when the case was decided in conference on November 27, 1869, at which time he concurred with the majority.

The majority concluded that the due process clause protects holders of contracts to the same extent that it does owners of real property. According to Chase, the clause (as well as other provisions of the Fifth Amendment) operates "directly in limitation and restraint of the legislative powers conferred by the Constitution." Justice Miller, for the minority of three, did not deny that the clause was a substantive limitation on the legislature. He objected that the effect on holders of contracts was incidental to the purpose of the Congress to further the war effort. President Grant subsequently appointed two justices who on May 1, 1871 in *Knox v. Lee*[35] joined with the three dissenters to reverse *Hepburn*. Writing for the majority in *Knox*, Justice Strong applied the same analysis to the due process issue as Miller had, and Chase followed his prior interpretation.

---

[32]Dred Scott v. Sanford, 60 U.S. (19 How.) 393, 450 (1857).
[33]Baltimore v. Pittsburgh and Conellesville Railroad, 2 F. Cas. 570, No. 827 (C.C.W.D. Pa. 1865).
[34]75 U.S. (8 Wall.) 603 (1870).
[35]79 U.S. (12 Wall.) 457 (1871).

One of the dissenting justices in *Hepburn* was Swayne, and he and newly appointed Justice Bradley voted with the majority in *Knox*. Neither should be considered antagonistic to substantive due process. On the contrary, both contended in their dissents in the *Slaughter-House Cases*,[36] which was decided the following year, that the Fourteenth Amendment's due process clause secured property and economic interests. On the issue of protecting vested property interests, these two justices would probably have agreed with the four who had made up the majority in *Hepburn*. In *Knox*, Bradley filed a concurring opinion, arguing that Congress had full power to enact the disputed legislation. He did not discuss due process directly. Presumably Swayne agreed, although he did not file a separate opinion in either case.

At the state level, due process clauses were also applied to strike down legislative interferences with property. A leading pre-Civil War decision on due process at the state level was *Wynehamer v. People*,[37] an 1856 New York case involving a state penal statute forbidding the sale of intoxicating liquors owned at the time of enactment (except for medicinal and religious purposes) and requiring the destruction of such as were intended for sale. *Wynehamer* declared that the statute violated the state constitution's due process clause. New York's highest court held that the clause protected the prerogatives of ownership; that is, while some regulation is possible, said one of the justices, "where [property] rights are acquired by the citizen under the existing law, there is no power in any branch of the government to take them away."

The most influential commentator in the period following the ratification of the Fourteenth Amendment, Justice Thomas Cooley of the Michigan Supreme Court, also asserted that due process secured property rights. In the first edition of his famous book on constitutional limitations, published in 1868, he concluded that government can violate due process by the limitations it imposes

> and not [by] any considerations of mere form. . . . When the government, through its established agencies, interferes with the title to one's property, or with his independent enjoyment of it, and its act is called in question as not in accordance with the law of the land, we are to test its validity by those principles of civil liberty and constitutional defense which have become established in our system of law, and not by any rules that pertain to forms of procedure merely. . . . Due process of law in each particular case means, such an exertion of the powers of government as the settled maxims of

[36]83 U.S. (16 Wall.) 36 (1872).
[37]13 N.Y. 378 (1856).

law sanction, and under such safeguards for the protection of individual rights as those maxims prescribe for the class of cases to which the one in question belongs.[38]

Cooley conceded that private rights to property may be interfered with by any branch of government:

> The chief restriction is that vested rights must not be disturbed; but in its application as a shield of protection, the term "vested rights" is not used in any narrow or technical sense, as importing a power of legal control merely, but rather as implying a vested interest which it is equitable the government should recognize, and of which the individual cannot be deprived without injustice.[39]

He went on to discuss those property interests protected by due process (or its equivalent, law of the land) clauses. Thus, according to this authoritative commentator, due process at the time the Fourteenth Amendment came into being provided substantive safeguards for property interests; Cooley rejected the view that due process had no more than procedural significance in civil matters. As previously indicated, this position was probably accepted by a majority of the U.S. Supreme Court then and in many subsequent years.

Understandably, due process did not remain limited to securing vested interests. Deciding the issue on a case-to-case basis, as is typical of American jurisprudence, the Supreme Court enlarged the protections of the due process clauses to include, by 1897, the liberty to contract for the production, distribution, and sale of goods and services. In *Allgeyer v. Louisiana*, Justice Peckham explained the unanimous ruling:

> The liberty in [the Fourteenth Amendment's due process clause] means not only the right of the citizen to be free from the mere physical restraint of his person, as by incarceration, but the term is deemed to embrace the right of the citizen to be free in the enjoyment of all his faculties: to be free to use them in all lawful ways; to live and work where he will; to earn his livelihood by any lawful calling; to pursue any livelihood or avocation, and for that purpose to enter into all contracts which may be proper, necessary and essential to his carrying out to a successful conclusion the purposes above mentioned.[40]

The Court thus eliminated the dubious distinction between property and contract rights, a distinction that cannot be supported in terms of either personal freedom or public welfare.

---

[38]Thomas M. Cooley, *A Treatise on the Constitutional Limitations*, reprint of 1868 edition (New York: Da Capo Press, 1972), p. 356.

[39]Ibid., pp. 357–58.

[40]Allgeyer v. Louisiana, 165 U.S. 578, 589 (1897).

V. Conclusion

Due process does not bar all governmental restraints in the area it impacts; it forbids unjustified restraints. This is consistent with long-held Anglo-American conceptions about the limits of governmental powers. Thus Blackstone defined civil liberty as "no other than natural liberty so far restrained by human laws (and no farther) as is necessary and expedient for the general advantage of the public."[41] Similarly, Justice Washington asserted in *Corfield* that the fundamental liberties he designated belonged by right to citizens of all free governments, but were "[s]ubject nevertheless to such restraints as the government may justly provide for the general good of the whole." Rep. Bingham accepted these views but likely would have demanded that a very high burden of proof be borne by the government in justifying a restraint.

The inquiry usually conducted by the U.S. Supreme Court in the economic due process cases between 1897 and 1937 was consistent with the Framers' understanding of the due process clause of the Fourteenth Amendment. It was also a logical progression of American law on the subject. By 1897 the technical definition of due process, in the normal course of adjudication, had gone from the inclusion of vested property rights (in the 1860s) to comprehending contracts of employment. This development was not antagonistic to the basic rationale of due process nor to an unrealistic extension in meaning. Constitutional adjudication does not preclude sensible movement in interpretation. Thus, when *Lochner* was decided in 1905, the constitutional outcome should have been the same, whether the interpretation relied on the judicial or the Framers' meaning of due process. In either case, it is clear that economic liberties are firmly rooted in the due process clause of the Fourteenth Amendment.

[41]Blackstone, *Commentaries*, vol. 1, pp. 121–22.

PART II

PROPERTY RIGHTS, ACTIVISM, AND THE JUDICIAL PROCESS

7

A PROPERTY RIGHTS APPROACH TO JUDICIAL DECISION MAKING

Wesley J. Liebeler

I. Introduction

Ronald Coase's discussion of the railroad train strewing sparks as it steamed its way across the English countryside has had a profound effect on the way we think about the law.[1] The relevance of Coase's model to torts and environmental law is clear, and it has been widely applied in those fields.[2] His treatment of the problem of social cost, however, provides a useful approach to a much wider range of legal problems. In this paper I briefly restate his basic points, supplement them with Harold Demsetz's theory of property rights, and apply the result to a number of different legal issues.

Professor Coase specifically examined "those actions of business firms which have harmful effects on others."[3] One example is the situation in which sparks from a locomotive set fire to crops along the track. Most would instinctively conclude that the railroad had "caused" the losses resulting from these fires. A court sharing these instincts and confronted with a tort action by farmers whose crops had burned would probably make the railroad pay the entire loss. When we finish reading Coase however, we know that the loss was "caused" just as much by the flammables along the track as it was by the sparks.

The author is Professor of Law and John M. Olin Distinguished Scholar at the University of California at Los Angeles.

[1]Ronald Coase, "The Problem of Social Cost," *Journal of Law and Economics* 3 (October 1960): 1–44.

[2]See, for example, William M. Landes and Richard Posner, "Causation in Tort Law: An Economic Approach," *Journal of Legal Studies* 12 (January 1983): 109–34; John Brown, "Toward an Economic Theory of Liability," *Journal of Legal Studies* 2 (June 1973): 323–50; Mark Grady, "Proximate Cause and the Law of Negligence," *Iowa Law Review* 69 (January 1984): 363–450; Mark Grady, "A Positive Theory of Negligence," *Yale Law Journal* 92 (April 1983): 799–830 and authorities cited in Grady, "Proximate Cause," notes 1–3.

[3]Coase, "Social Cost," p. 1.

Coase showed that the configuration of crops grown along the track and the steps taken by the railroad to control spark emissions will be the same no matter how the court decides the case, as long as the costs of dealing between the railroad and the adjoining farmers are low.[4] Suppose the court held the railroad liable. If it were cheaper to install spark arresters than to pay the farmers to leave a strip of land fallow along the tracks, a rational railroad would install them. If the opposite were true, however, the railroad would presumably pay the farmers to leave the strip fallow.[5]

Suppose, however, that the railroad is absolved. If it is cheaper to leave the strip fallow than stop the sparks, the farmers will leave the strip fallow rather than have their crops burned each year. If the value of the crops that can be grown on the strip exceeds the cost of spark arresters, however, the farmers would be smart to plant the strip in crops and pay the railroad to stop the sparks.

The solution to the conflict between the railroad and the farmers need not involve all spark arresters and no strip of fallow land or vice versa. A combination of steps by both parties to reduce the cost of fires is in fact more likely. If transaction costs are low, there is no reason to suppose that the parties will not reach a solution that leaves them all about as well off as they could be under the circumstances.[6] When the parties improve their own positions in this way, they also increase the total wealth of society as a whole.

While Coase dealt specifically with harmful externalities, his analysis also is relevant to beneficial externalities. Either type of externality produces a misallocation of resources as compared to that which would exist if the externality could be efficiently eliminated.[7] To the extent that it is cost effective, therefore, judicial (and other public) decisions should try to eliminate externalities of both types.

We can extract three guides for judicial decision making from this elementary story of sparks and crops. Judicial decisions would make it easier for private parties to reduce the total cost of dealing with reciprocal claims to scarce resources if they (1) defined property

---

[4]More precisely, given zero transaction costs, the allocation of relevant resources would be the same no matter how the court decided the case. See Coase, "Social Cost," pp. 6–7. See also, Harold Demsetz, "Toward a Theory of Property Rights," *American Economic Review* 57 (May 1967): 347–73.

[5]One way for the railroad to do this, of course, would be to buy such a strip of land from those who own land adjoining the tracks.

[6]See Elizabeth Hoffman and Mathew Spitzer, "The Coase Theorem: Some Experimental Tests," *Journal of Law and Economics* 25 (April 1982): 73–98.

[7]Externalities could be "efficiently" eliminated whenever the costs of doing so were less than the benefits.

rights precisely, (2) unambiguously assigned such rights, and (3) decided cases in ways that otherwise tended to reduce private transaction costs.[8]

An additional guide to decision making emerges from situations in which the costs of dealing in markets exceeds the possible gains from such transactions. A court's decision in these cases is more important than it is in cases where the parties can reallocate resources by private contract. Inefficiencies created by an "erroneous" decision will tend to persist until the legal rule is changed to produce a more efficient result. Even though an inefficient legal rule provides incentives for its future challenge,[9] the social cost of "wrong" decisions will be greater than in those cases where transaction costs are low enough to permit changes by private contract.

Where transaction costs are high, courts could increase society's wealth by assigning property rights as closely as possible to the way in which they would be allocated by the affected parties themselves, assuming that transaction costs were low enough to permit market exchanges.[10] Coase recognized that the government could act as a "super-firm" to raise the value of production in cases where transaction costs were intractably great. He noted that unless the arrangement of rights established by the legal system was the one that brought "about a greater value of production than any other," the costs of market transactions might be so great as to prevent that "optimal arrangement of rights" from being achieved.[11]

The specification of property rights that maximizes social wealth at one time need not produce the same result when conditions change. Harold Demsetz makes this point in his explanation of how private property rights in land developed among Indians engaged in the fur trade.[12] Private property in land was not common among the early American Indians. Not only have anthropologists noted the existence of such property among the Indians of Eastern Canada but they also

---

[8]Increasing the predictability of results in future legal cases is one example of how courts could act to reduce such costs. Professor Coase states: "Of course, if market transactions were costless, all that matters (questions of equity aside) is that the rights of the various parties should be well defined and the results of legal actions easy to forecast." Coase, "Social Cost," p. 19.

[9]See Paul Rubin, "Why Is the Common Law Efficient?," *Journal of Legal Studies* 6 (January 1977): 51–64; George Priest, "The Common Law Process and the Selection of Efficient Rules," *Journal of Legal Studies* 6 (January 1977): 65–83.

[10]See Harold Demsetz, "When Does the Rule of Liability Matter?," *Journal of Legal Studies* 1 (January 1972): 13–28.

[11]Coase, "Social Cost," p. 16.

[12]Demsetz, "Toward a Theory of Property Rights," pp. 349–50.

have shown a close relationship between its development and the rise of the commercial fur trade.

Before the fur trade became important, Indians hunted beaver and other game on commonly held land. Since there was no general control over this hunting, no one had an incentive to invest in increasing or maintaining the stock of game. While there was clearly an externality present (hunting by one Indian could impose some harmful effects on others), it was not a serious problem because there was enough game available to satisfy local demand.[13]

Demsetz suggests that the rise of the fur trade significantly raised the value of furs to the Indians and sharply pushed up the scale of hunting. These changes increased the impact of the externalities associated with hunting on commonly held land. Demsetz says: "The property right system began to change, and it changed specifically in the direction required to take account of the economic effects made important by the fur trade."[14]

The property rights system changed so as to recognize private property rights in land. In Eastern Canada this change reduced the problems associated with overhunting:

> Forest animals confine their territories to relatively small areas, so that the cost of internalizing the effects of husbanding these animals is considerably reduced. This reduced cost, together with the higher commercial value of fur-bearing forest animals [as compared with plains animals, which were not associated with private property rights in land], made it productive to establish private hunting lands.[15]

Demsetz suggests that "property rights arise when it becomes economic for those affected by externalities to internalize benefits and costs."[16] He suggests that new property rights will tend to emerge "in response to changes in technology and relative prices."[17] A simple example can be constructed by applying Demsetz's analysis to the case of sparks and crops discussed by Coase. An equilibrium set of property rights that might have been developed between the railroad and adjoining landowners would be upset by changes in technology that made it cheaper to build effective spark arresters. Similar effects would result, for example, from the advent of diesel engines, relative

---

[13]Demsetz states that "these external effects were of such small significance that it did not pay for anyone to take them into account." Ibid.

[14]Ibid., p. 350.

[15]Ibid., p. 351.

[16]Ibid., p. 352.

[17]Ibid., p. 348.

increases in the demand for crops, changes in agricultural productivity and other similar developments.

The effects of these changes would be taken into account by the private transactions of the affected parties if transaction costs were relatively low. If transaction costs were high, however, a change in legal rules would be necessary to reallocate resources efficiently in response to changes in underlying technological or demand conditions. As always, these changes in legal rules would increase social wealth to the extent that they replicate the allocation of resources that would result from the choices of the affected parties themselves, assuming that transaction costs were low enough to permit such choices to be expressed in market exchanges.

It is useful to apply these ideas to some current problems in antitrust law, to the question of judicial review of economic regulation, and to some free speech problems under the First Amendment.

II. Property Rights and Antitrust Analysis

I want to apply the analysis sketched above to the antitrust law governing relationships between suppliers and their resellers—a law that has been confused and inconsistent for a long time.[18] To lead into that discussion, however, I want to show that the principles outlined above were operative at the very beginning of Sherman Antitrust Act jurisprudence and, indeed, even prior to that time, in the common law of restraint of trade. Once this fact has been demonstrated, it will be evident that the application of these principles to modern antitrust problems is part of a long-honored tradition. It is not simply a recent invention of so-called Chicago economists.

The Early Law

In developing the Ancillary Restraints Doctrine in *Addyston Pipe & Steel*,[19] Circuit Judge William Howard Taft noted that at one time the common law had proscribed all restraints of trade. After a time, however, "it became apparent to the people and the courts" that trade would be improved if certain restraints of trade were enforced. Taft discussed five specific restraints:

1. A seller's agreement not to compete with a buyer of a business so as to protect the transfer of good will;

---

[18]See White Motor Company v. U.S., 372 U.S. 291 (1963); U.S. v. Arnold, Schwinn & Co., 338 U.S. 365 (1967); Continental T.V., Inc. v. GTE Sylvania, Inc., 433 U.S. 36 (1977); Wesley J. Liebeler, "Intrabrand 'Cartels' Under GTE Sylvania," *UCLA Law Review* 30 (October 1982): 1–51.

[19]U.S. v. Addyston Pipe & Steel Co., 85 Fed. 271 (6th Cir. 1898).

2. An agreement by dissolving partners not to compete in such a way as to reduce the value of partnership assets distributed amongst them;

3. An agreement of partners not to compete with each other or the partnership pending the existence of the partnership;

4. A buyer's agreement not to use property transferred by a seller in competition with the seller;

5. An employee's agreement not to compete with his employer after the end of the employment.[20]

Two important points emerge from Taft's discussion of this change in the common law. First, the recognition of property rights is based on a cost-benefit analysis. Each of the property rights created when the five types of contracts which Taft discussed came to be enforced reduced externalities. By enforcing these contracts, the law permitted the returns from certain activities to be obtained by those who engaged in them, thereby encouraging those activities to be undertaken. These property rights would not have been enforced, however, if the courts had not been able to conclude that the social benefits of the activities encouraged by such enforcement exceeded their social costs. This conclusion flows not only from the reasons that Taft gave for generally enforcing these contracts but also from the reasons that he gave for not enforcing either "naked" restraints of trade or certain of the above contracts when it appeared that they were being used to create a "monopoly."

In considering Taft's explanation of why the common law came to enforce the above contracts, consider first a seller's contracts not to compete with buyers of his business. Taft wrote:

> It was of importance *as an incentive to industry and honest dealing in trade* that, after a man had built up a business with an extensive good will, he should be able to sell his business and good will to the best advantage, and he could not do so unless he could bind himself by an enforceable contract not to engage in the same business in such a way as to prevent injury to that which he was about to sell.[21]

The inability to create a property right so as to transfer goodwill in connection with the sale of a business would prevent both buyers and sellers from obtaining full returns from their investments. The sellers would not be able to transfer the goodwill they had created while operating the businesses. This would reduce the number of

[20]Id. at 280–81.
[21]Id. at 280; emphasis added.

businesses sold and reduce the investment in producing customer satisfaction that creates goodwill in the first place. The inability of buyers to obtain a return on their investment in purchased goodwill would reinforce both of the effects just described. The existence of these externalities would reduce consumer welfare. It appears that the benefits of a system of property rights that eliminates these externalities without producing other harmful effects exceeds its costs.[22]

The cost-benefit underpinnings of property rights also are shown by the types of arrangements that the law refused to countenance. Taft noted that contracts to sell a business and its goodwill or to create a partnership or corporation would be illegal if they were "only part of a plan to acquire all the property used in one business by one management with a view to establishing a monopoly."[23] The mere tendency of the provisions of a contract to restrain competition, however, was not enough to make it illegal. There had to be an actual intent to monopolize; the restraint of competition had to be the main purpose of the contract and "the transfer of property and good will, or the partnership agreement, . . . merely ancillary and subordinate to that purpose."[24]

Taft also held naked restraints of trade to be illegal. Naked restraints were those not ancillary to the main and lawful purpose of a contract or those that were broader than necessary to protect the parties in effecting that main purpose. Today these arrangements are illegal per se; they have a potential to restrict output and do not have any significant efficiency creating capacity.

Agreements aimed at monopoly of the type discussed above[25] and naked restraints of trade have one thing in common: It is almost

---

[22]The fact that the recognition of property rights turned on the outcome of a social cost-benefit analysis also appears from Taft's treatment of agreements not to compete among partners who were dissolving their relationship. He wrote: "It was equally *for the good of the public and trade,* that when partners dissolved, and one took the business or they divided the business, that each partner might bind himself not to do anything in trade thereafter which would derogate from his grant of the interest conveyed to his former partner." Id. at 280, emphasis added.

Enforcing contracts like this eliminated externalities. Taft's focus on *"for the good of the public and trade"* clearly indicates his view that the common law came to enforce such contracts between dissolving partners because the effect was to reduce net social costs or to increase net social benefits. Similarly, enforcement of agreements between partners not to compete pending the existence of the partnership was justified on the grounds that it would promote the formation of businesses "useful to the community." Id. at 280–81.

[23]Id. at 291.

[24]Id.

[25]Taft seems to have referred to a monopoly whose main purpose is the restriction of output. It is one formed by acquisition and merger, not one that developed through

certain that their social costs will exceed their social benefits. Their very purpose is to create external harmful effects that would be eliminated if transaction costs were low enough to allow the interests of all affected parties to be taken into account. In holding them to be illegal, the law eliminated externalities and moved toward a more efficient allocation of resources.

The second important point to emerge from Taft's discussion is that the common law changed in response to underlying social and economic conditions in ways that were consistent with Demsetz's hypothesis that "property rights arise when it becomes economic for those affected by externalities to internalize benefits and costs."[26] As Taft noted, "After a time it became apparent to the people and the courts that it was in the interest of trade that certain covenants in restraint of trade should be enforced."[27] Taft did not mean by this that hitherto obscure ideas had suddenly become clear. He meant, rather, that conditions had changed so that the benefits of enforcing these contracts—at least where monopoly was not involved—came to exceed the costs.[28]

It is not hard to see the general nature of these changes. Society's movement from farms and villages to towns and cities, from *Gemeinschaft* to *Gesellschaft*, had the same kinds of effects as the rise of the fur trade had on the Indians of Eastern Canada. Covenants not to compete so as to facilitate the transfer of goodwill were not needed when the business was handed down from father to son, generation after generation. Indeed, goodwill itself is an asset of greater value in an impersonal society (*Gesellschaft*) than in one where the relevant actors have known each other most or all of their lives and expect to deal with each other again and again in the future (*Gemeinschaft*). Goodwill, or brand-name capital, is a method of providing information about expected future performance. It is not as important in the village as it is in a society where dealings span wider horizons and where the number of localized repeat transactions is likely to be fewer.

"natural" growth. It must be shown that the acquisitions were only part of a plan to establish a monopoly, and the actual intent to monopolize must appear. If its main purpose is the restriction of output, its costs, by definition, will exceed its benefits. See Oliver Williamson, "Economies as an Antitrust Defense: The Welfare Tradeoffs," *American Economic Review* 58 (December 1968): 18–36; Wesley J. Liebeler, "Market Power and Competitive Superiority in Concentrated Industries," *UCLA Law Review* 25 (1978): 1260–61.

[26] Demsetz, "Toward a Theory of Property Rights," p. 352.
[27] 85 Fed. at 280.
[28] Id.

The movement away from the close-knit, traditional relationships of earlier common law times toward a more impersonal, market-oriented society made the older rules inefficient, just as the development of diesel engines would prompt a revision of the relationship between the railroad and the adjoining farmers. New externalities developed or became more pronounced. As a result new opportunities for gains from trade appeared; it became economic for the affected parties to internalize benefits and costs. The common law changed its views on the value of certain restraints of trade *because their social value had in fact changed.*

We can see from *Addyston Pipe* that from the very beginning of antitrust jurisprudence, the question of what property rights the legal system would recognize was resolved on the basis of cost-benefit analysis. Property rights would be recognized when the social benefits of the activities encouraged by such recognition exceeded their social costs. Another way to view the process described by Taft is to say that the law recognized those property rights that tended to internalize the costs and benefits of economic activities. By doing this the law enabled people to increase consumer welfare by their own voluntary exchanges.

The problems raised by restricted distribution systems are similar to those Taft confronted in *Addyston Pipe*. This is an important point, and once it is understood, attempts to loosen the antitrust strictures against restricted distribution arrangements can be seen as part of an antitrust tradition going back to the very beginnings of American antitrust law.

Restricted Distribution Systems

Lester Telser first described the central economic problem that suppliers attempt to solve by limiting the behavior of their resellers.[29] The clearest legal recognition of this problem appeared in *Continental T.V., Inc. v. GTE Sylvania, Inc.*[30] In this case the Supreme Court noted that restrictions on distributors could be used to induce investment in "promotional activities or to provide service and repair facilities necessary to the efficient marketing of their [the manufacturers'] product."[31] The Court said:

> Because of market imperfections such as the so-called "free-rider" effect, these services might not be provided by retailers in a purely

[29]Lester Telser, "Why Should Manufacturers Want Fair Trade?," *Journal of Law and Economics* 3 (October 1960): 86–105.
[30]433 U.S. 36 (1977).
[31]433 U.S. at 55.

competitive situation, despite the fact that each retailer's benefit would be greater if all provided the services than if none did.[32]

The "so-called 'free-rider' effect," of course, is an externality. In Telser's paradigm, one retailer provides point-of-sale product information to a consumer, and the consumer takes it and buys the product from another retailer who offers lower prices because it does not incur the costs of providing such information. The case of *Klor's, Inc. v. Broadway-Hale Stores, Inc.*[33] provides a striking example of this effect. In this case the Broadway maintained a showroom to display major household appliances. Klor's sold the same appliances next door, from a store that had nothing in it but catalogs. No extended explanation is needed to understand the problem created by this arrangement.[34]

The free-rider problem can be solved if some sort of property right can be created in the product information produced by individual distributors. The externality can be eliminated if resellers who produce information can exclude other distributors from its use.

It is a mystery why the law has made this so difficult to do, but it has.[35] Manufacturers seek to induce the production of product information by retailers because they believe that some consumers wish to purchase it. There is no reason to suppose that resources used to produce such information are inherently less productive than resources devoted to the production of consumer satisfaction (goodwill) in general.[36] Even if there were such a reason, it would not make sense for the law to prevent parties from obtaining a full return on their investment in the former. Only by facilitating such a return can we even know how much "promotional activities" at the retail level consumers actually desire, or if they desire any at all.

---

[32]Id.

[33]359 U.S. 207 (1959).

[34]Problems such as this one will be more severe—that is, will cause greater externalities—as consumer products become more complex and as consumer income increases. Other things being equal, high-income consumers will be more likely than lower-income consumers to buy product information than produce it for themselves. The Demsetz theory of property rights suggests that changes such as this (increased product complexity and increased value of consumer time) will tend to prompt a change in the property rights system in locally produced product information. This may help explain the persistence that suppliers seem to demonstrate in getting their resellers to produce this sort of information.

[35]See, for example, Monsanto Co. v. Spray-Rite Service Corp., 104 S.Ct. 1464 (1984).

[36]The problem of "monopoly" or "naked restraints of trade" is no more likely to be present in the latter case than in the former. There is, therefore, just as much reason to recognize property rights in locally produced product information as in general goodwill.

The approach that Taft used in *Addyston Pipe,* therefore, readily solves the economic problem presented in the restricted distribution cases. When this approach is fully understood, it also becomes clear that that case is legal precedent for the general legality (enforceability) of contracts that parties make to create property rights in local product information. Indeed, *Addyston Pipe* can be viewed as general support for the legality of all business arrangements aimed at eliminating externalities.

III. Property Rights and Judicial Review of Economic Regulation

The history of the decline of economic due process is too familiar to need recounting here.[37] Many constitutional scholars who otherwise strongly favor market processes oppose significant expansion of judicial involvement in such matters. This is partly because they believe there are no intelligible standards to assess the constitutionality of economic regulation. In the absence of such standards, judges would simply be substituting their own views about the desirability of particular pieces of economic regulation for those of the legislature.

The lack-of-standards argument could be a considerable objection to a renaissance of judicial scrutiny of economic regulation if it were true, but it is not true. In this section I will sketch the standards for judicial review of economic regulation that are implicit in the property rights approach described above.

Standards for Judicial Review of Economic Regulation

Suppose the Supreme Court applied the same *verbal* standard in reviewing economic regulation that it now applies to regulation of speech and the press.[38] Government restrictions on economic freedom would be unconstitutional unless the government could show that they served a compelling state interest.

Our problem is to provide operational content for the expression "compelling state interest" as applied to economic regulation. It is hard to see how there can be a compelling state interest in adopting an economic regulation that could not make the affected parties better off *in their own view of the matter* than they would have been

---

[37]See Bernard H. Siegan, *Economic Liberties and the Constitution* (Chicago: University of Chicago Press, 1980), pp. 3–23. Siegan offers a powerful argument that the courts should expand the scope of their review of economic regulation.

[38]Under the present view, these and other so-called fundamental liberties are thought to be more important than the right to try to earn a living in the calling of one's choice. See, for example, City of New Orleans v. Dukes, 427 U.S. 297 (1976).

without the regulation. If this is true, then the first standard that emerges from the analysis outlined above is that there cannot be a compelling state interest in regulation that prevents people from expressing their own choices in situations where there are no persistent, significant third-party effects. There will not be any such effects where affected parties are able to conduct market exchanges at relatively low costs. If the railroad and the adjoining landowners could readily deal with each other on the issue of sparks and crops, there would be no legitimate reason for the state to interfere.

This first standard would outlaw economic regulation unless it addressed situations characterized by significant external costs or benefits and intractably high transaction costs. While this conclusion is perfectly straightforward from an analytical standpoint, its effect is quite far-reaching. It would invalidate an enormous amount of existing regulation and prevent a great deal more. The list of government acts that would be thrown out by this first standard is so long that it makes one ask again if the analysis that leads to it is correct. It is.

A second standard emerges from Coase's suggestion that it might be efficient for government to act as a "super-firm" when there are significant externalities and intractably high transaction costs. Government would make the affected parties best off in such cases if it allocated resources in the same way the parties would if there were zero transaction costs.

This formulation suggests that economic regulation could not be justified unless it produced results roughly consistent with those that the affected parties would reach through private bargains, assuming zero transaction costs. This does not mean that courts should second-guess the state on the general terms of regulation that plausibly meets this test. It does suggest, however, a considerable difficulty in discovering a compelling state interest in regulation that could not plausibly claim to produce effects resembling those that would have emerged from private bargains among the affected parties, assuming zero transaction costs.

This standard implies the existence of three categories of regulation, each of which, interestingly, has an analogue in antitrust law.

Regulation in the first category is like private agreements that are illegal per se. It resembles a negative sum game in that it necessarily reduces the total wealth of society. Because it has such an effect, this type of regulation, by definition, could not emerge from dealings between the affected parties in a hypothetical world of zero transaction costs. Not only is there no compelling state interest in this type of regulation but there is no legitimate state interest in it at all.

A second category of regulation applies to situations in which private transactions might not necessarily take place even in the assumed zero-transaction-cost environment. That is, there may not be any gains from trade available even if transactions could be made at no cost to the affected parties. It differs from the first category of regulation, in which it is known a priori that no mutual gains from trade would be available from private transactions among all affected parties that produced results similar to the regulation, even assuming zero transaction costs. In this second category of regulation, the availability of gains from trade is an empirical question: Such gains may or may not be available. The antitrust analogue is the category of private arrangements the legality of which is assessed under the rule of reason.

Regulation in the third category applies to situations in which significant zero-transaction-cost gains from trade are clearly available. The antitrust analogue here consists of private arrangements that would be legal per se or not be a matter of antitrust concern at all.

The nature of these categories can be made clearer by citing some examples. Regulation in the first category would include state laws which prohibit automobile manufacturers from establishing new dealerships or relocating existing ones without giving notice to existing dealers within the market area. If any of those dealers object, the manufacturer must obtain the permission of a state agency to open the new dealership.[39] Another example is the North Dakota statute requiring a corporation operating a pharmacy to have a majority of its stock owned by registered pharmacists actively engaged in its management and operation.[40] Still another is the Maryland statute prohibiting major refiners from operating retail service stations in that state.[41]

The above regulations were all recently upheld by the Supreme Court, in spite of the fact that the obvious purpose in each was to protect a narrow special interest group from competition. Such reg-

---

[39]See New Motor Vehicle Board v. Fox, 439 U.S. 96 (1978). At least 17 other states have adopted similar statutes. For an empirical estimate of the welfare loss prompted by these statutes, see Richard Smith II, "Franchise Regulation: An Economic Analysis of State Restrictions on Automobile Distribution," *Journal of Law and Economics* 25 (April 1982): 125–58.

[40]See North Dakota State Board of Pharmacy v. Snyder's Drug Stores, Inc., 414 U.S. 156 (1973).

[41]See Exxon v. Maryland, 437 U.S. 117 (1978). This case, the two cases cited in notes 39–40, and other similar cases are discussed in Siegan, *Economic Liberties*, pp. 191–203.

ulation creates externalities by establishing a property rights system that necessarily inflicts harmful effects on some *without producing equalizing benefits for others.*[42] Regulation like this involves more than a wealth transfer from one group to another. Like the traditional private cartel that is illegal per se under the antitrust laws, it necessarily produces a net social loss.[43] Coase's description of the government's role as a "super-firm" that could internalize naturally occurring external effects is as far as it could be from the role of the state in adopting this type of regulation.

An example of regulation in the second category may be found in *Linmark Associates v. Township of Willingboro.*[44] This case involved a successful challenge to the constitutionality of a local ordinance that prohibited the posting of "For Sale" or "Sold" signs on property within the township. The existence of condominiums or private subdivisions where developers offer provisions even more restrictive than the *Willingboro* ordinance suggests that gains from trade might have been available to the affected parties (had they been able to interact in our hypothetical zero-transaction-cost world).

The third category includes regulation dealing with situations in which significant gains from trade are clearly available, again assuming zero transaction costs. Properly designed regulation in this context would conform to Coase's concept of the "super-firm" that attempts to allocate resources efficiently where both transaction costs and external effects are high. Environmental pollution is perhaps the most obvious example.

My analysis does not answer the question of which, if any, of these three types of economic regulation the courts "should" hold unconstitutional, and this question is certainly one on which reasonable people could legitimately disagree. I do not address the question in detail here because my principal purpose is simply to show that a property rights approach provides considerable guidance to the kind of standards that could be applied to constitutional review of economic regulation were the courts to move in that direction.

If the scope of judicial review were expanded, however, regulation in the first of the three categories described above would be, to say

---

[42]It might be appropriate in these cases to view the regulations as a transaction between the benefited special-interest group and the state. The "others" on whom harmful external effects were visited would be those whose interests were not fully taken into account in the transaction by which the regulation was "purchased."

[43]This type of regulation produces allocative losses identical to those produced by private cartels. Indeed, regulation in this first category could be viewed as a cartel established by the state.

[44]431 U.S. 85 (1977).

the least, a most attractive candidate for increased scrutiny. If the same standard were applied to economic regulation that is now accorded to the so-called fundamental liberties, most or all regulation in the second category and some in the third category would also become constitutionally suspect.[45]

It is hard to disagree with Professors Bernard H. Siegan and Richard Epstein that some expansion of judicial review of regulation that deprives us of important freedoms is in order. The analysis that I have outlined above suggests that state action which produces the same or more harmful effects as private arrangements that would be per se illegal under the antitrust laws would be a good place to start.

IV. Property Rights and the First Amendment

Many free speech cases raise the same problem confronted by the railroad and the adjoining landowners. In both types of cases the parties compete for the use of a scarce resource. In Coase's paradigm the railroad wants to emit sparks, which the adjoining landowners do not want. In many free speech cases the parties at whom the speech is aimed view it in the same way that farmers view sparks from the locomotive. They do not want to receive the speech any more than the adjoining landowners want to receive sparks. The problem in all these cases is to find a solution that minimizes the social cost of these encounters.

Coase's solution is just as relevant to free speech cases as it is to the railroad case. Where transaction costs are low, courts should define and assign property rights to assist private parties reach a solution that is most satisfactory to all those involved. Where transaction costs are high, courts should assign rights so as to approximate the result that the affected parties would produce through private bargains in a zero-transaction-cost world.

---

[45]Cases in the third category are the only ones that would involve a balancing problem of constitutional dimensions. Cases in the second category, such as *Willingboro*, also will involve balancing, but only on the question of whether the regulation produces net social gains. The constitutional balancing issue will arise only if the existence of such gains is clear and they are significantly large. Here it will be necessary to make some kind of tradeoff between freedom and increased efficiency, and there clearly will be times when the claims of increased efficiency will be paramount over those of freedom. No sensible society, for example, would leave its members free to drive heavily polluting automobiles until it is on the verge of having everyone wear gas masks to survive. At the margin these tradeoffs will be difficult to make. How much economic gain would justify how much restriction of freedom is a question of judgment about which economic analysis has little or nothing to say. My own view is that freedom counts for considerably more than economic efficiency. Happily we do not often have to make the choice between the two.

In this section I consider examples of each case, in the order described above.

Accommodation Where Transaction Costs Are Low

A series of cases extending from *Marsh v. Alabama*[46] to *PruneYard Shopping Center v. Robins*[47] raises questions about the extent to which owners of company towns and shopping centers can exclude those who wish to speak, picket, or otherwise express themselves. In *Marsh* the Supreme Court held that the owners of a company town could not prevent a Jehovah's Witness from distributing leaflets on its streets. It extended this rule to a privately owned shopping center in *Food Employees Local 590 v. Logan Valley Plaza, Inc.*[48]

The Court later backed away from the proposition that the First Amendment guarantees speakers access to privately owned shopping centers, overruling *Logan Valley* in *Hudgens v. NLRB*.[49] In *Prune-Yard*, however, the Court affirmed the California Supreme Court's holding that the liberty of speech clauses of the California constitution "protect speech and petitioning, reasonably exercised, in shopping centers even when the centers are privately owned."[50]

The Court reasoned quite formalistically in these cases, and as a result it never confronted the underlying conflict that exists between different parties for the use of scarce resources. The majority in *Marsh*, for example, thought the important question was whether the company town was enough like "any other American town" to justify applying the rules governing attempts by municipalities to restrict speech on public property. For example, Justice Hugo L. Black wrote:

> Except for [ownership by a private corporation] it [the company town] has all the characteristics of any other American town. The property consists of residential buildings, streets, a system of sewers, a sewage disposal plant and a "business block" on which business places are situated. A deputy of the Mobile County Sheriff, paid by the Company, serves as the town's policeman. Merchants and store establishments have rented the stores and business places on the business block and the United States uses one of the places as a post office from which six carriers deliver mail to the people of Chickasaw and the adjacent territory. . . .[51]

[46]326 U.S. 501 (1946).
[47]447 U.S. 74 (1980).
[48]391 U.S. 308 (1968).
[49]424 U.S. 507 (1976).
[50]23 Cal. 3d 899, 910, 592 P.2d 341, 347; 153 Cal. Rptr. 854, 860 (1979).
[51]326 U.S. at 502–03.

The existence of a sewage system has little to do with the issue. No more relevant was the language in *Logan Valley*. The Court noted the similarities between *Marsh's* business block and the Logan Valley shopping center and concluded that "[t]he shopping center here is clearly the functional equivalent of the business district of Chickasaw involved in *Marsh*."[52]

These similarities are beside the point. Suppose we have two towns identical in all respects except that in one of them the shopping area, streets, and similar resources are "privately" owned, in the sense that their owner can maximize returns from them—that is, will respond to the perceived market demands of interested parties. In the other town those resources are "owned" by the municipality, the representatives of which do not have a direct financial incentive to allocate those resources to their most highly valued uses.

In terms of deciding cases such as *Marsh* and *Logan Valley*, this difference between the two towns is more important than their similarities. When property rights are precisely specified and held in a few hands, transaction costs are likely to be lower than if such rights are not clearly specified or are widely held. Since the owner of the "common areas" of the privately owned town can obtain any increase in value of those resources prompted by his actions, he will act to improve such value until the marginal cost of improvement equals the marginal revenue therefrom. If proselytizing by Jehovah's Witnesses increases the value of the town, the owner of the common areas has a direct incentive to permit it. If not, he has an equally strong incentive to prohibit it.

These direct incentives will not exist where changes in the value of common areas are not visited directly on some utility maximizing entity. They will not, accordingly, be present (or will be reduced) in the usual case, in which common areas are owned by a municipal corporation administered by elected officials. These officials have no particular incentive to determine whether the residents of the town value their peace and quiet more than the Witnesses value their efforts to convert, or vice versa. An optimum resolution of the possible conflict between residents and putative speakers, therefore, is less likely when the common areas are owned by the municipality than when they are privately owned.

If common areas are privately owned and the cost of transactions between that owner and the residents are relatively low, it is hard to see what legitimate interest the government has in intervening. Why would the owner of Chickasaw, Alabama, exclude Jehovah's

[52]391 U.S. at 318.

Witnesses if the affected parties valued the presence of the Witnesses more than their absence?[53]

This market system for deciding between the claims of speech and repose is even more relevant to the shopping center cases, in which transaction costs appear even lower, than in the case of the company town. The shopping center tenants want the shopping center to be attractive to prospective customers. If the customers value being accosted by Jehovah's Witnesses while shopping, the stores have every incentive to let their landlord know. Since the shopping center owner wants his tenants to be happy, as long as the benefits of that joy exceed its costs, there is no reason why the landlord would not admit the Witnesses to the shopping center. If these parties believe, however, that shopping will be more pleasant without the Witnesses, as seems likely to be the case, social costs are minimized by their exclusion. The Witnesses are free, of course, to compensate the shopping center and its tenants for the costs that their presence imposes on others, and if they do so, these profit maximizers could be expected to respond accordingly.

It might be argued that the social interest in free speech overrides the above analysis. As a fellow traveler of the libertarians, I have no interest in opposing free speech, but I do believe that the free speech protected by the First Amendment must be speech offered by a willing speaker to a willing audience. That is what Congress may make no law abridging. The First Amendment does not require anyone to listen to a Jehovah's Witness or anyone else.

The problem presented by such cases as *Marsh* and *Logan Valley* is essentially an economic one. It is a problem of measuring choice. The problem arises because audiences are not perfectly divisible. If we could somehow distinguish the shoppers who want to be approached by Jehovah's Witnesses from those who do not, and segregate them in some way so that only those who so desired would be exposed to the Witnesses' message, everyone would agree that no First Amendment problems were involved. No one wants to prevent those who want to receive the message from receiving it. The problem is to avoid the costs that arise when those who do not want to receive the word are accosted.

---

[53]Suppose the owner is a devout Catholic who places a negative value on the message of Jehovah's Witnesses. He might want to exclude them even if their presence would increase the value of his property, that is, even if the residents on balance prefer to have them present. The owner's vote, however, counts too. Are not the affected interests properly measured if the owner values excluding the Witnesses more than his residents value their being present and he, accordingly, does exclude them? The owner pays for his preferences by forgoing an increase in the value of his property.

Where transaction costs are low and property rights can be precisely specified, the market will solve this problem of allocating scarce resources better than any other method. The decision as to whether to admit the Jehovah's Witnesses is no different in principle from the decision on how best to lay out the location of the stores in the mall. In both cases the shopping center owner and the tenants want to make their customers as happy as possible, as long as the costs of doing so do not exceed the benefits.

The market cannot operate unless the relevant property rights are assigned to some party who can either include or exclude the activity that produces conflicting costs and benefits. A legal requirement that all speakers be admitted to the shopping center creates a situation in which no one has the right to exclude that activity. No matter how much the shopping center owner, the tenants, and the customers want to exclude either speakers in general or particular speakers, they cannot do so. There is no way that private arrangements of any kind can resolve these conflicting claims to the same scarce resource. This suggests that *Marsh, Logan Valley,* and *PruneYard* (in the California Supreme Court) were all wrongly decided. The Supreme Court was right when it overruled *Logan Valley* in *Hudgens.*

The foregoing analysis has one other important implication for cases such as *Marsh* and *Logan Valley.* The interests of putative speakers on the one hand and customers or residents on the other could better be accommodated if we permit distinctions between speakers on the basis of the content of their speech. A market in which consumers can buy Rice Krispies in individual boxes rather than by 24-box cases is obviously more efficient than one in which they cannot.

Shoppers in different towns and shopping centers will have different tastes for speech just as they have different tastes for other goods. We all might be happy with the League of Women Voters seeking to register new voters. Responses to the American Nazi Party would be more negative. Other speakers would produce different responses in different places. These varying demands for different kinds of speech cannot be accommodated unless the law is capable of making distinctions on the basis of content.

An approach that bans such distinctions makes sense when applied to encounters between willing speakers and a willing audience. That is where true First Amendment problems arise. It does not make sense where we are trying to minimize the social costs of encounters such as those described above. We would recognize immediately the error of a rule prohibiting the railroad from emitting any sparks, coupled with a ban on contracting between the railroad and the adjoining landowners. So too with a rule that banned contracting and permitted the railroad to emit as many sparks as it wished. If left to contract freely, the railroad and the adjoining landowners would often reach a result in which the railroad reduced its sparks somewhat and the adjoining landowners took some precautions, too.

If the analogy between the railroad paradigm and the conflict between speakers and unwilling listeners is correct, then everyone could be better off if the parties were left to make these decisions on their own. People's preferences will be more nearly matched if we let the market reflect their views on different types of speech.

The shopping center discussion is just one example of the property rights approach to speech issues. For another, consider a problem posed by my colleague Steve Shiffrin, who asks whether, without liability, Mercedes Benz could truthfully advertise that Frank Sinatra drives a Mercedes automobile or whether *Time* could advertise that Sinatra is a regular reader of that periodical.[54] Shiffrin answers his own questions as follows:

> Assuming enough disclosure to avoid deception, I think Mercedes Benz and Time, Inc. should have the right to tell the public which public figures buy their products and that the public has a right to be told that information without the permission of the public figure. Few would seriously regard these as intimate details of a public figure's private life. The issue is whether public figures should be able to license (or worse, not license) use of this true information by commercial entities. In the absence of deception, what is being weighed is the freedom to communicate the truth against the creation of a property interest allowing the public figure to control the dissemination of truth for his or her own profit. For those concerned about the "unjust" enrichment of the vendors, I counter that it is "unjust" only if one views the name selling business as more important than freedom of speech. There are good reasons, I think, to create private property rights in items from clothing to cars; and there are good reasons to be debated about the creation of the private property in the means of production. But the creation of a commercial appropriation or right of publicity tort in examples one and four [the Mercedes Benz and *Time* cases] seems to be a clear case of limiting freedom of speech in pursuit of excessive capitalism.[55]

The issues here should not be posed in terms of weighing freedom of speech against the name-selling business (something done for profit). Passing this pejorative formulation, Shiffrin's case involves

[54]Steven Shiffrin, "The First Amendment and Economic Regulation: Away From a General Theory of the First Amendment," *Northwestern Law Review* 78 (December 1983): 1212–83.

[55]Ibid., pp. 1257–58, n. 275.

nothing more than two groups competing for the use of scarce resources, just like the railroad and the adjoining landowners. Sinatra cannot have his privacy at the same time that the public is told about his driving and reading habits. The relevant question in this case is not about free speech; it is whether consumers value the information more than Sinatra does or vice versa. Mercedes Benz and *Time* are middlemen between Sinatra and the public. If *Time* could make more money by advertising that Sinatra reads the magazine, it would be willing to pay almost all of it to Sinatra to get his permission to run the ad. Sinatra will refuse if he values his privacy more than *Time's* consumers value information about his reading habits (measured roughly by the amount of money *Time* would make by running the ad). That should be the end of the story, but the end can be reached only if Sinatra is given a property right to prevent the use of his name by others.

Accommodation Where Transaction Costs Are High

Not much need be said about this case, since the analysis parallels the one sketched in Section II above. Courts deciding speech cases involving unwilling parties and high transaction costs should try to reach results consistent with those the affected parties would reach if they could make exchanges in a hypothetical zero-transaction-cost environment.

It is worth noting that the argument against prohibiting content-based distinctions outlined above applies as much when transaction costs are high as when they are low. A legal approach that treats an American Legion parade down the main street of Skokie, Illinois, in the same manner as it treats a Nazi parade is blind to the basic issues involved. I am not suggesting that the Nazis could be prevented from hiring a hall in Skokie and delivering their message to those who might wish to attend.[56] While there are no doubt some externalities involved in that case too, there is no direct attempt to impose a message on unwilling listeners as would be involved in a Nazi march down Main Street. Permitting distinctions based on content would allow the interests of affected parties to be more closely accommodated than if such distinctions were proscribed.

V. Conclusion

It is not surprising that a property rights approach to judicial decision making can help resolve difficult issues in antitrust or in

---

[56]Content regulation is inappropriate where speakers have taken reasonable steps to protect unwilling listeners from being subjected to the undesired message. The property rights problem is effectively solved by the self-selection process involved in either going to the hall or remaining absent.

reviewing economic regulation. It is more surprising, however, that this cost-benefit approach to establishing legal rules can illuminate difficult free speech issues as much as it does. This approach is as general as it is powerful. The three areas discussed above are only examples of its reach.

Aside from being useful, the property rights approach is attractive because it focuses on voluntary exchange between private parties. Even where transaction costs are too high for such private exchanges to occur, the approach leads courts to try to replicate the result that would occur if such exchanges were possible. It not only provides a mechanism for resolving competing claims to scarce resources but it does so on the basis of individual integrity and personal choice. It is hard to think of an approach for which more could be claimed.

COMMENT

PROPERTY RIGHTS AND THE JUDICIARY
Louis De Alessi

Introduction

In his paper Professor Liebeler considers judicial decisions that affect the definition, assignment, and exchange of rights to the use of resources. Noting that a decision that facilitates the flow of these rights to their highest-valued use increases the wealth of society, he proposes that the courts apply three criteria to reduce externalities. First, if transaction costs are negligible, the courts should enforce voluntary contracts. Second, if transaction costs are significant, the courts should assign (and enforce) property rights the way the parties themselves would have chosen if transaction costs had been low. Third, if circumstances change, perhaps because of an increase in the demand for some rights or a decrease in the cost of enforcing them, the courts should take account of the change and decide cases with the objective of reducing transaction costs to private parties. Liebeler illustrates these criteria within the context of antitrust and freedom-of-speech cases and argues that legal precedent supports the adoption of his policy recommendations.

Liebeler's application of economic theory is well grounded and straightforward, leaving little scope for critical commentary. Accordingly, after the almost obligatory caveat regarding the distinction between positive and normative economics, this comment will turn to an important issue not addressed by Liebeler: the nature and consequences of the property rights that characterize the judiciary itself.

Positive and Normative Issues

Liebeler's paper is concerned with both positive and normative issues. Keeping them separate avoids two possible pitfalls: (1) rejecting positive analyses on the misconception that they reflect normative values,

The author is Professor of Economics at the University of Miami's Law and Economics Center in Coral Gables. He gratefully acknowledges the helpful comments on this paper made by Robert J. Staaf.

and (2) accepting normative prescriptions on the misconception that they represent positive conclusions.

Consider first the range of positive analyses, defined simply as the application of economic theory to predict or explain the economic consequences of a change in circumstances.[1] Following Coase (1960), Liebeler examines the effect of differences in transaction costs on the exchange of rights to the use of resources that are fully allocated and privately held. This analysis does not contain any value judgments among its axioms or conclusions. Thus it is purely positive in scope and intent. Following Demsetz (1967), Liebeler next examines the effect of changes in the state of the world on the evolution of institutions used to control the definition, assignment, enforcement, and exchange of rights to the use of resources. This application of economic theory is also value free and represents a simple exercise in positive economics.

On the other hand, consider Liebeler's proposal that the courts, in the presence of significant transaction costs, assign the rights to the use of resources so as to reduce externalities. The assignment of private property rights to one party rather than another affects the welfare of the individuals. Accordingly the proposal clearly entails a value judgment. As Liebeler recognizes, therefore, whether or not the courts should accept the proposed criteria is a normative judgment about which economic theory is silent—keeping in mind, of course, that positive economics generates much of the information used for normative purposes.

Value judgments are a necessary ingredient of any choice. All choices, whether private or collective, ultimately pivot on the subjective value that each chooser attaches to each of the alternatives at hand. Liebeler's proposal that economic efficiency be taken as the dominant criterion in judicial decision making is offered as an alternative to the present welter of special interest regulations and diverse value judgments by judges and other regulators. Viewed from this perspective, the proposal can be attractive, particularly within the context of antitrust whose objective presumably is economic efficiency.

A brief aside on free speech may be useful. Much of the continuing confusion regarding the boundaries of free speech seems to arise from the failure to distinguish between (1) the governmentally unrestricted right to acquire, through voluntary exchange, the use of resources with which to present a viewpoint to a willing audience (the right, for example, to hire a hall from a willing owner and give a talk to those who choose to attend) and (2) the governmentally

---

[1]See, for example, De Alessi (forthcoming).

enforced right to be given the use of resources with which to express that viewpoint (the right, for example, to be given access to a public building to give a talk or the right to equal time on television). The First Amendment presumably is concerned with (1) rather than (2), a position consistent with Liebeler's approach on this issue.

Property Rights, Incentives, and Judicial Discretion

This section explores the property rights that characterize the judiciary and thus affect the criteria that judges in fact choose to apply in making their decisions. That is, it attempts to answer the question: What are the nature and consequences of the structure of property rights, embedded in judiciary institutions, that determine the incentive structure faced by judges?

The choices of decision makers within business and government organizations are subject to constraints ultimately enforced in the economic or political marketplace (De Alessi 1980). Accordingly individual preferences typically are subordinated, in varying degrees determined by the structure of property rights and the costs of transactions, to the achievement of organizational goals (De Alessi 1982). Constraints within the judiciary appear to be weak and organizational goals unclear, implying that judges enjoy broad discretionary authority.

Consider first the constraints on the federal judiciary (Landes and Posner 1975). Federal judges are appointed by the executive branch; have life tenure, with turnover typically occurring only at death or retirement; receive salaries that are independent of individual performance, whether the latter is measured by case load, quality of decisions, or any other criterion of productivity; and are subject to relatively weak monitoring by the legislature and executive branch, with gross malfeasance or dereliction of duty effectively being the only grounds for disciplinary action or removal.

Although individual performance does not affect the relative salaries of judges within the same cohort (district court judges, for example) it may affect the probability of promotion of lower court judges to a higher court, with the attendant higher income and prestige. The evidence on this point is not clear. Higgins and Rubin (1980) have shown that the probability of being reversed on appeal, a measure of performance, does not provide a constraint. Promotion, however, is not determined by judges who sit in the higher court and who would view the reversal record of a candidate as an index of the threat he or she would pose to the existing majority coalition. Rather, promotion is determined by government employees within the executive branch who would view a judge's decisions—and reversals—

as either good or bad depending upon whether they facilitated or hindered the administration's policies. As Samuels (1975) notes, courts are a political phenomenon.

The formal constraints faced by state and local judges are only slightly more binding than those faced by federal judges (Landes and Posner 1975). State and local judges may be elected rather than appointed, typically have shorter terms of office (only one state has life tenure), typically earn salaries that are independent of performance and lower than those received by federal judges, and are subject to relatively weak monitoring by the legislature and the executive branch. To the extent that a judge comes up for reelection or reappointment, he or she may be expected to be more sensitive to the desires of the appointing authority or the electorate. A recent econometric study of congressional voting behavior, for example, indicates that as reelection time approaches, U.S. senators are more likely to vote according to the wishes of their constituents than according to their own preferences (Kalt and Zupan 1984). Thus state and local judges may be expected to be more responsive than federal judges to political pressure, although they still have considerable scope for discretionary behavior.

The comments so far suggest that pecuniary rewards within the judiciary effectively are divorced from judicial performance. This separation lowers the cost of nonpecuniary sources of utility, and, predictably, judges will consume more of them. Such sources of utility include prestige, power, and the advancement of a judge's own view of the public interest.

In practice the exercise of discretionary authority by federal judges and, at least, state judges seems to be constrained by the legal precedents that characterize a case. New precedents evolve slowly, and typically they are justified at length as correcting a deviation from the proper line of precedents and in any case as reflecting what the law had meant all along.

The maintenance of precedent in the absence of a change in underlying conditions decreases uncertainty and is clearly a "good" produced by the judicial system. Indeed, the establishment and maintenance of precedent is an important capital investment (Landes and Posner 1980). Higgins and Rubin (1980), however, have found that the probability of reversal does not affect the probability of promotion; thus it is not clear why individual judges have the incentive to be constrained by precedent. Conjectures include competition from other jurisdictions (for example, among federal courts and between federal and state courts) and from the legislature, as well as the existence of nonpecuniary sources of utility, such as prestige.

That nonpecuniary considerations matter is suggested by the observation that at least federal and higher-court state judges could receive much higher pecuniary rewards in private practice. Further research, including studies using data provided by the growing use of private judges (Cooter 1983, Rubin 1983), would be useful in providing better insights into judicial behavior.

A number of scholars have examined the extent to which the common law, reflecting judicial interpretation, is efficient in the sense that its rules evolve to yield a more efficient allocation of resources.[2] The findings, however, are mixed and provide little confidence that, at least in recent times, the common law has moved toward efficient rules.[3]

There is also a very extensive literature concerned with the extent to which the law ought to adopt criteria of economic efficiency (for example, the Hofstra Symposium 1980). Much of the debate over efficiency has stemmed from the failure of many legal scholars to grasp the distinction between normative and positive economics (at least some writers appear to view all economics as normative). The debate also has stemmed from the enthusiasm of other legal scholars for the beacon that efficiency provides in an otherwise uncharted and tempestuous sea of ad hoc legal doctrines, from the fascination of economists with welfare criteria, and from some general confusion over the meaning and relevance of efficiency (De Alessi 1983).

Finally, the reason for an independent federal judiciary deserves closer study. It especially should be noted that the degree of independence decreases as the jurisdiction shifts from broader (for example, federal) to narrower (for example, local) levels (Landes and Posner 1975). The importance of an independent judiciary was recognized as early as 1776 by Adam Smith. Such a system, said Smith, would help insulate judges from politics and "make every individual feel himself perfectly secure in the possession of every right which belongs to him" (p. 681). Landes and Posner (1975), meanwhile, have conjectured that an independent judicial system is intended to enforce special interest legislation. Buchanan (1975), commenting on their paper, concurs that the purpose of independence, whatever it may be, is not to provide "unique guardians of some mystical 'public interest' " (p. 903), and he adds that "ethical norms should not be determining factors in judicial decisions" (p. 903). In a recent conversation with the author, R. J. Staaf built on Smith's insight and the

---

[2]See, for example, Posner (1971), Rubin (1977), Priest (1977), Goodman (1978), and Landes and Posner (1980).

[3]See, for example, Komesar (1980).

seminal work by Buchanan and Tullock (1962) to suggest that an independent judiciary effectively enforces fundamental rights through an implicit rule of unanimity: A single dissenting citizen can sue to have a majority-supported legislative act declared unconstitutional.

An independent judiciary, of course, does not imply that judges' compensation must be independent of performance. Thus, for example, Smith (1937, pp. 677–81) proposed that judges be paid out of fees charged for administering justice. The fees would be collected after a decision had been rendered (thereby providing incentive for speedy decisions) and put into a fund from which each judge would be paid in proportion to the amount of time spent on judicial activities, such compensation apparently being in addition to a small base salary. Smith added that "Public services are never better performed than when their reward comes only in consequence of their being performed, and is proportioned to the diligence employed in performing them" (p. 678).

Conclusion

The analysis presented in this comment suggests that judges enjoy considerable discretionary authority. Accordingly the instruments available to affect the quality of judicial decision making—especially at the federal level—seem clear: Revise the existing institutional framework to provide a preferred structure of incentives and, more important in the short run, appoint judges whose track record reveals the desired view of the public interest.

References

Buchanan, James M. "The Independent Judiciary in an Interest-Group Perspective: Comment." *Journal of Law and Economics* 18 (December 1975): 903–5.

Buchanan, James M., and Tullock, Gordon. *The Calculus of Consent.* Ann Arbor: University of Michigan Press, 1962.

Coase, Ronald H. "The Problem of Social Cost." *Journal of Law and Economics* 3 (October 1960): 1–44.

Cooter, Robert D. "The Objectives of Private and Public Judges." *Public Choice* 41 (1983): 107–32.

De Alessi, Louis. "The Economics of Property Rights: A Review of the Evidence." *Research in Law and Economics* 2 (1980): 1–47.

De Alessi, Louis. "Nature and Consequences of Private and Public Enterprises." *Minnesota Law Review* 67 (October 1982): 191–209.

De Alessi, Louis. "Property Rights, Transaction Costs, and X-Efficiency: An Essay in Economic Theory." *American Economic Review* 73 (March 1983): 64–81.

De Alessi, Louis. "Nature and Methodological Foundations of Some Recent Extensions of Economic Theory." In *Economic Imperialism: The Economic Method Applied Outside the Field of Economics*. Edited by Gerard Radnitzky and Peter Bernholz. New York: Paragon Publishers, forthcoming.

Demsetz, Harold. "Toward a Theory of Property Rights." *American Economic Review* 57 (May 1967): 347–59.

Goodman, John C. "An Economic Theory of the Evolution of the Common Law." *Journal of Legal Studies* 7 (June 1978): 393–406.

Higgins, Richard S., and Rubin, Paul H. "Judicial Discretion." *Journal of Legal Studies* 9 (January 1980): 129–38.

Hofstra Symposium. "Symposium on Efficiency as a Legal Concern." *Hofstra Law Review* 8 (Spring 1980): 485–770. "A Response to the Efficiency Symposium." *Hofstra Law Review* 8 (Summer 1980): 811–972.

Kalt, Joseph P., and Zupan, Mark A. "Capture and Ideology in the Economic Theory of Politics." *American Economic Review* 74 (June 1984): 279–300.

Komesar, Neil K. "Legal Change, Judicial Behavior, and the Diversity Jurisdiction: A Comment." *Journal of Legal Studies* 9 (March 1980): 387–97.

Landes, William M., and Posner, Richard A. "The Independent Judiciary in an Interest-Group Perspective." *Journal of Law and Economics* 18 (December 1975): 875–901.

Landes, William M., and Posner, Richard A. "Legal Change, Judicial Behavior, and the Diversity Jurisdiction." *Journal of Legal Studies* 9 (March 1980): 367–86.

Posner, Richard A. "Killing or Wounding to Protect Property Interests." *Journal of Law and Economics* 14 (April 1971): 201–32.

Priest, George L. "The Common Law Process and the Selection of Efficient Rules." *Journal of Legal Studies* 6 (January 1977): 65–82.

Rubin, Paul A. "Why Is the Common Law Efficient?" *Journal of Legal Studies* 6 (January 1977): 51–63.

Rubin, Paul A. "The Objectives of Private and Public Judges: Comment." *Public Choice* 41 (1983): 133–37.

Samuels, Warren J. "The Independent Judiciary in an Interest-Group Perspective: Comment. *Journal of Law and Economics* 18 (December 1975): 907–11.

Smith, Adam. *An Inquiry into the Nature and Causes of the Wealth of Nations*. 1776. Reprint. New York: Modern Library, 1937.

8

LEGISLATIVE ACTIVISM, JUDICIAL ACTIVISM, AND THE DECLINE OF PRIVATE SOVEREIGNTY
Roger Pilon

The Decline of Private Sovereignty

With his *Economic Liberties and the Constitution*,[1] Professor Bernard H. Siegan has thrown the gauntlet down to the judiciary, and to the intellectual and political community that surrounds it, to show why in the case of our economic liberties we have strayed so far from our beginnings. In the beginning, he says, was the Constitution, and it was the word. Its authors, inspired by the higher law, by the natural law and natural rights traditions and by the common law of England, and chastened by their own recent experience with the English Crown, set forth a plan for ordered liberty that protected economic and noneconomic liberties alike. Little more than a decade earlier, during the course of which they secured their independence, these Founders had declared to the world, in a conclusory way at least, their philosophy of government: "[T]hat all Men are created equal, that they are endowed by their Creator with certain unalienable Rights, that among these are Life, Liberty, and the Pursuit of Happiness—that to secure these Rights, Governments are instituted among Men, deriving their just Powers from the Consent of the Governed. . . ."[2] It was to set these "self-evident truths" in stone, more or less, that the Founders drew up a written Constitution, designed to guide and constrain our institutions of government on into the future.

Over the next century and a half the Constitution did this reasonably well, although the execution of the plan was often less than perfect, to be sure. Whether we point to slavery, to the erosion of

---

The author is Director of Policy for the Bureau of Human Rights and Humananitarian Affairs at the Department of State. The views expressed in this paper are those of the author, not necessarily those of the Reagan administration.

[1]Bernard H. Siegan, *Economic Liberties and the Constitution* (Chicago: University of Chicago Press, 1980).

[2]Declaration of Independence.

riparian rights or strict liability in torts,[3] to the "public interest" exception to freedom of contract as formulated in 1877 in *Munn v. Illinois*,[4] to the passage of the Sherman Act,[5] or to the *Euclid* zoning decision of 1926,[6] there were numerous examples of our having strayed from the mark. Nevertheless, for the most part the system worked as it was intended to work. In particular, legislative inroads on private rights in property and liberty were regularly reviewed and almost as regularly rejected by the courts of the land. Thus the tyranny of the majority, which the Founders had learned to fear from their readings of Plato and Aristotle, Lord Coke and Montesquieu, as well as from their own direct experience, never came to pass in any far-reaching form. Whereas the legislature and the executive were the mark of self-government, the court stood as the bulwark of our liberties.

Over the past 50 years, however, the situation has been very different. Professor Siegan points to the decision of the Supreme Court in *Nebbia v. New York*,[7] handed down in 1934, as signaling "the approaching end of economic due process, which actually terminated three years later"[8] with the Court's decision in *West Coast Hotel v. Parrish*.[9] In announcing its decision in *Nebbia*, which upheld the conviction of a store owner who had sold two bottles of milk at a price below that set by a milk control board recently instituted by the New York State legislature, "the majority held that the due process guarantee demands only that the law be not unreasonable or arbitrary and that it have a substantial relation to the object sought to be achieved."[10] Thus did the "rational relation" test emerge, which is tantamount to the most minimal level of judicial review. As Professor Siegan observes, "[b]ecause every economic regulation serves some purpose"—in *Nebbia*, to guarantee a "reasonable return" to milk producers and dealers—the rational relation standard essentially presupposes judicial withdrawal."[11] Those who would thereafter exercise their traditional economic liberties would find, he concludes, that the American government consisted of only two, not

[3]See Morton J. Horwitz, *The Transformation of American Law, 1780–1860* (Cambridge, Mass.: Harvard University Press, 1977).

[4]94 U.S. 113 (1877).

[5]Sherman Antitrust Act, ch. 647, 26 Stat. 209 (1890) [current version at 15 U.S.C. §§1–7 (1982)].

[6]Village of Euclid v. Ambler Realty Co., 272 U.S. 365 (1926).

[7]291 U.S. 502 (1934).

[8]Siegan, *Economic Liberties*, p. 139.

[9]300 U.S. 379 (1937).

[10]Siegan, *Economic Liberties*, p. 139.

[11]Ibid., p. 265.

three, branches. In fact, although the Court has continued to strike down economic regulations that infringed on certain "fundamental" rights, such as expression or privacy, since 1936 not one economic regulation has been invalidated on due process grounds.[12]

With the advent of judicial restraint in the economic area there began, of course, the legislative activism that gave us the New Deal institutions we have all come to know so well. Not that these institutions had not begun slowly to emerge during the Progressive Era, from the thinking of which they drew much of their intellectual support; but now, unrestrained by the need to consider any but the Court's preferred rights, they grew and prospered, regulating and restraining enterprise as never before, touching every facet of our lives. At all levels of government, legislators, executives, and bureaucrats set out in pursuit of the public interest, driven by the majoritarian pulse—or worse, but more likely, by the interests that would ensure their continuance in office. Policy, not principle, became the *raison d'être* of government, as legislators and executives alike measured their stock by the number of bills they had introduced, the number of benefits they had bestowed.

But the story does not end there, of course, for even before the legislature and executive had gotten their second wind in the form of the Great Society, the Court rediscovered its activist past—not in the area of economic liberty as set forth in the Constitution, to be sure, but in the uncharted sea of social and welfare rights. Armed with an egalitarian sword, the Court began carving out whole areas of entitlement, cutting deeply once again into those economic liberties the legislature had not yet gotten around to skewer. As if pressed by a double phalanx, economic liberties were now under assault on both sides. On one hand the courts would do little to prevent the legislature and executive from reordering property and economic liberty in the name of "social justice." On the other hand the courts undertook their own program of "social justice," discovering and inventing rights alike, rights the Founders had never even imagined.

In all of this, of course, the public domain has grown larger as the domain of private sovereignty has declined. This has taken place in two basic ways. First, through countless regulatory schemes at the federal, state, and local levels, direct restrictions have been imposed on rights of property and contract, ranging from zoning regulations to barriers to entry and exit, control of terms, control of product, and on and on—restrictions so myriad that a brief list could not begin to

[12]Ibid., pp. 265–66.

convey their scope. Second, to support these regulatory schemes as well as the growing number of redistributive schemes, substantial increases in the level of taxation have been required. With each increase in the level of transfers from private to public hands, the scope of private sovereignty has necessarily declined. Not that each of us is not entitled, under specified conditions, to some part of this growing public pie. Indeed, the pie has spawned a whole industry aimed at helping us to maximize our piece, whether in the form of agricultural price supports, tax write-offs, research grants, public education, use of public ski resorts, public television—what have you. It would be fatuous, however, to suppose that even those who learn to manipulate the rules enjoy anything like the sovereignty they would enjoy were goods and services not open to public disposition.

The Conservative Response: Deference to the Legislature

Now in light of this history, one might assume that the conservative community that is otherwise inclined toward economic freedom would be of one voice, urging the Court to resurrect the substantive due process that so long enabled it to stand athwart the legislative, majoritarian drive, that enabled it to frustrate interest in the name of right. This is not the case, however. In fact, the subject of judicial review has sharply divided conservatives, as witness the papers presented at a recent Federalist Society symposium on judicial activism.[13]

In general, those conservative critics of the Court who nonetheless eschew substantive due process have been driven by the judicial activism of the past 30 years—and in particular by the Court's decisions on abortion, busing, school prayer, and criminal law—to what often appears to be a deep-seated antipathy to the federal judiciary especially and hence to federal judicial review as such: Thus the score and more of bills in Congress over the past few years aimed at limiting Supreme Court and lower federal court jurisdiction over specified kinds of cases, arguably permitted under Article III, section 2 of the Constitution.[14] Not that these critics would abolish all judicial

[13]"A Symposium on Judicial Activism: Problems and Responses," *Harvard Journal of Law and Public Policy* 7 (1984): 1–108.

[14]See especially the following: Charles E. Rice, "Withdrawing Jurisdiction From Federal Courts," *Harvard Journal of Law and Public Policy* 7 (1984): 13–15; Patrick McGuigan, "Withdrawing Jurisdiction From Federal Courts," *Harvard Journal of Law and Public Policy* 7 (1984): 17–21; Lino A. Graglia, "The Power of Congress to Limit Supreme Court Jurisdiction," *Harvard Journal of Law and Public Policy* 7 (1984): 23–29.

review; rather, "large categories of cases,"[15] as one put it, would be removed to state courts for review, thus circumventing the Supreme Court's incorporation doctrine under which it applies the provisions of the Bill of Rights to state action through the Fourteenth Amendment. Antipathy aside, therefore, it is their rejection of the incorporation doctrine,[16] together with their belief that the Constitution protects only those rights articulated therein,[17] that leads these critics to the conclusion that the Supreme Court has no authority to decide various of the questions it lately has decided. As one put it:

> Virtually any group, therefore, that seeks to limit the power of the Court on any issue for any reason has my support. To limit the Court's power in any regard is to take a most important step toward restoring this country's political and social health.[18]

This points, then, to the direction that many of these conservative critics would take. At heart they are small "d" democrats who would place in the hands of the people and their elected representatives— preferably at the state and local level—many of the questions that now are decided by the Supreme Court. Although judicial review at the state level is reserved, judicial restraint is the recommended posture. "If the judges of any state should fail to eschew judicial law-making and the Supreme Court's plainly baseless 'interpretations' of the Constitution," said one, "it would be up to the people of the state to see to their judges."[19] Indeed, judicial review "as understood and practiced today," this critic contends, is "the major obstacle to our maintenance of a system of democratic, decentralized government."[20]

In truth, however, we need not go beyond the Supreme Court itself to discover the conservative strain that defers to the legislature. Well-known for this view, for example, is the Court's leading conservative,

---

[15]McGuigan, "Withdrawing Jurisdiction," p. 18.

[16]Rice, "Withdrawing Jurisdiction," pp. 13–14; McGuigan, "Withdrawing Jurisdiction," p. 18. See generally Raoul Berger, *Government by Judiciary: The Transformation of the Fourteenth Amendment* (Cambridge, Mass.: Harvard University Press, 1977); for a devastating critique, see Edwin Vieira, review of *Government by Judiciary*, by R. Berger, *Law & Liberty* 4 (Fall 1978): 1–6.

[17]See, for example, Rex Lee, "Legislative Questions and Judicial Questions," *Harvard Journal of Law and Public Policy* 7 (1984): 38. Compare with Joseph Story (Associate Justice of the Supreme Court, 1812–45), *Commentaries on the Constitution of the United States* (New York: Da Capo Press, 1970), pp. 715–16: "[The Bill of Rights] presumes the existence of a substantial body of rights not specifically enumerated but easily perceived in the broad concept of liberty and so numerous and so obvious as to preclude listing them."

[18]Graglia, "The Power of Congress," p. 24.

[19]Ibid., p. 28.

[20]Ibid., p. 23.

Justice William H. Rehnquist. Thus in *Virginia State Board of Pharmacy v. Virginia Citizens Consumer Council*,[21] a 1976 opinion that struck down a Virginia statute prohibiting pharmacists from advertising the prices of prescription drugs, thereby carving out a degree of First Amendment protection for commercial speech, Justice Rehnquist wrote the lone dissent, denying that the Constitution in any way prohibited the state legislature from regulating such speech. In echo of Justice Holmes's famous dissent in *Lochner v. New York*,[22] Mr. Rehnquist averred that "there is certainly nothing in the United States Constitution which requires the Virginia Legislature to hew to the teachings of Adam Smith in its legislative decisions,"[23] a comment presaged some four years earlier when he observed, in *Weber v. Aetna Casualty & Surety Co.*,[24] again in dissent, that the freedom of contract doctrine, thought by the Court in the first part of this century to be part of the Fourteenth Amendment's guarantees, had received its "just deserts" in 1937 in *West Coast Hotel v. Parrish*.[25]

Writing more recently in this vein, the newest court conservative, Justice Sandra Day O'Connor, has indicated her own deference to the legislature in *Hawaii Housing Authority v. Midkiff*,[26] a 1984 decision upholding a Hawaii statute that permits the state to condemn private land, not so that it may be converted to public use but so that it may be purchased by the private tenants who occupy it. In overturning the decision of the Ninth Circuit, which had held that "it was the intention of the framers of the Constitution and the Fifth Amendment that this form of majoritarian tyranny should not occur,"[27] Justice O'Connor, writing for a unanimous court, commended "judicial restraint," adding that "the Court will not substitute its judgment

---

[21]425 U.S. 748 (1976).

[22]198 U.S. 45, 75 (1905): "I strongly believe that my agreement or disagreement [with the economic theory on which this decision is based] has nothing to do with the right of a majority to embody their opinions in law. ... The Fourteenth Amendment does not enact Mr. Herbert Spencer's Social Statics. ... [A] constitution is not intended to embody a particular economic theory, whether of paternalism and the organic relation of the citizen to the State or of *laissez faire*."

[23]Virginia State Board of Pharmacy v. Virginia Citizens Consumer Council, Inc., 425 U.S. 748, 781 (1976) (Rehnquist, J., dissenting).

[24]406 U.S. 164 (1972).

[25]Id. at 179–80. See also Judge Robert H. Bork, "Tradition and Morality in Constitutional Law," The Francis Boyer Lectures on Public Policy, American Enterprise Institute, 1984, p. 5: "If one may complain today that the Constitution did not adopt John Stuart Mill's *On Liberty*, it was only a few judicial generations ago, when economic laissez faire somehow got into the Constitution, that Justice Holmes wrote in dissent that the Constitution 'does not enact Mr. Herbert Spencer's Social Statics.' "

[26]467 U.S. 229 (1984).

[27]Midkiff v. Tom, 702 F.2d 788, 790 (1983).

for a legislature's judgment as to what constitutes a public use 'unless the use be palpably without reasonable foundation.' "[28] Just what will follow from this sweeping decision remains to be seen; but clearly, the eminent domain powers of states and municipalities have been substantially enlarged.

Stepping back from these conservative arguments, it is easy enough to appreciate their animating force; for the Court has indeed invented rights in recent years—although not as many, perhaps, as the critics suggest. Nevertheless, when the Court legislates rather than decides, when it makes policy rather than finds law, however difficult this pair of distinctions may be to articulate and apply, there is a sense of rule without authority, of self-government usurped, especially when the Court frustrates the clear and substantial will of the majority. Wielding, as it has, a new doctrine of substantive due process, though seldom calling it that, the modern Court has imposed its values on vast areas of our society. These conservatives are understandably reluctant, then, to resurrect the old substantive due process, even if they do think it in some sense legitimate.[29] For this would serve only to legitimate much of what the modern Court has done. Better to go the route of political legitimacy, they say, for only thus will the authority of the Court to legislate be undercut.

Having said all of that, however, there remains a deep sense of unease; for ours has never been a pure democracy. Our concern for the rights of the minority, especially when we find ourselves members of that minority, has always been at the core of our respect for judicial review. Speaking at the Federalist Society symposium mentioned earlier, and to the proposals for withdrawal of certain subjects from Supreme Court jurisdiction, Deputy Solicitor General Paul Bator characterized these arguments as "unconstitutional in spirit," even

---

[28]467 U.S. 229, 241 (1984), citing United States v. Gettysburg Electric R.Co. 160 U.S. 668, 680 (1896).

[29]Many think substantive due process less than legitimate, of course. See, for example, the remarks of William French Smith before the Federal Legal Council, Reston, Va., on 29 October 1981, p. 3: "It is clear that between *Allgeyer v. Louisiana* in 1897 and *Nebbia v. New York* in 1934 the Supreme Court engaged in—and fostered—judicial policy-making under the guise of substantive due process. During this period, the Court weighted the balance in favor of individual interests against the decisions of state and federal legislatures. Using the due process clauses, unelected judges substituted their own policy preferences for the determinations of the public's elected representatives." See also Smith, "Urging Judicial Restraint," *American Bar Association Journal* 68 (1982): 59–61: "In the era that has come to be epitomized by the decision in *Lochner v. New York*, . . . it was conservatives who urged judicial activism under the banner of due process to strike down popular enactments. Judges read their personal predilections into the flexible terms of the Constitution, at the expense of the policy choices of the elected representatives of the people" (p. 60).

if they did turn out to be constitutional in fact. As such, he added, they detract "from our valid criticism of the Court."[30] Indeed, he continued, the Framers would be "shocked" by some of these suggestions, for they assumed

> that a federal government and a federal system needs an institution that has the authority to make uniform authoritative pronouncements of federal law. That assumption is well documented. The Supreme Court did not just invent it.[31]

If judicial review is an essential part of our Constitution, then, if it goes to the core of our system of ordered liberty, the central question before us should be whether there is a principled way through the thicket that surrounds it. Or is it all rather a matter of the shifting sands of constitutional jurisprudence? More precisely, just what are the roots of the authority of the Court? For that matter, what are the roots of the authority of the legislature, or of the sovereign generally?

The Roots of Political Authority

Clearly, an inquiry into the foundations of judicial review takes us ultimately not simply to questions of constitutional theory but to questions of political and moral philosophy as well. Yet how could it be otherwise, for what were the Founders if not moral and political philosophers, drawing upon the thought of the ancients and moderns alike to set in train not simply a legal order but a legal order that reflected an overarching and abiding moral order.[32] What, after all, were the self-evident truths of which the Declaration speaks if not the truths of moral reason. That all men are created equal and that they are endowed by their Creator with certain unalienable rights are hardly empirical truths! Moreover, if governments are instituted among men to secure their rights, those rights could scarcely be the product of positive law. Rather, they preexist government; government's function is to recognize and secure them, not to create them.

The principal business of moral philosophy, then, is to discover and set forth the whole truth about our moral rights and obligations, to articulate and justify those universal principles of reason from which our moral rights and obligations are derived, as well as to

---

[30]Paul Bator, "Withdrawing Jurisdiction From Federal Courts," *Harvard Journal of Law and Public Policy* 7 (1984): 31.

[31]Ibid., p. 32.

[32]See, for example, Edward S. Corwin, *The "Higher Law" Background of American Constitutional Law* (Ithaca, N.Y.: Cornell University Press, 1955); Bernard Bailyn, *The Ideological Origins of the American Revolution* (Cambridge, Mass.: Belknap Press, 1967).

inquire about those value considerations that add meaning and rich-
ness to the stark world of self-referring rights. The principal business
of political philosophy, in turn, is to derive from the conclusions of
moral philosophy those principles and institutional arrangements
that will justly secure our rights in an imperfect world. In the course
of this discussion, of course, I will be able to say only a little about
these vast subjects before returning to the questions that immediately
concern us. Nevertheless, I hope that what I do have to say will help
to illuminate those questions.

Individual Rights

There are at least two ways to undertake the discovery of the truths
of moral philosophy. The more ambitious approach takes one to the
deepest reaches of logic, epistemology, action theory, and ethics in
order to derive the basic moral truths, from which the casuistry then
proceeds by drawing upon the vast experience of the common law,
if not by way of justification, at least by way of illumination.[33] More
modestly, one might proceed by a series of minimal presumptions
and shifting burdens-of-proof, leading, if not to the greater certitude
of the more ambitious approach, at least to the relative certitude that
flows from there being no better conclusion in view.[34] In either case,
however, if we proceed in the classical liberal tradition of methodological individualism (by far the most modest presumption), the
basic conclusions we derive are fairly Biblical in their simplicity,
however complex may be the arguments necessary to their derivation, on one hand, or to their application on the other. Stated as
obligations, correlative to which are rights in others, they are (1) As
between generally related individuals—common law strangers—do
not take what does not belong to you; (2) As between specially related
individuals, keep your agreements; and (3) Failing in either one or
two, give back what you have wrongly taken or wrongly withheld.[35]

---

[33]For examples of the more ambitious approach, see Alan Gewirth, *Reason and Morality*
(Chicago: University of Chicago Press, 1978); Roger Pilon, "A Theory of Rights: Toward
Limited Government," Ph.D. dissertation, University of Chicago, 1979.

[34]For an example of this approach, see Richard A. Epstein, "Possession As the Root of
Title," *Georgia Law Review* 13 (Summer 1979): 1121–43.

[35]The distinction between general and special relationships stems from H. L. A. Hart,
"Are There Any Natural Rights?" *Philosophical Review* 64 (1955): 175–91. I have
derived the conclusions set forth above, together with a number of applications, in my
doctoral dissertation, "A Theory of Rights," as well as in the following: "On Moral and
Legal Justification," *Southwestern University Law Review* 11 (1979): 1327–44; "Order-
ing Rights Consistently: Or What We Do and Do Not Have Rights To," *Georgia Law
Review* 13 (1979): 1171–96; "Corporations and Rights: On Treating Corporate People
Justly," *Georgia Law Review* 13 (1979): 1245–1370; "On The Foundations of Justice,"

What could be simpler? Again, the derivation of these conclusions as well as their application in manifold factual contexts is often exceedingly complex. At its core, however, the theory of human rights is elegantly simple, which is undoubtedly as it should be.

Notice, then, that all of our rights are reducible to property. John Locke, who more than anyone else can be said to have been America's philosopher, was perfectly correct, therefore, when he spoke of "Lives, Liberties, and Estates, which I call by the general Name, *Property*."[36] Notice also that all rights, however more particularly described, are derived from this fundamental root—and indeed are merely instances of it.[37] Notice finally that with certain rare exceptions, the theory of rights is perfectly consistent, yielding no conflicting rights and hence requiring no "balancing" of rights, whatever that may mean; for as individuals move from being generally related to being specially related, the rights they newly create replace those they have just alienated—thus is consistency preserved.[38]

The Anarchist's Challenge

Well, what has all of this to do with judicial review? Quite a bit. But we are not ready to proceed there just yet. First we have to address the question of political authority to which our question on judicial review led. We have to discover just what the roots of political authority are, whether it be the authority of the judge, the legislator, or the executive.

In addressing this issue, I am going to take what some may think a radical approach, because only so will we get to the heart of the matter. It will not do, for example, to stop at the Constitution, for ours is only one among many such arrangements, each of which must be justified against the moral principles just outlined in order to be ultimately satisfying. When we generalize the question, however, we are taken straightaway to the state-of-nature theory that dominated the moral and political thought of the 17th and 18th centuries, upon which the Founders drew so heavily, and to the ultimate ques-

---

Intercollegiate Review 17 (1981): 3–14; "Capitalism and Rights: An Essay Toward Fine-Tuning the Moral Foundations of the Free Society," *Journal of Business Ethics* 1 (1982): 29–42; "Property Rights, Takings, and a Free Society," *Harvard Journal of Law and Public Policy* 6 (1983): 165–95.

[36]John Locke, "The Second Treatise of Government," in *John Locke: Two Treatises of Government*, edited by Peter Laslett, rev. ed. (New York: Mentor, 1965), §123 (original emphasis); see also §87. I have indicated the theoretical foundations of this point in Pilon, "Ordering Rights Consistently," pp. 1178–82.

[37]Compare with footnote 17 of this paper and the accompanying text.

[38]See Pilon, "Corporations and Rights," p. 1286.

tion of political philosophy, the anarchist's challenge: By what right does one man have power over another? If we can answer that question we will have solved the basic problem of political philosophy.

Now it will not do, by way of answer, to point to the good deeds the ruler does, certainly not in the American tradition of individual rights. For as every student of the common law knows, mere receipt of benefit does not entail creation of obligation: Common law strangers are obligated only to leave each other alone, not to affirmatively conform to the will or wishes of others, even when they receive gratuitous benefits from those others. Benefactors, therefore, have no more rights than they would have had they done nothing at all. Indeed, the whole democratic thrust has been directed against beneficent and maleficent rulers alike. Democracy is not a cry for good rule but a cry for self rule.[39]

The foundations of political obligation are located, then, not in consequences, even good ones, but in process; and process is legitimate when rights are respected—in particular, when power over others arises through consent. As the Declaration of Independence makes clear, governments derive their *just* powers "from the consent of the governed." That, and only that, is the source of their legitimacy. But how could it be otherwise? If our basic right is one of private sovereignty, of sovereignty over what is ours—our lives, liberties, and estates—then any authority in another over what is ours must have arisen in such a way as to be consistent with our basic moral right. To be legitimate, that is, any such power must have been consented to by those over whom it is exercised, just as with any ordinary contract. Otherwise, the power exercised by that other over what is ours violates our right to be sovereign over our dominion: It is mere power, not authority. Only *we* have the right to alienate our sovereignty, in whole or in part. When others alienate our sovereignty without our consent, they take what is ours, they alienate our unalienable rights.

Social-Contract Theory

This explicates, of course, the moral foundations of the social-contract theory that dominated classical liberal thought in the 17th and 18th centuries. The power of the sovereign is legitimate only when grounded in the consent of the governed. But here we have to be careful. For it was never enough, on the classical view, that consent be manifest by the conduct of periodic elections among the

---

[39]See Isaiah Berlin, "Two Concepts of Liberty," in *Four Essays on Liberty* (Oxford: Oxford University Press, 1969), especially pp. 129–31, 162–66.

people. Indeed, by themselves, periodic elections yield no answer at all to the question why the majority that emerges from the process should have power over the minority; for by its very vote the minority indicates it does *not* consent to the issue in question. At common law, parties who cannot come to a meeting of the minds simply walk away. Should it be any different here? Surely the numbers carry no intrinsic moral weight, not if individual rights mean anything at all. Nor does the right of the minority to leave the territory—*its* territory—carry any weight either (the "love it or leave it" argument); for the question here, the basic question, is what right the majority has to put the minority to a choice between two of its entitlements—its right to remain where it is, and its right not to come under the rule of the majority. Clearly, the argument from periodic elections alone merely replicates the original problem, with "majority" and "minority" replacing "ruler" and "subject."

On the classical view, then, the obligation of the minority to conform to the will of the majority could be justified only by pointing to prior unanimity, to the prior consent of all to be bound thereafter by the results that flowed from the various decision procedures settled upon through that prior unanimous consent. Only when we give our prior consent to be bound by the outcome of an election, that is, can we be said to be obligated to abide by that outcome. Indeed, we need look no further than Article VII of the Constitution to see this point: "The Ratification of the Conventions of nine States, shall be sufficient for the Establishment of this Constitution *between the States so ratifying the Same*" [emphasis added]. Clearly, those states that did not ratify the Constitution could not have been bound by it, no matter how small a number they may have been. It is prior unanimous consent, then, that gets the whole game going, that justifies the structure, the decision procedures, and the whole apparatus through which legislators, executives, and judges ultimately derive their authority.

But here, precisely, is the rub. For as a matter of pure historical fact, there never was any such consent. We never did come together in that grand primordial field to yield up our unanimous consent, not to mention some consent capable of binding our heirs. At best, in the American context, our ancestors, or some majority of them, sent their representatives to the various state conventions, where majority rule prevailed again, presumably, to yield unanimity as regards the *states*. But surely that is not the consent that binds those who voted "nay" at some stage in the process, to say nothing of those who played no part at all in the process. Nor will the argument from tacit consent suffice: "You stayed, therefore you are bound." For again, by what right are we put to a choice between leaving or coming under another's rule? The anarchist, in short, has thrown down the gauntlet, and not even the recent and brilliant work of Robert Nozick in his award-winning *Anarchy, State, and Utopia* has succeeded in overcoming the challenge.[40]

None of this is to argue, of course, that no state enjoys even the relative acceptance of its citizens, or that there are not different degrees of consent in different states at different times. Nor is it to argue that there are not immense practical reasons for coming in out of the state of nature, which Locke and others carefully catalogued. I fully expect, in fact, that in any realistic world these arguments would "carry the day," even if we did have a full appreciation of the ultimate inadequacy of social-contract theory. But it is important to recognize that although they would likely carry the day, arguments from relative consent and from prudence, strictly speaking, do not go to the core of the moral issue, a point we most keenly appreciate when we are in the minority on some important question about which the majority is just wrong—morally wrong. At that point the argument from prior consent looks painfully pale.

What the anarchist has done, then, is help us to appreciate the tenuousness of the consent that undergirds political authority—*all* political authority. He has helped us to see, that is, that there is an air of illegitimacy that ineluctably surrounds *any* public undertaking. For even that quintessential public undertaking, the securing of our rights, is done in violation of the rights of those who would prefer to secure their rights themselves rather than pay the state for the service. We are forcing our association upon such individuals, which by our own standards we have no right to do. If this is true for so basic a service as securing rights, then *a fortiori* it is true for the countless services the modern state provides.

Now I realize that the 20th-century mind, accustomed as it is to viewing the state as a vehicle for doing good, is likely to find these conclusions disquieting, especially since they come not from economics but from ethics. But the anarchist is simply reminding us, albeit in a more searching way, of an insight the Founders keenly

---

[40]Robert Nozick, *Anarchy, State, and Utopia* (New York: Basic Books, 1974). On anarchism generally, see Robert Paul Wolff, *In Defense of Anarchism* (New York: Harper & Row, 1970). Decision theorists have pointed to quite different problems that surround the theory of democracy, including the observation that majoritarian procedures rarely yield majoritarian preferences. See, for example, Kenneth Arrow, *Social Choice and Individual Values*, 2d ed. (New Haven, Conn.: Yale University Press, 1963); William H. Riker, "Implications From the Disequilibrium of Majority Rule for the Study of Institutions," *American Political Science Review* 74 (1980): 432–46.

appreciated—that the state is a necessary evil, to which powers are to be given only when absolutely necessary.[41] He is urging us, in short, to reflect before we ask the state to do something for us.

From Process to Substance: The Search for Legitimacy

As a theoretical matter, then, when we heed what the anarchist is saying, two important results follow. First, we get the presumptions right. When we recognize the inherent illegitimacy of all political power, that is, a heavy burden is placed upon those who would urge public undertakings to show why those undertakings must be public, why the ends sought, however desirable, must be sought through public institutions. Second, and perhaps more important, we get the focus right. When we recognize our inability to satisfy the unanimous consent condition—when we recognize, that is, the illegitimacy that surrounds the very majoritarian decision process—the moral force of the argument from majority rule is positively undercut; as a result, our focus is shifted away from the process approach to legitimacy and toward the substantive approach. Process will not carry the day; substance must.

These results have two important corollaries. First, when we get the presumptions right, when we place a heavy burden upon those who would pursue ends through government institutions to show why, the presumption amounts to saying that since all government undertakings involve forced associations, government should be doing as little as possible. Second, when we get the focus right—on substance rather than process—we are encouraged to recognize that since government undertakings cannot be justified by considerations of process, by considerations of majority rule, for all government undertakings entail violating the rights of those who would not be associated with them, then whatever is undertaken through government must violate as few *additional* rights as possible. Since the undertaking enjoys no ultimate legitimacy from considerations of process, that is, whatever legitimacy it enjoys must be derived from the fact that no additional rights are violated by its execution. Otherwise the undertaking is twice illegitimate. Thus a policy of securing rights, if executed without violating any additional rights, would be right violating only with respect to those who would prefer to perform

---

[41]See William Stoebuck, "A General Theory of Eminent Domain," *Washington Law Review* 47 (1972): 553–608: "In essence, Lockean social-contract theory says this: . . . Government is a servant, necessary but evil, to which its subjects have surrendered only what they must, and that grudgingly. . . . [H]is was the accepted theory of government when the [Constitution] was being hammered out" (pp. 585–86).

this function themselves, those who are thus forced to have the government perform the service for them.[42]

Substantive Due Process

Now these several considerations can be drawn together, and we can return to the questions we left earlier, through a brief thought experiment as to what possibly could be the meaning of the due process clauses of the Fifth and Fourteenth amendments. The Fourteenth Amendment clause, for example, reads as follows: "nor shall any State deprive any person of life, liberty, or property, without due process of law." The problem, of course, is to determine the meaning of "due process of law," for with due process of law, presumably, a state may deprive a person of life, liberty, or property.

Let us assume initially that the clause has a purely procedural meaning, however difficult that assumption may be to sustain in the mind's eye; and ignore, for purposes of this experiment, all other clauses in the Constitution, however relevant. Presumably, then, if a state, through its duly elected and appointed officials, following duly enacted law, decides to hang a man for no other reason than that it wills to do so, it may hang him, for due process will have been followed. But this cannot be right, you say. Oh but it can! If all we mean by "due process of law" is mere procedure, then a man will be wrongly hanged only when the relevant officials hang him without first having gone through the procedural niceties. Our disquiet derives, of course, first from our inability to fully comprehend what mere procedural conformance would mean in a case such as this—after all, you cannot simply will a man hanged; there must be notice (of what behavior is illegal), charges, evidence, and so forth—and second, from our sense, implicit in our inability to comprehend "mere procedure," that "due process of law" cannot mean "mere procedure." While procedural correctness is a *necessary* condition for due process of law, that is, it is not a *sufficient* condition. In addition, due process of law requires substantive correctness.[43]

[42]Notice how this second corollary qualifies the first. If government undertakes a policy of securing our rights, for example, in connection with which it prohibits most self-help remedies, it cannot then do "as little as possible," as called for in the first corollary. Once it disables its citizens, that is, even if only by degree, government may thereby bind itself to do a great deal by way of executing the responsibility it has taken on.

[43]Notice, then, that "procedure" has two aspects, both of which involve substantive moral rights. First, "due process" may refer to the political process—legislative, judicial, or executive—through which the relevant law has been established, which involves the substantive rights discussed earlier. Second, "due process" may refer to the legal process—executive, judicial, or even legislative—through which that law is executed,

But now suppose our state wants to hang its man, again following all due process, but not simply because it wills to do so but because he parts his hair on the left, or because he is a Jew, or because the state needs to reduce the size of its population, or because the man is genetically unfit. Here, at least, there are substantive considerations; one could even say there is policy. But clearly, not any substance will do. We now have both procedure and substance, both due process and due process of law, if you will, but we have the wrong law. Yet how do we know this? As an historical matter, of course, my examples are not entirely far-fetched.

To try to get to the bottom of how we know this, let us assume now that our state wants to hang its man because he stole a dollar, or because he stole a million dollars, or because he maimed another for life, or because he murdered another. Getting closer? Clearly something is different in this series of examples. Here, unlike with the earlier examples, the man has *done* something, something wrong. By violating the right of another he has alienated a right of his own, meaning that others may treat him in ways that otherwise they may not. How do we know this? Not as a matter of policy, not because some legislature, reflecting the will of the majority, decided that we had a right to treat such a person differently than would be the case had he done nothing at all—which suggests that if the legislature had decided otherwise, then we would not have had that right. No, we have this knowledge as a matter of pure reason. These conclusions are contained in and derivable from the theory of rights mentioned earlier. If we are ever to get clear, therefore, about the substantive element in "due process of law," it is absolutely essential that we get clear about the substantive theory of rights; for this is the theory that tells us what we may or may not do to another, whether as

---

which also involves substantive rights, notwithstanding that some of these substantive rights are called "procedural rights."

Notice further that the word "law" in "due process of law" is systematically ambiguous, denoting either the positive law or the higher, moral law. This distinction is crucial; for if, indeed, all we do mean to denote by "law" when we speak of "due process of law" is the positive law, then the state *may* simply will its man hanged—provided the positive law permits this. As long as such "law" satisfies the system's criteria for being positive law—as opposed to social custom, say, or moral law—it will be law within that system. That law would not conform to the *higher* law, of course, and so would not be *morally* justified. Could the authors of the Fifth and Fourteenth amendments have meant "mere" law when they wrote "due process of law"? (see Siegan, *Economic Liberties.*) Can we? On criteria for establishing the existence of positive law, and on legal positivism generally, see H. L. A. Hart, *The Concept of Law* (Oxford: Clarendon Press, 1961).

individuals or as public officials.[44] It is the theory that provides the substantive element in "due process of law."

"Due process of law," then, is more than mere process; and it is more than process plus any substance. It is process plus that substance that tells us when we may or may not deprive a person of his life, liberty, or property. As we saw earlier, however, that substantive element is justified not because it reflects the will of the majority, not because it has been determined by some democratic process, but because it is derived from principles of reason. (But see the discussion in the next paragraph.) We have no right to hang a man simply because he is a Jew, even if a substantial majority of the legislature says that we may. We do have a right to treat a person who has stolen a dollar differently than otherwise we may, even if a substantial majority of the legislature says that we may not. These are not matters of will or of policy; they are matters of reason.

Now it is not without reason that I selected that last series of examples, for it serves to draw out an important point, a point that qualifies these conclusions ever so slightly—or better, shows where considerations of value or will enter the picture at last. It is a conclusion of reason that we may treat a man who has done something wrong differently than otherwise we may. And it is a conclusion of reason that the treatment must in some sense equal the wrong. But just what treatment will equal or rectify the wrong is often not a matter of reason. When determining appropriate punishment, then, as well as a good many compensatory remedies, we have to leave the realm of reason, strictly speaking, and move into the realm of value. Here, however, subjectivity enters; reasonable men will disagree about values as they should not about rights if those rights are derived from ultimate principles of reason. Accordingly, when we reach those points in the theory of rights where value determinations are necessary—as with remedies, or with questions about where exactly to draw the line between one man's right to quiet enjoyment of what is his and another man's right to active use of what is his—then we have genuine questions of policy. Precisely what punishment fits a given crime, therefore, or how much particulate matter a factory shall be permitted to emit are questions of value, not of rights; accordingly,

---

[44]Public officials, after all, even if they did derive their powers from the consent of the governed, could not have rights that individuals did not first have to yield up to them. Where would they have gotten such rights? See Nozick, *Anarchy, State, and Utopia*, p.6.

they are questions properly put to all of the people and hence to the legislature, to be decided by the prevailing standards of the time.[45]

As we have seen, then, if a state may hang a man only with due process of law and "due process of law" takes its meaning from the theory of rights—in particular, in the case at hand, from the principle that no man may be hanged unless he has done something to alienate his right against being hanged—then clearly the state has no right to hang a man in order to advance medical science, say, or to make an example of him to those who know nothing of his innocence, or to prevent some great social harm being perpetrated by the mob that mistakenly thinks him guilty. For these grounds for hanging amount to nothing less than *using* him in order to achieve some "social good." That is precisely what our rights prohibit others from doing—from using us for their own or even for society's greater good.[46] Recall that only *we* can legitimately alienate our rights; others have no right to do so, no matter how noble their motives or worthy their ends.

But if these conclusions hold in the case of depriving a man of his life, do they hold any less when we deprive a man of his liberty or property in order to achieve some "social good"? The Fourteenth Amendment makes no distinction at all between "more valuable" and "less valuable" rights. It says simply that no state shall deprive a person of life, liberty, or property without due process of law. If a man has done something to alienate his right in his life, liberty, or property, then by due process of law we may take that over which he no longer holds a right. Absent that condition, however, we have no right to take what rightly belongs to him. We have no right, for example, to take the liberty of a store owner to set his milk prices at whatever level he chooses, even if taking that liberty *would* accomplish the great social good of guaranteeing a "reasonable return" to milk producers and dealers. Nor do we have a right to redistribute Hawaiian land from owners to their tenants in order to cope with "oligopolistic market structures," even if those tenants do compensate the owners. For in neither case have those from whom we are taking done anything to justify our taking. If indeed we *must* take

---

[45]I have discussed some of these issues more fully in "Criminal Remedies: Restitution, Punishment, or Both?" *Ethics* 88 (1978): 348–57, and in "Corporations and Rights," pp. 1276–77, 1333–39. See also Richard A. Epstein, "Nuisance Law: Corrective Justice and its Utilitarian Constraints," *Journal of Legal Studies* 8 (1979): 49–102.

[46]This was the fundamental Kantian insight; see, for example, Immanuel Kant, *Groundwork of the Metaphysic of Morals*, translated by H. Paton (New York: Harper & Row, 1964). For an application, see Charles Fried, "Fast and Loose in the Welfare State," *AEI Regulation* 3 (May/June 1979): pp. 13–16 (proposal to require lawyers to do *pro bono* work as a condition of licensure).

what does not belong to us—in order to achieve some *compelling* social good—then at a minimum we should pay for what we have taken.[47] But the power of eminent domain is exercised by necessity, not by right. In recognition of this, at least, we pay. Should it be any different when we take a man's liberty? Why should *he* bear the costs of *our* pursuit of the "social good"? Indeed, is this not the welfare state on its head: not the few drawing from the many but the many taking from the few?

Now it should be noted here that had the *Nebbia* Court overturned the New York statute that prohibited the milk dealer from lowering his prices, it would not have been "making policy" or "imposing its values" on the citizens of New York. Rather, it would have been deciding the case according to the law, the higher law—not some arbitrary or spurious "higher law" that stands in *opposition* to the Fourteenth Amendment, but the rational theory of rights that is the higher law that stands *behind* the Fourteenth Amendment. The Court would have been saying simply that you cannot take a man's liberty when he has done nothing to warrant it. Moreover, far from denying to the citizens of New York their right to govern themselves, the Court would have been saying only that those citizens must exercise their right in such a way as not to violate the rights of some among them.[48] We are fortunate, in short, that our Constitution—unlike, say, the Soviet Constitution—sets out precisely those rights that reflect the background, higher law, albeit in a general way only. That higher law is one of structure, of framework—of rights that both permit and constrain our pursuit of values, whether as individuals or collectively. But the higher law is not "neutral," any more than any of the truths of reason, strictly speaking, are "neutral." Rather, it is the law of individual freedom, of private sovereignty, and hence of laissez-faire capitalism, the pronouncements of Justices Holmes, Rehnquist, and many others to the contrary notwithstanding. Some may value those rights, others may not. But there is all the difference in the world between our rights and our values, between those moral relationships we derive from principles of reason and those attitudes we hold, pro and con, toward the various things of the world. The failure to make this distinction, the failure to distinguish the objectivity of the one

---

[47]For a development of this principle with respect to the notorious Fifth Amendment "taking issue," see Pilon, "Property Rights, Takings, and a Free Society."

[48]Notice, however, how limited is our "right to govern ourselves (collectively)." If we take individual rights seriously, that is, there is not much room left for the pursuit of "public policy." This is a corollary, of course, of the conclusions developed in the previous section of this paper. Compare with footnote 29 above and the accompanying text, and the text accompanying footnote 45.

from the subjectivity of the other, can only lead, as it has in this century, to the most far-reaching of confusions.

Restoring the Judiciary

Needless to say, a judiciary untrained in these matters and driven by the darkest days of the legal realist movement would understandably, perhaps, have lost its confidence. Unable to discern that due process of law is ineluctably substantive and that all the rights we legitimately have are there to be drawn from the Constitution, they turned over to the legislature—the domain of interest and will— what was properly theirs to perform in the domain of reason. Having thus abandoned reason to will, they grew lethargic in their passivity until at last, witnessing the fun and profit the legislature seemed to be having pursuing the public good, they took up their own pursuit of that good, until today we are fairly awash with the public good.

Well, this will not change until we get back to basics. We will not unshackle the great engine of enterprise until we get the issues straight, until we recognize that the issue, ultimately, is not one of political legitimacy, of which branch of government has more authority to decide—for no branch enjoys the legitimacy that deeply satisfies. Nor is the issue one of values—individual or social, static or evolving. Rather, as it has always been, the issue, in the end, is one of right and wrong—of what it is, in particular, we may do to another by right. And that issue will be finally resolved neither by reading the Constitution literally or even narrowly, whatever those idioms may mean, nor by divining the intent of its authors, however felicitous that intent may have been, but only by going behind the Constitution to the rigorous, analytical theory of rights that alone can legitimately inform its broad texture, that alone can justify our resort to force, which is what government, in the end, is all about.

All of which reminds me of a remark I made to a colleague some years back, that judges should know their philosophy. "Know their philosophy?" my worldly friend replied. "You're lucky to find one who knows his law!" But how could it be otherwise. Our land today is papered over with law—often inconsistent, often downright ridiculous—so much law that no one in a lifetime can master it all. Yet the attempt, or the need, will keep a judge from turning to the things that matter, to the deep and abiding principles of reason and ethics that could help to order it all, that could help to roll it back, that could help to extricate the judiciary from its present intellectual impoverishment. In this, however, the judge needs our help. For let us be candid: at its best, his is a difficult and lonely job. In every system there are points at which the rule of law depends critically upon the rule of men. One such point in our system, a critically important point, is on the occasion of judicial review. We can make this occasion less difficult, less lonely, by creating a climate of opinion that encourages the judge to do what in the end is the only thing he should do—the right thing. We need to encourage the judge, in short, not to do less but to do better.

9

JUDICIAL PRAGMACTIVISM: A DEFINITION

Randy E. Barnett

judicial, *adj.* 1. of judges, law courts, or their functions. . . .

pragmatism, *n.* . . . . 3. a system of or tendency in philosophy which tests the validity of all concepts by their practical results.

activism, *n.* the doctrine or policy of being active or doing things with energy or decision.

—Webster's New World Dictionary

Introduction

When I was in law school, the students were constantly being prodded by the professors to take sides between the judiciary and the legislature when the two institutions came into conflict. The judicial activists among us sided with the judiciary, while the judicial passivists among us sided with the legislature. In those days the activists tended to be liberals and the passivists were mainly conservatives, although the *Lochner* decision[1] was effectively used by our professors to confound both the liberal-activists and the conservative-passivists among us. As a person whose primary concern was with protecting the rights of individuals to control the use of their bodies and the use and disposition of their possessions, I was never very comfortable in either camp.

In constitutional matters, where legislative or executive branches of government sought to encroach upon these rights, I usually found myself rooting for the judicial activists—as, for example, when

---

The author is Associate Professor of Law at the Illinois Institute of Technology, Chicago-Kent College of Law.

[1]Lochner v. New York, 198 U.S. 45 (1905). This was a decision in which the Supreme Court struck down, as violative of the due process clause of the Fourteenth Amendment, a state statute regulating the maximum hours that a baker may work.

studying the famous cases of *Nebbia v. New York*,[2] *Griswold v. Connecticut*,[3] or *Roe v. Wade*.[4] In private law matters, where the encroachment most often came from the judiciary, I usually found myself siding with the judicial passivists—as, for example, in such a case as *Williams v. Walker-Thomas Furniture Co.*[5] So what was I? Was I a judicial activist or a judicial passivist or—worse yet, from my point of view—was I simply an unprincipled vacillator, as in one who "waves to and fro," shows "indecision," or is "irresolute?"[6]

In this paper I suggest a third approach to the choice between judiciary and legislature that is no less principled than either pure activism or passivism, but it is principled in a different way. It is a view I call "judicial pragmactivism." *Webster's New World Dictionary* defines the word "judicial" as an adjective meaning "of judges, law courts, or their functions."[7] The third definition of "pragmatism" in *Webster's* is "a system of or tendency in philosophy which tests the validity of all concepts by their practical results."[8] Finally, "activism" is defined therein as "the doctrine or policy of being active or doing things with energy or decision."[9] Judicial pragmactivism, then,

---

[2]291 U.S. 502 (1934). In Nebbia v. New York the Supreme Court refused to strike down a state statute that attempted to regulate the minimum and maximum retail prices of milk. This case represents the dawn of an era that rejected judicial activism on behalf of "economic liberties" that was associated with the so-called Lochner era in favor of extreme deference to the will of the legislature.

[3]381 U.S. 479 (1965).

[4]410 U.S. 113 (1973). This case and Griswold v. Connecticut are taken as representing a renewed interest in protecting so-called fundamental rights from legislative regulation under the due process clause of the Fourteenth Amendment. Roe v. Wade concerned a statute making it a crime to procure an abortion; Griswold v. Connecticut concerned a statute that criminalized the private use of contraceptives. Both statutes were struck down by the Supreme Court. Thus far, economic liberties have not been considered by the Court to be "fundamental rights" requiring enhanced scrutiny under the due process clause.

[5]350 F.2d 445 (1965). In this case the United States Court of Appeals for the District of Columbia retroactively applied a recently enacted statute, 28 D.C. Code §2–302 (1965), which permitted a court to refuse to enforce an "unconscionable" contract, to a contract made before the enactment of the section.

[6]From the definition of "vacillate" found in *Webster's New World Dictionary* (1968), p. 1606.

[7]Ibid., p. 792.

[8]Ibid., p. 1146. *The Oxford English Dictionary*, vol. 8 (1970) offers the following helpful definition of pragmatism as its fourth meaning: "the method of testing the value of any assertion that claims to be true, by its consequences, i.e. by its practical bearing upon human interests and purposes" (p. 1225).

[9]*Webster's*, p. 15.

can be defined as follows:

> *judicial pragmactivism, n.* a system of philosophy or jurisprudence
> that tests the validity of a decision concerning the appropriate sphere
> of judges or law courts by its tendency to actively achieve a practical
> result or results.[10]

Judicial pragmactivism is not to be confused with "moral pragmatism." Pragmatism as a moral philosophy claims insight into the choices among ends. Judicial pragmactivism has nothing to say about the ends of law. It applies only to the choice of means to achieve ends that may be established in numerous and nonpragmatic ways, and even then it applies only to the limited choice between the judiciary or the legislature as the appropriate means to these ends. To a judicial pragmactivist, neither judicial activism nor judicial passivism is correct all the time. Sometimes activism is justified; at other times passivity is warranted. Which stance is appropriate in what instance must be decided by determining both the likely consequences of each for the parties at hand and the potential effect of this choice on future parties. And how they distinguish good consequences from bad consequences will differentiate pragmactivists from each other.

Different Kinds of Pragmactivism

A judicial pragmactivist favors whichever forum is more likely, in a particular instance, to secure fundamental moral principles. Where the consequences of judicial initiative are more in harmony with a pragmactivist's basic principles than the consequences of deferring to the legislature, judicial initiative is favored; where the consequences of deferring to the legislature are more in harmony with the pragmactivist's basic principles than judicial initiative, judicial deference is favored. Jurisprudential confusion arises, though, not only from a failure to recognize judicial pragmactivism as a respectable and principled view of the relationship between the judiciary and the legislature; it also arises from a failure to adequately acknowledge distinctions among pragmactivists.

Judicial pragmactivists differ with one another about which principles should be employed to distinguish "good" consequences from "bad" consequences. Some pragmactivists seek to advance certain

[10]So far as I know, I have coined this term. If it turns out that this expression has already been taken, I stand ready with a substitute: "judicial practivism." Let me suggest the following definition for this term: "judicial practivism, *n.* a synonym for judicial pragmactivism."

ends that other pragmactivists find abhorrent. The principles about which they disagree are usually easily discernible and can be made the subject of rational discourse and sometimes even ultimate resolution. Furthermore, the differing principles of different pragmactivists can account for their coming out on different sides of a choice between the judiciary or legislature in a particular case.

For example, one may be an efficiency pragmactivist and argue that judges should acquiesce to the legislature when a statute leads to the efficient outcome but should blaze new creative legal trails when a statute is inefficient. The consequence against which judicial intervention is assessed is whether the goal of efficiency is served or disserved by judicial intervention or by judicial deference. Or one may be an equal-wealth pragmactivist favoring only those departures from statutes and precedent that serve to equalize the material possessions of all and favoring passivism where statutes and precedents are having this effect. The consequence against which judicial intervention is assessed is whether the goal of material equality is served or disserved by judicial intervention or by judicial deference.

Lastly, one may be a rights pragmactivist. According to this view, judges should passively follow the public and private law when it is in accord with the property rights[11] of all persons (as would be the case with much of both the common law and most, if not all, of the rights enumerated by the Constitution of the United States). On the other hand, a judge should "make" new law when the preexisting law inadequately respects or protects these individual rights. In no event where well-defined rights of an individual are at stake should a judge yield in the defense of these rights to the will of the legislature.

A rights pragmactivist's view of the judiciary is based on the idea that the courts exist to do justice; that justice is determined by correctly identifying the rights of the parties to a lawsuit; that these rights are determined not solely by reference to the positive or enacted law, but are based on a more fundamental moral status; that because the violation of any person's rights is unjust, when a person has a right, this means that the court should respect that right and enforce it; and that failure by a court to respect and enforce a right is itself an injustice.[12]

---

[11]The term "property rights," as I use it, includes not only the right to use and alienate external possessions but also the right to control the use of one's body or person as well. I explain this usage at greater length in Barnett, "Why We Need Legal Philosophy," *Harvard Journal of Law and Public Policy* 8 (Winter 1985): 1–18. These are the rights to which I am referring when the term "individual rights" is used in the following discussion.

[12]Of course, to fully appreciate such a position, much more needs to be said about it

In short, unlike those who would favor the legislature as a matter of principle—such as, for example, the principle of "majority rule"—judicial pragmactivists assert that when the issue concerns the enforcement of fundamental rights, the choice between the judiciary and the legislature is to be governed by determining which institution will most expediently protect individual rights in a particular case. Whichever branch will best secure individual rights is the branch deserving of deference. Such a decision involves at least two kinds of issues: (1) which institution is likely to achieve the correct outcome in the case at hand, and (2) what effect is this choice likely to have on the ability of others to enforce their rights in the future.

The second of these issues can be affected by the sorts of institutional analysis we are accustomed to in matters of this sort—that is, an analysis that stresses the inherent qualities of the institution. Such phrases as "the least dangerous branch" or "expression of the majority's will" or "the ability of an institution to engage in fact finding" come to mind. It is here that we must be concerned about minimizing the possible errors in each direction—that is, the errors that will result from judicial activism as compared with the errors that will result from deference to the legislature.[13]

When employing a word whose root is "pragmatic," it is important to make clear where the assessment of consequences is being made to show that an approach called "rights pragmactivism" is not a contradiction in terms. A rights pragmactivist does not ask which *outcome* of a particular case has the "best" consequence, as a pragmatist would.[14] Rather, he or she asks which *institution*—judi-

---

than is possible here. Among other things, one would need to know the moral foundations for such rights, their contents, how they comport with a "rule of law" approach to adjudication, the means by which they may be identified, and the type of legal order that is best suited to enforce them.

I discuss each of these issues at greater length elsewhere. See Barnett, "Why We Need Legal Philosophy"; and "Pursuing Justice in a Free Society: Power v. Liberty," *Criminal Justice Ethics* 4 (Summer/Fall 1985): 50–72; and "Pursuing Justice in a Free Society: Crime Prevention and the Legal Order," *Criminal Justice Ethics* 5 (Winter/Spring 1986): 30–53.

The rights-based approach to justice and social order described in the text of this paper has received wide attention in recent years. I summarize recent intellectual developments in this direction and attempt to put them in a historical context in Barnett, "Contract Scholarship and the Reemergence of Legal Philosophy" (review essay), *Harvard Law Review* 97 (March 1984): 1225–36.

[13]See Richard A. Epstein, "Judicial Review: Reckoning on Two Kinds of Error," this volume, ch. 3.

[14]Except insofar as consequences enter into determining what rights we have. I have briefly discussed how consequences and rights may fit together in Barnett, "Public Decisions and Private Rights" (review essay), *Criminal Justice Ethics* 3 (Summer/Fall

ciary or legislature—is more likely to secure the correct outcome, namely, the enforcement of the fundamental rights of the parties and of others in the future. The rights pragmactivist then chooses the enforcement mechanism accordingly.

We are pragmactivistic in a similar manner when we formulate rules governing the admission of evidence. The rules that make up the law of evidence are not ends in themselves, but are always instrumental in achieving the other more fundamental ends of the judicial process.[15] We know that the enforcement of a rule of evidence will sometimes lead to mistaken outcomes, but we rightly fear that a relaxation of evidentiary rules to permit judicial "discretion" will create more frequent and more serious mistakes.[16] Just as the choice of evidentiary rules is instrumental in achieving the fundamental goals of the judicial process, to a rights pragmactivist the choice between the judiciary and the legislature is always to be assessed by its potential effects on the enforcement of individual rights.

Outcomes versus Rationales

The rights of future parties will not only be affected by the outcome of a particular case; they may also be affected by the reasons given for that outcome. A rights pragmactivist may favor the outcome of judicial activism because it is consistent with and protects individual rights, both of the parties and of others in the future, while still

---

1984): 50–62. See also John Gray, "Indirect Utility and Fundamental Rights," *Social and Political Philosophy* 1 (Spring 1984):73–91, which discusses the consequentialist component of the concept of individual rights.

[15]At least three ends or functions of the judicial process are needed to explain most of evidence law: (1) the justice function, which is the effort to discover the historical truth about an event that has occurred sometime in the past; (2) the fairness function, which is the effort to satisfy the parties and the community that the truth has been discovered, and therefore that justice has been done; and (3) the adversary function, which is the attempt to harness the self-interest of the parties to a lawsuit to achieve the first two functions.

[16]For a brief explanation of the difference between a legal system based on rules and one based on (cost-benefit) balancing, and the advantages of the former, see Mario J. Rizzo, "Rules versus Cost-Benefit Analysis in the Common Law," this volume, ch. 10, especially pp. 232–43.

It is important to note that the analogy between rights pragmactivism and evidence law employed in the text of this paper compares the choice between branches of government with the choice among rules of evidence to show that (1) both types of choices are pragmatic or instrumental in their nature, and (2) a correct choice in either area will minimize, but not eliminate, all error. The analogy is not offered to suggest that the choice between branches of government should be governed by rules of the sort that should govern the law of evidence. If no workable set of rules could be identified that would indeed minimize rights violations, a rights pragmactivist would reject this suggestion.

insisting that the rationale proffered by the judge for the outcome is woefully deficient. Therefore, although judicial intervention may be favored on pragmactivist grounds to secure an individual's rights, the rationale for a judicial decision may still be criticized because it is an incorrect analysis of the rights in issue.

In the case of *Griswold v. Connecticut*,[17] for example, the United States Supreme Court found that a state statute criminalizing the use of contraceptives infringed upon what the Court said was every citizen's constitutional "right of privacy."[18] A rights pragmactivist may strongly deny that any person has a right to privacy as such.[19] Nonetheless, rights pragmactivists may still oppose any retreat from *Griswold* if this would mean upholding a statute restricting the right to exercise choice in the area of birth control, even though the articulated rationale for the outcome might in their view be quite wrong.

Similarly, because of what they believe are the rights of women to control their bodies, even at the expense of other human beings who may reside within, rights pragmactivists may still embrace the precedent of *Roe v. Wade*[20] (which respects and enforces the rights of women to exercise choice in the area of abortion) while always being careful to distance themselves from supporting a putative right to privacy.

A rights pragmactivist, on balance, may favor the exercise of judicial "lawmaking" here because it furthers the securement of certain individual rights, even though the court may be stating the wrong reason for its decision. At the same time, it should be stressed, a complete assessment of the consequences of this choice in a particular case must take into account the danger to the security of other rights that a decision based on erroneous grounds may create. In rare cases a rights pragmactivist may be forced to oppose the

---

[17]381 U.S. 479 (1965).

[18]Id. at 486: "We deal with a right of privacy older than the Bill of Rights—older than our political parties, older than our school system."

[19]As a positive matter, a rights pragmactivist may contest the claim that there exists a constitutional right of privacy. The Constitution does not mention any such right, and the argument that it is implicit in the Constitution is belied by the nearly 200 years of constitutional jurisprudence during which some well-respected members of the Supreme Court have managed to overlook its presence.

As a normative matter such a right is extremely problematic in that, if applied broadly, it can undermine other rights, such as property rights, that support free speech and a free press. See, for example, Cox Broadcasting Corp. v. Cohn, 420 U.S. 469 (1975), which struck down a state restriction on the publication of a rape victim's name obtained from public records, but refused to decide whether "the State may ever define and protect an area of privacy free from unwanted publicity in the press" (id. at 491).

[20]410 U.S. 113 (1973).

"correct" outcome, when a wrong rationale for that outcome places other rights in serious jeopardy. Such a judgment is a matter about which reasonable people are likely to differ.

Pragmactivism and the Constitution

Judicial pragmactivism also takes a pragmatic approach to the Constitution. It views a constitutional framework as instrumental to other more fundamental principles. How a pragmactivist views the deference that a judge should pay to the Constitution of the United States depends, therefore, upon how he views the Constitution. Where the Constitution is viewed as a positive embodiment of the principles of right and wrong held by the pragmactivist, then he would be very deferential to the Constitution and would, on normative grounds, argue that others should be as well. Where this is not the case, only small weight would be placed on the words of the Constitution.

In the case of *Hawaii Housing Authority v. Midkiff*,[21] for example, equal-wealth pragmactivists would cheer on the Supreme Court's deference to the state legislature's attempt to take land from some and give it to others, allegedly in contravention of the "takings clause" of the Fifth Amendment.[22] Efficiency pragmactivists would have to ponder the effects on competition of having so much land in so few hands, balanced against the costs of undercutting the certainty of the landowner's property rights. Rights pragmactivists, who view the takings clause as an integral part of the Constitution's protection of property rights,[23] would simply be aghast at the injustice done by the Court's disregard of this constitutional provision.

If a rights pragmactivist agreed with such scholars as Richard Epstein that the Constitution is a largely successful enunciation of the requirements of a free society based on individual rights to life, liberty, and property,[24] then he or she would favor extreme deference

---

[21] 81 L.Ed.2d 186 (1984).

[22] The Fifth Amendment of the Constitution states, in part: ". . . nor shall private property be taken for public use, without just compensation."

[23] See, for example, Richard Epstein, "Not Deference, but Doctrine: The Eminent Domain Clause," *Supreme Court Review* 11 (1983): 351–80.

[24] This view is suggested by Epstein's analysis of the takings clause (ibid., p. 351):

> As a matter of practical politics and high political theory, one of the central functions of government is to create a stable legal order in which all individuals may securely use their talents and possessions. In order to meet this minimum condition of social order, it has been seen necessary, at least in the American constitutional system, to develop a complex system of checks and balances to prevent the aggrandizement and abuse of official power by any single group of individuals.

This theme is developed further in Epstein's book, *Takings: Private Property and the Power of Eminent Domain* (Cambridge, Mass.: Harvard University Press, 1985).

to the words and spirit of the Constitution. If one believes that the Constitution does not justify the political power it creates,[25] but that, given the necessity of such power, it provides an appropriate framework of limitations on its use, then one would still be quite deferential to the words and spirit of the Constitution.

Moreover, a rights-pragmactivist who is sympathetic to the Constitution on the normative ground that the scheme it enacts is harmonious with individual rights would advocate that the judiciary "actively" strike down legislation that violated the rights enumerated or implicit[26] in the Constitution or that undermined the framework it enacted.[27] By the same token, such a rights-pragmactivist would bitterly oppose any invention of new constitutional "rights" which a judge might find congenial.[28]

If, on the other hand, one agreed that political power was evil but disagreed with the frequently made assertion that it is necessary, then much of the political framework provided by the Constitution would be highly suspect. A rights pragmactivist who took this approach may still contend that deference to many of the political provisions of the Constitution—the balance of powers framework for example—is prudent in the absence of a politically feasible alternative, but that once that alternative became available, deference to the Constitution should melt away. Still other provisions—for example, those giving Congress the right and obligation to coin money or to establish post offices and roads[29]—would not be entitled to even this prima facie deference.

Judicial pragmactivism also assists an understanding of the endless wrangling about the proper mode of constitutional interpretation. Suppose that rights pragmactivists who view the U.S. Constitution as providing an effective framework to protect certain individual

---

[25]See, for example, Roger Pilon, "Legislative Activism, Judicial Activism, and the Decline of Private Sovereignty," this volume, ch. 8.

[26]I defend the view that the judicial protection of "property rights" derived from centuries-old, judge-made "common law" principles is implicit in the "historical Constitution" in Randy E. Barnett, "Are Enumerated Constitutional Rights the Only Rights We Have? The Case of Associational Freedom," *Harvard Journal of Law and Public Policy* 10 (forthcoming).

[27]See, for example, Epstein, *Takings*, p. 281, where he argues that "[t]he New Deal *is* inconsistent with the principles of limited government and with the constitutional decisions in a wide diversity of cases."

[28]See, for example, Epstein, *Takings*, pp. 306–29, challenging the constitutionality of "welfare rights" and concluding that it "is not possible to design a stable set of institutional arrangements for transfer payments to satisfy the just-compensation requirement of the eminent domain clause."

[29]See U.S. Constitution, art. I, §8.

rights (and not others) are correct in their *descriptive* assessment. If so, then honest pragmactivist advocates of principles inconsistent with this framework—equal-wealth pragmactivists, for example— have but two responses. They can either reject adherence to the Constitution on normative grounds or they can try to pursue their normative ends by espousing a loose "living constitution" mode of interpretation to escape the constraints of the document.

Rights pragmactivists, on the other hand, would "strictly construe" the Constitution, justifying this mode of constitutional interpretation on the normative grounds that the "original" or "historical" (I would say "actual") constitutional framework is basically right. The debate would then be joined on this *normative* level. In this way the controversy concerning the proper mode of constitutional interpretation can be seen as a purely pragmactivist debate.

While I am only defining (and not defending) judicial pragmactivism in this paper, there is one concern that is worth considering because it may impede the willingness of some to accept the pragmactivist position as a reasonable alternative to passivism or activism. A critic may ask: Do we really want to encourage judges to interpret constitutional provisions in light of their vision of rights or justice or whatever? Is not the constitutional *process* a sufficiently important value that we should not permit it to be "undermined" by a judge's opinion of *substantive* matters?[30] It will take but a moment's reflection to realize that this concern depends as much upon a substantive assessment of the Constitution as the assessment called for by judicial pragmactivism.

The critic of pragmactivism who says a judge should never (or only rarely) sacrifice the constitutional process in pursuit of substantive ends, but should instead urge that the Constitution be changed or perhaps should resign from the bench, can assert this position only on the assumption that the constitutional framework in existence advances the critic's favored substantive concerns. In other words, the critic is asserting that the Constitution is sufficiently well done and that to let a judge undermine a piece of it here will cost us a lot more elsewhere. On balance, therefore, we will be "worse off" if such meddling is permitted. However, one can make the judgment that the Constitution is well done and that meddling with it will make us better off or worse off only with respect to a substantive standard of good and bad that must be external to the Constitution itself, a standard that the critic does not disclose.

---

[30]I thank Earl Ravenal for inducing me to respond to this widely held concern.

Thus what appears at first glance to be a process-oriented position that eschews substantive judgments conceals what is mainly a substantive assumption about the merits of the Constitution; that is, that the Constitution is too good to let individual judges tamper with it. The critic of pragmactivism turns out to be simply taking an extreme pragmactivist position: that letting judges intervene to pursue ends will invariably end up defeating the ends we should be seeking. What the critic of pragmactivism is not making clear is the extraconstitutional standard of evaluation that led to this conclusion. Once this standard is made explicit, a rational and essentially pragmactivist analysis of the critic's position is then possible.

The conclusion that a substantive assumption underlies this facially process-oriented concern can be tested by seeing whether, if the substantive assumption is changed, we feel as confident about the process claim. Suppose we are in a country where a statute that sanctions genocide or apartheid has just been passed in accordance with all constitutional requirements. Do we really think that a judge who is asked to uphold such a statute should put the interest of the "constitutional order" above the fundamental preconstitutional rights of the affected persons? Must a judge in that society "follow" the constitution or resign from the bench when such serious rights violations are at stake? Do we deny to the military officer—a person who is part of a rigid command structure—who transports people to a concentration camp the defense that he was "only following orders," while allowing a judge—our last guardian of justice—to escape responsibility by asserting what amounts to the same thing?

A rights pragmactivist answers "no" to each of these questions. A judge has no legal duty to follow orders that are manifestly unjust,[31] whether these commands are spoken by a dictator or are written on a piece of parchment that bears the heading of "constitution." And a judge may have a moral duty to thwart the operation of such orders. If the concept of law includes a duty of obedience, despite the fact that they are sanctioned by a constitution, such unjust "laws" are not truly laws at all.

Therefore, even if the Supreme Court correctly interpreted the Constitution in *Korematsu v. United States*,[32] it was wrong nonetheless for the Court to permit the internment of innocent citizens of

---

[31]The word "manifestly" is used to rebut any prima facie duty to obey the positive law that may arguably exist. Such a duty can be asserted on the pragmactivist grounds that the fallibility and self-interest of individuals require the societal recognition in practice of a (rebuttable) presumption that duly enacted rules of conduct are valid.

[32]323 U.S. 214 (1944). This ruling upheld the constitutionality of the internment of United States citizens of Japanese descent.

Japanese descent. When they refused to strike down such a statute, these Supreme Court justices—their titles ringing hollow in this context—may have thought themselves to be acting pragmatically. They may have believed that the executive branch would not have complied with a decision that enforced the rights of the victims of this statute and thwarted the will of the majority. They may even have shared the majority's fears and believed that the preservation of the nation forced them to neglect the rights of the internees. Nevertheless a rights pragmactivist would suggest that they had abdicated their judicial responsibility.

Conclusion

This paper defines judicial pragmactivism as the jurisprudential mean that lies somewhere between the extremes of judicial activism and passivism. In my view, it is a position that others are attempting to both articulate and defend.[33] My purpose here is not to present a systematic defense of this position, but rather to identify it as an alternative position that is both principled and worthy of consideration.

Judicial pragmactivists see decisions concerning the allocation of lawmaking responsibility between the courts and the legislature as secondary to more fundamental matters of principle. They see the problem of which institution is to be preferred as one that concerns means and ends in a contest where the ends must take priority over the means.

Pragmactivists differ over what principles to adhere to—such as equality of wealth, efficiency, or the protection of individual rights. They also may disagree about how the balance of errors made by either the legislature or the judiciary in pursuit of these principles should be struck. However, they agree that decisions about which branch of government should prevail should not be made without taking account of the consequences of this allocation on the implementation of the principles they view as fundamental.

Finally, the version of pragmactivism that elevates the protection of individual rights to a central place in its view of society can be identified as a distinct brand of pragmactivism called rights pragmactivism. Rights pragmactivists stand somewhere between activists and passivists. They are extremely cautious about the creation of new rights or "entitlements" by an activist judiciary seeking ultimately to achieve social policy at the expense of the genuine property rights

---

[33]See, for example, Epstein, "Not Deference"; Pilon, "Legislative Activism"; and Peter H. Aranson, "Judicial Control of the Political Branches: Public Purpose and Public Law," this volume, ch. 4.

that secure our liberty. At the same time, however, rights pragmac-tivists are hard-pressed to justify sacrificing these individual rights on the altar of judicial restraint. Their credo is *"judicial activism in pursuit of liberty is no vice; judicial restraint in pursuit of justice is no virtue."*

COMMENT

A PUBLIC CHOICE PERSPECTIVE ON JUDICIAL PRAGMACTIVISM

Charles K. Rowley

In his interesting paper, Randy Barnett defines *judicial pragmactivism* as "a system of philosophy or jurisprudence that tests the validity of a decision concerning the appropriate sphere of judges or law courts by its tendency to actively achieve a practical result or results" (p. 207).

Barnett is careful to avoid associating judicial pragmactivism with any particular moral philosophy, with any claim to an insight into the choice among ends. Rather, its scope is restricted to the choice of means, specifically to the choice between the legislature and the judiciary, as the appropriate means to any desired objectives, whether based on efficiency, wealth equalization, or rights. Of course, Barnett has objectives of his own, evidently the pursuit of rights. However, concern in this paper is with the choice between instruments and not with the attainment of some specific moral philosophy.

Barnett's starting point is the perennial debate among students in law school concerning the dominance of the judiciary or the legislature when these two institutions come into conflict. Concerned by the observed tendency of students to opt for outright activism or passivism of one branch or the other, Barnett offers pragmactivism as a "no less principled" approach to conflict resolution. Specifically, a judicial pragmactivist favors whichever forum is more likely, in a particular instance, to secure his fundamental moral principles.

Evidently, such a viewpoint has consequences for constitutionalism in a country like the United States which is governed by a written constitution and whose system of government rests on strictly delegated authority. In this respect, Barnett assumes a controversial position for pragmactivism, namely, that it should apply to the Constitution itself and not merely to the interpretation of the Constitution. Judicial pragmactivism "views a constitutional framework as instru-

---

The author is Professor of Economics at the Center for Study of Public Choice, George Mason University.

mental to other more fundamental principles"; and where the pragmactivist does not accept the principles embodied in the Constitution, "only small weight would be placed on the words of the Constitution" (p. 212).

In this respect, Barnett accords to the alienated pragmactivist the
right to deny even prima facie deference to the provisions of the U.S.
Constitution. In so doing, he denies the importance of the constitutional process as an overriding value, permitting that value to be
undermined by the pragmactivist's opinions on substantive matters.
Since this issue goes to the very heart of the strict constructionist
versus the living constitution debate, I make no apology for centering
my comment upon its detailed evaluation.

The Logic of Constitutionalism

Pragmactivism in the sense defined (though not of course endorsed)
by Barnett is completely alien to anyone who has assimilated two
important insights of the public choice school, first presented by
James M. Buchanan and Gordon Tullock in their seminal work on
the logic of constitutionalism, *The Calculus of Consent* (1962).

The first such insight is the contractarian notion of a Constitution
determined (or subsequently endorsed) as nearly as possible on the
basis of universal consent—a higher-order catallaxy that predeter-
mines the nature of decisionmaking in a constitutional democracy
and, indeed, that explicitly conditions and constrains the institutions
of participative democracy. In such a vision, those who subsequently
find themselves alienated from the Constitution are expected to work
through the amendment procedures established by that Constitution
and to seek out the consensus for their viewpoints necessary for
constitutional adjustment. There is no place for legislative or judicial
adjustment. There is no place for constitutional subversion via
manipulation of the lower-level machinery of governance.

The second insight is the recognition that *homo oeconomicus* thrives
not only in private markets but also within the political marketplace—that the omniscient and impartial servant of the public good
is a figment of the Platonic imagination. This insight that man for the
most part is myopically self-seeking in the lower-level political market reaffirms the importance of the public choice school's constitutional perspective. For even if individuals predominantly self-seek
in their capacities as politicians, bureaucrats, or members of special
interest groups, they may prove capable of rules selection at the
higher constitutional level on the basis of a more farsighted, if yet
solipsist, vision. In such circumstances, lower-level self-mutilation

may be bounded by constitutional constraints imposed by individuals upon themselves via a calculus of consent.

Judicial Pragmactivism versus Constitutionalism

Judicial pragmactivism runs directly counter to the safeguards provided to society by constitutionalism. The very forces of rent seeking which so characterize the lower order polity are launched under pragmactivism against the U.S. Constitution itself. In one sense, Barnett has done no more than enunciate a philosophy that already has an overwhelming presence in U.S. society. Pragmactivism is the sine qua non of would-be rent seekers and rent protectors in an increasingly transfer-oriented society. Special interest groups scarcely require a definition for an approach that is the rationale for their continued existence. Nevertheless, they will not ignore support from constitutional lawyers when they sense that it is forthcoming.

Flirting with Pragmactivism

The important issue here addressed, therefore, is whether Barnett is simply defining an approach, as the title of his paper certainly suggests, or whether he is urging its adoption as a procedural device. On this, he walks the tightrope with not inconsiderable expertise. He does not attempt to present a systematic defense of judicial pragmactivism; but he does identify it as "an alternative position that is both principled and worthy of consideration" (p. 216). In my view, he is lured almost away from strict constructionism by an overwhelming desire to restore rights where they have been eroded by activist judicial interpretation of the U.S. Constitution. As one who shares his love of liberty, nevertheless I believe that he should rely upon the Constitution itself in its strictest interpretation rather than flirt with the pragmactivism of the living constitution.

Barnett has expressed elsewhere the view that for any constitution to be genuinely authoritative, it must enact a system which is basically "just."[1] The Constitution must be evaluated and interpreted according to this standard. Although he does not elaborate specifically on the definition of "just," it is evident that Barnett follows Richard Epstein (1985) in accepting that the historical Constitution did enact a justifiable scheme but that important elements of the original scheme have long been written out of the Constitution by the Supreme Court. Furthermore, like Epstein, Barnett accepts the

---

[1]See Barnett's letter to Dorn (1986) and also his forthcoming article in the *Harvard Journal of Law and Public Policy* (1987).

view that the Constitution was historically conceived as a mechanism for protecting individual rights within a Lockean perspective.

Barnett, however, takes a yet more fundamental view of the rights issue and is tempted to endorse pragmactivism despite a sixth sense that warns him of the dangers inherent in such an approach. In his view, individual rights precede the formation of a government, with constitutional government a means to the end of protecting these rights which are viewed as pre-existing and "natural." Textual references do not refute Barnett's position, as the following sample serves to illustrate:

> We the People of the United States, in Order to . . . establish justice . . . and secure the Blessings of Liberty to ourselves and our Posterity, do ordain and establish this Constitution for the United States of America [Preamble].

> No state shall . . . pass any Bill of attainder, ex post facto Law, or Law impairing the Obligation of Contracts . . . [Art. 1, sec. 10].

> The enumeration in the Constitution, of certain rights, shall not be construed to deny or disparage others retained by the people [Amend. IX].

> The powers not delegated to the United States by the Constitution, nor prohibited by it to the States, are reserved to the States respectively, or to the people [Amend. X].

> No State shall make or enforce any law which shall abridge the privileges and immunities of citizens of the United States; nor shall any State deprive any person of life, liberty or property, without due process of laws; nor deny to any person within its jurisdiction the equal protection of the laws [Amend. XIV].

Evidently, the U.S. Constitution established the federal system of government on an explicitly derivative basis. The powers not delegated by the Constitution, nor prohibited by it to the States, remain with the States or with the people. The importance attached to rights by the Founding Fathers, as illustrated above, permeated the notes and documents whence the Constitution was drafted, was enunciated in the Constitution itself, and was consolidated later by the Bill of Rights. This emphasis cannot be ignored in a strict constructionist interpretation of the U.S. Constitution, though it is stretching the evidence somewhat to claim that it is the sole rather than the predominant outcome of the 1787 convention, as subsequently amended.

Dangers of Judicial Pragmactivism

It is for this latter reason that I am opposed to judicial pragmactivism in the sense defined by Barnett. Strict constructionism will not always result in Supreme Court decisions that place rights lexico-graphically ahead of "fairness" or "efficiency" as Constitutional pre-rogatives. Where it does not do so, there is a natural temptation to subvert the Constitution. However, once the Constitution is invaded by judicial activism, however laudable the objectives, the credibility of that document as a contractual defense against the myopia of in-period politics is inevitably eroded. The opportunities thus provided for judicial policymaking will not go unnoticed either by presidents who wish to force through extra-legislative objectives or by oppor-tunists who seek their routes into the bench in order to subvert the Constitution. It is a fundamental misreading of human nature to suppose that judges have no personal policy agenda that they will attempt to impose once constitutional constraints have been suffi-ciently weakened (Kimenyi, Shughart, and Tollison 1985).

Those who favor judicial pragmactivism over strict constructionism thus expose the U.S. polity to all the weaknesses that permeate the European parliamentary democracies. They lend their voices, in however limited a fashion, to those individuals such as Ronald Dwor-kin (1985), Lawrence Tribe (1985), and perhaps even Richard Epstein (1985) who are impatient with the slowness and uncertainties of the amendment process and who seek out instead more expeditious returns from a suitably reconstructed Supreme Court. Courts can be stacked from the viewpoint of several alternative ideologies, not all of which are favorably impressed by the importance of liberty.

Of course, strict constructionism should not be viewed as locking the judiciary into acceptance of the precedents of earlier activism by Supreme Court justices. It requires instead that the judges be ruled by the wording of the Constitution, together with the notes and textual interpretations that surround it, to the extent possible in a rapidly changing environment. Only where the Constitution is truly silent should law-making rather than legal interpretation emanate from the bench. Even then, if the issues are suitably important, constitutional amendment is the preferred route for those who embrace the American dream of a country which still offers the promise of wealth creation combined with the preservation of liberty under constitutional constraint.

References

Barnett, Randy E. Letter to James A. Dorn, 31 July 1986.

Barnett, Randy E. "Are Enumerated Constitutional Rights the Only Rights We Have? The Case of Associational Freedom." *Harvard Journal of Law and Public Policy* 10 (forthcoming 1987).

Buchanan, James M., and Tullock, Gordon. *The Calculus of Consent*. Ann Arbor, Mich.: University of Michigan Press, 1962.

Dworkin, Ronald. *A Matter of Principle*. Cambridge, Mass.: Harvard University Press, 1985.

Epstein, Richard A. *Takings: Private Property and the Power of Eminent Domain*. Cambridge, Mass.: Harvard University Press, 1985.

Kimenyi, M. S.; Shughart II, W. F.; and Tollison, R. D. "What Do Judges Maximize?" Center for Study of Public Choice Working Paper, September 1985.

Tribe, Lawrence H. *Constitutional Choices*. Cambridge, Mass.: Harvard University Press, 1985.

10

RULES VERSUS COST-BENEFIT ANALYSIS IN THE COMMON LAW

Mario J. Rizzo

> When they speak so resonantly of "public policy," do lawyers have the slightest idea what they're talking about?
>
> —B. A. Ackerman[1]

I. Introduction

The relation between economic liberty and the judiciary is far broader than that evident from those areas of law that are explicitly concerned with policy. Everyone recognizes this interrelation in antitrust, securities regulation, environmental policy, labor law, and countless other areas. In each of these it is universally accepted that as long as we have law it must be based on specific policy goals. The idea of economic legislation that is policy-neutral is a contradiction in terms. In the 20th century this emphasis on policy considerations has spread to all areas of the law including the classic common law fields (Prosser and Keeton 1984, pp. 15–20). Economic policy factors (as well as other forms of policy) are said to be relevant to the formulation of society's contract, property, and tort rules. The fundamental purpose of this paper is to demonstrate that this need not be the case. The common law, that is, judge-made private law, can be policy neutral in the sense that it need not impose a specific hierarchy of values on society. It can restrict itself to the provision of abstract rules that enhance the possibilities of an order in which individuals can pursue and attain their own goals. In other words, the purpose of this paper is to show that we can eliminate, or at least drastically reduce, consideration of specific public policy questions even in

---

The author is Associate Professor of Economics at New York University. He wishes to thank the Earhart Foundation and the Sarah Scaife Foundation for financial support in preparing this paper. He also acknowledges the Civil Liability Program at the Yale Law School for providing him with a congenial atmosphere during the spring of 1984 in which to think about the issues discussed in this paper.

[1]Ackerman (1984, p. 22).

those areas where we must have law. The judiciary can promote economic and other forms of liberty by returning to the classic common law adherence to abstract rules and eschewing the now-fashionable balancing of economic or social interests.

The remainder of this paper is organized as follows. In Section II we argue that there is a lack of appreciation of the principle of spontaneous order among many economists and most legal theorists. This principle is central to understanding the nature of a policy-neutral legal system. In Section III we show that the function of the pure common law is to promote such a spontaneous order of individual actions. Section IV demonstrates that the common law is itself a spontaneous order that is not the result of conscious direction.[2] Section V elucidates the concept of an abstract or general rule by contrasting it with the idea of interest balancing. Section VI illustrates the tension between rules and balancing in the law of negligence, while Section VII demonstrates the superior rule-orientation of strict liability in tort. In Section VIII, we offer a brief discussion of a recent and important explanation for the decline in the common law's emphasis on rules, and in Section IX, we present some concluding remarks.

II. Decline of Spontaneous Order in Economics and Law

The concept of spontaneous order is a general principle of social organization that once commanded widespread recognition in economics and significant adherence in legal theory. In economics it has been best known in the form of Adam Smith's "invisible hand." The system of natural liberty—the free interaction of individual producers, merchants, and consumers—would tend to yield socially beneficial outcomes, as if by an invisible hand. During most of the 20th century, however, the principle of spontaneous order has been out of favor with the majority of the economics profession.

In recent years there has been a revival of interest in spontaneous ordering forces, but most economists still remain skeptical. Among general equilibrium theorists, especially, these forces have been given an interpretation that renders the principle entirely useless. Frank Hahn, for example, identifies the invisible hand with the formal model of general equilibrium developed by Kenneth Arrow and Gerard Debreu (Hahn 1973, p. 324):

[2]Sections II and III draw heavily on, and in some respects expand, the seminal work of F. A. Hayek (1973, 1976, 1979).

When the claim is made—and the claim is as old as Adam Smith—that a myriad of self-seeking agents left to themselves will lead to a coherent and efficient disposition of economic resources, Arrow and Debreu show what the world would have to look like if this claim is to be true. *In doing this they provide the most potent avenue of falsification of the claims* [emphasis added].

The Arrow-Debreu general equilibrium construct is based on extremely stringent assumptions: perfect information and foresight, complete futures markets, perfect divisibility, and a host of other technical requirements. When these assumptions are met, it can be shown that an unregulated system results in a Pareto-efficient allocation of resources. In the real world, however, the assumptions are not even remotely satisfied, and hence an "efficient" disposition of resources is not possible. Thus, argues Hahn, the claims of Adam Smith and other spontaneous order theorists must be false, because the necessary conditions for the realization of these claims are absent.[3] Hahn's argument is held together, though, by a weak logical link: the identification of the principle of spontaneous order with the Arrow-Debreu formal construct. On the contrary, the principle has little to do with and is far broader than its general equilibrium representation. The lesson to be drawn from Hahn's remarks is not the illusory character of the spontaneous order principle, but rather the intellectual aridity of the general equilibrium style of thought (Coddington 1975; Demsetz 1969).

The concept of spontaneous order has never dominated legal theorizing to the extent it once dominated economics. Even so staunch an advocate of economic liberty as Jeremy Bentham thought of law solely in terms of conscious design. Law, for Bentham, was "a command issuing from the requisite source" (Bentham 1973a, p. 155) or, more specifically, "the will of the sovereign in a state" (Bentham 1973b, p. 157). In modern times the Benthamite banner was held, although in far more sophisticated fashion, by the great legal realist Roscoe Pound. Pound thought of law as an instrument for the satisfaction of specific human desires and for the rational balancing of those desires when they conflict. He believed that the instrumental character of law could be more perfectly attained "if we have a clear picture before us of what we are seeking to do and to what end" and insofar "as we consciously build and shape the law" (Pound 1954, p. 45). Pound saw the entire history of law as a gradual unfolding of this vision (p. 47):

---

[3]Hahn is guilty of a logical error. The assumptions of the Arrow-Debreu construction are merely sufficient conditions for an efficient allocation of resources (Hausman 1981, p. 152). The absence of these conditions does not imply inefficient resource allocation.

> For present purposes I am content to see in legal history the record of a continually wider recognizing and satisfying of human wants or claims or desires through social control: a more embracing and more effective securing of social interests; a continually more complete and effective elimination of waste and precluding of friction in human enjoyment of the goods of existence—in short, a continually more efficacious social engineering.

F. A. Hayek, on the other hand, has seen the development of the law as a manifestation of spontaneous ordering forces. For Hayek the idea of consciously building and shaping law completely misconstrues the nature of the common law process (however accurately it may describe administrative law). The common law is a system that is grown or evolved, not a system that is made. It is an order quite unlike the changeless equilibrium of Arrow and Debreu or the system of conscious compromises produced by Pound's realist judges. The common law is a dynamic order that allows for and even promotes change. It is also an abstract order that is unbound by the specific value hierarchies or compromises of its judges. The purpose of the law is to promote "that abstract order of the whole which does not aim at the achievement of known particular results but is preserved as a means for assisting in the pursuit of a great variety of individual purposes" (Hayek 1976, p. 5).

Hayek applies the principle of spontaneous order to the legal system in two different but interrelated ways. First, he uses it to explain the function of a pure common law system; second, he uses it to elucidate the process by which that system grows or adapts to change. There is thus both a functional and dynamic aspect to Hayek's theory, and each aspect is necessary for understanding his concept of a legal rule. These aspects of the spontaneous order approach are explored in the following two sections.

III. Function of the Common Law

Authority and Legitimacy of the Common Law

Hayek's fundamental model of the common law is one of purely private rule creation. The law and the courts are not creations of the sovereign but rather are evolved institutions within which all individuals, including the sovereign, must operate. The common law antedates legislation, and it draws on preexisting implicit societal rules or customs, as well as on previous judicial decisions (Hayek 1973, p. 72). It is by deference to this preexisting opinion that the common law judge can lay claim to authority and legitimacy. People respect his judgments because, in part, they see in those judgments the crystallization of commonly held moral views.

The legitimacy of the law is also enhanced by the abstract character of the rules that the judges draw upon and that is manifest in their opinions. A defendant is not subject to a particular judgment because of his personality or individual circumstances, but because his conduct belongs to a certain general class that is deemed legally relevant. Jones, for example, may be prima facie liable to Smith for the latter's injuries because Jones hit Smith, and thus his behavior is subsumed into a general class of causal relationships, *A* hit *B* (Epstein 1973, pp. 166–71). All who act in this way—not only Jones—are subject to liability. On the basis of their perception of the general rule, people grow to expect a certain outcome in a particular class of cases. These expectations are then reinforced by the continual application and reinforcement of the rule in future cases (Hayek 1973, p. 98).

Nature of the Order

Because the common law is abstract (that is, in all cases of a given type, independent of particulars, a certain consequence follows), it gives rise to expectations that are similarly abstract. Suppose we say that valid contracts require consideration. This rule does not assist us in predicting the specific content of future contractual relationships. It does, however, help us in forming reasonable expectations about the overall character of these relationships. By voluntarily complying or failing to comply with this and other contractual rules, an individual can widen or narrow the range of his protected domain. Inasmuch as he validly contracts, his claims on others become, as it were, an extended "property right" (just as their claims on him become part of their extended property rights).

The order thus engendered by common law rules is an abstract order, one in which only general features of individual interaction are constant through time. The abstract order of expectations consequently enhances, but does not guarantee, the coordination of individual plans. Or, to put matters another way, the order coordinates the *pattern* of plans and activities, rather than the particulars of those plans and activities (O'Driscoll and Rizzo 1985, ch. 5).

An abstract order ensures certain expectations, but permits others to be disappointed. Individuals may (forward) contract today for 1986 soybeans in the hope that the spot price at that future time will be higher than the contract price. The common law does not seek to ensure anyone's expectations about the future price of soybeans. "The task of rules of just conduct can . . . only be to tell people which expectations they can count on and which not" (Hayek 1973, p. 102).

Even if it were in some sense desirable to ensure all expectations, it would be impossible to do so. The necessary condition for the fulfillment of some expectations is the disappointment of others (Hayek 1973, p. 103). For example, we could not be continually supplied with the products we want (and expect) if producers refused or could not change their behavior in the light of new circumstances. It might even be physically impossible for them to continue as before if resource constraints significantly change. Paradoxically, change of the particulars within an abstract order is vital to the maintenance of that order. "It will only be through unforeseeable changes in the particulars that a high degree of predictability of the overall results can be achieved" (Hayek 1973, p. 104). For Hayek, then, uncertainty with respect to certain features of our environment is necessary for certainty with respect to other features.

The most we can expect from a system of abstract rules is that, on balance, individuals will be able to pursue their own purposes more effectively within the system than outside of it. The role of the common law, therefore, is not to enshrine any particular hierarchy of specific ends, but rather to "maximize the fulfillment of expectations as a whole," and thus to promote the achievement of as many individual ends as possible (Hayek 1973, p. 103).[4] The pure common law system is "purposeless" and does not seek to achieve specific social goals or to balance them when they are in conflict.

IV. The Common Law Process

Hayek has both a micro and macro analysis of the common law process. The macro story, based on a Darwinian survival mechanism, is not extremely relevant to understanding those aspects of legal rules in which we are interested, and so we do not pursue it here.[5] The micro story, on the other hand, does shed considerable light on our subject by elucidating the judicial decision-making or reasoning process that gives rise to common law rules.

The process or, perhaps more exactly, the method of arriving at decisions in a common law system does not rest on deduction from a closed and limited set of explicit premises. It is based instead on "trained intuition" that draws on the unarticulated rules of society and adapts the reasoning and results of previous cases (Hayek 1973,

---

[4]In the second volume of *Law, Legislation and Liberty* Hayek clarifies somewhat this idea of maximizing the fulfillment of expectations. "A policy making use of spontaneously ordering forces . . . must aim at increasing, for any person picked out at random, the prospects that the effect of all changes required by that order will be to increase his chances of attaining his ends" (Hayek 1976, p. 114).

[5]Hayek argues that a society based on a system of abstract rules will prosper relative to those societies that do not rely on such ordering mechanisms (Hayek 1979, pp. 153–76).

pp. 116–17). The common law judge makes decisions in new cases on the basis of analogies with earlier cases (Levi 1949) and with simpler hypothetical situations in which there is a clear right answer.

The process of common law reasoning has important implications for the nature and function of the rules it generates. To see this clearly, it is useful to trace the evolution of rules in a specific area of law. One important area that is currently undergoing significant change is that of negligent infliction of emotional distress.[6]

The doctrine that originally prevailed in the 19th century was the "impact rule." To recover for his emotional distress, the plaintiff also had to be physically injured by the defendant. Without such physical impact, no recovery was allowed. In time the courts began to interpret the impact requirement more and more liberally. Eventually, even the slightest physical contact could be construed as sufficient to allow recovery for emotional distress. This loosening of the impact requirement transformed it into what many felt was a meaningless formality. Still worse was the apparent injustice of permitting recovery for emotional distress to one who had been simply scratched and denying such recovery to one who had narrowly escaped being killed by a truck.

Consequently the impact rule gave way to the "zone of the physical danger" doctrine. Under this approach, if the plaintiff had been in danger of physical injury, he could recover for his emotional distress even if he escaped actual physical harm. The logic of the new rule, however, seemed to be that only emotional distress arising out of fear for one's *own* safety could be compensable. Suppose, for example, the plaintiff had been in a situation where he narrowly escaped physical injury and, at the same time, saw his children physically injured. Could he recover for fear of his *children's* safety? By the strict logic of the zone rule, he could not. The courts were then faced with the impossible task of apportioning the plaintiff's distress between the two sources: fear for his own safety and fear for that of his children. Most courts, of course, never even tried to do this. As a consequence it began to appear rather awkward for plaintiffs, who were themselves in the zone of danger, to recover for their distress over the safety of others, while plaintiffs not in personal danger could not recover. The distress was, after all, the same in both cases. Accordingly, some states (for example, California, Hawaii, and Massachusetts) shifted to a broader "bystander rule." Mothers, fathers, and possibly other close relatives could now recover for the emotional distress suffered

---

[6]For a survey of the development of the law in this area see Epstein, Gregory, and Kalven (1984, pp. 1049–83).

upon seeing their child or relative physically injured in an accident. In California the bystander rule requires that the plaintiff contemporaneously observe the accident, be physically close to it, and be a close relative of the person injured. As should be apparent, this rule also contains the seeds of its further development. How should the courts decide, under the bystander rule, a case in which the mother of a child happens on the scene of an auto accident three minutes after her child is killed? The image of a mother seeing her child in a pool of blood may provide ample "justification" for extending the rule to cases of "almost contemporaneous" observance.

Our story could go on, but doubtless the reader can now imagine possible extensions himself. The important point to appreciate is that analogous reasoning provides a dynamic whereby the law develops, changes, and adjusts. While the problem of recovery for emotional distress is extremely difficult and current developments may well be unfortunate, this brief doctrinal history is a vivid illustration of two important and related theoretical insights. The pure common law process is both incremental and purposeless. Observe that in none of the developments sketched above was there a sharp break with what had been the previous rule. The process of change is as close to a continuous development as one is likely to see in human affairs.

The purposelessness of the process, although somewhat more difficult to appreciate, is nonetheless the crucial element in our analysis. The current state of the law of emotional distress could not have been predicted or directed when the impact rule was the prevailing doctrine. There are two reasons for this (Hart 1977, p. 125). First, and primary, is the indeterminacy of judges' aims. Judges do not start out with a clear objective function to which they then fit the facts of each case. Instead, they reason by analogy or similarity with already decided cases. Second, due to our inability to predict future fact patterns, even if judges had tentative policy goals, they could not foresee the full consequences of any rule they might adopt. These consequences would obviously differ in different concrete situations and judges would be forced, at least in large part, to adhere to rules irrespective of their specific consequences in order to ensure the stability of the legal order. These two factors in effect guarantee that a common law system will tend to be dominated by what to outsiders must seem to be myopia. This "myopic" vision is really the working of the spontaneous order principle and a manifestation of the purposeless of the common law.

V. Rules versus Balancing

The abstract character of the common law is intimately related to the tension between rule-oriented methods and cost-benefit or balancing methods of resolving disputes. The more abstract a legal order is, the more heavily it depends on rules. Recall that the function of an abstract order is to maximize the fulfillment of individual expectations and plans rather than to impose upon society a particular hierarchy of ends. When the legal system engages in the balancing of interests or, equivalently, of social costs and benefits, it produces at best a particularistic order that supplants the ends sought by individuals with the ends desired by the courts. Rules, on the other hand, enable the legal system to adopt a more neutral position on the pursuit of private interests.

The need for rules is predicated on our ignorance (Hayek 1976, pp. 8–11). A utilitarian or balancing framework would require us to trace the full effects of each (tentative) judicial decision, and then evaluate it against the particular utilitarian standard adopted. It is, however, no mean feat to determine these effects in view of the substantial information problems and uncertainties likely to face a court (Hayek 1976, pp. 19–20; Rizzo 1980a, 1980b). There also are substantial interactive effects among decisions and rules that are often impossible to discern. Rules must therefore be applied in particular cases regardless of the hypothesized or "guessed-at" consequences. The very unpredictability of these consequences requires adherence to the given rule (Hayek 1976, pp. 16–17). If the law cannot systematically achieve specific social goals, then the best it can do is provide a stable order in which individuals are free to pursue their own goals. The unpredictability of a rule's effects in a concrete situation is the price we must pay so as to achieve predictability of the abstract order.

Much of the above discussion of rules versus balancing is couched in stark terms of contrast. This is because we are comparing, as it were, the ideal typical rule with ideal typical balancing. Admittedly, real-world legal systems simply tend to move in the one direction or the other. All legal doctrines are an admixture of rules and balancing. Both ideal types cannot be achieved in practice for what are surprisingly the same reasons. A thoroughgoing cost-benefit approach to law is impossible because, as we have seen, we are not always able to determine adequately the consequences of specific judgments. Similarly, an unflinching rule-oriented approach will inevitably break down because unfamiliar factual situations will make the meaning of any previously announced rule unclear. At the same time, attempts to apply a rule rigidly to novel situations may appear patently unjust from the perspective of the more basic implicit (or unarticulated) rules that guide society. Thus the critical question concerns the

direction in which the system tends—either toward more rules or
more balancing.

VI. Negligence: Rules and Balancing

In this section and the following section, an analysis of two alternative theories of tort liability is used to illustrate the difference
between a rule-oriented system and a system that rests on interest
balancing. In the present section the tension between rules and
balancing within a theory of negligence is explored; in the next
section the analysis is extended to encompass the role of rules in a
system based on strict liability. The purpose in both sections is to
clarify the precise nature of an abstract legal order and the kind of
rules it generates.

Negligence Congealed into Rules[7]

At its core the concept of negligence in tort is far more compatible
with the balancing approach to dispute settlement than with the rule-
oriented approach. Nevertheless, the late 19th century and early 20th
century law and legal theory struggled to put reins on negligence
liability. While notions of "due care" or "the care undertaken by the
reasonable man" invite the weighing of costs and benefits according
to some social calculus, many theorists were prone to interpret these
generalities in ways that minimized discretion. As Oliver Wendell
Holmes recognized, when "the elements are few and permanent, an
inclination has been shown to lay down a definite rule" (1963, p.
102). Under static conditions it is possible to interpret the due care
standard in terms of simple rules of thumb. Thus what was formerly
a factual matter of jury determination becomes, in effect, a matter of
law or a legal rule. Henry Terry made the point succinctly: "[A]lthough
negligence is . . . always in its own nature a question of fact, a number
of positive rules of considerable generality have been evolved, that
certain conduct in certain circumstances is or is not negligent per se
. . . When one of these rules applies, the question of negligence is
really one of law" (1915–16, p. 50). Illustrative of these rules is the
exhortation to "stop, look, and listen" at railroad crossings. Failure
to do so could easily be construed as "negligence per se." The
acknowledged function of these evolved rules of negligence was to
promote certainty in the legal order by reducing the case-by-case
discretion of juries. "[T]he tendency of the law must always be to
narrow the field of uncertainty" (Holmes 1963, p. 101).

---

[7]This subsection and the following two subsections are strongly influenced by the work
of G. E. White (1980).

In addition to rules of thumb for negligence determination, the turn of the century saw efforts aimed at developing rules of proximate causation. Subsequent to a showing that the defendant's conduct fell below the due care standard, it still remained to demonstrate that his negligence was the legal cause of the plaintiff's injuries. If the method by which causation was established left room for a substantial amount of discretion, then most of the certainty that had been won at the initial stage through the use of rules would be lost at the subsequent stage. Joseph Beale and others tried to extract from the common law decisions certain rules or patterns of causal reasoning so as to constrain the use of discretion in later cases (Beale 1919–20). Among Beale's rules for determining the proximate consequences of an act were:

> [A] direct result of an active force is always proximate [p. 644].
>
> Though there is an active force intervening after defendant's act, the result will nevertheless be proximate if the defendant's act actively caused the intervening force [p. 646].
>
> [W]here defendant's active force has come to rest in a position of apparent safety, the court will follow it no longer; if some new force later combines with this condition to create harm, the result is remote from defendant's act [p. 651].

Rules such as these in the form of a judge's instructions to the jury, it was supposed, could reduce the range of their discretion. "The law does not place in the hands of the jurors power to decide that the causal relation may be inferred from any state of facts whatever. . . . It is for the judge to say whether the jury *can* reasonably so find" (Smith 1911–12, p. 306).

Assumption of Risk

The rule of assumption of risk functioned to narrow still further the scope for discretion generated by negligence liability. A plaintiff who had voluntarily assumed the risk of the type of injury he actually suffered could not recover even from a negligent defendant. Under 19th century evidence law, the burden of proof was on the plaintiff to show that he had not assumed the risk of his own injury (Warren 1894–95, p. 461). If he were not able to meet this burden, he would be barred from bringing a suit based on the negligence of the defendant. In fact, under such circumstances, there can be no negligence on the part of the defendant: There is no duty of care owed to those who assume the risk of injury (Warren 1894–95, pp. 458–59).

The plaintiff's assumption of risk effectively barred recovery whether it was "reasonable" or "unreasonable." Unlike the defense of contributory negligence where the reasonableness of the plaintiff's conduct is crucial, assumption of risk is a strict rule (Epstein 1974, pp. 185–201). It does not require any balancing of the social costs and benefits of the plaintiff's activity. All that matters is whether the risk was knowingly encountered and assumed.

The assumption of risk rule, taken in conjunction with the allocation of the burden of proof to the plaintiff, completely eliminated the need for any balancing whatsoever in a significant number of negligence cases. The plaintiff's case for recovery could be extinguished without any serious determination of the defendant's negligence simply by the plaintiff's failure to prove that he had not assumed the risk. Thus it is quite likely that a coal miner, who presumptively knows the risks of his occupation, would be barred from seeking compensation for a "typical" mining accident. Similarly, the plaintiff who sees defendant's automobile precariously wobbling at the edge of a cliff and yet decides to have a picnic on the grass below would be unsuccessful in an attempt to recover if the car hit him. In both of those cases the issue would be settled without worrying about the reasonableness of either party's behavior.

The general and abstract character of a strictly applied assumption of risk rule was clearly seen by many legal theorists at the turn of the century. Francis Bohlen, for example, summarized the dominant view: Assumption of risk "is a terse expression of the individualistic tendency of the common law, which . . . regards freedom of individual action as the keystone of the whole structure. Each individual is left free to work out his own destinies [sic]; . . . the common law does not assume to protect him from the effects of his own personality and from the consequences of his voluntary actions or of his careless misconduct" (Bohlen 1906–07, p. 14). The rule of assumption of risk thus makes any view of the social value of the plaintiff's actions or goals completely irrelevant to the resolution of the dispute.

Particularistic Negligence

Rule-oriented negligence was based on an abstract universal conception of duty (White 1980, pp. 16–18; Terry 1915–16, p. 52). The duty of care owed by the reasonable man was, with few exceptions, to everyone in the community. Thus, the utility of the defendant's general class of conduct was balanced against the general class of harms it might cause, and not merely the particular harm it did cause. From this perspective, certain types of conduct could be viewed as negligent in a broad category of circumstances; it would be unnecessary to reconsider the negligence of these types of conduct in each and every set of circumstances in which they recurred. The rules of thumb discussed above are consequently intimately related to the abstract universal conception of negligence.

In more recent times, however, a particularistic concept of negligence has emerged. This has been fundamental to the breakdown of a rule-oriented approach. In *Palsgraf v. Long Island Rail Road*,[8] Cardozo applied particularistic negligence to what was to become one of the most discussed set of facts in modern legal history. Two men were late for a train and ran to catch it as it was leaving the station. The first reached the train with no mishap; the second, who was carrying a package, seemed as if he was going to miss it. At that point one guard on the train pulled him aboard, while another guard on the platform pushed him onto the train. In the process the package he was carrying became dislodged. Unbeknownst to the guards it contained fireworks, and exploded upon hitting the ground. The force of the explosion tipped over some scales at the other end of the platform, injuring Mrs. Palsgraf.

Cardozo focused on the defendant's conduct relative to the particular harm that occurred, the injury to Mrs. Palsgraf. The conduct of the defendant had to be balanced against the likelihood of harm to the plaintiff. Since the ex ante likelihood of injury to Mrs. Palsgraf was undoubtedly miniscule, Cardozo found no negligence *relative to her*. The abstract view of negligence, on the other hand, would balance the defendant's conduct against the likelihood of harms to all members of society. Thus, possible harm to the man carrying the package, other trainmen, and those in the immediate area, as well as persons standing in Mrs. Palsgraf's position, would be considered. Consequently the conduct would be found either negligent or not relative to a large number of possible harms. Hence such a determination could be applicable to possible future cases with similar fact patterns. To single out, as Cardozo did, the particular harm that did occur fragments the entire process of negligence determination. Now the question becomes the utility of the defendant's conduct relative to each harm that occurs, *taken separately*. The rule orientation that Holmes and others had hoped to inculcate in the law of negligence was seriously compromised.

It is possible to preserve, at least formally, the abstract quality of negligence while undermining it through the doctrines of proximate causation. Consider the view, expounded by Arthur Goodhart, that liability for negligent acts should extend only to the foreseeable consequences of those acts (Goodhart 1931, p. 114). This idea accomplishes at the causation stage exactly what Cardozo's analysis accom-

[8]248 N.Y. 339, 162 N.E. 99 (1928).

plished at the duty stage. While the defendant might have violated a duty of care because of the general class of harms that could stem from his behavior, Goodhart's proximate cause doctrine would require a particularistic causal analysis. After establishing that the defendant had indeed been negligent (in the abstract universal sense), we would then proceed to determine whether the particular harm that occurred was foreseeable to the reasonable defendant. Since "foreseeability" generally refers not only to foresight but to a complete cost-benefit balancing, we are in effect balancing the utility of defendant's conduct against the prospect of a particular harm to a specific plaintiff (for example, Mrs. Palsgraf). Thus, by a circuitous route, we have returned to the particularistic concept of negligence.

The price of adopting this concept indirectly, however, is a loss of analytical coherence. What sense does it make to perform the cost-benefit balancing twice—once with respect to the general class of possible harms and then with respect to the specific harm alleged? (Hart and Honore 1959, pp. 234–48). Presumably the latter is contained in the former and is one of the reasons that the defendant's conduct was found negligent (if indeed it was). Nevertheless, the bifurcation of the balancing process clearly directs the analysis away from the overall potential consequences of an act to the specific, more nearly unique, consequences. The critical determination of liability turns on the foreseeability of those consequences.

Today, while many courts and tort theorists might refuse to go along with Cardozo's and Goodhart's formulations of particularistic negligence, they do accept their emphasis on the dominance of balancing considerations. Prosser and Keeton, for example, take a totally policy view of proximate causation, and hence, ultimately, of the entire law of negligence. "The real problem, and the one to which attention should be directed, would seem to be one of social policy: whether defendants in such cases should bear the heavy negligence losses of a complex civilization, rather than the individual plaintiff" (Prosser and Keeton 1984, p. 287). The solution to this problem, in their view, depends on such policy considerations as risk spreading, relative avoidance costs, and the desirability of promoting or retarding certain kinds of industrial development. The rules of proximate causation have all been tried and found wanting. "There is no substitute," we are told by Prosser (1953, p. 32), "for dealing with the *particular facts*" (emphasis added).

VII. Strict Liability as a System of Rules

While theorists and judges in the late 19th and early 20th centuries attempted to reduce the scope for discretion in negligence law, they were constrained in their efforts by the simple fact that negligence fundamentally involves the balancing of interests. Strict liability principles, on the other hand, fit far more naturally into a rule-oriented approach. These principles, long a fundamental part of the common law, have been developed into a general theory of tort liability by Richard Epstein (1973, 1974, 1975). His theory seeks to extract from the common law those traditions that are most consistent with rule-based protection of individual domains.

This brief discussion is not intended to constitute a comprehensive analysis of strict liability, but to merely demonstrate that, in its broad outlines, Epstein's system appears to be precisely the kind of rule-based abstract order about which Hayek has written.

Prima Facie Case

Under strict liability the plaintiff's prima facie case is established when he shows that the defendant has injured him in any of four patterns of causal relationship. These "causal paradigms" are (1) A hit B, (2) A frightened B, (3) A compelled C to hit B, and (4) A created a dangerous condition that resulted in harm to B (Epstein 1973). Unlike negligence, strict liability does not require implicit or explicit balancing in the prima facie case. The plaintiff is not claiming that, weighing the costs of avoidance against the likelihood of harm, the reasonable person would not have injured him. Instead he is merely asserting the fact of his injury at the "hands" of the defendant. The causal claims of the prima facie case function to protect, in a strict fashion, existing individual domains defined generally in terms of clear physical boundaries.

Causal Defenses

The causal paradigms that constitute plaintiff's case against the defendant can also be used as defenses against that case (Epstein 1974, pp. 174–85). The very strictness of the causal claims, prima facie, implies that these claims, when raised against the plaintiff, provide a sufficient answer. A causal defense means in effect that the plaintiff really injured himself.

Consider the following simple situation: (1) A hit B (prima facie case); (2) B compelled A to hit B (defense). The defense of compulsion, if proved, means simply that the plaintiff's own conduct compelled the blow. A was therefore merely an instrument of B's injuring himself (Epstein 1974, pp. 174–75). Note that in both the prima facie case and defense no balancing of social costs and benefits takes place. There is simply a factual assertion of the defendant's invasion of the plaintiff's domain, answered by another factual assertion that the "invasion" was self-inflicted. The other causal paradigms also can be used in a similar way as defenses. Since the same underlying principle of strict defenses with no balancing is at work in these cases as well, the analysis is not pursued here.

Trespass as a Defense

There are also noncausal defenses under strict liability. One of them is assumption of risk in its strict form, unrelated to contributory negligence (discussed above in the analysis of a rule-oriented negligence system). The other noncausal defense is trespass (Epstein 1974, pp. 201–13). The ancient action of trespass functioned to protect the plaintiff's proprietary interests in his own body, his movable possessions, and his land. As such it was simply the corollary of individual autonomy. In a system of strict liability, trespass to land, for example, states a sufficient prima facie case. The plaintiff has a right to expect the defendant to keep off his land regardless of the costs of avoidance. Thus the trespass action is strict. Used as a defense it is an assertion of exclusive possession that shifts the risk of injury to the plaintiff.

Consider the following situation: (1) A created a dangerous condition that resulted in harm to B (prima facie case); (2) B trespassed on A's land (defense). This defense is sufficient to overcome the prima facie allegation. Thus, if the crane on the defendant's land fell on the plaintiff as he trespassed, the latter's action for damages would fail. The plaintiff had no right, prima facie, to be on the defendant's land. Had he stayed off, there would have been no injury and hence no prima facie case at all. The trespass defense also is strict in the sense that the plaintiff's inability to stay off the land is an insufficient reply to the defense. An infant trespasser, for example, cannot successfully plead his diminished ability to avoid the defendant's land. In general the plaintiffs have no right to shift the burden of their problems or deficiencies to the defendant. While it may not be the "fault" of the infant that it trespassed, it is certainly not the "fault" of the defendant either.

The strict quality of the trespass defense means that there is no question of balancing the costs of trespass avoidance with those of greater safety precautions by the defendant. His property right does not depend on whether he or the plaintiff were the "cheaper cost avoider" of the accident. Under strict liability principles, property rights are protected by rules and are not subject to the compromises of balancing considerations.

White (1980, p. 229) argues that Epstein's system implicitly introduces a form of balancing in the sense that, for example, the right to be free of trespass is accorded a higher status than the right to be free of the effects of the defendant's dangerous condition. Of course, all decision making involves the balancing or weighing of alternative courses of action; consequently, so long as there is any kind of dispute settlement, there will be weighing in this sense. This is not the sense, however, in which the term "balancing" is customarily used. Rather, the term is used to refer to two kinds of activity. First, there is the particularistic or case-by-case weighing of social costs and benefits, which is the essential thrust of the modern law of negligence. Second, even where there is an attempt to apply "rules," the balancing approach evaluates them by reference to specific (particularistic) social goals. Thus, the increasing tendency to impose liability on defendants in product cases has been interpreted as an attempt to achieve a greater degree of risk spreading (since manufacturers are assumed to pass liability costs on to all purchasers of the product). Rules in this area of law, such as defendant liability for "foreseeable misuse" of products, are therefore to be evaluated with respect to the risk-spreading goal. In other areas of law, however, there may be different goals and consequently different standards of evaluation. In all cases, then, balancing is a particularistic form of weighing because it often requires a case-by-case analysis of costs and benefits and because these costs and benefits are defined in terms of the pursuit of specific social goals.

The evolution of an order of priority among abstract rules is part of the overall process in which the rules themselves develop. In fact a rule is not fully defined unless its priority with respect to other rules is also determined. A rule is best viewed as a *complex* of pleadings and counterpleadings that ultimately establish a result. The system of law thus evolves as a whole in which the various parts interact with each other. Therefore, the order of priority among rules or pleadings, like the overall system itself, is not specific-goal directed; it is "purposeless." Judges do not know the particular outcomes produced by a given hierarchy of rules. All they know (and need to know) is that there is a *meta-rule* by which, for example, trespass is a sufficient defense to the allegation that the defendant created a dangerous condition that resulted in harm.

The function of a clearly defined priority of rules is identical to the function of the system itself. A complex of pleadings and counter-pleadings with no clear relationships in the form of an adequate prima facie case, sufficient defense, and sufficient reply to the defense, etc. would not produce an abstract order of expectations. Property owners, for example, would be unsure about whether trespassers could impose costs on them if something untoward were to happen on their land. The answer would all hinge on the outcome of a balancing endeavor. "The most frequent cause of uncertainty is probably that the order of rank of the different rules belonging to a system is only vaguely determined" (Hayek 1976, p. 24). In contrast, a system of strict liability implies a legal framework in which both the prima facie case and subsequent pleadings are all strict and accordingly largely free from the vagaries of cost-benefit balancing.

VIII. Common Law Process and Rules Revisited

Earlier in this paper it was argued that the pure common law process produces abstract rules that do not impose a particular hierarchy of ends on society, but simply facilitate the attainment of various individual ends. To some readers this may appear at odds with the recognition that contemporary doctrines in common law areas have been formulated increasingly in terms of interest balancing. The resolution of this paradox lies in understanding that we do not have a pure common law system. Indeed, as Hayek himself recognizes, it may be impossible to avoid certain legislative adjustments or "corrections" of evolved rules (Hayek 1973, pp. 88–89). Nevertheless, the degree to which the common law system is "contaminated" by outside influences is crucial to understanding the kinds of doctrines that have developed. While a detailed analysis of this issue is outside of the scope of this paper, it is important to at least mention a recent interesting, and probably correct, explanation of the change in the common law.

Ackerman (1984, pp. 9–18) argues that the rise of the administrative state in general and New Deal legislation in particular transformed a more nearly rule-based common law into one that became increasingly reliant on the balancing of social interests. Specific-goal-oriented legislation, passed in an ad hoc piecemeal fashion, destroyed the idea of law as a seamless web. Judges, lawyers, and litigants now had to be content with heterogeneous pockets of law with different, and frequently conflicting, policy goals. Indeed, many pieces of legislation were themselves each motivated by conflicting policies and so tradeoffs became a way of life. The growth of administrative agencies and of administrative law necessarily introduced a level of bureaucratic discretion that the law had not known before. This discretion is precisely in the form of balancing costs and benefits of one kind or another. That the legislature could delegate discretionary authority to various agencies means that, in a real sense, the agencies both interpret and "evolve" a type of law that is quite alien to the common law tradition. This tradition now found itself to be only one part of a triune legal system that also included heavy reliance on statutes and bureaucratic discretion.

Inevitably pressure mounted for a consistent mode of analysis in all three areas. Any legal system that continued to adhere to a rigidly dichotomized method of reasoning would, in the long run, incur the extremely heavy costs of increased complexity. There is little doubt that both the statutory/administrative and common law domains would have to interact because, while the law may not be a seamless web, society and the order of actions governed by law are so constituted. Consequently the balancing mode of reasoning and specific-goal orientation quickly rose to prominence in the "abstract common law."

IX. Concluding Remarks

In this paper it has been argued that it is possible to have a policy-neutral common law. This claim has been elucidated by contrasting rule-oriented and balancing approaches to law in the context of negligence and strict tort liability. Finally, it was suggested that the rise of the administrative state is at least partly responsible for the decline in legal rules.

References

Ackerman, B. A. *Reconstructing American Law*. Cambridge, Mass.: Harvard University Press, 1984.
Beale, J. H. "The Proximate Consequences of an Act." *Harvard Law Review* 33 (1919–20): 633–58.
Bentham, J. "What a Law Is." In *Bentham's Political Thought*. Edited by B. Parekh. New York: Barnes and Noble, 1973a.
Bentham, J. "Source of a Law." In *Bentham's Political Thought*. Edited by B. Parekh. New York: Barnes and Noble, 1973b.
Bohlen, F. "Voluntary Assumption of Risk I." *Harvard Law Review* 20 (1906–7): 14–34.
Coddington, A. "The Rationale of General Equilibrium Theory." *Economic Inquiry* 13 (December 1975): 539–58.
Demsetz, H. "Information and Efficiency: Another Viewpoint." *Journal of Law and Economics* 12 (April 1969): 1–22.
Epstein, R. A. "A Theory of Strict Liability." *Journal of Legal Studies* 2 (January 1973): 151–204.
Epstein, R. A. "Defenses and Subsequent Pleas in a System of Strict Liability." *Journal of Legal Studies* 3 (January 1974): 165–215.
Epstein, R. A. "Intentional Harms." *Journal of Legal Studies* 4 (June 1975): 391–442.
Epstein, R. A.; Gregory, C. O.; and Kalven, H. *Cases and Materials on Torts*. 4th ed. Boston, Mass.: Little, Brown and Company, 1984.

Goodhart, A. "The Palsgraf Case." In his *Essays in Jurisprudence and the Common Law*, pp. 129–50. Cambridge, England: Cambridge University Press, 1931.

Hahn, F. H. "The Winter of Our Discontent." *Economica* 40 (1973): 322–30.

Hart, H. L. A. *The Concept of Law*. 1961. Reprint. Oxford, England: Clarendon Press, 1977.

Hart, H. L. A., and Honore, A. M. *Causation in the Law*. Oxford, England: Clarendon Press, 1959.

Hausman, D. M. *Capital, Profits and Prices: An Essay in the Philosophy of Economics*. New York, N.Y.: Columbia University Press, 1981.

Hayek, F. A. *Law, Legislation and Liberty: Rules and Order*. Chicago, Ill.: University of Chicago Press, 1973.

Hayek, F. A. *Law, Legislation and Liberty: The Mirage of Social Justice*. Chicago, Ill.: University of Chicago Press, 1976.

Hayek, F. A. *Law, Legislation and Liberty: The Political Order of a Free People*. Chicago, Ill.: University of Chicago Press, 1979.

Holmes, O. W. *The Common Law*. 1881. Reprint. Edited by Mark DeWolfe Howe. Boston, Mass.: Little, Brown and Company, 1963.

Levi, E. H. *An Introduction to Legal Reasoning*. Chicago, Ill.: University of Chicago Press, 1949.

O'Driscoll, G. P., and Rizzo, M. J. *The Economics of Time and Ignorance*. Oxford, England: Basil Blackwell, 1985.

Pound, R. *An Introduction to the Philosophy of Law*. 1922. Reprint. New Haven, Conn.: Yale University Press, 1954.

Prosser, W. L. "Palsgraf Revisited." *Michigan Law Review* 52 (November 1953): 1–32.

Prosser, W. L. , and Keeton, W. P. *Prosser and Keeton on the Law of Torts*. St. Paul, Minn.: West Publishing Company, 1984.

Rizzo, M. J. "Law amid Flux: The Economics of Negligence and Strict Liability in Tort." *Journal of Legal Studies* 9 (March 1980a): 291–318.

Rizzo, M. J. "The Mirage of Efficiency." *Hofstra Law Review* 8 (Spring 1980b): 641–58.

Smith, J. "Legal Cause in Actions of Tort II." *Harvard Law Review* 25 (1911–12): 303–27.

Terry, H. "Negligence." *Harvard Law Review* 29 (1915–16): 40–54.

Warren, C. "Volenti Non Fit Injuria in Actions of Negligence." *Harvard Law Review* 8 (1894–95): 457–71.

White, G. E. *Tort Law in America: An Intellectual History*. New York: Oxford University Press, 1980.

COMMENT

COMPATIBILITY OF LEGAL RULES AND COST-BENEFIT ANALYSIS
Steve H. Hanke

To set the stage for the remarks that follow, a brief summary of Professor Rizzo's position is in order. He judges a legal system to be superior if it is policy-neutral (does not impose a particular hierarchy of ends on society) and if it facilitates the attainment of individual, private goals. If it is based exclusively on abstract rules, Professor Rizzo asserts that a system of common, judge-made, private law represents such a superior legal system. By way of contrast, he rejects as being inferior, any legal system that employs cost-benefit analysis (a balancing of interests). To develop his argument, Professor Rizzo makes use of the common law of torts. For the assignment of liability in this field, he favors the application of a strict liability rule, rather than negligence systems that require the use of cost-benefit analysis.

Although I accept Professor Rizzo's position concerning the proper role of a legal system, I question certain aspects of his analysis. To illustrate the importance of the deficiencies in Professor Rizzo's analysis, we can turn to the common law of contracts. The instrumentality used to assign liability in breach of contract cases is not cost-benefit analysis. Instead, a strict liability rule is applied.[1] Thus, for liability to be imposed on a breaching party, a victim of a breached contract does not have to prove that the cost to him exceeds the benefit to a breaching party.

It appears that the assignment of liability in breach of contract cases conforms to the requisites of a rule-driven, common law system that is devoid of cost-benefit analysis. But, this is not the case. Even though cost-benefit analysis is not employed at the time when liability is assigned, it is an integral part of the common law of contracts. For example, the strict liability rule is used in contract law because

---

The author is Professor of Applied Economics at The Johns Hopkins University.
[1]There are exceptions to this statement, but they are extremely rare. For example, contracts can be discharged because of lack of consideration, mutual mistake, fraud, incapacity, duress, and impossibility.

a breaching party can prevent or insure against a breach at a lower cost than can a victim. Given this cost-benefit calculus, which is based on standard, economic efficiency criteria, the strict liability rule provides an effectual and efficient means of assigning liability.[2] To put it another way, the strict liability rule is nothing more than the instrument used to administer a system of law that is driven by cost-benefit analysis.

After liability is assigned in breach of contract cases, the proper remedy must be determined. The common law of contracts employs two remedies. The most common remedy requires the breaching party to pay damages to the victim of a breach, where the damages are equal to the victim's lost profits. However, for certain cases (real estate transactions and others that involve the transfer of "unique" goods), specific performance is required.[3] The choice of the appropriate remedy depends on the direct application of cost-benefit analysis.

In most cases, the application of cost-benefit analysis reveals that a specific performance remedy would create economic waste. For example, when a victim's lost profits from a breach are less than the net costs to the breaching party of performing a contract, it is wasteful to require specific performance. In these cases, the common law of contracts (the application of cost-benefit analysis) promotes economic efficiency by allowing a breaching party to discharge his obligations by paying a victim damages. This remedy leaves a victim as well off as if a contract had not been breached, while it leaves a breaching party better off than if a specific performance remedy would have been required.[4]

The specific performance remedy is reserved for those cases in which it is impractical to apply cost-benefit analysis. For example, when contracts involving real estate or "unique" goods are breached, it is difficult to determine a victim's damages because market prices systematically understate a victim's losses.

Unlike the assignment of liability in breach of contract cases—where the application of a single rule yields results that are consistent

---

[2]In the context of Professor Rizzo's paper, it is important to mention that Professor Posner (1977) demonstrates that common, judge-made, private law has evolved in a spontaneous way, and that it is driven by a cost-benefit calculus that is based on standard, economic efficiency criteria.

[3]See Rubin (1981).

[4]It should be mentioned that a breach will not occur, even when a potential breaching party anticipates losses from the performance of a contract, in those instances when a potential victim's losses from a breach are anticipated to exceed the net costs to the potential breaching party of performing a contract.

with the direct application of an efficiency-based, cost-benefit analysis—a single rule for the determination of remedies is inappropriate. To maintain consistency between an efficiency-based, cost-benefit analysis and the instrumentality chosen to administer the law, the common law of contracts allows for two possible remedies for breached contracts. The choice of the appropriate remedy depends on the direct application of cost-benefit analysis.

The common law of contracts reveals serious shortcomings in Professor Rizzo's analysis. Without cost-benefit analysis, how would we be able to know whether a strict liability rule is or is not a superior way to assign liability in breach of contract cases, or how would we be able to determine whether a damage payment or specific performance is the appropriate remedy for discharging liability for a breached contract?

By rejecting cost-benefit analysis, Professor Rizzo fails to provide a means to determine the appropriate instrumentality for administering the law. In consequence, Professor Rizzo is left in an untenable position, since he has no way to determine whether one abstract rule is superior to another; without cost-benefit analysis, all rules must be assumed to be equally desirable.[5]

Rules (instrumentalities used to administer the law) and cost-benefit analysis are not mutually exclusive; they are necessarily related. Therefore, contrary to Professor Rizzo's assertions, the fundamental issue is not a choice between rules and cost-benefit analysis. Rather, it is the determination of the appropriate criteria that should be used to guide cost-benefit analysis.[6] In the final analysis, Professor Rizzo's failure to address the issue of cost-benefit criteria represents the fatal flaw in his argument.

References

Bowles, Roger A. *Law and the Economy.* Oxford: Martin Robertson & Co., Ltd., 1982.

Posner, Richard A. *Economic Analysis of the Law.* 2nd ed. Boston: Little, Brown and Co., 1977.

Rubin, Paul H. "Unenforceable Contracts: Penalty Clauses and Specific Performance." *Journal of Legal Studies* 10 (June 1981): 237–47.

[5]It goes without saying, that, by rejecting cost-benefit analysis, Professor Rizzo also fails to establish a means to determine when rules do and do not provide appropriate instrumentalities for administering the law.

[6]For a summary of some of the cost-benefit criteria that could be used, see Bowles (1982, pp. 47–52).

COMMENT

SIMPLICITY VERSUS COMPLEXITY IN THE LAW
Glen O. Robinson

I agree with Professor Rizzo's basic view that the law should facilitate individual self-realization. I wish I could stop there and say that my disagreement with Rizzo's analysis is a matter of mere detail. Unfortunately almost everything of importance here lies in the details, and on most of these details my view of the legal order appears to be different from Rizzo's. I say "appears to be" advisedly; I cannot be sure, for there are portions of his argument that I find difficult to follow.

Spontaneity versus Order

My difficulty arises early in the paper. Rizzo, following Hayek, views the common law as central to the notion of "spontaneous order." While "spontaneous order" is not defined, I interpret the general intent of it to be a scheme that strongly favors individual ordering over collective choice. Although I have a similar preference, that preference does not get me very far in resolving the hard questions. The expression "spontaneous order" is itself rather misleading in glossing over a fundamental tension between two important themes: "spontaneity," interpreted as individual freedom, plainly conflicts with "order," interpreted as protecting one individual against the effects of another's freedom.

The conflict between these two notions cannot be erased by the simple conjunction of opposing terms. The problem after all is not semantic—a mere matter of defining one end of the conjunction so as to embrace its opposite end. It is a matter of substantive philosophical principle: When must individual liberty yield to the demands of order, and vice versa? I would not pause on this point if I thought Rizzo's use of the phrase was simply ornamental—as with Cardozo's famous phrase "ordered liberty." The problem I have with Rizzo's phrase is that he wants it to carry the burden of a particular view of the legal system and of legal rules. I do not think it can carry that burden.

The author is John C. Stennis Professor of Law at the University of Virginia.

Spontaneous Order and Common Law

For Rizzo, as for Hayek, there is a special affinity between spontaneous order and the common law, but the affinity is not well explained. We are told that the model of the common law is one of "purely private rule creation," as distinct from legislation that is a matter of sovereign power.

This view of law confuses form with substance. To be sure the common law frequently does embody a scheme of private ordering, as Rizzo illustrates with an example of contract law. The private ordering, however, inheres in the substantive body of the law and not in the form in which it is implemented. Contract law is no less private ordering when it is codified by the legislature (as in the case of the Uniform Commercial Code) than when it is uncodified. Conversely, tort law is no less a scheme of public ordering according to collective norms when enforced through common law rules than when codified in statutes.

The common law process may be more conducive to individual freedom than legislation insofar as it is more flexible in adapting legal rules to particular circumstances. The accommodation of different situational demands permits a wider range of individual action based on the environment and circumstances in which action is taken. This accommodation serves the interest of individual freedom in permitting actors to vary their conduct in light of the needs and interests of different situations as opposed to invariant rules that command or forbid behavior without regard to different social contexts. But I doubt this is quite what Rizzo has in mind as a defense of the common law, because this accommodation depends on rules that adjust to the balance of interests in each case and it is precisely such a balancing of interests that Rizzo attacks. This point brings me to Rizzo's central argument for "purposeless," "abstract," "policy-neutral" legal rules.

Policies and Rules

For Rizzo the preeminent virtue of the common law process is its "incremental" and "purposeless" character. The first, as he notes, is fairly obvious: It is the quintessential feature of the common law that legal rules evolve from adjudication of individual disputes, not from singular, simple declarations of sovereign will.

The second aspect, as he also observes, is "more difficult to appreciate." Part of the problem may be semantic. For Rizzo the common law is "purposeless" insofar as judges' aims in rendering decisions are indeterminate and the consequences of their decisions are not entirely foreseeable.

I do not think this is a useful way to think about the matter. It is not a question of whether the common law judge acts purposefully but according to what purpose he acts—specifically whether the judge renders decisions entirely within the framework of existing legal material or whether he appeals to policy considerations of efficiency or fairness that are not bounded by strictly legal material. I take the thrust of Rizzo's argument to be an endorsement of the former—an argument for what can be loosely described as a "formalist," as opposed to a "positivist," conception of the judicial role. If I interpret him correctly, Rizzo's arguments parallel those of Ronald Dworkin (1977), although they are articulated in a rather different manner.

I agree with this model of adjudication up to a point, although it seems to me that Dworkin—and, by my interpretation, Rizzo—both exaggerate the difference between rules and policy. It may be that judges are expected to decide cases according to principles found in or derived from legal materials such as precedent, statutes, and constitutional rules. These materials, however, often provide no clear guidelines for the disposition of particular "hard cases," to use Dworkin's phrase. Indeed, even in relatively "easy" cases, the selection of which "relevant" legal materials to be interpreted involves a degree of subjective value preferences that we cannot and do not expect judges to forego. As Judge Henry Friendly once remarked, we expect judges to be neutral but not sterile when they don their judicial robes. The conception of a judge sifting through conflicting arguments of legal principle, guided only by some vision of abstract legal principle, with no thought to whether the principle makes any sense in terms of contemporary social policy (as reflected in the case *sub judice*) brings to mind Aristotle's conception of God as pure thought thinking about itself. However interesting such a conception, it cannot have much practical force in law.

Rizzo's idealized depiction of the common law process bears no resemblance to the legal system I know. His example of the evolution of the law on negligent infliction of emotional distress suggests an almost effortless dynamic in which pure principle (as precedent) unfolds itself. One would not think from his description that judges who participated in this legal evolution ever gave a thought to policy considerations underlying negligence liability. That is very hard to imagine. By what pure "principle" (that is, principle of logical interpretation uncontaminated by social policy consideration) could it have been deduced that a mother who witnesses her child being run over by a car can recover from her emotional distress but a mother who does not witness it but hears an impact and her child's scream cannot? Simple interpretivism of "principle" in Rizzo's sense gives us very little guidance, unless we make conscious reference to the social policies embedded in the rules—the precedent—before us. However, even that will not quite do without some reference to contemporary conditions (and policies), for otherwise we would be forever stuck with the original rule; Rizzo's much-admired common law "dynamic" would be a stasis. In short, some evaluation of policy and law as an instrument of policy, as well as principle, seems to me the essential motive force of change.

The rigid distinction between interpretivism and positivism implicit in Rizzo's (and Dworkin's) model of common law adjudication is thus unrealistic. In any case, adhering to a rule-based model of adjudication does not necessarily proscribe interest balancing in the way Rizzo supposes. A rule may explicitly incorporate a policy based on interest balancing according to some set of standards set down in the rule. A judge who then proceeds to balance does not depart from principled, rule-based jurisprudence. A judge who, faithful to the principles of negligence law, balances the benefits and costs of a particular activity is perfectly faithful to the model of rules. He would depart from that model only if he applied social criteria that were not embraced within the set of material that we identify as the relevant legal universe in which he is supposed to act. (Notice incidentally that "balancing" does not necessarily entail a utilitarian framework as Rizzo appears to imply; even within a deontological framework, it is necessary to accommodate conflicting rights, and in practical terms such an accommodation can be understood only as an exercise in "balancing.")

At this point Rizzo appears to go beyond the model of rules explicated by Dworkin, for he appears to perceive some inherent vice in balancing even if balancing is embraced by a formal legal rule. I cannot really tell what that vice is; it seems to be a notion that the weighing of individual variables (interests or rights) in specific contexts is incompatible with principled jurisprudence. In this regard Rizzo seems to equate principled jurisprudence with the purely formalistic application of general rules (precedent). His endorsement of Epstein's (1973) strict liability model for tort law illustrates Rizzo's own conception of the law.

General and Individual Justice

I do not want to explore Epstein's particular model of strict liability. I have grave reservations about it on moral as well as practical grounds, but those reservations are only tangentially relevant here in that Rizzo's argument for fixed rules with formalistic application transcends any particular field of law.

I have some sympathy for Rizzo's argument, although it is a sympathy grounded more in pragmatism than in high principle. Adjudications that involve individualized balancing (of "interests" or of "rights") are costly. In a complex world, rules cannot "fit" each and every case. We must accept some misfits simply because the costs of trying to achieve individualized "justice" would swamp any possible gains in terms of fairness or efficiency.

The costs of ad hoc balancing lie not simply in the administrative cost of individualization, but also in the erosion of the force of the rule. Ad hoc adjudications increase uncertainty of enforcement as a consequence of judicial variation. They also encourage strategic behavior by private parties to avoid the application of the rule through loopholes in the law. Furthermore, they invite judges and juries to substitute their preferences for particular outcomes for "principled" interpretation of rules. The greater the degree of individualization, the greater the opportunity for erosion of both the effectiveness and the legitimacy of rule.

Administrative costs and rule erosion may justify a system of legal rules and enforcement that is, more or less, insensitive to individual cases. Our law is full of illustrations. Per se rules in antitrust law are one notable example. So too are a wide variety of statutory offenses that impose a fixed, "strict" liability. Even tort law, which relies fundamentally on ad hoc enforcement, puts limitations on individualized determinations. The question is how much further to advance the supremacy of generic rules over individualized adjudication. I do not pretend to have an answer, but I do have a couple of vagrant biases.

It is not easy to generalize about the vice and virtue of generalization. Two areas of law—antitrust and tort law—can illustrate the point.

For most of its modern history—since World War II at least—the dominant trend in antitrust has been toward development of fixed rules applied without excuse or exception. The per se rule against price fixing is the most prominent but not the only case in point. The underlying premise of this trend was that it would decrease the cost of enforcement and increase the effectiveness of antitrust rules. The record on this issue is by no means unambiguous, but two things seem evident. First, the difficulty of clearly defining the metes and bounds of the so-called per se rules has led to costly adjudication over the boundary question. The rule that price fixing is illegal per se may be simple and relatively less costly to enforce than a rule of reason that would weigh the social utility of the action in the light of each context. But what, after all, is "price fixing"? (Anyone who thinks this an easy question save only in the simplest case needs a tutorial in antitrust law.) No doubt we could refine and clarify the definitional question so as to minimize disputes, but the more we do so, of course, the greater the probability of an egregious misfit in applying the rules to individual cases. In fact, many critics of antitrust think that is precisely what has happened with the per se jurisprudence in antitrust.

Second, the pervasive use of per se rules in antitrust has not necessarily led to a more principled jurisprudence. In fact, the often arbitrary character of the per se rules has been the despair of thoughtful antitrust scholars. The more arbitrary the per se rule, the more it has induced selective enforcement by public enforcement agencies and, on occasion, judicial invention, precisely to avoid what would otherwise be irrational results. As one can see from a scanning of the case reports, however, such efforts do not prevent all irrational results.

Much the same point can be made about per se rules in tort law. Rizzo appears to have some nostalgia for the 19th-century tort law insofar as it sought to adhere to simple, abstract, and rather fixed liability rules. It is beyond the scope of this comment to consider how well those rules really worked in that simpler age. Suffice it to say that I find it difficult to understand how it could be thought to be any more "principled" or just or cost effective than the law of modern times.

Irrespective of that point, consider for a moment the modern experience with per se tort rules. The attempt to develop clear and sensible per se rules for tort law has emerged most prominently in the area of products liability. The manufacturer of a "defective product" is strictly liable—liable per se. So the simple rule says. On closer examination, however, the simple rule is very deceptive. Laying aside all of the many exceptions that have been created to make the simple rule sensible, the very meaning of the rule in its per se form is problematical. What is a "defective product"? Is a microbus defective if its front end collapses on impacts at speeds of 20 miles per hour? What about a rotary lawnmower that keeps on running while an impatient user reaches underneath the blade housing to remove a branch? Is a bottle of perfume defective if it does not disclose that its contents are inflammable? These examples could be expanded indefinitely, but the point should be clear: The same definitional problems that have thwarted the seeming simplicity of antitrust per se rules have had a similar effect on per se tort rules.

Likewise, in other areas of the law, the harder we strive for simplicity, the more we exacerbate the "misfit" between the rule and the problems to be addressed. Ultimately, if we go far enough, we will have only barren form or mindlessly mechanical rules that cannot command any practical or ethical respect.

Conclusion

Life is complex. No doubt we could simplify it somewhat. No doubt simplifying our legal world would be a useful beginning. However, I think the kind of abstract simplicity that Rizzo seeks in the common law world generally is a delusion. It cannot be achieved without intolerable sacrifice to the integrity of the law and the social justice for which the law is supposed to be designed.

References

Dworkin, Ronald. *Taking Rights Seriously*. Cambridge, Mass.: Harvard University Press, 1977.

Epstein, Richard A. "A Theory of Strict Liability." *Journal of Legal Studies* 2 (January 1973): 151–204.

11

THE CONSERVATIVE JUDICIAL AGENDA: A CRITIQUE
Doug Bandow

Introduction

The 20th century has been distinguished by the ubiquitous growth of the state so that today virtually no facet of a citizen's life is free from state intervention. Equally dramatic has been the transformation of the judiciary. Entrusted by the Founding Fathers with the protection of individual liberty, the courts more often tear down than build up the barricades to state growth.

The New Deal proved to be the watershed in modern American jurisprudence. Until about 1937, conservative judges typically invoked a variety of constitutional provisions to strike down federal intervention in the marketplace; it was liberals who denounced the courts for their unwarranted interference with the democratic process. For example, in 1932 law professor Louis Boudin, in his book *Government by Judiciary*—ironically the same title used 45 years later by Raoul Berger for his conservative critique of judicial activism—contended that "the actual practice of the courts is to declare any law unconstitutional of which they strongly disapprove, whatever the reason of such disapproval, and quite irrespective of the actual provisions of the Constitution."[1] Boudin thought the "judicial power," as he termed it, would be difficult to control, but he was hopeful: "I believe that the people of the United States are not ready to abdicate their right to self-government."[2]

Within five years, the Supreme Court had surrendered to the Democrats who dominated the executive and legislative branches,

---

The author is Senior Fellow at the Cato Institute and former Special Assistant to the President for Policy Development in the Reagan administration. He also served as Deputy Assistant Director for Legal Affairs in the Office of Policy Development and is a graduate of Stanford Law School.

[1]Louis Boudin, *Government by Judiciary* (New York: William Godwin, Inc., 1932), p. vi.

[2]Ibid., p. x.

upholding all manner of federal economic regulation. Throughout the 1950s and 1960s the Supreme Court, under Chief Justice Earl Warren, went even further, engaging in what Berkeley political scientist Martin Shapiro describes as "a consistent and comprehensive constitutionalization of the New Deal's fundamental vision of social justice."[3] In becoming an activist policymaking branch, the federal judiciary increasingly took the initiative where elected officials—and the electorate—refused to act.

At the same time, however, the Supreme Court also sought to slow the tide of repressive legislation spawned by the cold war, as well as to combat police and prosecutorial abuses in the criminal process. This steady judicial resistance to majoritarian pressures from the right, and not, ironically, the judiciary's failure to protect economic freedom, turned conservatives against the judicial branch, even though they had once championed the role of the courts in placing constitutional rights beyond legislative reach.

In 1968 Richard Nixon made the federal courts an issue, campaigning to restrain its judges. But despite Nixon's four appointments to the Supreme Court, that body maintained roughly the same liberal course charted during the New Deal. The Court now lacks the ideological consistency that characterized it during the Warren era—its activism has been called "rootless" and "centrist" by Columbia University law professor Vincent Blasi—but it continues to be more sensitive to civil liberties than either Congress or the executive, while refusing to intervene in economic issues even where the other branches of government are acting in ways not authorized by the nation's governing document.[4]

A new challenge to the judicial role has been issued by the Reagan administration, which, says Attorney General Edwin Meese, wants to reestablish "a jurisprudence that seeks to be faithful to our Constitution—a jurisprudence of original intention."[5] Indeed, control of

[3]Martin Shapiro, "Fathers and Sons: The Court, the Commentators, and the Search for Values," in *The Burger Court: The Counterrevolution that Wasn't*, ed. Vincent Blasi (New Haven: Yale University Press, 1983), p. 219.

[4]Vincent Blasi, "The Rootless Activism of the Burger Court," in *The Burger Court*, p. 211.

[5]Edwin Meese III, address before the District of Columbia Chapter of the Federalist Society Lawyers Division, 15 November 1985. Trying to discern the "original intent" of specific constitutional provisions—the stated goal of conservatives such as Meese—is fraught with difficulty, as Steven Macedo has demonstrated in his recent book *The New Right v. the Constitution* (Washington, D.C.: Cato Institute, 1986). This does not mean, however, that the intent of the Framers is irrelevant; instead, it must be viewed in a broader context.

"The invocation of intent," writes Richard Epstein in his foreword to Macedo's book,

the federal bench has become a partisan issue as Senate Democrats increasingly challenge administration nominees.

Reagan's campaign to restrain judicial policymaking may be more effective than Richard Nixon's, because this administration appears to be giving judicial philosophy much greater emphasis in the appointive process. But Reagan, and conservatives more generally, will not succeed in installing a judiciary more "faithful to our Constitution," in Meese's words, so long as they fail to appreciate the clear constitutional mandate for judges to act to protect personal liberty, economic as well as civil. The judiciary has a key role to play in the American system, a role that could be destroyed by a careless response to the judicialization of civic life.

The Judiciary's Misguided Activism

The most literal function of the courts is to adjudicate private and public disputes. When the judiciary intervenes in public conflicts, its overriding duty is to protect the individual from the state.[6] The other branches of government, of course, also have a responsibility to uphold individual rights, but the Framers of the Constitution expected elected officials to be more susceptible to the influence of special interests and runaway majorities. The courts were to provide the necessary balance, proving to be, in the words of James Madison, "an impenetrable bulwark against every assumption of power in the legislative or executive."[7]

However, the judiciary was vested with the role of defining, not redefining, constitutional liberties. Judges take an oath "to support this Constitution," not to enforce the one they wish the Founders

---

"can stand for the position that the text of the Constitution has to be the sole source of judicial authority, for if the text cannot constrain unelected judges, then very little else can" [p. xiii]. The evaluation of intent then involves a study of the text of the Constitution as common language dictates, with an understanding of the Lockean tradition that helped shape the Framers' document, that is, a tradition in which individual liberty was put at the forefront and the state's task was to protect property and other rights.

[6]See, for example, Bernard Siegan, *Economic Liberties and the Constitution* (Chicago: University of Chicago Press, 1980), p. 11. Former Solicitor General Rex Lee has argued that "the Constitution has only one purpose: the protection of individual rights. Under this view, the allocation of power among the various components of government is just another and, indeed, a more efficient, means of achieving that solitary end." Rex Lee, "Legislative and Judicial Questions," *Harvard Journal of Law and Public Policy* 7 (Winter 1984): 35.

[7]Quoted in Archibald Cox, "Don't Overrule the Courts," *Newsweek* (28 September 1981): 18. Adam Smith extolled the virtue of an independent judiciary, believing it would "make every individual feel himself perfectly secure in the possession of every right which belongs to him." Adam Smith, *An Inquiry into the Nature and Causes of the Wealth of Nations* (New York: Modern Library, 1937), p. 681.

had written. The reason for this is obvious: the purpose of a written Constitution, argued Supreme Court Justice Hugo Black, was "to make certain that men in power would be governed by law, not the arbitrary fiat of the man or men in power," even if they be high-minded judges.[8]

Thus, conservatives are correct insofar as they criticize judges for creating "rights" that are inconsistent with what Harvard University political scientist Stephen Macedo terms "the other values and goals in the Constitution."[9] Though not all constitutional provisions are equally clear, judges often have distorted well-founded concepts, such as equal protection, and issued decisions with but a tenuous connection to the text of the Constitution, let alone the purpose for which it was adopted—to limit the power of government.[10]

In this way the judiciary has substituted an ideology of egalitarian social justice, enforced by an ever-expanding federal establishment, for the limited government/individual freedom framework established by the nation's Founders. The negative rights of protection against government have given way to positive rights of access to government benefits, in effect, the right to use government against other citizens.

The most egregious example of judicial overreaching was the invalidation of state abortion laws in *Roe v. Wade* by the Supreme Court in 1973. From the Fourteenth Amendment, the Court created out of whole cloth a constitutional right to an abortion, which was approved by states with restrictive abortion statutes in force. The Warren Court also moved a long way, observes Shapiro, "toward creating constitutional rights to at least minimum levels of subsistence, housing, and education and to the administrative fairness and legal services that would ensure access to welfare state services."[11]

The overall effect of this form of judicial intervention has been to greatly reduce the freedom of individuals not represented in court—virtually everyone other than the litigants—necessarily encroaching upon the concept of negative rights embodied in the Constitution. An institution that was to have been an "impenetrable bulwark" for individual liberty instead has frequently joined the legislative and executive branches in expanding government intervention.

---

[8]In re Winship, 397 U.S. 358, 384 (1870) (Black, J., dissenting).

[9]Macedo, *New Right*, p. 12.

[10]See, for example, Richard A. Epstein, *Takings: Private Property and the Power of Eminent Domain* (Cambridge, Mass.: Harvard University Press, 1985), pp. 143–45.

[11]Shapiro, "Fathers and Sons," p. 219.

Yet conservative legal analysis stops with criticism of *Roe v. Wade.* The problem is simply defined as one of judges being too "active," so the solution is to restrict the power of the courts to block decisions taken by legislative or popular majorities. Thus, says Macedo, New Right activists, in particular, "advocate a new majoritarianism and a fundamental narrowing of judicial protections for individual rights."[12]

Such an approach necessarily leads to a restrictive view on civil liberties. More curious, however, is the fact that the dominant legal philosophy of conservatives—who profess to value economic liberties—makes judicial protection of such freedoms virtually impossible. Not only do conservatives propose no remedies to bring the courts back to the activist role intended by the Founders, in enforcing the Constitution's expressed protections of economic rights, but new restrictions on court decision making would explicitly bar such intervention. Indeed, many conservatives have endorsed the judiciary's abandonment of economic freedom during the New Deal; former Attorney General William French Smith called past Supreme Court decisions protecting property rights an example of judges reading "their personal predilections into the flexible terms of the Constitution."[13]

But it is clear that the Framers intended the Constitution to protect economic liberty: "government is instituted to protect property of every sort," wrote Madison.[14] For nearly 150 years, from 1790 to 1937, the Supreme Court regularly struck down coercive legislative enactments. Far from being an example of judicial adventurism, the judiciary was merely fulfilling its unequivocal constitutional role.

Only when faced with Franklin Roosevelt's threat to "pack the court" did the Supreme Court begin upholding legislative intrusions in the marketplace under the so-called rational basis test. Professor Robert McCloskey observed that "it is hard to think of another instance where the Court so thoroughly and quickly demolished a constitutional doctrine of such far-reaching significance."[15] As a result,

---

[12]Macedo, *New Right*, p. 1.

[13]William French Smith, "Urging Judicial Restraint," *American Bar Association Journal* 68 (January 1982): 60.

[14]James Madison, "Property," in vol. 4, *Letters and Other Writings of James Madison* (Philadelphia: J. B. Lippincott, 1865), pp. 478–79. For more comprehensive analyses of the intent of the Framers in this regard, see Siegan, *Economic Liberties*, pp. 24–82; Epstein, *Takings*, pp. 7–31; and Robert Goldwin and William Schambra, eds., *How Capitalistic is the Constitution?* (Washington, D.C.: American Enterprise Institute, 1982).

[15]Robert McCloskey, "Economic Due Process and the Supreme Court: An Exhumation and Reburial," *Supreme Court Review* (1962): 36.

individuals face an almost impossible burden to convince the judiciary to intervene to protect their property/economic rights, even where explicit constitutional protections apply. This "judicial passivity" is the obverse of "judicial activism," yet it is a problem that conservatives do not consider.

For instance, the commerce clause, which restricts federal regulation to business "among the several states," has been interpreted to allow federal control of essentially any economic activity within a state, however minor. And in a Depression-era case the Court vitiated the contract clause, which bars states from "impairing the obligation of contracts."[16]

The courts have broken down explicit constitutional limits on the power of the federal government to tax. The origination clause requires "all bills for raising revenues" to originate in the House of Representatives; the purpose is to force the body of Congress most responsive to the electorate to take the lead in hiking taxes.[17] However, the Fifth Circuit Court of Appeals overruled this constitutional doctrine, arguing that it should not "intrude into the deliberative process of Congress" to enforce the Constitution.[18]

Another constitutional dead letter is the uniformity clause, which requires taxes to "be uniform throughout the United States." Despite this clear prohibition on discriminatory taxation, the Supreme Court allowed the so-called windfall profits tax on oil to stand even with its exemption of certain classes of Alaskan oil. The Court reversed a district court decision striking down the levy, ruling that Congress had "wide latitude in deciding what to tax."[19]

The erosion in the Fifth Amendment's explicit "public use" restraint on government seizure of private property has been equally serious. In *Hawaii Housing Authority v. Midkiff* (1984), the Supreme Court essentially abrogated the eminent domain clause, ruling that the legislature's action need only be "rationally related to a conceivable public purpose" to withstand constitutional scrutiny.[20] It is difficult to imagine anything not passing muster under such a nonstandard: both the appropriation of local sports franchises and money-losing

---

[16]Home Building & Loan Association v. Blaisdell, 290 U.S. 398 (1934). In 1977, however, the Court partially resuscitated the provision in U.S. Trust Co. v. N.J., 431 U.S. 1 (1977).

[17]Ronald Zumbrun and Sam Kazman, Brief of Appellant in Texas Association of Concerned Taxpayers, Inc. v. U.S. (mimeo, no. 84-5021, 6 February 1985), pp. 18–21.

[18]Texas Association of Concerned Taxpayers v. U.S., 772 F.2d 163 (1985).

[19]U.S. v. Ptasynski, 462 U.S. 74, 84 (1983).

[20]Hawaii Housing Authority v. Midkiff, 467 U.S. 229, 241 (1984).

firms to prevent their closure have been under active litigation in several states.

In all of these economic rights cases, the judiciary has failed to uphold the constitutional principles of property and contract. Instead, the Supreme Court has yielded to majoritarianism. In the field of economic rights, then, one might say that the Court has deferred to the political branches and pursued a *misguided* activism, that is, an activism that has strayed from the Framers' principle of limited government—the judiciary has been remarkably activist in the sense of abrogating explicit constitutional provisions intended to restrain government and protect economic liberties. The judiciary's refusal to protect property rights is no more consistent with even the narrow interpretation of the Framers' "original intent" advanced by conservatives like Meese than is the invention of rights to government benefits. As Bernard Siegan points out, "the judiciary has no authority to eliminate constitutional protections for economic liberty."[21]

The judicial role, therefore, has been seriously distorted in two ways, with courts intervening where they should not—in the area of social rights—and failing to act when they should—in the area of economic liberties.[22] The common thread to simultaneous judicial activism and passivity is support for an expansive public sector by the very institution that was intended to preserve the freedoms of the Constitution. It is in this sense that the Court's behavior might well be called "misguided judicial activism," that is, activism not to protect property rights but to rearrange and attenuate them.

The lapse of judicial protection for property rights, broadly defined to include both civil and economic liberties, is a serious problem. Where judges treat the nation's fundamental law as an archaic and irrelevant parchment, they destroy the basis for the secure protection of any right. The government becomes one of men, not laws, where those who control the judiciary control our freedom, economic and civil. Overall, we are poorer and less free due to half a century of constitutional misinterpretation by the courts.

The key to reversing judicial policymaking without destroying the courts in the process is to adopt a package of reforms that changes the reward structure facing judges and restricts their power, but does not eliminate the degree of independence necessary for them to fulfill their constitutional responsibility of protecting individual liberty. There is no simple answer, and, unfortunately, few conserva-

---

[21]Siegan, *Economic Liberties*, p. 319.

[22]See Epstein, "Judicial Review: Reckoning on Two Kinds of Error," this volume, ch. 3.

tives, especially those in the populist camp, have demonstrated the sensitivity to individual liberties necessary to draft a program consistent with the judicial framework established by the Framers. Conservative activists want to use majoritarian institutions to block judges from expanding the welfare state and social liberties, but in doing so they would make it even more difficult for courts to protect economic freedom.

Reforming the Judiciary: The Conservative Agenda

There are almost as many conservative proposals for judicial reform as there are conservative activists. But the common theme to the activities of the Reagan administration as well as the populist Free Congress Foundation is reducing the authority of judges to intervene in any public policy matter, especially where the executive and legislative branches have already spoken. Most of the suggested controls would bar judges from acting even where the Constitution justified their doing so.

The conservative judicial agenda can be divided into five broad categories: ideology and appointments, restrictions on law suits, institutional limits on judges, political pressure on judges, and resistance to judicial rulings.

Ideology and Appointments

The debate opened by the Reagan administration over the proper role of the courts is intended not only to build political support for the President's program, but also to displace the activist legal philosophy that permeates the profession, from law schools to the bench. Reagan has used the Justice Department as litigant to press his judicial philosophy as well. The Solicitor General's office has used its special relationship with the Supreme Court to press for less judicial policymaking (so far without much success), and William French Smith vowed that the department would exercise "self-restraint" by refusing to "advance arguments that promote judicial activism even when those arguments might help us in a particular case."[23]

Moreover, the administration is using the appointment process to transform the federal bench. When he leaves office in January 1989, Reagan will have appointed roughly half the federal judges, a larger percentage than any other president during this century except Franklin Roosevelt and Dwight Eisenhower. Moreover, the Justice

---

[23]Smith, "Urging Judicial Restraint," p. 61.

Department's selection process, though no more partisan than that of past presidents, places greater emphasis on ideology.

Restrictions on Lawsuits

The courts are able to intervene only in cases or controversies brought before them; they have no authority *sua sponte* to assert their power. Thus, some observers have proposed to curb judicial activism by reducing the range of lawsuits in which judges can impose their policy preferences. Today's conservatives harken back to Progressive President Theodore Roosevelt when he argued that the people "should be taught that the right way to get rid of a bad law is to have the legislature repeal it, and not to have the courts by ingenious hair-splitting nullify it."[24]

Since most litigants are unlikely to voluntarily give up after their third time at bat, so to speak, they will be dissuaded from going to court only if the judicial process is changed to deny them redress. Today a number of doctrines can prevent courts from even deciding cases: ripeness, mootness, justiciability, political question, review preclusion, standing, prudential considerations, and so on. Among the more important of these doctrines is "standing," which requires litigants to suffer a measureable injury that may be remedied by a court ruling. Tightening the standing requirement, either judicially, as the Burger Court has done in several cases, or legislatively, as Congress did when it passed the Administrative Procedures Act of 1966, would help reverse the surge in lawsuits.[25]

Institutional Limits on Judges

Although the Reagan administration has not attacked the judicial institution itself, many conservative activists believe that the only way to restrain judicial activism effectively is to radically reshape the very exercise of judicial power. One means of doing so would be to broadly restrict the power of the courts through a constitutional amendment allowing, for example, the other branches of government to overrule judicial decisions. William Stanmeyer, president of the Lincoln Center for Legal Studies, proposes making "it as hard for the court to amend the Constitution as it is for the people."[26] He

[24]Theodore Roosevelt, "President's Annual Message to Congress," *Congressional Record*, 43, part 1 (8 December 1908): 21.

[25]Gary McDowell, "A Modest Reform for Judicial Activism," *The Public Interest* no. 67 (Spring 1982): 6–8; Bruce Fein, "The Indecision of the Burger Court," *District Lawyer* 4 (6 May 1980): 50–51.

[26]William Stanmeyer, "Governing the Judiciary," in *A Blueprint for Judicial Reform*, ed. Patrick McGuigan and Randall Rader (Washington, D.C.: Free Congress Research and Education Foundation, 1981), pp. 50–51.

favors a constitutional amendment to empower Congress to nullify federal and state court rulings that overturn federal statutes. Another proposal, first seriously advanced in 1923, is to require the courts to attain a super-majority to strike down federal statutes.

Some conservatives, unwilling to directly challenge the doctrine of judicial supremacy, have suggested using constitutional amendments to reverse specific court decisions. In 1980, for example, California voters passed Proposition 1, amending the state constitution to foreclose the expansive judicial interpretation of the state equal protection clause, under which judges were ordering busing in cases where federal law did not require it. A similar approach has been suggested to restrain federal judges on specific subjects, such as prayer in public schools or busing to promote a racial balance.

Because constitutional amendments are difficult to pass, conservatives in Congress also have sought to restrict court power by statute. Congress can strike legislatively at constitutional activism by reasserting its authority over judicial procedures, such as the availability of declaratory relief. Statutory changes, however, generally cannot directly reverse a constitutional ruling; no amount of redrafting could validate a statute banning abortion.

Nevertheless, two different kinds of legislative attempts have been made to reverse decisions that courts claim are rooted in the Constitution. One method is to substitute congressional standards for judicial enactments. Section 5 of the Fourteenth Amendment provides that "Congress shall have power to enforce, by appropriate legislation, the provisions of this article." Based on this authority, in 1982 the Senate approved legislation to forbid federal courts from requiring busing of students more than five miles or 15 minutes from their homes for racial reasons.[27] Another attempt to use Congress' enforcement power was the Human Life bill, which would have defined "person" within the meaning of the Fourteenth Amendment to protect the life of the unborn; this legislation never passed the Senate.

Conservatives have also endorsed proposals, based on Article III, section 2 of the Constitution, to withdraw specific areas of jurisdiction from the federal courts, thus preventing them from considering cases involving particular issues or constitutional provisions. Legislation to strip the federal courts of jurisdiction over school prayer cases reached the Senate floor in both 1982 and 1985, only to be blocked first by a filibuster and then voted down.

---

[27]Steven Roberts, "Antibusing Moves Passed by Senate After Long Fight," *New York Times* (3 March 1982): A–1.

Political Pressure on Judges

Some conservatives believe that abstract procedural reform will prove inadequate to redress the decades-long shift in power toward the judicial branch, and therefore recommend that judges intent on making policy be themselves judged on the soundness of their decisions. Although courts do not precisely follow the election returns, as was suggested by the fictitious Mr. Dooley, they do trim their sails to meet new political winds. In 1937, for instance, Roosevelt threatened to pack the court and thereby transform its rulings: "I do not know much about law," he said, "but I do know how to put the fear of God into judges."[28]

A wide range of political pressures could be applied to the judiciary. Conservative groups, particularly at the local level, have attempted to evaluate judges, publicize court rulings, and generally hold the judiciary accountable for its decisions. The Washington Legal Foundation, a conservative public interest law firm, has published a "Court Watch Manual" to encourage citizen oversight of the judiciary.

Some conservatives have proposed increasing the legislative accountability of judges by changing the procedure to remove errant jurists from office. The House may impeach and the Senate remove federal judges, but the process is cumbersome and rarely used. Moreover, impeachable offenses generally are thought to involve criminal or corrupt conduct rather than exceeding judicial authority. In contrast, most states have commissions to review judges' performance, although there too the grounds for disciplinary action involve traditional forms of misconduct or disability.

In light of such sentiment, some legislators have suggested expanding existing mechanisms for removal of judges to include abuse of power. In 1979 Rep. Robert Dornan introduced a bill to make ordering government expenditures without legislative approval grounds for impeachment; Senator John East's Judicial Reform Act of 1982 proposed to define the constitutional requirement of "good behavior" to authorize a judge's ouster for usurpation of legislative or executive power. It is unclear, however, whether impeachment, constitutionally, can reach political charges and whether the "good behavior" provision is anything more than an exhortation for judges to do good.[29] Alternatively, Congress could propose to amend the Constitution to

[28]Quoted in Robert H. Jackson, *The Struggle for Judicial Supremacy* (New York: A.A. Knopf, 1941), p. 190.
[29]Jules Gerard, "A Proposal to Amend Article III: Putting A Check on Antidemocratic Courts," in McGuigan and Rader, *Blueprint*, pp. 220–21.

create an entirely new disciplinary procedure, one less cumbersome than impeachment, such as a federal judicial panel modeled after state systems. A complementary change, which also would require a constitutional amendment, would be to end life tenure for judges by appointing them for a specific term and requiring reconfirmation by the Senate, if not renomination by the President.

Finally, some conservatives support amending the Constitution to make federal judges face the voters. Fifteen states use some variant of the "Missouri Plan," under which judges are appointed and subject to a retention vote by the electorate. In California, for example, Supreme Court and appellate court judges must receive a majority vote to remain in office. Washington University law professor Jules Gerard has proposed a constitutional amendment to make Supreme Court justices subject to a national retention election and to have appellate and district court judges voted on by residents of their respective circuits or districts.[30]

Resistance to Judicial Rulings

If all else fails, the ultimate response to judicial overreaching is disobedience. The power of the judiciary is based on respect: Alexander Hamilton called it "the least dangerous" branch because it possessed neither the executive's sword nor the legislature's purse. In the main, courts must rely on voluntary compliance by the public and their elected representatives.

However, today even vigorous critics of the Court are reluctant to urge resistance. The administration apparently decided not to appoint University of Texas law professor Lino Graglia to the U.S. Court of Appeals in part because in 1979 he allegedly counseled parents to defy a court busing decree, a charge Graglia denies.[31] And while Rep. Robert Dornan, a controversial conservative, authored a book challenging the doctrine of judicial supremacy and urging the legislative and executive branches to exercise their independent responsibilities to interpret the Constitution, he did not explicitly recommend that Congress or the President defy judicial decisions.[32]

Yet resistance to court rulings has not been infrequent. In the 1857 *Dred Scott* decision the Court purported to void the power of Congress to limit the spread of slavery into new states and the authority

[30]Ibid.

[31]Philip Shenon, "Opposed by Bar, Professor Fades as Judge Choice," *New York Times* (7 August 1986): A–1.

[32]Robert Dornan and Csaba Vedlik, *Judicial Supremacy: The Supreme Court on Trial* (New York: Nordland Publishing International, 1980), pp. 106–107.

of "free states" to free slaves brought into their jurisdictions. But, relates historian Allan Nevins, "when the Republicans took control of the government, the decision was set aside quietly, completely, and forever."[33]

Defiance of *Brown v. Board of Education* was massive; more sustained, if not as well publicized, has been disregard for Supreme Court decisions on religious education and prayer in public schools. Perhaps the clearest case of presidential insubordination is provided by *Worcester v. Georgia,* wherein the Court decided, in 1832, that Georgia had no power to pass laws concerning Indians living on Indian territory in the state. President Andrew Jackson refused to use federal troops to enforce the ruling, reportedly saying "John Marshall has made his decision; now let him enforce it."[34]

The Conservative Judicial Agenda and the Constitution

The development of a court reform package that reverses judicial policymaking in a manner consistent with the original constitutional scheme requires recognition that the Constitution not only allows, but requires, judges to intervene in certain circumstances. Thus, while some limits on judges' power are warranted, such restrictions should not eliminate the degree of independence necessary for judges to execute their responsibility to protect individual liberty. However, many of the conservative proposals for controlling the courts would, if anything, lead farther away from the constitutional principles of property and contract by subjecting individual rights to legislative and popular majorities. Each of the conservatives' five proposals for judicial reform is now evaluated in this light.

Ideology and Appointments

Since the ultimate responsibility to fulfill the courts' constitutional mandate lies with the judges themselves, the least painful solution to today's "judicial crisis" would be for judges to return to their proper role of acting as bulwarks against expanding governmental power. Consequently, reforming prevailing judicial philosophy is an eminently sensible goal. Unfortunately, however, unless the dominant conservative philosophy recognizes the need for judicial inter-

[33]Allan Nevins, *The Emergence of Lincoln,* vol. 1 (New York: Charles Scribner's Sons, 1950), p. 115.

[34]Lawrence Baum, *The Supreme Court* (Washington, D.C.: Congressional Quarterly Press, 1981), p. 207.

vention to protect economic liberties, it will still leave judges far afield from their constitutionally intended role.

The administration's efforts to appoint people who share a particular judicial philosophy, too, is legitimate. Competence, judicial temperament, and other virtues should be considered, of course, but the potential judge's personal philosophy regarding the role of the judiciary and the Constitution should be paramount. Indeed, a well-articulated philosophy is itself a form of competence, for it demonstrates whether a prospective appointee can fulfill his constitutional duties.[35]

The most serious limitation on the administration's campaign to impose its ideology on the judiciary is that Reagan's appointees do not appear to understand the dual nature of the activism problem; that is, that judges are simultaneously creating unconstitutional rights by their activism on the social benefits front and destroying constitutionally sanctioned property rights by their failure to protect economic liberties—which may be viewed as misguided activism in the sense of actively undermining fundamental economic rights to private property and freedom of contract. It is unclear whether Reagan's conservative judges will solve the first problem, but they clearly will worsen the second: the *Midkiff* opinion, written by Reagan's first Supreme Court appointee, Sandra Day O'Connor, illustrates the problem. Reagan's other appointees to the Court, William Rehnquist and Antonin Scalia, have equally limited and constitutionally incorrect views of the propriety of "judicial activism" to protect economic freedom.[36]

Restrictions on Lawsuits

The fundamental problem with reducing the range of lawsuits to prevent judges from imposing their policy preferences is that doing so prevents citizens from seeking legitimate judicial intervention to protect their rights, particularly economic liberties. For example, potential residents often are unable to gain standing to challenge exclusionary local zoning ordinances; taxpayers have had similar

---

[35]The views of nominees on particular issues should not be controlling. Senators grilled Sandra Day O'Connor about her opinion of abortion at her 1981 confirmation hearings, but whether she is "pro-life" or "pro-choice" is irrelevant. What is important is her conception of the role of the Court, both whether it should make policy determinations as it did in Roe v. Wade, and whether it should defer to the political branches as it did in Hawaii Housing Authority v. Midkiff, forgoing its obligation to protect private property rights in the process.

[36]See *Scalia v. Epstein: Two Views of Judicial Activism* (Washington, D.C.: Cato Institute, 1985).

problems in disputing allegedly unconstitutional expenditures and taxes. The issue is not open access to the courts, but judges failing to follow the Constitution; the solution, therefore, is to return the judiciary to its proper role, not to restrict the right to sue.

Institutional Limits on Judges

The conservative search for institutional reform is not unreasonable, since promoting a new legal ethic will take years, and some judicial abuses are likely to persist regardless of the prevailing legal philosophy. According to West Virginia Supreme Court Justice Richard Neely: "No judge with an ounce of conviction about anything is willing to forbear from achieving substantive and really quite unbalanced results in deference to some vague and perhaps vapid theory."[37] So long as some judges manipulate legal principles to advance favored ends, the judicial institution itself must be reformed to reduce both the incentive and power of judges to intervene indiscriminately.

However, the challenge is not simply to limit court power; it is to restore the intended constitutional balance, in which judges are to play an important role. Thus, judicial controls should deter courts from creating apocryphal rights, as well as allow the judiciary to protect genuine rights.

Constitutional changes allowing majoritarian institutions to reverse the courts would certainly limit the ability of judges to constitutionalize their personal preferences about social policy. But the cost in lost liberty from enacting popular override mechanisms would be too high; giving Congress the final say would make it impossible for the courts to place basic constitutional rights beyond the reach of elected officials and the public. The unfortunate reality, argues attorney Mark Pulliam, is that "individual rights, in particular property rights, are susceptible to abuse from unrestrained, hostile majorities."[38]

Narrower restrictions on judicial decisionmaking, such as the California antibusing amendment, are less dangerous and therefore are justified so long as they are limited to cases where the courts have clearly exceeded their constitutional authority. A federal amendment requiring courts to use the rigorous "strict scrutiny" test in evaluating all legislation, including economic regulation, would restore most of the fundamental economic freedoms abandoned by the courts.

Statutory limits on the courts, by giving the legislature greater control over rights explicitly protected by the Constitution, do not

---

[37]Richard Neely, *How Courts Govern America* (New Haven: Yale University Press, 1981), p. 148.

[38]Mark Pulliam, "Two Faces of Judicial Review," *Policy Review* 20 (Spring 1982): 166.

seem consistent with the original constitutional scheme. For example, even if Congress' authority to enforce the Fourteenth Amendment transcends that of the courts (which is by no means obvious) no rights would be secure if legislators could regularly redefine the reach of America's fundamental law. Former Solicitor General Archibald Cox argues, "even if the pro-abortion decisions are wrong, it would be worse to accept the principle that bare majorities in the Senate and House of Representatives, with the approval of the President, can change the Constitution by simple legislative definitions."[39]

Equally dangerous are efforts to strip the federal courts of jurisdiction over hotly contested issues. First, the constitutional parameters of the jurisdiction clause are unclear. Congress' authority is not plenary, despite the late Senator East's claim that "of course, we have the power to set the jurisdiction of the court."[40] For example, New York University law professor Lawrence Sager argues that Congress cannot deprive the Supreme Court of jurisdiction in such a way as to impair the courts' "essential function," particularly the review of state actions to ensure compliance with the federal Constitution.[41] Congress also probably could not manipulate court jurisdiction to achieve an unconstitutional end, such as depriving someone of life, liberty, or property without the due process of law; other limitations may apply as well.

In any case, stripping the courts of their jurisdiction is unconstitutional in spirit, "anticonstitutional," says Reagan's Solicitor General Charles Fried, "if not unconstitutional."[42] For the fundamental problem is not that the courts have improperly asserted jurisdiction, but that they have ruled incorrectly. Indeed, the precedent set by withdrawing jurisdiction likely would be more harmful than the court decisions targeted for reversal, as it would undermine the ability of courts to safeguard any individual rights.[43]

---

[39]Cox, "Don't Overrule the Courts," p. 18.

[40]Remarks of Senator East, in *A Conference on Judicial Reform: The Proceedings*, ed. Patrick McGuigan and Claudia Keiper (Washington, D.C.: Free Congress Research and Education Foundation, 1982), p. 30.

[41]Lawrence Sager, "Foreword: Constitutional Limitations on Congress' Authority to Regulate the Jurisdiction of the Federal Courts," *Harvard Law Review* 95 (November 1981): 43–57.

[42]Charles Fried, "Limiting the Courts," *Orange County Register* (17 November 1981): A–23.

[43]One of the precedents cited by conservatives who favor restricting court jurisdiction is the Norris-La Guardia Act, which abrogates an otherwise protected economic right by barring court enforcement of "yellow dog" (nonunion) contracts.

Political Pressure on Judges

Not surprisingly, the more courts are exposed to majoritarian pressures, the more is the damage that can be done to the judicial institution and its ability to uphold rights that the Founders thought important enough to include in the Constitution.

Increasing public scrutiny of court operations is entirely appropriate. Moreover, since judges have demonstrated that, when given unreviewable power to be exercised in obscure ways, they will abuse their positions, improved procedures to remove errant jurists from office are justified. Giving Congress greater authority to discipline federal judges does entail some risks of the legislature acting unreasonably. In 1964, for example, Congress, angered by recent Supreme Court rulings, increased the salaries of Supreme Court justices by substantially less than those of other federal judges. Nevertheless, past experience suggests that Congress would not act precipitously against individual judges, however much it would like to reverse their decisions.

Ending life tenure for judges, too, is a modest way of trimming court power without unduly restricting judicial independence. Lengthy appointments of, say, 10 or 15 years, which would extend far beyond the normal presidential or congressional term, would guarantee judicial autonomy while assuring some political accountability to other government institutions.

In contrast, making federal judgeships elective could place potentially crippling political pressure on the courts. Retention elections, where judges face no opposition but merely require a majority yes vote, pose some danger. California Chief Justice Rose Bird and two other court members were defeated in the November 1986 retention election, a contest overrun with interest groups from all sides. However, the California court was a special case: it had given a distinctly partisan flavor to rulings regarding everything from the death penalty to tax limitation to reapportionment. Gubernatorial appointment and 12-year terms provide the justices in that state with significant independence, while giving voters a periodic opportunity to rectify judicial excesses and making judges ultimately answerable to someone. As journalist Mickey Kaus notes, "there is nothing inherently dangerous or scary about asking the people, once every six years or so, to vote yes or no on judges. . . . There is no sense in which . . . that's a threat to anybody's constitutional liberties."[44]

---

[44]Remarks of Mickey Kaus, in McGuigan and Keiper, *Conference on Judicial Reform*, p. 66.

Contested elections, on the other hand, could easily discourage judges from carrying out their legitimate role. It is true that incumbent judges in contested races are regularly returned to office as well, usually without serious challenge. In fact, a study of Missouri's experience after implementing "merit selection" and retention votes to replace contested, partisan elections found that the changes had little effect on the composition of the bench.[45]

But courts are to protect fundamental individual liberties from majority abuse, and a contested election, particularly a partisan race, turns a judge into just another politician, forcing him to raise money, seek support from interest groups, and campaign. Voters do retaliate, however infrequently, against judges for unpopular decisions. The Los Angeles superior court judge who initially decided that city's busing case, based on standards enforced by his state's highest court, was defeated for reelection. Judges also may find their candidacies at the mercy of political parties as well as voters. In Chicago and New York City, for instance, the local Democratic organizations choose the municipal judiciary. Such factors affect judicial decision making: at a symposium organized by the Federalist Society, some California justices were frank in discussing how elections affected court assignments and the release of their decisions.[46]

In short, judges respond to sustained pressure; after the Civil War, during the New Deal, and at the height of the cold war the Supreme Court has retreated from policies that placed it in conflict with Congress. Unfortunately, the result has usually been to lower the barriers protecting individual liberty. Thus, directly turning majoritarian forces loose on the judiciary, as many conservatives would do, could destroy the judicial branch, at least as the Founders intended it to function. And this certainly would not promote Meese's "jurisprudence of original intention," let alone be consistent with the broader understanding of the Constitution's principles and purpose advanced by scholars such as Epstein, Macedo, and Siegan.

Resistance to Judicial Rulings

If there is a case for defiance of the courts, it is rooted in the fact that the executive and legislative branches, no less than the judiciary, have a duty to interpret and uphold the Constitution. Today, at least, there is no one empowered to check the courts when they act uncon-

---

[45]J. Anthony Kline, "Merit Selection: The Pursuit of an Illusion," *California State Bar Journal* 55 (October 1980): 422.

[46]"Politicization of the Courts: Balancing the Need for Judicial Independence Against the Need for Judicial Accountability," *Harvard Journal of Law and Public Policy* 6 (Summer 1983): 330–34.

stitutionally. If other mechanisms fail, disobedience may be the only way to protect the values embodied in America's governing document.

However, resistance is the ultimate check on responsible as well as irresponsible judges. Indeed, virtually every major instance of disobedience to court authority, aside from the *Dred Scott* case, has involved one branch or level of government refusing to allow its power to be constricted. Rarely have the legislature or executive resisted judicial rulemaking in an attempt to protect individual liberty. Under these circumstances, widespread resistance to the courts would destroy the most important guardian of our basic freedoms.

Restoring Judicial Balance

Conservatives are correct in arguing that the courts have improperly usurped power: many judges are effectively rewriting the Constitution to replace the right to protect one's property with the right to seize another's property. But no analysis of judicial activism is complete without acknowledging that the Constitution requires a principled judicial activism in the sense of court intervention to uphold genuine guarantees of individual liberty.[47] Richard Epstein has observed that judges are now committing "two kinds of errors: the error of commission . . . and the error of omission. . . . This second type of error—the failure to intervene when there is strong textual authority and constitutional theory—cannot be ignored."[48]

Therefore, in reforming the judiciary it is not enough to reduce judges' power, for that would leave Americans even more subject to abusive majorities. Instead, it is necessary to restore the judicial institution to its proper role of protecting individual rights against abuse by the political branches.

Court reforms must be severe enough to circumscribe judges intent on remaking society; jurists must lose both the institutional incentive and authority to overreach their intended role. Executive and legislative abuses are constrained both by the popular will and judicial review; judicial excess, however, is restricted by little other than the sense of propriety on the part of the judges themselves. The constitutional scheme simply does not envision any branch or level of government exercising unaccountable power. And while preserving the independence of the judiciary deserves a high priority, so does protecting the integrity of our market economic system.

---

[47]For a discussion of the need for a "principled judicial activism," see Macedo, this volume, ch. 5, pp. 131–34.
[48]Epstein, "Judicial Review," p. 45.

But the controls must not be so stringent as to destroy judicial autonomy. The courts must be free from improper interference by other institutions and popular majorities, since, observes Pulliam, "unbridled majoritarianism can be far more tyrannical than errant 'government by judiciary'."[49] Indeed, the difference between the legislative and judicial branches "is fundamental," explains Siegan:

> The legislature is the protector of the governor and the judiciary of the governee. The legislature equates the public interest with the creation of laws; the judiciary, with the preservation of liberty. Each must look to its constituency in the exercise of its responsibility. However, finality under our system must be with the branch of government charged with safeguarding liberty.[50]

A program of judicial reform consistent with the role of the courts in a free society is certainly achievable, if focused on three areas: constitutional interpretation, constitutional reform, and political accountability of judges.

Constitutional Interpretation

The debate over the constitutional role of the judiciary initiated by the Reagan administration has been valuable in bringing to the fore the question of constitutional interpretation and the courts. Though both traditional liberal and conservative views are flawed—judges are simultaneously doing too much and too little—the fact that legal philosophy is now an issue provides an opportunity to present a judicial paradigm more consistent with America's governing document.

Moreover, the Reagan administration's careful appointment process provides a model for future presidents to use in filling the bench. What is needed, however, is the selection of judges who are willing to act, not to create "welfare rights," mandate government expenditures, or seize control of school systems, but to simply say "no" when the government contravenes constitutional rights, whether economic or civil.

Constitutional Reform

New constitutional restrictions are needed, but more on the power of government in general than on courts in particular. Since the rise in judicial policymaking has been concomitant with the growth of state intervention generally, explicit constitutional limits on the authority of government would reduce the ability of the courts to promote public sector growth. For instance, former Reagan adviser

---

[49]Pulliam, "Two Faces," p. 166.
[50]Siegan, *Economic Liberties*, p. 317.

Martin Anderson has proposed an "Economic Bill of Rights" to restrict the power of government to tax and spend; such an amendment could also limit the state's power to abrogate contracts and condemn property.[51] A new, restrictive "general welfare" clause could block the use of government to redistribute wealth to clamorous interest groups.[52]

Narrower constitutional changes could be useful as well. A new "public use" provision that clearly circumscribes the government's eminent domain power, for example, would indirectly overrule *Midkiff*, a court decision at odds with the text and purpose of the Constitution pertaining to the protection of property rights. This amendment approach would unequivocally remedy the specific abuse addressed. Former American Bar Association president Robert Meserve observed, "if a clear majority of the people agree in the manner suggested by the Constitution, then the Constitution stands amended and the Supreme Court is told it's wrong."[53]

Political Accountability of Judges

Measures to increase moderately the political accountability of judges are needed. As Harvard University law professor Raoul Berger points out, "it is axiomatic that all wielders of power, judges included, ever thirst for more."[54] Thus, judges, like presidents and Congressmen, must be answerable to some other institution for their conduct. Making the judicial process more open, giving Congress a less cumbersome means of disciplining jurists, ending life tenure, and perhaps even providing for periodic retention elections, would all prune the enormous authority now wielded by judges without subjecting their decisions to direct electoral or legislative votes. This kind of reform would thereby reduce the potential for activist abuses by an independent government branch constrained by no one, but would not, as in contested elections, politicize decisions protecting fundamental rights.

Conclusion

The conservative assault on the courts is not without some cause; since the New Deal era the judiciary has tended to act in combination

[51]Martin Anderson, "An Economic Bill of Rights," in *To Promote Prosperity*, ed. John H. Moore (Stanford, Calif.: Hoover Institution Press, 1984), pp. 1–22.

[52]A thoughtful discussion of possible constitutional protections for economic freedom is presented in Richard McKenzie, ed., *Constitutional Economics: Containing the Economic Powers of Government* (Lexington, Mass.: Lexington Books, 1984).

[53]Remarks of Robert Meserve, in McGuigan and Keiper, *Conference on Judicial Reform*, p. 35.

[54]Raoul Berger, *Government by Judiciary: The Transformation of the Fourteenth Amendment* (Cambridge: Harvard University Press, 1977), p. 250.

with the so-called new class of professionals and bureaucrats to expand the public sector and the reach of every branch of government. But the tragedy of the "liberal" judicial philosophy of indiscriminate intervention should not be replaced by an equally flawed conservative standard of no intervention. Instead of destroying the effectiveness of the judicial branch, the courts must be redirected to their original role, that of safeguarding all forms of liberty from expansive government.

It was probably inevitable that once the political branches of government embarked on their interventionist march, the judiciary would follow. Accordingly, George Washington University law professor Arthur Miller has noted: "when the Court validated the New Deal in the 1930s and 1940s, it confirmed, rather than wrought, a revolution in American government."[55] Returning the courts to their proper role of safeguarding property rights, therefore, will require a change in the country's governing ideology—from embracing the welfare state to supporting the Founders' view of limited government.

Nevertheless, though "we cannot pretend that the New Deal never happened," observes Epstein, "we must strive to regain sight of the proper objectives of constitutional government and the proper distribution of powers between the legislatures and the courts, so as to come up with the kinds of incremental adjustments that might help us to restore the proper constitutional balance."[56] Such "incremental adjustments" are not provided by the typical populist or conservative judicial agenda. An alternative program, however, is available—one based on sound constitutional principles that would discourage judges from actively promoting the expansion of governmental power while allowing them to intervene to block improper government action. Implementing this form of court reform would make the Constitution function more as its Framers intended, and, not coincidentally, this approach would also come closer to achieving conservative Edwin Meese's professed goal of a "jurisprudence of original intent."

---

[55] Arthur Miller, *Toward Increased Judicial Activism: The Political Role of the Supreme Court* (Westpark, Conn.: Greenwood Press, 1982), p. 129.
[56] Epstein, "Judicial Review," p. 45.

PART III

RECENT ECONOMIC ISSUES IN THE COURTS

12

THE FTC AND VOLUNTARY STANDARDS

James C. Miller III

The vast majority of commercial transactions work well, without need for interference of any kind. In some cases, however, the market "fails," and regulation of some kind is warranted. But this need not be *government* regulation if industry self-regulation is superior. In this article I explain the theoretical reasons self-regulation may be superior to government regulation, give some examples of areas where self-regulation is currently working, and discuss the potential anti-trust pitfalls involved in self-regulatory activities.

Theoretical Advantages of Self-Regulation

Private sector solutions will frequently be superior to the alternative of government intervention, for several reasons. First, self-regulation directly involves the parties who will generally have the best institutional knowledge about the need for action and about the efficacy of various potential actions. Although government can always hire the technical expertise needed to draft complicated regulations, it will almost always be slower in perceiving the need for some action than will the participants in the relevant market.

Second, self-regulation is more flexible, and therefore is less likely to stifle innovation or excessively limit consumer choice. That is, once the government promulgates a regulation, it is more or less permanent. One of the most difficult challenges the administration has faced is changing existing rules. Old rules tend to acquire

The author is Director of the Office of Management and Budget. This paper was written while the author was Chairman of the Federal Trade Commission. The views expressed here are his own. Portions of this paper were originally presented at the White House Conference on Association Self-Regulation, Washington, D.C., 3 October 1984.

constituencies—on Capitol Hill as well as in the agencies—and it is very tough to change them.[1]

In the private sector, it is a bit different. When a rule becomes unnecessary, no one will follow it. If one set of standards is inefficient, a new organization will offer a substitute. Thus, rules developed through self-regulation are, in effect, subject to a *market test*. Finally, self-regulation generally results in the costs of such regulation being fully borne in the market in which the regulation is imposed. As we are well aware, the costs incurred by the government for some regulations are large. In most cases economic efficiency would dictate that these costs should be borne in the market that is regulated.[2]

Examples of Successful Self-Regulation

To be more specific, let me give three examples of areas where self-regulation is producing the kinds of benefits I have been discussing.

Product Standards And Certification

Consider product standard and certification programs. Today, we have some 32,000 privately developed standards, covering products ranging from nuts and bolts to computers and nuclear reactors. Approximately 700 organizations participate in the standards development process. These organizations bring together individuals who are experts in specific product areas, many of whom are employed by manufacturers or sellers of the products involved.

Private organizations also certify that products have been tested and meet a given standard. Frequently, testing is conducted by third parties such as independent laboratories; Underwriters' Laboratories is a familiar example.

Certification permits manufacturers to demonstrate efficiently that their products comply with relevant standards. One obvious benefit of these programs is to facilitate the introduction of new technology

---

[1]Mark Crain makes this point nicely in a recent op-ed in the *Wall Street Journal*: "Regulations, like products, become obsolete. Market forces take care of obsolete products, which means they find their way to the junkyard. The same cannot be said for obsolete government regulations, which tend to last long after they are moribund." W. Mark Crain, "Spinning Wheels on Old Safety Checks," *Wall Street Journal*, 25 September 1984.

[2]On a similar point, government agencies faced with budget constraints may act to minimize only the *enforcement* costs of regulation, even where this results in excessive *compliance* costs. This problem does not exist with self-regulation because both types of costs are borne by the market participants.

by enabling innovative manufacturers to demonstrate the safety or efficiency of new products.

More generally, standards and certification programs facilitate communication between buyers and sellers about complex product attributes. For example, consumers purchase motor oil with reference to standard viscosity grades—such as the familiar 10W-40—without having to understand the physics of oil viscosity. Similarly, building contractors can procure steel of desired corrosion-resistance simply by referencing relevant steel standards in a procurement contract—without having to become trained metallurgists. Obviously, transactions costs would be higher if consumers had to become experts in oil viscosity, or contractors in metallurgy. The existence of standards and certification lowers the costs associated with thousands of transactions every day.

Government itself relies heavily on private standards for regulatory and procurement purposes. For example, the Department of Defense refers to approximately 3,300 private standards in its procurement documents. Such federal reliance on private standards is likely to increase. Office of Management and Budget Circular A-119, "Federal Participation in the Development and Use of Voluntary Standards,"[3] establishes a policy preference in favor of the use of private standards and certifications by federal agencies. Its purpose is to increase government efficiency by reducing the need for government standards.

State and local jurisdictions may rely even more extensively on private standards. In most cases, these jurisdictions do not have the resources to undertake independent evaluations of the wide variety of products they use. Reliance on private-sector standards constitutes a cost-effective means of allocating their taxpayers' money.

Professional Self-Regulation

Another area where self-regulation is beneficial is in the professions. Such regulation has a long and honorable history. The American Medical Association (AMA) first established a code of ethics for its members in 1848. Since then, many other professional societies have established professional codes of ethics that can help protect consumers, other professionals, and third parties (such as insurers) from dishonest, dangerous, or otherwise unacceptable conduct. Association codes frequently prohibit false and deceptive advertising, proscribe improper business dealings with patients or clients, and set minimum standards to ensure professional competence. Responsible self-regulation is particularly important in the area of

[3]See 47 *Federal Register* 49496 (1 November 1982).

professional services because such services are often highly technical, and consumers may not be able to judge for themselves either the need for the service or its quality. Consumers would clearly suffer if they could not count on the credibility and competence of professionals.

Voluntary Advertising Standards

A third important area where self-regulation is working well is advertising. Advertisers, advertising agencies, and consumers have a shared interest in protecting advertising credibility, and it is not surprising that some of the most successful self-regulation programs are found in this area. For example, the National Advertising Division of the Council of Better Business Bureaus (BBB) administers a voluntary arbitration and correction mechanism. The BBB system allows for quick and efficient correction of questionable ads without the complicated and time-consuming legal maneuvering that accompanies government intervention.

To sum up, cooperative activities by industry and professional groups such as self-regulation can have substantial benefits for society. In addition, self-regulation is in many cases superior to government regulation.

Self-Regulation and the FTC

The Federal Trade Commission has worked to avoid impeding beneficial self-regulation. On the contrary, as I will discuss below, the FTC is actively involved in providing information on how self-regulatory groups can structure themselves to avoid problems with the antitrust and consumer protection statutes.

We must also recognize, however, that self-regulation (like government regulation) can be used to exclude competitors and otherwise limit competition. Not only must self-regulatory programs be vigilant against the types of excesses that mar government regulatory programs, they must also combat the temptation to abuse self-regulation to hinder competition. Indeed, where self-regulation involves the concerted actions of competitors, both the self-regulatory mechanism and the government must be especially wary.

There are two major problems that have concerned the FTC in this area. The first is suppression of information needed by consumers to make informed purchasing decisions. The second is the unreasonable exclusion of new products or new competitors from the market.

The best-known FTC action against suppression of information through self-regulation was its suit against the AMA.[4] The AMA's code of ethics once prohibited virtually all means of disseminating truthful information to consumers. By 1977, the code had been revised to allow certain forms of advertising, but it still prohibited statements that were "self-laudatory" or implied that the advertising physician had skills superior to those of other physicians. The Commission concluded that *all* advertising is to some degree self-laudatory. Thus, the continued ban on self-laudatory advertising really did not represent a very significant change from a virtual total ban. The Second Circuit Court of Appeals specifically upheld the Commission's conclusion that the restraints on self-laudatory advertisements justified the order issued in the AMA case.

In the order, the Commission recognized not only the virtues of truthful advertising, but the harms created by deceptive advertising.[5] Accordingly, it permitted the AMA to adopt and enforce rules designed to prevent such harmful advertising by its members.

Since the AMA case, the Commission has brought a number of other actions challenging private restrictions on the dissemination of truthful information, reaching consent agreements with a number of state and local medical and dental associations.[6] It has also intervened before state professional regulatory boards to suggest that limitations on the use of trade names by lawyers, for example, may hinder rather than help competition.

The potential that self-regulatory activities might be used to exclude new products or competitors is illustrated by two recent cases. In April 1981, the Commission filed an *amicus* brief in *American Society of Mechanical Engineers v. Hydro level.*[7] In that case, a member of the American Society of Mechanical Engineers (ASME) used his position within the organization to injure a competitor who manufactured an innovative boiler safety device. The Supreme Court held that ASME was liable for the anticompetitive actions of its member.

On July 26, 1984, the Commission accepted, subject to final approval, a consent agreement with the American Society of Sanitary Engi-

---

[4]94 F.T.C. 701 (1979), *aff'd as modified,* 638 F.2d 443 (2d Cir. 1980), *aff'd by an equally divided court,* 445 U.S. 676 (1982) (order modified, 99 F.T.C. 440 (1982) and 100 F.T.C. 572 (1982)).

[5]94 F.T.C. 1003.

[6]Washington, D.C. Dermatological Society, 102 F.T.C. 1292 (1983); Michigan Association of Osteopathic Physicians and Surgeons, 102 F.T.C. 1982 (1983); Association of Independent Dentists, 100 F.T.C. 518 (1982); Broward County Medical Association, 99 F.T.C. 622 (1982). See also American Dental Association, 94 F.T.C. 403 (1979) (consent order); *modified,* 100 F.T.C. 448 (1982); and 101 F.T.C. 34 (1983).

[7]456 U.S. 556 (1982).

neering (ASSE).[8] The complaint alleged that ASSE unreasonably restrained trade by refusing to extend standards coverage to an innovative plumbing valve produced by a small business. As a result of ASSE's refusal, sales of the innovative product may have been unduly restricted in numerous state and local jurisdictions that rely on ASSE standards.

I want to emphasize here that exclusion of a potentially competing product is not, by itself, a cause for antitrust action. In the vast majority of cases, the exclusion may be well justified. It is the basis for and extent of the exclusion that is the focus of antitrust analysis. Simply put, the exclusion should not be for the purpose of restraining competition. Nor should the exclusion exceed that which is reasonably necessary to achieve the legitimate goals of the standards or certification organization.

I also want to emphasize that these enforcement actions are not the preferred method of avoiding problems in the area of self-regulation—or, for that matter, in any area. The Federal Trade Commission's concerns are with ensuring compliance with the law and maximizing benefits to consumers. Especially in areas, such as self-regulation, where private action can create substantial benefits, the sue-first-and-ask-questions-later approach can cause great damage.

Indeed, the FTC has worked to promote an atmosphere where responsible industry self-regulation will flourish. One example is the Commission's recent advisory opinion on the American Academy of Ophthalmology's Code of Ethics.

The Academy, an organization of approximately 12,000 physicians who specialize in medical and surgical eye care, decided that it wanted to provide its members with specific guidance with respect to their professional conduct. The Academy wanted not only to address concerns about deceptive advertising, but also to touch on issues such as informed consent, unnecessary surgery, use of experimental procedures, and relationships with other health care providers.

After a draft of the code was approved by the organization's leadership, the Academy asked for a formal advisory opinion from the FTC. That draft—in the view of Commission's staff—*did* raise some antitrust concerns. But Academy representatives and FTC staff ulti-

---

[8]The consent agreement has been accepted subject to final approval in accordance with the Commission's Rules of Practice. Under the Rules, after consent agreements are accepted by the Commission, they are placed on the public record for 60 days for comment. After analysis and consideration of all comments, the Commission decides whether to make the agreement final. The comment period for the ASSE consent agreement closed on 13 October 1984.

mately worked out a proposed code that was approved by the Commission in June 1983.

Conclusion

Self-regulation by the private sector can create substantial benefits by facilitating the efficient organization and policing of market activities. By providing information, discouraging fraud and other undesirable activities, and providing a forum for market participants to communicate their legitimate common interests, self-regulatory activities ameliorate the problems of market failure emphasized by advocates of government regulation. Thus, self-regulation is in many cases a desirable alternative to government regulation.

The potential for anticompetitive abuses is also present in many self-regulatory activities, and government can and must play an active role in overseeing such activities. In the past, the FTC's oversight activities have emphasized litigation. More recently, the FTC has concentrated on working with self-regulatory organizations to arrive at solutions that provide for effective self-regulation while minimizing or eliminating potential antitrust problems. In so doing, the FTC is attempting to maximize the overall societal benefits from these activities, consistent with its statutory mandate.

13

PUBLIC CHOICE AND ANTITRUST
Robert D. Tollison

I. Introduction

The field of antitrust and industrial economics is one of the last bastions of the economics profession to be untouched by the public choice revolution. Economic analysis in this area proceeds in roughly the following way. First, the efficiency of market arrangements and organizations is analyzed. Second, those markets found wanting on the efficiency scorecard are assigned to government, through an antitrust case, to correct. The first step in this process is unobjectionable and represents one of the richest applied parts of modern economics. The second part is weak because it rests on a public interest theory of government. A market failure (monopoly) is found in the private sector, and government (an unexamined alternative) is invoked to correct it. Judges and antitrust bureaucrats are assumed to operate in the public interest, which in this case means the promotion of economic efficiency in the economy.

This is not a very useful way to approach antitrust (or any other) economic analysis. As a positive theory, it is wrong. As many critics have shown, the historical record of antitrust decisions will not support the public interest theory. If we are to understand the course of antitrust better, the behavior of the relevant actors must be made endogenous to our explanation of antitrust outcomes. As a normative basis for criticizing antitrust, the public interest approach is not very helpful. When all is said and done and government is not following one's conception of the public interest in antitrust, we are reduced to such tried and true nonsense as "better people make better government." Change the decision makers and the policy will change. This sounds good but it never seems to work. Government cranks along by an internal logic of its own, which in this case we do not know because we have not tried to find out what it is. If we want to

The author is Professor of Economics and Director of the Center for Study of Public Choice at George Mason University. He formerly served as Director of the Bureau of Economics at the Federal Trade Commission.

have a powerful critique of antitrust, the first thing that must be done is to achieve a positive understanding of how antitrust decision makers behave. Launched from such a platform, antitrust criticism and reform can be more effective.

My interest in this paper is to review the state of the (small) art with respect to developing a positive public choice theory of antitrust and to illustrate the potential of this approach. In Section II, I offer the reader a brief introduction to public choice. In Section III, I briefly outline the prevailing public interest approach to antitrust commentary. In Section IV, I survey some of the useful steps that have evolved in the literature away from the public-interest perspective. In Section V, I present some of the literature directly on the positive economics of antitrust and detail a couple of examples of the approach. Finally, in Section VI, I offer some concluding remarks.

One caveat is in order at the outset. I have not tried to be copious in my search of the literature. As a result, I have undoubtedly missed work that bears on the issues of this paper. My apologies are offered in advance for any glaring omissions.

II. Public Choice

"Public choice" refers to a revolution in the way government is analyzed. Before public choice, government was treated as exogenous to the economy, a benign corrector of the market economy when it faltered. After public choice, the role of government in the economy became something to be explained, not assumed. As a result of the public choice revolution, economists now place government failure alongside market failure as a useful category of analysis.[1]

What is public choice? I advance my own particular answer to the question. Public choice is an expansion of the explanatory domain of economic theory. Traditional economic analysis uses the apparatus of economic theory to explain the behavior of individuals in private settings. Public choice represents the use of standard economic tools (demand and supply) to explain behavior in nonmarket environments, such as government.

This expansion of economic theory is based on a simple idea. Individuals are the same people whether they are behaving in a market or nonmarket context. The person who votes also buys groceries; the workers in government bureaucracies do not have radically different temperaments from workers in corporations; and

---

[1]See Mueller (1979) and Buchanan and Tollison (1984) for useful surveys of public choice research.

so on. There is no Dr. Jekyll and Mr. Hyde dichotomy in economic behavior whereby we behave one way in the private sector and another way in the public sector. As a practical working hypothesis, individuals seek to promote their self-interest in any given situation. Public choice represents the application of this axiom to behavior in nonmarket settings. This approach has been employed by public choice analysts to explain the behavior of voters, bureaucrats, politicians, interest groups, and other political actors and organizations.

Obviously, this is not an argument that rational behavior in private and public settings leads to the same types of outcomes. The result of self-interest in government manifests itself in a different way than elsewhere because the constraints on individual behavior are different. The managers of a private corporation and a government bureau behave differently, not because they are different people but because the rules that govern their behavior are different. This is a simple but important point.

Finally, note that public choice closes the behavioral system of economic analysis (Buchanan 1972). It incorporates the behavior of government actors into economic theory, and it pushes us beyond the Pigovian fantasy that the market is guided by private interest and the government is guided by public interest. It is this step that is sorely needed in the field of antitrust and industrial organization.

III. The Antitruster's View of Government

There is a nearly unanimous tendency in antitrust commentary toward a public interest theory of government. In short, there is an implicit and unexamined view in the literature that antitrust decision makers are benign seekers of the public interest. If they knew better, they would do better. This case can be made without much effort by drawing selective references from the literature.

The primary U.S. antitrust statutes—the Sherman Antitrust Act (1890), the Clayton Antitrust Act (1914), and the Federal Trade Commission Act (1914)—are largely seen as being without economic motivation. Rather they are seen as efforts by the Congress to protect the public interest (Bork 1966, p. 7). Moreover, the role of the antitrust bureaucrats put in place by this legislation is seen as that of maintaining a competitive economy (Bain 1968, p. 515). Scherer (1980, p. 491) summarizes when he observes that antitrust is "one of the more important weapons wielded by government in its effort to harmonize the profit-seeking behavior of private enterprises with the public interest." In a similar vein Posner (1976, p. 4) suggests that the importance of economic efficiency as a social norm "establishes a prima facie case for having an antitrust policy." Neale and Goyder (1980, p. 441) put the matter as well as anyone when they observe that "it is tempting (and common) to regard the antitrust policy simply as a kind of economic engineering project."

I could go on in this vein, quoting famous students of antitrust of various ideological and methodological stripes, but the point is the same. Antitrust policy, whether discussed in terms of the origin of antitrust laws, the behavior of the antitrust bureaucracies, the behavior of judges, and so on, is predominantly discussed in public interest terms. The market fouls up; government corrects.

Of course, the public interest approach may be right, although the trenchancy of the antitrust critics with respect to selected policies and decisions seems to suggest that it is not. Moreover, the solutions that the public interest approach offers do not seem to work. The public interest approach says that more information or better people will lead to better antitrust. There is obviously some truth to such an argument, but it does not seem to be very important in the actual conduct of government affairs.

An alternative way to approach the problem is by the route of positive public choice. What can be said about the *actual* or *predicted* course of antitrust policy, as opposed to the *desired* course? By learning first about how antitrust decisions are actually made and how antitrust decision makers behave, we are surely in a better position to reform antitrust institutions—if that is what we want to do.

IV. Steps in the Right Direction

The idea that I espouse, the application of positive economics to antitrust issues, is not new. Efforts in this direction have just not been systematic, and they have been scattered around in the literature for some time. This section briefly reviews some of these early steps toward positive analysis.

Empiricism

One way to find out what antitrust authorities do is to look. In this spirit there have been several statistical studies of antitrust enforcement. The primary example is a paper by Posner (1970). Other studies include those by Stigler (1966), Gallo and Bush (1983), Clabault and Block (1981), Shughart and Tollison (forthcoming), Elzinga (1969), Asch and Seneca (1976), Hay and Kelley (1974), and Palmer (1972).

What can this approach teach us? Primarily, it can yield clues about the interworkings of the enforcement agencies. Shughart and Tollison (forthcoming), for example, study the incidence of recidivism in Federal Trade Commission (FTC) enforcement activities since 1914. They find that the rate of repeat offenses is very high, constituting about one-quarter of historical agency enforcement actions. Why is this rate so high? Is it because it is bureaucratically easier to keep track of and to prosecute the same firms over time (cost-minimizing bureaucrats), or is it because offenders find it worthwhile to violate the antitrust laws repeatedly over time? While these questions cannot be resolved on purely empirical grounds, the data point to an interesting process in FTC enforcement to be explained. This is one way in which the empirical study of antitrust can be useful.

As Posner (1970, p. 419) concludes, "antitrust enforcement is inefficient and the first step toward improvement must be a greater interest in the dry subject of statistics."

Organizational Behavior

Another way to find out what antitrust authorities do is to ask them. This is essentially what Weaver (1977) and Katzman (1980) have done in providing organizational studies of the Antitrust Division of the U.S. Department of Justice and the FTC respectively. Both of these authors base their analyses on extensive interviews with agency staff. The primary value of such studies is that they point the way to a bureaucratic model of agency behavior. Katzman, for example, finds that the desire to gain trial experience biases FTC lawyers toward shorter and less complicated initiatives as opposed to the FTC economists who are for the most part long-term employees with an interest in more time-consuming structural assaults on industry. The moral is that personnel turnover patterns may provide an important clue about agency behavior.[2]

Cost-Benefit Analysis

There has been an attempt to apply cost-benefit analysis to antitrust case-bringing activity. The basic paper here is by Long, Schramm, and Tollison (1973), with follow-up studies by Asch (1975) and Siegfried (1975). The thrust of applying the cost-benefit approach to antitrust is interesting. On the benefit side, industries are ranked according to their estimated degree of deadweight costs attributable to monopoly power. The cost side is represented by the costs of legal action by the government. Cases are then targeted according to a rule of marginal benefit equal marginal cost until the enforcement budget is exhausted.

[2]Also see Clarkson and Muris (1981) for an organizational-type study of the FTC.

There are many pitfalls in such an idealized approach to antitrust. At the theoretical level, it is not clear, for example, how deterrent effects should be treated in the case-allocation decision. At a practical level, reliable empirical estimates of monopoly deadweight costs are hard to obtain, and legal action against firms and industries based on such evidence is probably not sustainable (antitrust as economic surgery seems out of fashion). For such reasons no one has ever pushed very hard on applying the cost-benefit calculus to antitrust problems. Long, Schramm, and Tollison (1973), however, find that the actual cases brought by the Justice Department do *not* correspond to what a welfare-loss model would imply. In other words, *ceteris paribus*, cases are not brought where welfare losses are higher. This is fairly strong evidence that the goal of antitrust enforcement is not linked closely to the economist's conception of social welfare.[3]

V. Antitrust as a Problem in Positive Economics

The literature that takes the positive public choice approach to antitrust is small in quantity and admits of no easy organizing principle. In this section, accordingly, I first offer a brief survey of this literature and then produce two applications of the approach to illustrate more clearly its potentiality.

Explaining Antitrust

The papers using the positive approach fall mainly into two broad categories. In the first category are papers that apply the so-called interest group theory of government to antitrust. In the second category are papers that seek to identify the winners and losers from particular antitrust actions.

The interest group theory of government, in its modern form, is normally credited to Stigler (1971). This theory suggests the forces by which some groups win at the expense of others in the political process. Efforts to model antitrust in this spirit include Stigler's (1984) attempt to explain the origin of the Sherman Antitrust Act, Baxter's (1980) insightful paper on the political economy of antitrust, the work of Faith, Leavens, and Tollison (1982) and of Weingast and Moran (1983) on the influence of congressional committees on FTC activities, a paper by Amacher et al. (1985) on the countercyclical and cartelizing nature of historical antitrust enforcement activity, and

[3]In recent years the standard Harberger treatment of monopoly welfare loss has been modified by the concept of rent seeking. Briefly, rent seeking means that trapezoids and not triangles are the relevant geometrical unit of calculation for measuring welfare loss. For more details see Tollison (1982).

a paper by Higgins and McChesney (1983) explaining the FTC ad substantiation program in interest-group terms.

This small body of literature is distinguished by the development of a testable model of an antitrust process and a test of the model on available data. The main conclusion of this work seems to be that government works in this area much the same way as it works in others; namely, that antitrust is at least partly a veil over a wealth-transfer process fueled by certain relevant interest groups. Moreover, where the conventional wisdom points to policy failure to explain deviations in antitrust, this work suggests that the deviations are readily understandable as self-interested behavior under the relevant constraints. Thus, for example, the Robinson-Patman Act is not a mistake of antitrust policy but a rationally designed law to buffer certain firms against losses when aggregate demand falls.

The second category of positive literature looks directly at the wealth losses and gains from antitrust actions. These papers differ from those in the first category in that the unit of analysis is the firm and the concern is not with modeling the political process that guides antitrust. In a way this work can be seen as searching for important clues (who wins? who loses?) about the identity of the relevant interest groups that undergird antitrust activities. Important papers in this tradition are a study by Ellert (1976) of mergers and antimerger law enforcement, an examination by Burns (1977) of the famous oil and tobacco dissolutions in 1911, and a study by Ross (1984) of the origin of the Robinson-Patman Act suggesting that the wealth effects of the law and its enforcement transferred wealth from large chain stores to small firms and brokers. These papers are all heavily empir-ical, and, in particular, they employ capital market data to test hypotheses. This movement away from the reliance on accounting data is a heartening development in industrial organization research.

At base, then, the positive approach to antitrust analysis is repre-sented by a small body of literature. Although I have undoubtedly missed some papers and other efforts, my aim is not to be compre-hensive in reviewing the literature, but to show something about what has been done and, more important, what can be done.[4]

Dual Enforcement

Antitrust laws in the United States are enforced by the Antitrust Division of the Department of Justice and by the FTC. The critical

---

[4]I should also mention a particular effort to study the FTC that grew out of my experi-ence as director of the FTC's Bureau of Economics from 1981 to 1983. A group of my FTC colleagues and I undertook systematic studies of several aspects of FTC activities that will appear in Mackay, Miller, and Yandle (forthcoming).

literature on this dual enforcement system has been exclusively normative. Some observers have criticized the quality of FTC cases, and some have criticized the FTC internal procedure whereby commissioners sometimes sit as both prosecutors and judges for the same cases. Normally the brunt of dual-enforcement criticism is aimed at the FTC, with many calls being made for its abolition.

There is a prior problem, however, which is that of how well the dual-enforcement system works in practice. That is, what are the positive economics of dual enforcement? Higgins, Shughart, and Tollison (forthcoming) recently have tackled this problem. Their approach is simple. Dual enforcement can be modeled as an example of two bureaus competing with one another. Thus, Higgins, Shughart, and Tollison posit a model—the H-S-T model—of two budget-maximizing bureaus that behave according to Cournot output conjectures. The results of this analytical exercise are straightforward. Independent agency dual enforcement leads to more output (cases) per budget dollar than either single agency or collusive dual-agency enforcement. Begging the question for the moment of what is being produced, competition in government operates as it does anywhere else—it acts to increase output.

History provides a natural experiment for the H-S-T model. From 1890 to 1914 the Antitrust Division was the sole antitrust agency (single-agency enforcement). From 1914 to 1948 the FTC competed vigorously with the Antitrust Division (independent dual-agency enforcement). From 1948 to this day the two agencies have colluded under a liaison agreement with respect to who will bring what case or contest which merger (collusive dual-agency enforcement). Moreover, budget and output data are available for the two agencies for the years 1931 to the present. The model's implications about cases per budget dollar can therefore be tested.

Using the period 1932 to 1948 as the period of competition between the two agencies and the period 1948 to 1981 as the period of collusion, the H-S-T model has been used to compare mean annual case output, real budgets, and real output per budget dollar for the two agencies over the two periods. The authors have found that in the two periods, total cases remained roughly the same, but average cases per budget dollar fell substantially (by about half) in both organizations. This implies that more inputs were used per case in the period of collusion, or that, put another way, collusion led to increased rents to bureaucratic input suppliers (lawyers, economists).

Positive economics thus teaches us a familiar lesson in this application. For a given enforcement budget, independent dual enforcement will yield more cases per dollar spent. On such grounds one may mount a serious scientific case for dual enforcement without collusion; that is, for scrapping the so-called liaison agreement. There remains, however, a major question: Are these agencies producing "goods" or "bads"? If the latter (as the first part of this paper more or less argued), single or collusive dual-agency enforcement would be preferred on the grounds of restricting the output of a "bad." If the former, then competition between the two bureaus is the best policy. Either way, however, a positive understanding of the implications of dual enforcement provides a basis for knowing what to recommend.

Antitrust and Jobs

Time after time, regulatory programs have failed a cost-benefit test, and the econometric assault on regulation has spawned a significant regulatory reform movement in this country and abroad. For some reason, though, antitrust activities have largely escaped this type of careful, applied analysis.

In a recent paper Shughart and Tollison (1984) seek to take a first step toward remedying this situation. They propose to look at the impact of antitrust on the economy, and as a start, they look at the impact of antitrust on the level of unemployment. The purpose of this work is to try to achieve a preliminary understanding of how antitrust is related to basic economic welfare. Jobs seemed a good place to start in this regard.

The methodology used by Shughart and Tollison is quite simple. They searched the literature for a standard model of the unemployment rate in the United States and then augmented this model with a measure of antitrust activity—cases per real budget dollar brought per year by the Antitrust Division under the Sherman and Clayton Acts (a complete set of data is available for the 1947–81 period). Estimating this relationship by using ordinary least squares analysis reveals that over this period a 1 percent increase in Justice Department cases leads to a 0.17 percent increase in the economy's unemployment rate, *ceteris paribus*. Moreover, accounting for the fact that the aggregate economy and antitrust are jointly determined leaves this basic result intact.

The results yield to a natural interpretation. What Shughart and Tollison have found is an antitrust Phillips curve. When the model is run on definitions of expected (predicted) and unexpected (unpredicted) antitrust cases, it has been found that unexpected antitrust drives the result. This is analogous to unexpected money in the traditional Phillips relation. Furthermore, the numerical results are consistent in this specification of the problem. Using conservative estimates, the Shughart-Tollison study suggests that over the 1947–81 period, a 1 percent increase in annual enforcement activity added about 7,000 individuals to the mean stock of unemployed persons in the economy.

Now to the important question: How can this be? If antitrust causes unemployment in one sector, will not these workers and resources find employment in an untargeted sector? The answer is yes where antitrust activities are predicted. If antitrust actions are accurately forecast, the indicated resource adjustments will take place. It is the unexpected component of antitrust that causes unemployment.

Consider the following hypothetical situation. Suddenly the merger rules are changed for large tire firms. New mergers are challenged under stricter rules and old mergers are dissolved. Firms react by reducing the optimal scale of tire production, laying off workers as planned production falls. Unemployment rises during the adjustment period. Other industries face similar antitrust uncertainty, and they expand less as a consequence. Economywide, the unemployment rate goes up and stays up owing to the uncertainty over being targeted for an antitrust complaint. This simple Phillips curve theory explains the Shughart-Tollison results.

Some other points worth noting about these results are (1) they do some damage to the esteem with which the Sherman and Clayton Acts are held by most observers; (2) the Phillips curve explanation is quite consistent with the new learning critique of antitrust decisions, which suggests that antitrust normally attacks efficient firms or commercial practices; (3) the idea that antitrust is about equity suffers in this analysis; and (4) we are at some distance here from the public interest theory.

VI. Conclusion

The thesis of this paper is that we need to know how and why antitrust decision makers behave before we can make intelligent criticisms of antitrust policies; science must precede prescription if prescription is to be meaningful. My focus has been on enforcement officials. Judges also are important antitrust decision makers, but they have been largely exempt from the discussion. How do judges behave and why? The flat answer is that we simply do not know. We know that their antitrust decisions often evoke reams of criticism, but we have made almost no progress in developing a theory of judicial decision making in antitrust or any other area of the law.[5]

[5]See, however, the work of Landes and Posner (1975) on the independent judiciary.

So there is work, much work, to be done to achieve a fusion of public choice with antitrust law and economics. I predict that this work will emerge, and that it will provide a rich empirical basis for deciding whether antitrust is a boon or bane for the economy. Moreover, this work will help to cast the role of antitrust in more reasonable terms. Our choice in this area of government policy, as in all others, is between imperfect markets and imperfect government. In the public interest approach, government always gets a green light in antitrust. In the public choice approach, government will often face red and yellow lights, and a little bit more laissez faire will be allowed to prevail in the world.

References

Amacher, R. C.; Higgins, R. S.; Shughart, W. F., II; and Tollison, R. D. "The Behavior of Regulatory Activity Over the Business Cycle." *Economic Inquiry* 23 (January 1985): 7–19.

Asch, P. "The Determinants and Effects of Antitrust Policy." *Journal of Law and Economics* 17 (October 1975): 578–81.

Asch, P., and Seneca, J. J. "Is Collusion Profitable?" *Review of Economics and Statistics* 58 (February 1976): 1–10.

Bain, J. *Industrial Organization.* 2d ed. New York: John Wiley & Sons, Inc., 1968.

Baxter, W. "The Political Economy of Antitrust." In *The Political Economy of Antitrust: Principal Paper by William Baxter,* pp. 3–49. Edited by Robert D. Tollison. Lexington, Mass.: D. C. Heath & Co., 1980.

Bork, R. H. *The Antitrust Paradox.* New York: Basic Books, 1978.

Buchanan, J. M. "Toward Analysis of Closed Behavioral Systems." In *Theory of Public Choice,* pp. 11–23. Edited by J. M. Buchanan and R. D. Tollison. Ann Arbor: University of Michigan Press, 1972.

Buchanan, J. M., and Tollison, R. D., eds. *The Theory of Public Choice—II.* Ann Arbor: University of Michigan Press, 1984.

Burns, M. R. "The Competitive Effects of Trust-Busting: A Portfolio Analysis." *Journal of Political Economy* 85 (August 1977): 717–39.

Clabault, M. M., and Block, M. *Sherman Act Indictments, 1955–1980.* 2 vols. New York: Federal Legal Publications, 1981.

Clarkson, K. W., and Muris, T. J., eds. *The Federal Trade Commission Since 1970: Economic Regulation and Bureaucratic Behavior.* Cambridge: Cambridge University Press, 1981.

Ellert, J. "Mergers, Antitrust Law Enforcement and Stockholder Returns." *Journal of Finance* 31 (1976): 715–32.

Elzinga, K. "The Antimerger Law: Pyrrhic Victories." *Journal of Law and Economics* 12 (April 1969): 43–78.

Faith, R.; Leavens, D.; and Tollison, R. D. "Antitrust Pork Barrel." *Journal of Law and Economics* 25 (October 1982): 329–42.

Gallo, J. C., and Bush, S. "The Anatomy of Antitrust Enforcement for the Period 1963–1981." Manuscript. May 1983.

Hay, G. A., and Kelley, D. "An Empirical Survey of Price-Fixing Conspiracies." *Journal of Law and Economics* 17 (April 1974): 13–38.

Higgins, R., and McChesney, F. "Truth and Consequences: The Federal Trade Commission's Ad Substantiation Program." Manuscript. 1983.

Higgins, R. S.; Shughart, W. F., II; and Tollison, R. D. "Dual Enforcement of the Antitrust Laws." In *The Federal Trade Commission.* Edited by R. Mackay, J. C. Miller, and B. Yandle. Stanford, Calif.: Hoover Institution Press, forthcoming.

Katzman, R. A. *Regulatory Bureaucracy: The Federal Trade Commission and Antitrust Policy.* Cambridge, Mass.: MIT Press, 1980.

Landes, W. M., and Posner, R. A. "The Independent Judiciary in an Interest-Group Perspective." *Journal of Law and Economics* 18 (December 1975): 875–901.

Long, W. F.; Schramm, R.; and Tollison, R. D. "The Determinants of Antitrust Activity." *Journal of Law and Economics* 16 (October 1973): 351–64.

Mackay, R.; Miller, J. C.; and Yandle, B., eds. *The Federal Trade Commission.* Stanford, Calif.: Hoover Institution Press, forthcoming.

Mueller, D. C. *Public Choice.* Cambridge: Cambridge University Press, 1979.

Neale, Alan D., and Goyder, D. G. *Antitrust Laws of the U.S.A.* 3d ed. Cambridge: Cambridge University Press, 1980.

Palmer, J. "Some Economic Conditions Conducive to Collusion." *Journal of Economic Issues* 6 (June 1972): 29–38.

Posner, R. A. "A Statistical Study of Antitrust Law Enforcement." *Journal of Law and Economics* 13 (October 1970): 365–419.

Posner, R. A. *Antitrust Law, An Economic Perspective.* Chicago: University of Chicago Press, 1976.

Ross, T. W. "Winners and Losers Under the Robinson-Patman Act." *Journal of Law and Economics* 27 (October 1984): 243–72.

Scherer, F. M. *Industrial Market Structure and Economic Performance.* 2d ed. Chicago: Rand McNally, 1980.

Shughart, W. F., II, and Tollison, R. D. "The Employment Consequences of Antitrust." Manuscript. 1984.

Shughart, W. F., II, and Tollison, R. D. "Antitrust Recidivism in Federal Trade Commission Data: 1914–1982." In *The Federal Trade Commission.* Edited by R. Mackay, J. C. Miller, and B. Yandle. Stanford, Calif.: Hoover Institution Press, forthcoming.

Siegfried, J. J. "The Determinants of Antitrust Activity." *Journal of Law and Economics* 17 (October 1975): 559–73.

Stigler, G. J. "The Economic Effects of the Antitrust Laws." *Journal of Law and Economics* 9 (October 1966): 225–58.

Stigler, G. J. "The Theory of Economic Regulation." *Bell Journal of Economics* 2 (Spring 1971): 7–21.

Stigler, G. J. "The Origin of the Sherman Act." *Journal of Legal Studies* 14 (January 1985): 1–12.

Tollison, R. D. "Rent Seeking: A Survey." *Kyklos* 35 (1982): 575–602.

Weaver, S. *Decision to Prosecute: Organization and Public Policy in the Antitrust Division.* Cambridge, Mass.: MIT Press, 1977.

Weingast, B. R., and Moran, M. J. "Bureaucratic Discretion or Congressional Control: Regulatory Policymaking by the Federal Trade Commission." *Journal of Political Economy* 91 (October 1983): 765–800.

COMMENT

DECISION MAKERS DO MATTER
Kenneth G. Elzinga

To assume a position on the economics faculty at the University of Virginia in the 1960s was a remarkable experience. Public choice—as a new field of economics, as a new subculture within the economics profession, and as a new journal—was in first bloom.[1] Graduate students in economics at the University of Virginia, such as Bob Tollison and others, had more impressive publication records than most of the assistant professors, as James M. Buchanan challenged a group of students to take economic reasoning down new avenues and to submit the fruits of their inquiry to leading journals.

For those of us on the faculty outside the field of public choice, Virginia was also a perplexing place. If we had any previous acquaintance with the field of public finance, we thought of its concerns as being tax policy and fiscal policy. But at Virginia, the meat and potatoes of graduate courses in public finance were topics such as reward structures in bureaucracies and legislatures. Even those of us not doing public choice heard with interest, and shall I add even some pleasure, the howls of protest from political scientists as their turf was invaded by first a platoon, later a battalion, and now a division of public choice theorists. And, of course, many of these political scientists were eventually to throw down their arms and don the methodological uniform of the public choice economist.

Robert Tollison drank of that heady brew while a graduate student at the University of Virginia, and now is one of the discipline's leading brewmasters. It is almost a paradox for me, as one who has learned so much from Tollison (not an easy thing to admit since he

---

The author is Professor of Economics at the University of Virginia. He wishes to thank William Breit, James M. Buchanan, Henry G. Manne, James C. Miller, John H. Moore, and Gordon M. Stewart for their helpful comments in preparing this paper.

[1]The journal is *Public Choice*. When the publication first began in 1966, it was entitled *Papers on Non-Market Decision Making*. The original issue contained articles by Duncan Black, James S. Coleman, Otto A. Davis, M. A. H. Dempster, Aaron Wildavsky, E. A. Thompson, Gordon Tullock, and Richard Wagner. The journal became *Public Choice* with the Spring 1968 issue. For a summary of the origins and growth of public choice, see Tollison (1984, pp. 3–8).

is a former teaching assistant of mine), that I find myself in disagreement with the basic proposition of his paper, namely:

> When all is said and done and government is not following one's conception of the public interest in antitrust, we are reduced to such tried and true nonsense as "better people make better government." Change the decision makers and the policy will change. That sounds good but it never seems to work. Government cranks along by an internal logic of its own [p. 289].

This is vintage public choice dogma. It makes for wonderfully provocative classroom discussion. There is a lesson to these words that is very basic to the case for limited government. And for all I know, it may be empirically on the mark with regard to many government agencies. But not with regard to antitrust.

I cite these illustrations to support my case, drawn from the Antitrust Division of the Department of Justice, the Federal Trade Commission (FTC), and the federal courts. All belie the public choice axiom that better people do not make for better government.

A little more than a decade ago, the Antitrust Division embarked on a modest crusade against conglomerate diversification. Lawsuits against ITT, LTV, and Northwest Industries were prominently noted and often acclaimed by the press (Green et al. 1972, pp. 99–106). It was thought, in some circles, that the conglomerates would use their financial deep pockets to subsidize acquired subsidiaries, thereby lessening competition in these markets. Vertical mergers and loose-knit vertical arrangements were also regularly attacked. Indeed, as recently as the Carter Administration, vertical price fixing was viewed as a criminal offense by the assistant attorney general for antitrust.

Under the direction of William F. Baxter, the Antitrust Division attacked no conglomerate mergers. Horizontal mergers continued to be examined for possible anticompetitive offenses. But conglomerate mergers (and vertical mergers as well) were viewed as being inoffensive, even benign.

Note that this switch did not involve a change in political parties in the White House. A Republican occupied the presidency during the anticonglomerate campaign of Richard McLaren. A Republican commanded the executive branch during Baxter's regime. The office of assistant attorney general and its considerable perquisites were the same, the antimerger statute was unchanged, the budgetary process for the agency was the same; in Tollison's language, the "rules that govern their behavior" were the same. But the two men carried different ideas to the office. To argue, as Tollison does, that changing "the decision makers" to improve a bureau's performance "sounds good but it never seems to work" is to ignore the recent history of the Antitrust Division, where profound changes in enforcement direction have taken place—because, in large measure, a decision-maker made a difference.

For my second illustration, I turn to the counterpart agency, the FTC, where Tollison himself served until recently. I can only surmise that the diligence of his labors at the agency clouded for him the picture of what has occurred at the FTC that is contrary to the thesis of his paper. Once again, there were no statutory changes and no changes in the budgetary procedures by which the agency is funded. The FTC, now in its 70th year, should be a representative example, as Tollison puts it, of "government cranking along by an internal logic of its own." But when James C. Miller assumed the chairmanship, the crank, if there was one, became like a tiller. And the tiller's direction was changed notably.

As I understand one theme of the public choice literature, the directors of bureaus are presumed to behave purposefully, and while there may be several arguments in the bureaucrat's utility function, the maximization of the agency's budget is presumed to be dominant (Mueller 1979, pp. 156–67). Chairman Miller repeatedly violated this fundamental axiom of public choice theory by endeavoring to reduce the size of the agency's budget and even to eliminate the institution's field offices ("FTC Votes . . . ," p. 191; "FTC Regional Offices . . . ," p. 640). Moreover, he has authored opinions and taken administrative steps that have limited the potential for increasing litigation and the regulatory scope of the agency, thereby reducing the potential for larger staffs and budgets.[2] An acquaintance with the Jeffersonian principles of limited government and the principles of economics (principles in which Miller was instructed at the University of Virginia) explains the "internal logic" of Miller's enforcement themes, and in that sense his actions may be predictable. But they are not the actions of an "internal logic" of an agency that somehow "cranks along" heedless of those who head it.

The third example I select is that of the federal courts. Public choice, as Tollison concedes, has not been as fruitful in analyzing the behavior of courts as it has with regard to bureaus and legislatures. However, I shall argue that utilitarian maximizing principles will not capture, and may cause us to overlook, the proposition that in judicial decision making, ideas matter—and people count. It is not necessary to change an economic incentive structure to reform antitrust. Reform

---

[2]See, for example, the commission's opinion, *In the Matter of General Foods Corporation*, FTC Docket No. 9085 (6 April 1984) and the commission's resolution of the Borden ReaLemon case ("Divided FTC . . . ," p. 491).

has been happening for some time, and economic *ideas* have been the mover-and-shaker, not economic *inducements*.

One is tempted to cite the case of Aaron Director, whose influence first at the University of Chicago and later at the Hoover Institution has altered the way in which economic theory is used in antitrust analysis (Kitch 1983, pp. 181–95). Or one is tempted to cite the effect of the Areeda and Turner (1975) article on predatory pricing, which on one level affected the way courts view predation, but on a different and ultimately more influential level affected the eminence courts give to economic literature in reaching their decisions. Instead I shall mention the influence of Henry G. Manne who, for a generation now, has trained both law professors and judges in the elements of economic analysis.[3] As a result of the former effort, any student who now enrolls in a major law school ignorant of economics does so with temerity. And as a result of the second batch of students, the federal judges, it is increasingly with temerity that an antitrust lawyer argues a case ignorant of the economic issues and without casting the case in terms of economic analysis.

The point of my remarks is not to say that the reward structure of an institution does not matter, or that antitrust bureaucrats do not respond to economic incentives. The economic model of human capital accumulation explains very cogently the propensity of the young antitrust attorney to (1) want to begin a career with a government agency, (2) exhibit a strong desire to file cases, (3) be relatively unconcerned with remedy and relief in a particular case, and (4) not continue with the agency. For this reason and others, I am uncomfortable with even the appearance of being a critic of the public choice paradigm as applied to antitrust. So I take comfort in Seymour Siegel's story of the wise rabbi who told one disputant strongly holding to a particular view, "I think you're right." When the other party to the dispute protested, the rabbi said to him, "Well, you're right as well." And when both protested as to how each of them could be right, the rabbi said, "That's right too."

Tollison is right when he calls for making the actors endogenous to our analysis of antitrust outcomes. But I am right in suggesting that his statement, "looking for better people will not change the results," which was a favorite cry of the free market proponent at a time when free market proponents had little influence in government, is more a tactical argument than a proposition of inerrancy. A

---

[3]Done under the auspices of his Law and Economics Center, now at George Mason University.

more accurate statement, to which Tollison alludes later in his paper, is that if the output of the agency is a public bad, putting even good people in charge may not remedy the problem of government failure.[4]

After setting out the public choice approach to economic phenomena, Tollison contrasts this with the public interest approach, arguing that most antitrust observers naively have viewed the institution of antitrust in this latter context. He finds this disconcerting, in light of the "trenchancy of the antitrust critics with respect to [antitrust policies] and decisions," and he argues that this criticism suggests that the public interest approach does not hold. I am not so sure. Before Jonas Salk, physicians were distressingly unsuccessful in preventing poliomyelitis. But their failures were not the result of a lack of concern for their patients' health. Doctors were ignorant of the methods by which infantile paralysis could be prevented. In like fashion, antitrust authorities (and federal judges) in the recent past may have been ignorant of the free-rider effect in vertical distribution, uninformed of the existence of the market for corporate control and its implications for conglomerate mergers, not yet aware of the obstacles to successful predation, and unaware of the complex relationship between the concentration and efficiency. As economists, Tollison and I must be forgiving of them. For many who practiced the dismal science did not know of these economic characteristics either.

The important contribution of Tollison's paper is his review of the public choice approach to antitrust, and every bit as useful, his commentary on the studies that have been done.[5] Scholars as yet untutored in public choice will also appreciate his succinct manner in setting forth the approach of this form of analysis. I particularly appreciated his analysis of dual enforcement of the antitrust laws and the insights of the public choice approach to the coexistence of the Antitrust Division and the FTC, a duality long accepted by scholars who would never propose multiple Environmental Protection Agencies or Federal Communications Commissions. The possibility of reviving a Phillips curve for antitrust, a curve thought to be put to rest by devotees of rational expectations, is also provocative. It offers,

[4]Though even here the example of A. E. Kahn's presiding over the demise of the Civil Aeronautics Board, and his active encouragement of this regulatory agency's disappearance, could be cited as a notable counterexample.

[5]Tollison apologizes that his review of the literature may not be complete. Neither is my own. But one cost-benefit study, contemporaneous with the Long, Schramm, and Tollison (1973) article, that goes unmentioned is that of Leonard W. Weiss (1974, pp. 35–56). Weiss finds a more economical allocation of the enforcement resources of the Antitrust Division than do Long et al.

perhaps for the first time, the possibility that antitrust will be taken seriously at a macroeconomic workshop.[6]

Let me close by returning to my opening focus: the economics department at the University of Virginia. Also bringing luster to this department in the 1960s was G. Warren Nutter. In his last article in the *Journal of Law and Economics*, Nutter (1979) warned of excesses in the economizing paradigm. There is always the danger, not easily recognized from within the discipline, that unflagging application of the utility maximizing model leads to a nihilism or cynicism about human behavior. It borders on teaching this proposition: My taking any action is conditioned upon it being only in my narrow self-interest.

In the public choice paradigm, narrowly construed, it is as if Martin Luther had said at Worms, "Hier maximiere ich. Hier handele ich zu meinem eigenen Vorteil; ich kann nicht anders" ("Here I maximize. Here I behave in my self-interest. I can do nothing else."), instead of his famous statement, which says something quite different: "Hier stehe ich; ich kann nicht anders" ("Here I stand; I can do nothing else").

Luther was not calculating an expected lifetime earnings stream. Further, we can take grateful note that Professor Baxter did not ask, "Here I stand; how can I maximize the number of cases filed?" And Chairman Miller did not inquire, "Here I stand; how can I maximize my agency's budget?"

Tollison (p. 292) writes: "The public interest approach says that more information or better people will lead to better antitrust. There is obviously some truth to such an argument, but it does not seem to be very important in the actual conduct of government affairs." I disagree. One is not limited to contemporary antitrust affairs for other corroboration. A study of the Antitrust Division under Thurman Arnold also illustrates my point. There are times when you change the decision makers, and change *only* the decision makers, and the policy will change. As an academician, I find it heartening that decision makers can change, not because the institutional reward structure has been altered, but because ideas have consequences.

---

[6]The statement is not quite accurate. For about two decades there was significant interface between industrial organization economists and macroeconomic policy, by way of the study of administered prices in oligopolistic industries and their influence, if any, upon inflation. With the waning interest in antitrust as an anti-inflationary device, the Tollison paper suggests that antitrust endeavors may have employment consequences.

References

Areeda, Phillip, and Turner, Donald F. "Predatory Pricing and Related Practices Under Section 2 of the Sherman Act." *Harvard Law Review* 88 (February 1975): 697–733.

"Divided FTC Proposes Settlement of Predation Case Involving ReaLemon." *BNA Antitrust and Trade Regulation Report* 44 (3 March 1983): 491.

"FTC Regional Offices Contemplate Streamlined Operations With Less Staff." *BNA Antitrust and Trade Regulation Report* 44 (24 March 1983): 640.

"FTC Votes 3–2 To Close Three Regional Offices." *BNA Antitrust and Trade Regulation Report* 44 (27 January 1983): 191.

Green, Mark J., with Moore, Beverly C., and Wasserstein, Bruce. *The Closed Enterprise System*. New York: Grossman, 1972.

In the Matter of General Foods Corporation. Docket no. 9085. Federal Trade Commission, 6 April 1984.

Kitch, Edmund W., ed. "The Fire of Truth: A Remembrance of Law and Economics at Chicago, 1932–1970." *Journal of Law and Economics* 26 (April 1983): 163–234.

Long, William F.; Schramm, Richard; and Tollison, Robert D. "The Determinants of Antitrust Activity." *Journal of Law and Economics* 16 (October 1973): 351–64.

Mueller, Dennis C. *Public Choice*. Cambridge: Cambridge University Press, 1979.

Nutter, G. Warren. "On Economism." *Journal of Law and Economics* 22 (October 1979): 263–68.

Tollison, Robert D. "Public Choice, 1972–1982." In *The Theory of Public Choice—II*, pp. 3–8. Edited by James M. Buchanan and Robert D. Tollison. Ann Arbor: University of Michigan Press, 1984.

Weiss, Leonard W. "An Analysis of the Allocation of Antitrust Division Resources." In *The Antitrust Dilemma*. Edited by James A. Dalton and Stanford L. Levin. Lexington, Mass.: Lexington Books, 1974.

COMMENT

EFFICIENCY, LIBERTY, AND ANTITRUST POLICY

D. T. Armentano

Robert Tollison has written an interesting and thoughtful paper on how to critically evaluate antitrust policy. He first suggests that the public interest theory of antitrust enforcement makes little theoretical or empirical sense and we should discard it. He then argues that public choice theory—which has been useful in understanding governmental regulatory behavior—be applied to antitrust policy; after all, antitrust is regulation too. Finally, he devotes considerable attention to reviewing some of the empirical work from the public choice and interest group literature, as well as discussing the importance of recent attempts to measure the macroeconomic effects of antitrust policy. He concludes, correctly, that such evidence is probably necessary in any serious effort to reform antitrust policy in the United States.

The Antitrust Revolution

The intellectual effort to reform antitrust policy is well underway; thus Tollison's paper is both timely and important. There have been important breakthroughs in our theoretical understanding of how markets work, of how market performance affects market structure, of how private "restraints" that limit "free-riding" enhance market efficiency, and of how generally (with horizontal collusion being the primary exception) free markets tend to be efficient markets. In addition, there have been important empirical studies—the so-called new learning—that call into serious question the conventional beliefs and alleged evidence associating market concentration and poor economic performance (Goldschmid, Mann, and Weston 1974). Indeed, the weight of the new evidence has shifted the burden of proof entirely regarding this important issue (Brozen 1982). Finally, the antitrust authorities themselves, since roughly 1980, have embarked

---

The author is Professor of Economics at the University of Hartford.

on a new direction in antitrust policy that is generally coincident with the theoretical and empirical revolution now ongoing in industrial organization.[1]

One of the clear tasks that remains is a serious investigation of the incentives and behavior of the antitrust decision makers themselves. Especially relevant and useful would be information concerning the behavior of the regulatory authorities, the courts, and the administrative law judges. Tollison's call for more research in this much-neglected area is certainly welcome. Such information would help complete our understanding and criticism of antitrust policy, and would form the basis for an all-out political effort to reform (or repeal) antimonopoly law.

Public Interest versus Public Choice

There are some small bones to be picked with several of Tollison's arguments and some larger issues that need to be taken up concerning the scope of his paper and related matters.

Tollison's position on the public interest theory of antitrust would appear to be too extreme. We are told at one point that changing the decision makers to change policy "sounds good but it never seems to work"; at another point we are told that it is "tried and true nonsense" that "better people make better government." One can certainly be sympathetic with Tollison's skepticism on this issue, given our long and suffering experience with governmental mismanagement. However, it does seem clear that changing ideas and people has mattered in the quality of antitrust enforcement over the last few years. (Tollison himself has been an important part of that antitrust policy change at the Federal Trade Commission.) Whether these are long-run permanent changes is, itself, another matter entirely; if that matter is what Tollison has in mind with regard to his criticism, then his extremism may well be warranted. After all, the recent changes in antitrust policy are entirely administrative and the laws themselves are still firmly in place. It may be too early, therefore, to tell whether Tollison's extreme position on the public interest theory is as unwarranted as it first appears.

Antitrust and Liberty

A far more serious issue concerns Tollison's complete silence on matters related to economic liberty—the theme of the conference for

---

[1]See, for instance, the discussion in Meadows (1981) and the talk before the American Bar Association by Federal Trade Commission Chairman James C. Miller (1984).

which this paper was prepared. To put the matter succinctly: What is the relationship, if any, between economic liberty and the antitrust laws? As Tollison is silent on the entire issue, let us attempt to raise (but not answer fully) some of the relevant questions and issues.

It has been apparent from the start that the administration of the antitrust laws has posed serious difficulties for those committed to notions of individual rights, consent exchange, and due process. The laws, by their very nature, seem to interfere with and infringe directly on individual rights, on the freedom to transfer (or not transfer)—through consent exchange—legitimately held property or titles to property (Pilon 1979). Antitrust laws against price discrimination, merging, tying, price fixing, and even (free-market) monopolizing appear to prevent freely contracting parties from making, or refusing to make, certain contracts they believe to be in their best interests. There may be reason to prohibit or regulate such activity from some economic perspective; however, as we have argued, the theoretical case for prohibition and regulation in antitrust has been dramatically narrowed. Economic matters aside, these private activities do not violate any property rights in the ordinary use of the term—that is, they do not involve force, fraud, or misrepresentation—yet their regulation or prohibition by the state directly violates the property rights of the market participants. From a strict libertarian or natural rights position, therefore, the antitrust laws are inherently unjust. Even Adam Smith, despite all of his reservations about businessmen and price conspiracy, rejected any antitrust law on the grounds that its enforcement would not be "consistent with liberty and justice" (Smith 1937, p. 128).

In addition, there have always been serious due process problems associated with antitrust law and antitrust enforcement. Can we really know what it means to "reduce competition substantially"? Can we really know what it means to prohibit "unreasonable" restraints of trade? Can we really know what it means to prohibit "attempts to monopolize"? Can we even know what any given "relevant market" is or whether there is an "intent" to destroy "competition"? And can we know these things prior to any legal action and prior even to any alleged violation of antitrust law? If we surely cannot know these things, and most students of antitrust enforcement would agree that we cannot with certainty know these things, then antitrust "law" is capricious and arbitrary in the extreme, and those firms and individuals tried under it can hardly be said to have experienced any real "due process."[2] Thus part of the case to be marshaled against

---

[2]This has been most obvious in Federal Trade Commission enforcement of the Robinson-Patman Act (1936). See, for instance, Armentano (1982, ch. 6).

antitrust concerns itself with basic questions of economic liberty and fairness. Tollison might at least have made this a part of his recommended research agenda in the antitrust area.

Liberty and Efficiency

Existing antitrust law, as we have seen, is inherently hostile to the notion of individual property rights and consent exchange. The laws aim to enhance market efficiency, but inevitably they interfere with someone's liberty—the liberty, say, to price discriminate or to fix prices and divide markets. Can liberty and economic efficiency be reconciled?

Most who would accept existing antitrust law, or at least the minimalist prohibition on "naked" price-fixing agreements (Bork 1978), would appear to accept that some individual freedom (say the freedom to collude) must be sacrificed or traded off to preserve efficiency and competition. For example, agreements to restrain output—absent any other effects—are usually considered socially inefficient in that they would tend to raise market prices above marginal cost and create a deadweight loss for consumers (Liebeler 1978). The standard neoclassical approach therefore sees a conflict between efficiency and economic freedom, while recognizing that most free-market processes are socially efficient. Tollison generally appears to endorse the conventional welfare analysis (Tollison 1982).

Although the neoclassical theories of competition and efficiency are still widely accepted, there has recently been increasing criticism of the conventional theory and of its welfare implications (Rizzo 1980). Critics have argued that the standard view is a static and partial equilibrium analysis and, more seriously, that the conventional theory of efficiency assumes information concerning social costs and social benefits that is impossible, even in theory, to obtain (Rothbard 1979). The issue can be put as follows (Armentano 1983, pp. 9–10):

> The costs of an action are the subjective opportunities foregone by the person who makes the decision; the benefits are the subjective satisfactions. . . . Since costs and benefits are subjective they are not cardinally measurable. There is no standard unit of value that would allow the summing up of individual costs and benefits into social aggregates for comparison. Thus it is misleading to suggest that a rational antitrust policy can weigh the costs against the gains of restrictive agreements, and then decide which agreements are socially efficient and which are not.

If this methodological criticism of standard theory is valid, it creates important difficulties for any "rational" antitrust policy. Most discussions of a rational antitrust policy have assumed that the state should prohibit those agreements that have the likelihood of raising social costs without offsetting social benefits, that is, those agreements that are socially inefficient. However, if it is impossible, even in theory, to calculate social costs and benefits, then any hope for such a policy appears doomed to certain failure, regardless of the behavior of the antitrust decision makers.

If the standard theory of efficiency (and competition) has serious methodological difficulties, it may be useful to suggest some alternative approach to efficiency that may be relevant in discussions of antitrust policy. Such a theory, ideally, would seek to avoid the methodological pitfalls of the neoclassical approach, while at the same time permitting a reconciliation between economic liberty and efficiency. Indeed, such a theory might even be able to ground economic liberty solidly on scientific rather than purely normative considerations.

Alternative Perspectives on Efficiency

An alternative perspective, well within the neoclassical paradigm, would be to argue that all agreements (intend to) "lower costs" and that because opportunity costs are ultimately subjective and personal, such "savings" could always offset any so-called welfare losses (due, say, to higher prices). The easy assumption in antitrust has always been that the costs of "naked" collusive agreements greatly outweigh the benefits (if any), and that their flat prohibition per se is "efficient."[3] Yet if costs are subtle and subjective, such an easy antitrust conclusion may no longer be warranted. Market division agreements may end costly cross-hauling and advertising. Agreements between competitors (in transportation) may reduce information and transactions costs. Horizontal agreements that reduce risk and uncertainty can promote efficiency. Further, as only the parties to the agreement can evaluate the "cost savings" associated with agreement, no antitrust regulation of such activity could be rational.

An even bolder alternative to the standard theoretical approach would be a "plan-coordination" theory of efficiency. This theoretical perspective would hold that all voluntary agreements—including so-called restrictive agreements—are consistent with a process of efficiency in that they all aim, ex ante, to bring into coordination the respective plans of the market participants to the agreement. Because

---

[3]For a review of the law on price fixing, see Easterbrook (1983). His call for a "rule of reason" approach in price fixing is subject to all of the criticism just reviewed concerning the subjective nature of costs and benefits.

market information is never perfect, and because information is constantly changing, this process of plan coordination (through agreement) could never attain any final equilibrium. The end-state equilibrium, however, cannot be the focus of analysis (Hayek, 1972). The open-market process itself would continuously create powerful incentives to discover and use the best information available to correct plans that fall short of objectives (Sowell 1980). Thus an efficient market is an open market in which individuals are constantly learning, and one that tends to provide the widest scope and encouragement for private plan making, private plan correction, and private plan coordination.

This approach to efficiency would allow a condemnation of legal restrictions on competition (and on cooperation) independent of any neoclassical cost-benefit or welfare-loss calculations. Legal restrictions on trade and exchange would be harmful (inefficient) in that they would directly limit market information and the scope of voluntary plan coordination. In addition, this alternative approach to efficiency would encompass the (now) entirely troublesome "cooperative" agreements that can exist between "competitive" business organizations. Cooperation, so essential to any understanding of efficiency inside the firm, has always been suspect between firms because (according to conventional analysis) it tends to "reduce competition." Once we adopt a plan-coordination theory of efficiency, however, we are able to see rivalry and cooperation not as antagonists or opposites but as simply different elements in an entrepreneurial process of market plan coordination (Kirzner 1973). Presumably firms are in the process of minimizing their own costs either as rivals or as participants in some joint venture. As no outside observer is in a position to observe these costs, and as all voluntary agreements are consistent with plan-coordination efficiency, the determination to be rivalrous or cooperative can be left entirely up to the participants involved in these agreements. This insight ends the presumption that the Federal Trade Commission or some regulatory authority can ever judge rationally the social efficiency of any merger or joint venture.

Conclusion

A plan-coordination theory of efficiency and competition is not without difficulty; this is not meant to be an exhaustive treatment but merely a suggestive one. Recall the modest objectives: to avoid the methodological pitfalls of the standard welfare approach and especially to reconcile individual liberty and "efficiency." What is being argued here, in contrast to Tollison, is that some of the most important remaining questions in the antitrust area are theoretical rather than (necessarily) empirical. Knowledge of how antitrust decision makers behave is important, especially in any attempt to revise antitrust enforcement. Yet fundamental theoretical questions concerning the notion of "market failure" itself (apparently taken as a given in the Tollison paper) would appear to precede any concern with additional empiricism.

Tollison states that "we need to know how and why antitrust decision makers behave before we can make intelligent criticisms of antitrust policies." Perhaps so, but it can be argued instead that we need to rethink the entire notion of market failure and economic inefficiency before we can possibly understand the relevance of any additional empirical information, or even know what empirical information to seek. Any serious effort to reform or repeal antitrust will depend not so much upon antitrust impact studies—although they may be relevant—but upon a fundamental rethinking of theoretical questions concerning liberty and efficiency.

References

Armentano, Dominick T. *Antitrust and Monopoly: Anatomy of a Policy Failure*. New York: John Wiley and Sons, 1982.

Armentano, Dominick T. "Antitrust Policy: Reform or Repeal?" Cato Institute Policy Analysis, no. 21, Washington, D.C., 18 January 1983.

Bork, Robert H. *The Antitrust Paradox: A Policy at War with Itself*. New York: Basic Books, 1978.

Brozen, Yale. *Concentration, Mergers and Public Policy*. New York: Macmillan, 1982.

Easterbrook, Frank. "Fixing the Price Fixing Confusion: A Rule of Reason Approach." *Yale Law Journal* 92 (March 1983): 706–30.

Goldschmid, Harvey J.; Mann, H. Michael; and Weston, J. Fred, eds. *Industrial Concentration: The New Learning*. Boston: Little, Brown and Co., 1974.

Hayek, F. A. "The Meaning of Competition." In *Individualism and Economic Order*, pp. 92-106. Chicago: Henry Regnery Company, 1972.

Kirzner, Israel M. *Competition and Entrepreneurship*. Chicago: University of Chicago Press, 1973.

Liebeler, Wesley J. "Market Power and Competitive Superiority in Concentrated Markets." *UCLA Law Review* 25 (1978): 1243–50.

Meadows, Edward. "Bold Departures in Antitrust." *Fortune* 110 (October 1981): 52–54.

Miller, James C. "Report From Official Washington." *Antitrust Law Journal* 53 (1984): 5–13.

Pilon, Roger. "Corporations and Rights: On Treating Corporate People Justly." *Georgia Law Review* 13 (Summer 1979): 1245–1370.

Rizzo, Mario. "The Mirage of Efficiency." *Hofstra Law Review* 8 (Spring 1980): 641–58.

Rothbard, Murray N. "The Myth of Efficiency." In *Time, Uncertainty, and Disequilibrium*, pp. 90–95. Boston: D.C. Heath and Company, 1979.
Smith, Adam. *The Wealth of Nations*. New York: Modern Library, 1937.
Sowell, Thomas. *Knowledge and Decisions*. New York: Basic Books, 1980.
Tollison, Robert D. "Rent Seeking: A Survey." *Kyklos* 35 (1982): 575–602.

14

INSIDER TRADING AND PROPERTY RIGHTS IN NEW INFORMATION
Henry G. Manne

I have been dealing with the insider trading issue for over 20 years. I am happy to report that the tone of the discussion has changed dramatically over those years as a new generation of legal and economic scholars are now able to take a less emotional view of the topic. Not all of these newer and more sophisticated commentators agree with everything I wrote in 1966 in my book *Insider Trading and the Stock Market*, but that work apparently does now set the agenda for the debate, and we all know that the power to set the agenda may determine the outcome.

There is a different view today largely because people have been willing to look at insider trading as an issue that requires serious analytical work. However, one aspect of the topic has had much too little attention. This is the fundamental question of whether, even if economic welfare were maximized by the Security and Exchange Commission's (SEC's) insider trading enforcement program, we should give up the economic and human freedom involved in the nonregulated regime to gain those assumed benefits. I shall try to elaborate these noneconomic arguments along with the more traditional kinds in this paper.

Who Is Injured?

The most fundamental economic proposition in the whole topic of insider trading is that no shareholder is harmed by a rule of law that allows the exploitation of nonpublicized information about shares of publicly traded corporations. The naive argument in defense of the SEC's position on this subject is that if the shareholder had the information (good news) the insider had, he would not sell his shares.[1]

The author is Dean of the School of Law and Director of the Law and Economics Center at George Mason University.
[1]William Painter, review of *Insider Trading and the Stock Market*, by Henry G. Manne, *George Washington Law Review* 35 (October 1966): 146–60.

The rhetorical fallacy in this proposition kept much of the early debate at fever pitch, so let me explain why it is a fallacy.[2] The statement compares the behavior of an "outside" shareholder who is in possession of valuable information with one who is not. Unfortunately for the proponents of this view, however, that is not the relevant comparison. The real question is whether the person wanting to sell shares for exogenous reasons would behave differently *before the information has been disclosed* if insiders are or are not allowed to trade on the information. Obviously every shareholder would like to have access to more valuable information, just as he would like to have access to more wealth. But there is no reason to believe that the rule about insider trading will have any effect on the time of his sale, which is the critical issue in the matter. Obviously the argument demonstrates no injury to any prepublication interest that should be protected.

The modern academic literature now recognizes that there is no significant economic harm to any identifiable group of investors from insider trading. The serious literature does not even address that question anymore. The SEC still makes the "fairness" argument[3]— the argument that it is not fair for some people to have property and others not to have it—but most scholars now understand the intellectual merit of that kind of argument.[4]

There is a related point that is more an exercise in legal than in economic logic, but the end result is the same. The argument is that insiders, by using information that has not been disclosed previously to shareholders, are violating a fiduciary duty or an implied contractual obligation to the shareholders.[5] The question-begging aspect of this proposition should be immediately apparent. The question at issue is whether or not it is desirable to have just such an implied contractual provision or fiduciary obligation. One cannot argue meaningfully to a conclusion from such a question-begging proposition. Again this problem does not seem to plague current writing on this subject as it did some 20 years ago.

---

[2]For an elaboration of this argument, see Henry G. Manne, "Insider Trading and the Law Professors," *Vanderbilt Law Review* 23 (December 1969): 547, 551–53.

[3]See, for example, John M. Fedders and Michael Mann, "Waiver by Conduct versus Fraud," *Wall Street Journal*, 21 December 1984, p. 18.

[4]But see Victor Brudney, "Insiders, Outsiders, and Informational Advantages under the Federal Securities Laws," *Harvard Law Review* 93 (December 1979): 322–76.

[5]Richard Jennings, review of *Insider Trading and the Stock Market*, by Henry G. Manne, *California Law Review* 55 (October 1967): 1229–35.

The Efficient Stock Market

The next fundamental economic argument, one no economist has ever denied, is that insider trading will always push stock prices in the "correct" direction.[6] That is, the effect of insider trading will always be to move a share's price towards the level correctly reflecting all the real facts about the company. There is a debate on how quickly insider trading will do this and what the impact of insider trading is on the timing of public disclosure. But there is no debate on the basic proposition, and the economic logic underlying it is straightforward. The price of any commodity reflects individuals' subjective measurements of a good's utility. But individuals' subjective measurement of the value of any good is obviously a function of information they have about that commodity. A nugget thought to be iron oxide is discovered to be gold. That discovery tells us that the "market" will put a higher value on the nugget than was previously thought to be true. And that is precisely the process by which insider trading (or for that matter any informed trading, whether by insiders or not) will shift stock prices in the correct direction. The direction is "correct" simply because it reflects more valid information. Obviously the process whereby markets process information into prices is conceptually and institutionally quite complicated,[7] but happily this matter, as it relates to insider trading, is not in dispute.

What is new since I first made this argument is a tremendously increased sensitivity to the importance of "correct" stock prices, or of an efficient market. Dependent functions include, for instance, investment decisions, the allocation of capital, the market for corporate control, and the market for managers. Each of these requires correct stock prices to function effectively. I might add that the welfare of the many economists basing their work on the accuracy of stock market pricing is also at risk.

Information as Compensation

In my 1966 book I made another economic argument that I believe has had too little attention from mainstream neoclassical economists considering large, publicly held corporations. It was a matter Joseph Schumpeter first raised as a fundamental failing of the large corpo-

[6]See Hsiu-Kwang Wu, "An Economist Looks at Section 16 of the Securities Exchange Act of 1934," *Columbia Law Review* 68 (February 1968): 260–9.

[7]See, for example, Frank Easterbrook and Daniel Fischel, "Mandatory Disclosure and the Protection of Investors," *Virginia Law Review* 70 (May 1984): 669–715; Ronald Gilson and Reinier Kraakman, "The Mechanisms of Market Efficiency," *Virginia Law Review* 70 (May 1984): 549–644.

ration: that it did not by its nature encourage or reward entrepreneurship,[8] probably because appropriate compensation devices for entrepreneurs were unavailable in the large corporate system. I pointed out that for all the psychological tendencies that do exist for bureaucratization of large corporations, insider trading does provide one possibility for appropriate entrepreneurial compensation.[9] Only the Austrian economists in recent years have attempted to develop the theme of the entrepreneur,[10] though little effort has been directed to the form-of-compensation problem as such. Other commentators have, however, recognized the general compensatory implications of the rule for or against insider trading. Particularly Professors Fischel and Carlton have noted that allowing corporate insiders early access to information is indeed a form of compensation and one which, through familiar Coase theorem logic, is going to be paid in any event.[11] Professor Easterbrook, on the other hand, has concluded that allowing insiders to trade will encourage them to manage the company without sufficient concern for the shareholders' aversion to risk.[12] This argument, however, is presented without reference to the countervailing incentives managers already have to behave in too risk-averse a fashion.

We could not talk intelligently about the costs and benefits of the SEC's rule without at least noting the high compliance and escape costs from rules against insider trading. The lawyers advising corporations, shareholders, and others today on how to avoid the risks of an SEC complaint do not come cheaply. Furthermore, the fact there is so much money potentially available means that people will use inefficient devices to exploit the information if straightforward methods are apt to be discovered.[13] For instance, they will ship the information overseas and perhaps trade through an obscure mutual

---

[8]Joseph A. Schumpeter, *Capitalism, Socialism, and Democracy* (New York: Harper & Row, 1942), p. 134.

[9]Manne, *Insider Trading*, pp. 138–41.

[10]See, for example, Israel M. Kirzner, *Competition and Entrepreneurship* (Chicago: University of Chicago Press, 1978).

[11]Dennis Carlton and Daniel Fischel, "The Regulation of Insider Trading," *Stanford Law Review* 35 (May 1983): especially 861–66.

[12]Frank Easterbrook, "Insider Trading, Secret Agents, Evidentiary Privileges, and the Production of Information," *Supreme Court Review* (1981): 309–65. But see Richard Leftwich and Robert Verrecchia, "Insider Trading and Managers' Choice Among Risky Projects," CRSP Working Paper no. 63, University of Chicago Graduate School of Business, August 1983.

[13]Harold Demsetz, "Perfect Competition, Regulation, and the Stock Market," in *Economic Policy and the Regulation of Corporate Securities*, ed. Henry G. Manne (Washington, D.C.: American Enterprise Institute, 1969).

fund or a Swiss bank.[14] Delays in disclosure and a variety of barter arrangements also add to the real costs of these rules.

Enforcement Problems

The SEC has recently given convincing evidence of its own inability to police its rules against insider trading, particularly where foreign funding of such trades may be involved. Mr. John M. Fedders, Director of the SEC's Division of Enforcement, has proposed a rather extraordinary exportation of American law to foreign jurisdictions, particularly Switzerland. Under his proposal any purchase or sale of securities in the United States would automatically carry with it a waiver of the applicability of foreign secrecy laws.[15] The real effect of this is likely to be to force Swiss banks, which are unlikely to give up the advantages of bank secrecy, to refuse in the future to finance trading in American stocks. A more classic use of regulatory apparatus to restrain foreign competition would be hard to imagine. And for the U.S. Securities and Exchange Commission even seriously to consider such an idea can only mean that it is severely frustrated in its efforts to bar insider trading.

This argument is revealing in another regard since it suggests that there may be greater political pressure from some important SEC constituency than has been generally realized. After all, everyone understands today that insider trading is in the nature of a "victimless crime." Somehow it seems unlikely that such extraordinary pressures would be mounted by the SEC merely to police Swiss bankers' morality. We shall return subsequently to this point.

The enforcement problems I have just been referring to are inherent in the SEC's insider-trading rule. The ability to detect the practice will always be difficult, and when the gains that can be realized from the practice, discounted by the risk of being apprehended, are compared to the potential costs, many people will have the incentive to trade on inside information. But there is an even more fundamental reason why there can never be significant enforcement of a rule against the profitable use of new information in the stock market.

Most of us think that insider trading only takes place when the officers or other insiders, as in the classic *Texas-Gulf Sulfur*[16] case, place an order with their brokers to buy stock before important new

---

[14]Henry G. Manne, "Offshore and On—The SEC's Reach Threatens to Exceed Its Grasp," *Barron's* 2 November 1969, p. 1.

[15]Fedders and Mann, "Waiver by Conduct."

[16]SEC v. Texas Gulf Sulphur Co. 401 F. 2d. 833 (2d Cir., 1968) cert. denied, 404 U.S. 1005 (1971).

information about the company is disclosed publicly. That kind of trading may have some price impact, but we cannot be sure a priori how much impact it will actually have, if it will have any at all.[17] Given modern portfolio theory,[18] the assumption is that the demand curve for any given company's stock is extremely elastic. Thus even large purchases of a stock will not necessarily have an immediate and noticeable effect on its price since many other stocks are seen as perfect substitutes for this one in other investors' portfolios. This elasticity, however, is never perfect and, in general, heavy purchases or sales of a stock eventually will have an effect on its price.

In fact, many people who exploit new information do not buy additional stock; rather, they simply *do not sell*.[19] If the stock is already in their portfolio, it may be sold or not as conditions dictate. However, with inside information, they know when *not* to sell any of their present holdings. Refraining from selling stock that would otherwise have been sold has exactly the same economic effect on market price as a decision to buy that same number of shares. But there is one crucial legal distinction: A failure to sell cannot be a violation of the SEC's Rule 10b-5, because there has been no securities transaction. The SEC might like to punish people for what is in their head, but under the present state of law they cannot.

The upshot of all this is that people can make abnormal profits in the stock market simply by knowing when *not* to buy and when *not* to sell. They will not make as much perhaps as if they could trade on the information more efficiently, but nonetheless they will still make supra-competitive returns. And this is a form of insider trading that no one can do anything about. It may also be the dominant method of using inside information.[20]

Civil Liberties Issues

The amount of insider trading actually occurring, as compared to the amount effectively policed by the SEC, suggests a serious civil liberties problem in this area. As our national experience with prohibition demonstrated, it is difficult to give government enforce-

---

[17]See Henry G. Manne, "Economic Aspects of Required Disclosure Under Federal Securities Laws," in *Wall Street in Transition: The Emerging System and Its Impact on the Economy*, ed. H. Manne and E. Solomon (New York: New York University Press, 1974), p. 21.

[18]See generally Eugene Fama, *Foundations of Finance: Portfolio Decisions and Securities Prices* (New York: Basic Books, 1976).

[19]This argument was first elaborated in Manne, "Economic Aspects."

[20]Ibid., p. 78; and see Gilson and Kraakman, "The Mechanisms of Market Efficiency."

ment agencies vast discretionary powers over large numbers of people without that power being abused. If large numbers of people are regularly violating a particular law, that law becomes a device by which government powers may be used abusively through selective enforcement.

We have no direct evidence that the SEC has used its powers in an abusive fashion, but we should not have to wait for a situation to develop before recognizing the danger. Two recent cases are certainly suggestive. In 1984 the SEC brought an action against Mr. R. Foster Winans, then in charge of the *Wall Street Journal's* "Heard on the Street" column, for trading on information that would appear subsequently in the column.[21] Mr. Winans bore little resemblance to the usual insider, since he was not privy to any valuable market information about the company for which he worked. The SEC claimed that his "misappropriation" of the *Journal's* information was sufficient to run him afoul of its Rule 10b-5. The more fundamental legal question here seems to be the right of the SEC to expand its own jurisdiction into an area of law that has been traditionally a matter of state enforcement. However, the specter of regulation of reporters' behavior, including their financial activities, has certainly been taken as a warning shot by many thoughtful commentators. And while the Winans matter cannot be viewed in itself as a threat to freedom of the press, the fears expressed by some journalists do not seem entirely without justification.

Also in 1984, an Assistant Secretary of Defense, Mr. Paul Thayer, was forced to resign his government post in order to defend against a charge of insider trading. No one has suggested that the SEC's powers were being used against Mr. Thayer by his political enemies within the government. And yet, he had been the center of some heated political controversy in the months before the SEC's charge, and again, even though the reality of political abuse may not be present in this case, the potential is certainly clear. Given that many (most?) individuals of substance and of active business experience before assuming government positions could be colorably charged with a violation of Rule 10b-5, the danger of lodging this kind of power in a government agency is again brought home.

The matter involving Mr. Thayer raises still another civil liberties issue in connection with insider trading enforcement. We also should be concerned about potential abuses of individuals' right to privacy, unless some strong countervailing interest is to be served. In the

---

[21]See John C. Boland, *Wall Street's Insiders* (New York: Wm. Morrow & Co., 1984), p. 58.

famous *Dirks* case,[22] the U.S. Supreme Court ruled that in order to show a violation of Rule 10b-5, the SEC had to show that a person giving out the information got some benefit in return. The SEC found that Mr. Thayer had not used the undisclosed information himself to buy stock, and therefore he had made no profits in the stock. However, he did receive "sexual favors" from a woman to whom he gave the news.[23] A goodly number of insider trading cases have been found to involve intimate or close family relationships,[24] undoubtedly reflecting some form of payment. The SEC's rule seems to lead this government enforcement agency ineluctably into these areas. But these relationships are only examined by government agencies at a price we probably should not pay. There are subtle yet real dangers to liberty lurking in this "ethical" rule.

Contracting Out

We have already noted that insider trading is a victimless crime, with only amorphous and rhetorical claims about the "integrity of the market" to justify its prohibition. But there is further internal evidence suggesting intellectual hanky-panky in connection with this campaign by the SEC. Consider the fact that no corporation is allowed to adopt rules, even broadly publicized, specifying that its insiders are authorized to engage in insider trading. That is, no one may in effect contract out of the SEC's rule. The SEC's defenders have great difficulty in showing any reason why this should be a mandatory rather than elective rule. There once were in fact a few companies that adopted their own internal rules against insider trading, before anyone at the SEC had even thought of the subject in its modern form. Clearly, however, the overwhelming number of companies, when they were perfectly free to contract their way into such a rule, did not do so. This failure of corporations to design internal rules against insider trading could not have been an accident or oversight. Indeed, as Professors Fischel and Carlton have recently argued,[25] given industrial competition and efficient capital markets, this is a very strong indication that a rule against insider trading would actually be harmful to shareholders. But, as we shall see, the SEC may be responding to other interests by not allowing companies to contract out of the present rule.

---

[22]Dirks v. SEC 463 U.S. 646 (1983).
[23]See Boland, *Wall Street's Insiders.*
[24]Ibid., ch. 1.
[25]Carlton and Fischel, "The Regulation of Insider Trading."

It has been argued that SEC enforcement of a mandatory rule is necessary because the companies themselves are incapable of enforcing an internal rule on the subject.[26] That could also explain why they did not voluntarily adopt such a rule earlier. But there are two peculiarities to this. One is the explicit factual assumption that the SEC could do a better job of ferreting out insider trading than could a corporation that wanted to enforce such a rule against its employees. But corporations could surely detect activities, particularly repeat activity of heavy trading, very quickly.[27] And the enforcement record of the SEC is nothing to brag about. Market studies clearly show that there is vastly more of this activity than the SEC has uncovered.[28] But the SEC's public relations staff is good at telling the world what efficient policemen they are.

The second peculiarity stems from the argument that the SEC should enforce this rule for companies that would like to have it but who cannot do it themselves. Clearly at some price they could do it, so why should the SEC be using taxpayer's money to subsidize corporations in that fashion? No "economy of scale" or public goods argument can justify a rule, even if the corporations want it. But, of course, they do not want it. And this "gift" from the SEC is no subsidy if it has no value to the companies. The argument simply will not wash.

Political Interests

It seems fairly clear then that the economic, moral and legal arguments are very strong against the SEC's stand on insider trading. There remains then only one area of investigation, and that is a political one. Ever since George Stigler elaborated the modern "interest theory" of regulation,[29] scholars have been well-advised in seeking the explanation for a particular regulatory position to ask who would be benefitted most by the rule. Ethical and economic welfare arguments aside, who stands to benefit most if in fact the arguments for enforcement against corporate insiders carry the day?

[26]Easterbrook, "Insider Trading."

[27]Michael Dooley, "Enforcement of Insider Trading Restrictions," *Virginia Law Review* 66 (February 1980); 1–83.

[28]See authorities cited in Carlton and Fischel, n. 12, p. 59.

[29]George J. Stigler, "The Theory of Economic Regulation," *Bell Journal of Economics and Management Science* 2 (1971): 3–21. Revised and reprinted in G. Stigler, *The Citizen and the State: Essays on Regulation* (Chicago: University of Chicago Press, 1975).

If we know the answer to that question, we will have an important insight into what is really going on here.[30]

The answer starts with some economic aspects of the partial enforcement of economic regulations. Naturally we cannot have perfect enforcement of any economic regulation, since enforcement is not costless. Indeed no one argues for perfect detection and conviction of every inside trader. But since partial enforcement is a fact of life, we will find that some potential violators will be more risk-averse than others. People who value their personal reputations highly will not take the risk of being indicted or charged by the SEC, and they will pull out of the competition for "illegal" information. As they do, the supply of the service they had been providing will be reduced, and those left will thereby profit more.[31]

Prohibition is the best known example of how this scenario unfolds. When the mom-and-pop liquor stores were closed, the progenitors of modern racketeers took over the industry, and they liked the monopoly rents they received by the restriction of competition afforded by the police. Therefore, they actively opposed repeal of prohibition. Something similar is happening here. It is difficult to know the exact alternative channels for the flow of new information, but it is very valuable and it is going somewhere. Look for the supporters of the rule, and you will have a good idea of who benefits from it.

It is not too hard to find some suggestive evidence to support the hypothesis that investment bankers and their related functionaries are trying to get valuable information that would otherwise go to corporate insiders. Maybe corporate insiders do not look like mom-and-pop liquor-store owner types, but the economics of the two situations is identical.

What we are likely seeing in this whole insider trading binge is another attempt by regulation to reallocate wealth,[32] in this case the value of information from one set of users, corporate officials, to the financial service people who are the next in line to gain access to information before the public does. It is not surprising then that when information goes through the bankers' hands first, for "security analysis," it is no longer "illicit" inside information. Now it is the "data" the financial analysts use to make their evaluation of stocks. But no amount of semantics can change the fact that if insiders cannot

[30]I am indebted to Jonathan R. Macey for this excellent argument.
[31]See Herbert Packer, "The Crime Tariff," *American Scholar* 33 (Autumn 1964): 551–57. Note that this argument does not apply easily to most common types of crime, but it seems particularly apposite in all areas of victimless crime.
[32]See Richard Posner, "Taxation by Regulation," *Bell Journal of Economics and Management Science* 2 (Spring 1971): 22–50.

use the information, these functionaries will get it and use it to their advantage more quickly than anyone else.

There have, of course, been suggestions before that the SEC has long performed a valuable function for leading firms in the investment banking industry.[33] It is also noteworthy that elite Wall Streeters have long supported the SEC in its campaign against insider trading, though it is difficult to believe that sophisticated financial experts are really taken in by the "integrity of the market" argument or the traditional fairness position on insider trading. It is more likely that the SEC has again proved that it is no different from other agencies that have protected competitors instead of consumers.

[33]See Manne, "Economic Aspects."

COMMENT

CIVIL LIBERTIES AND REGULATION OF INSIDER TRADING
Nicholas Wolfson

This comment focuses on the significant civil rights issues raised by insider trading, as pointed out by Henry Manne. In particular, I will focus on Manne's concern that the government action against the journalist, Mr. R. Foster Winans, has significant implications for the safeguarding of civil liberties. The fact that the government is moving into sensitive areas affecting civil liberties may well be the most serious problem raised by the Justice Department and the Securities and Exchange Commission's enforcement of insider-trading regulations.

The Winans case was not a typical insider case, in that Winans was not privy to inside information about the corporations he was discussing.[1] At the time of the incidents Winans was one of the writers of the famous *Wall Street Journal* "Heard on the Street" column. The column was so well followed that it appeared to have an impact on the price of stocks about which it was concerned. Favorable stories often led to price increases; negative commentary often had the opposite effect. Winans knew in advance the type of report his column was going to contain on specific stocks. The news in his column was public in the sense that it was based on public sources and data. The act of putting this information together in coherent form and publishing it in the prestigious column of a well-known newspaper often led to a price impact. Winans was not accused of either omitting newsworthy material about the corporations or writing falsely about the stocks he covered. He and his confederates, rather, benefited from "scalping": They bought stock shortly before publication of the column and sold out at profit immediately after publication and the predictable price rise. The only news that was secret was the timing of his article and the fact that they would buy and later sell.

The author is Professor of Law at the University of Connecticut School of Law.
[1]United States v. Carpenter, 791 Fed. 2d. 1024 (1986).

Legal Doctrine on Insider Trading

As a result of two recent Supreme Court cases[2] and several court of appeals opinions the legal doctrine governing insider trading can be summarized as follows: Certain individuals have an affirmative duty to disclose so-called material secret information to a prospective buyer or seller of stock. The affected individuals are those with fiduciary duties to prospective buyers or sellers. Therefore, corporate officers and directors are covered, since under traditional corporate law they have a fiduciary duty to shareholders. Hence, when they trade in the open market they must first disclose material news about the issuer before they can trade with antifraud impunity. However, Winans had no such fiduciary duties; he was not a corporate insider of the issuers about which he wrote. He was, in legal jargon, a stranger to them.

Even if Winans did not violate that fiduciary duty, the Securities and Exchange Commission (SEC) could rely on the so-called misappropriation doctrine to bring Winans to justice. Since the *Wall Street Journal* had a policy forbidding scalping and Winans knew of it, he violated his obligation to his employer when he scalped. He misappropriated his special relationship or access to the *Journal* in connection with his purchases of stock. That misappropriation of the *Journal*'s own confidential schedule of forthcoming publications was a Rule 10b-5 fraud in connection with the purchase of stock; hence a criminal violation of the rule and the statute.[3]

Arguably, Winans also violated the journalist's special relationship of trust and confidence with his readers and, therefore, could also have been said to have violated Rule 10b-5 for that reason. Such an interpretation, however, would require a relatively radical judicial construct since it would impose Rule 10b-5 responsibilities on all journalists across a wide range of behavior. That theory was not presented in the criminal case. Naturally, public disclosure in advance by Winans of his plan could defeat any fraud action against him.

First Amendment Issues

If under the misappropriation doctrine Winans's failure to disclose his financial interest in his column and schedule of publications supports an SEC criminal fraud action, then First Amendment issues are clearly raised. The government is, in effect, instructing the news-

---

[2]Chiarella v. United States 445 U.S. 222 (1980); Dirks v. SEC 463 U.S. 646 (1983).
[3]Ironically the *Wall Street Journal* itself could lawfully have bought stock on its unpublished story, since the newspaper cannot misappropriate its own information or access.

paper reporter that advance disclosure of his financial interest—that is, the scalping scheme—or alternatively, refusal by the newspaper to run the story, would vitiate any criminal fraud action by the government. In this sense the government is dictating the nature of news disclosure, or the contents of his story.

The slippery slope argument is especially strong in this area. Once we grant the constitutional validity of a Winans prosection based on the misappropriation doctrine, we open the door to government regulation of all forms of communication. One could envision, for example, major newscasters on radio and television having to disclose in advance their financial or personal interest in any story, or suppress coverage altogether. For example, if television reporter X owns a stock interest in steel corporations, he must disclose that interest prior to his news coverage of steel strikes. Further, if he is a liberal or a conservative, the government could require that advance disclosure of his alleged bias be made. This would be an intrusion into the content of news that appears to raise serious First Amendment issues.

The contrary argument will be made that SEC regulation of insider fraud, even in the context of a newspaper reporter, is part of financial regulation of so-called commercial speech as distinguished from political speech. Under well-known constitutional doctrine the government may—under certain circumstances defined in the cases—regulate commercial speech, particularly commercial speech that has a tendency to deceive.[4] Indeed the government may regulate in advance the content of commercial speech as well as pursue after-the-fact fraud cases.

An initial question is the definition of commercial speech. Most commentators agree that advertisement of a product or service in connection with its sale is commercial speech. Clearly the advertisement of toothpaste would fit that definition. Some may argue that speech which is closely intertwined with economic self-interest is commercial speech. The broader definition is impossible to sustain because so much of so-called political speech is always closely connected to the proponent's economic self-interest. In the Winans case, presumably, the SEC would assert that his scalping scheme was a commercial transaction, and a statute requiring full disclosure of this self-interest is a form of permissible regulation of commercial speech. But this is a far stretch from the example of a corporation selling and advertising toothpaste or drugs. The government argues in the Winans case that a reporter's self-interest must be disclosed in connection

---

[4]See, for example, Central Hudson Gas & Electric Corporation v. Public Service Commission, 447 U.S. 557 (1980).

with an editorial or news story or news commentary he is about to write in a publicly disseminated newspaper. This amounts to government dictation of the content of news.

SEC Regulation of Financial News

It is fruitful to step back, at this point, and view the entire picture of SEC regulation of financial news. One of the principal areas of SEC regulation is proxy solicitation. The SEC mandates certain disclosure in connection with corporate shareholder meetings and under appropriate regulations forbids fraud in connection with proxy regulation.[5] Somehow, it has escaped the notice of the courts that this activity amounts to an astounding regulation of the political processes of one of the most important organizational structures in American life.

The expressed purpose of SEC proxy regulation is to foster shareholder democracy in the governance of publicly held corporations. Shareholder meetings are not infrequently characterized by strife between competing groups on issues of policy or electoral slates. This is a fairly common phenomenon of other organizations such as political parties, bar groups, medical groups, church organizations, and the like. Yet the SEC, through the laws it administers, asserts its right to regulate the content of campaign material put out by opposing directorial slates in corporate internal political battles. By any stretch of the imagination, this does not fit the customary definition of commercial speech. It appears a fairly obvious effort to censor in advance the activities of citizens who are exercising their constitutional right to freely associate.

The second major area of SEC regulation is the system that governs mandatory disclosure and fraud in connection with corporate sale of stock to the public for the purposes of raising capital.[6] Again, the SEC asserts that this is an instance of appropriate regulation of commercial speech. Yet, as in the proxy arena, the similarities to customary commercial speech are not so obvious on close analysis. Take the XYZ corporation that advertises and sells toothpaste. The advertisement for the product is clearly an example of traditional commercial speech. Now assume that same corporation sells shares of common stock. Each share of stock constitutes a bundle of legal rights in a private organization, a corporation. In that sense each share of stock is the same as a membership in the American Bar Association or the

---

[5]See generally, Thomas Lee Hazen, *The Law of Securities Regulation* (St. Paul, Minn.: West Publishing Co., 1985), ch. 11.
[6]Ibid, ch. 2.

Democratic party. Imagine a government regulation that mandated the kinds of disclosure the Democratic party could make in soliciting adherents to its purposes. That would appear a direct violation of the First Amendment. The only distinction between the corporation and other organizations must rest on the commercial, that is, economic self-interest of the organization. But as we have observed before, self-interest is an overly wide net that will sweep up in its embrace virtually all of human discourse.

Essentially, the SEC system of mandatory disclosure and fraud regulation concerning corporate sales of stock constitutes the regulation of speech of a major private form of free association in the American system. Its justification, as mentioned above, lies exclusively in the assertion that corporations, unlike other groups such as the NAACP and the Republican party, are motivated by economic self-interest.

A third area of SEC regulation involved investment advisers. A recent Supreme Court decision addressed that issue.[7] Christopher Lowe was the president and principal shareholder of Lowe Management Corporation, which had been registered as an investment adviser with the SEC as required by the Investment Advisers Act of 1940. Lowe was convicted of several criminal offenses that constituted grounds under the statute for revocation of the corporation's registration. None of the offenses or SEC allegations, however, went to the truth or falsity of Lowe's financial newsletter. The SEC revoked the corporation's registration for publishing its newsletter, and thereby its permission to publish investment advice, but the Supreme Court held that the corporation was still covered under the statutory exemption from registration for bona fide newspapers.

It appears clear that the Court reached its somewhat strained statutory conclusion because it feared that a different statutory interpretation would involve First Amendment issues. The concurring justices argued on direct constitutional grounds that the statute was intended to cover Mr. Lowe and his corporation, and, as such, it violated the First Amendment protection against prior restraint. The justices argued that a licensing requirement for an impersonal financial newsletter was to be distinguished from one-on-one personal investment advice. The latter was conduct and, therefore, could be regulated constitutionally by the SEC. The concurring justices did not have to decide whether the newsletter was political or commercial speech. They argued that even if it were commercial speech, the

---

[7]Lowe v. SEC, 105 S. Ct. 2557 (1985).

prepublication regulatory restraint was excessive and beyond what was necessary and appropriate for the government to exercise.

Implications for Civil Liberties

It is significant that certain justices questioned on constitutional grounds a broad licensing requirement for impersonal financial newsletters. Winans, of course, was a reporter for a bona fide newspaper, certainly an impersonal means of communication. It would appear that the SEC and Justice Department's misappropriation doctrine, discussed above, constitutes a form of prohibited licensing requirement for the journalistic profession, since it mandates disclosure by reporters of alleged self-interest, or alternatively, the suppression of their stories.

Even when we consider insider trading by nonjournalists, the same civil liberties concerns are significant. Insiders are compelled to make disclosures about the issuer prior to trading in the stock. The nature of what they must disclose is vague and governed by an elusive "materiality" standard. It is often difficult to distinguish between stock market rumor or gossip and illegal inside information. Moreover, even parties far removed from the initial transfer of "inside information"—the so-called tippees of tippees of insider tippors— may be regulated by the doctrine.

The rationale is that failure to disclose by an insider or tippee is commercial speech and, therefore, subject to considerable regulatory control. The stock certificate, however, as noted above, represents a membership interest in an organization. Therefore, that regulatory structure resembles government censorship of a voluntary association's communications by it or its members to its members and approaches a dangerous government interference with the right of individuals to freely associate. Certainly civil libertarians would detest a governmental requirement that regulated the contents of congressional speeches or the speeches of political party members. Congressmen have a passionate selfish interest in reelection. Yet, the First Amendment prevents government censorship of their reelection speeches. There appears less convincing reason than commonly believed to distinguish corporate-related speech, whether connected to an immediate share transaction or not, from the self-interested speech of elected officials.

In conclusion, I believe Manne was correct in raising civil liberties issues in connection with the government's insider trading case against R. Foster Winans. By alerting us to these important issues, Manne has performed a useful service and opened a new avenue for future research.

15

MISTAKEN JUDICIAL ACTIVISM: PROPOSED CONSTRAINTS ON CREDITOR REMEDIES

Simon Rottenberg

Introduction

In a system of liberty, the smallest possible number of constraints is put on the rights of individuals to participate in exchange transactions and to define the terms on which exchange is consummated. In such a system, judges will be active in the review of legislative constraints on exchange in order to assure consistency with constitutional prescriptions of individual liberty. Judges will also be active in either compelling performance or requiring that compensation be given to those who suffer losses from nonperformance where exchange arrangements have been entered into without deception, fraud, or coercion.

What is *not* consistent with a system of liberty is behavior by judges in which they, themselves, become instruments of constraint upon parties engaged in consensual transactions. We depend upon judges to enforce contracts. If they refuse to enforce some contract terms, contracting parties are compelled to refrain from the use of those terms in the design of contracts and to select contract characteristics that will be enforceable at law. The altered contract terms had been available, in any case, and had been rejected in favor of the alternative that judges had refused to enforce. Thus, contracting parties are jointly made worse-off by judicial constraint on their freedom to contract. In addition, if the judges are not sensitive to the altered behavior that their decisions induce, they may generate consequences that are not consistent with, and are perhaps the opposite of, what the judges intend.

Such a case of mistaken judicial activism made its appearance in a Supreme Court decision affecting the law of creditor remedies, rendered in the early 1970s. That decision was followed by a number of

---

The author is Professor of Economics at the University of Massachusetts at Amherst.

conforming lower court decisions, until the Supreme Court sustantially reversed after only a few years.

It is that case of a proposed revision of creditor-remedy law, its pretended defenses, and its predicted consequences, if the revision had survived in law, that will be discussed in this paper.

Some exchanges are consummated instantaneously and others spin themselves out over time. It is sometimes efficient for payment to be made now for commodities that will be delivered later, or for commodities to be delivered now for payment to be made later, or for agreements to be made now for delivery and payment to be made simultaneously at some later moment of time.

One of the central purposes of the law of contract is to permit activities and exchanges to sort themselves efficiently into instantaneous and time-consuming or lagged boxes. If the courts, as instruments of the state, did not enforce contract commitments, private systems of enforcement might still evolve. But the cost of enforcement would be substantially higher, in both private and social senses, and resources would tend to be skewed toward activities that are instantaneously consummated; inefficiency would be systematically introduced into the system.

In the absence of constraint, the market will tend to produce contract forms that are consensually and mutually acceptable to the contracting parties. Obnoxious contract arrangements will tend not to survive because they will be shunned by the side that they offend. Contract arrangements that are found to persist over a long period exhibit, by their survival, that they are joint welfare maximizing.

The judges, sometimes operating from ideological perspectives, have put limits, or sought to put limits, upon what might be consensually arranged by uncoerced contracting parties by defining what they will and will not enforce and by defining the procedures of enforcement that must be followed.

Those judicial constraints will be examined in the context of the law of creditor remedies of installment sellers whose capital is put at peril by defaulting buyers. Both, decisions that are settled law and decisions of lower courts that were reversed on appeal will be examined since this paper proposes to expose both the rationale and the predicted consequences of alternative rules of creditor-remedy law. Members of the set of alternative rules appear in lower court decisions even if they have not made their way into settled law.

Traditional Creditor Remedy Law

The law of secured transactions derives from the practice of ancient Rome and Greece, appears in the common law, and is codified in the

Uniform Commercial Code, which has been adopted by all states except Louisiana. A secured creditor may, if the buyer defaults, take possession of the collateral, if he can do so without breach of the peace. If the collateral is, for example, an automobile standing in the street, the creditor may resort to self-help repossession. He takes the car, without notice, hearing, and neutral judgment that repossession is warranted. If the collateral is furniture or appliances in the buyer's home, the creditor may not resort to self-help repossession, since crossing the threshold has been construed to breach the peace. In such cases, the standard practice for generations has been that the creditor makes an *ex parte* declaration to a clerk of court that repossession is warranted and, on the basis of that declaration, a writ of replevin is issued, also without notice, hearing, and neutral judgment, and an agent of the state, such as a sheriff, is paid by the creditor to execute the repossession.

If a buyer believes that repossession was not warranted, *he* may bring suit for recovery of the collateral and for damages he has suffered as a consequence of the repossession.

Clauses permitting repossession on these terms and in this way have commonly and conventionally appeared in contracts agreed to by buyers and sellers upon the execution of exchanges.

Recent Court Decisions

Summary prejudgment processes as a creditor remedy, when it involves state action, was struck down by the Supreme Court in *Sniadach v. Family Finance Corp. of Bay View*[1] for failure to meet the procedural due process requirements of the Fourteenth Amendment. The Fourteenth Amendment says that no *state* may "deprive any person of . . . property without due process of law." If a debtor has had property taken from him to satisfy debt to a creditor, a claim that he has been denied due process in the taking has no standing unless he can show that the property was taken under the terms of state law, or that it was taken by an agent of the state, or that the taking was otherwise "under cover of state action." When a creditor takes a debtor's property to satisfy debt and this is done under terms of a contract, without involving action by the state, constitutional due process prescriptions do not apply.

Sniadach owed Family Finance $420 under a promissory note. Family Finance garnished his wages and Sniadach's employer, under Wisconsin state law, withheld half the wages owed him. The machin-

[1]395 U.S. 337 (1969).

ery of garnishment was set in motion when a clerk of court issued a summons at the request of the creditor's lawyer; notice of garnishment was given to the debtor at the same time as it was given to his employer.

The Supreme Court held that Sniadach had been denied the right to be heard and, therefore, that he had been denied constitutional procedural due process. Justice Douglas, in the Court's opinion, said:

> A prejudgment garnishment of the Wisconsin type may as a practical matter drive a wage-earning family to the wall. Where the taking of one's property is so obvious, it needs no extended argument to conclude that absent notice and a prior hearing this prejudgment garnishment procedure violates the fundamental principles of due process.[2]

Following *Sniadach*, summary prejudgment remedies came to be challenged in many parts of the country and many courts struck down remedies that did not give prior notice and provide for a hearing when debtors were deprived of property under state law. In *Fuentes v. Shevin*,[3] the Court extended the *Sniadach* principle to conditional sales contract remedies when an agent of the state was an instrument for the execution of a writ of replevin.

Margarita Fuentes, a resident of Florida, bought a gas stove from Firestone Tire and Rubber Co. and, later, a stereophonic phonograph, under conditional sales contracts that gave Firestone title to the merchandise but permitted Mrs. Fuentes to possess and use them unless and until she defaulted on payments for them. Firestone filed a claim in small claims court alleging that Mrs. Fuentes had defaulted and, simultaneously, obtained a writ of replevin ordering a sheriff to seize the goods at once. The goods were seized without prior notice to Mrs. Fuentes, without hearing, without opportunities to her to offer defenses, and without the judgment of a neutral person that repossession was warranted. The conditional sales contracts had provided that, in the event of default, the creditor may "take back" or "repossess" the merchandise.

In the court's opinion, it was held that "prejudgment replevin provisions work a deprivation of property without due process of law insofar as they deny the right to a prior opportunity to be heard before chattels are taken from their possessor."[4]

---

[2]Id. at 341–42.
[3]407 U.S. 67 (1972).
[4]Id. at 96.

Two years after *Fuentes*, in *Mitchell v. W. T. Grant Co.*,[5] the Supreme Court modified (Justice Stewart, dissenting, said it "overruled") *Fuentes*. In *Mitchell*, the Court held that it was acceptable for agents of the state to take household appliances from a debtor, on behalf of a creditor who claimed default in repayment of debt, even in the absence of notice and hearing, if the state's agent was supervised by a judge, rather than a court functionary.

Grant sold Mitchell a refrigerator and other appliances. A balance of $547 was unpaid and overdue. Grant had a vendor's lien on the goods. A city court judge in New Orleans, based on a petition and affidavit, and without prior notice or opportunity for hearing being given Mitchell, signed a writ of sequestration and the constable of the court seized the merchandise. Mitchell filed a motion to dissolve the writ, claiming that the seizure violated the due process clauses of the state and federal constitutions. The Court demurred on grounds that the Louisiana seizure "provides for judicial control of the process from beginning to end" and "Mitchell was not at the unsupervised mercy of the creditor and court functionaries."[6]

Shortly after the *Fuentes* decision, a number of cases were brought challenging self-help repossession under contracts permitting such repossession. The challenges asserted that state enactment of the Uniform Commerical Code permitting private persons to self-help repossess under contract terms constituted action under color of state law and, therefore, caused self-help repossession to be covered by the procedural due process requirements of the Fourteenth Amendment. Petitioners were successful in some of the lower federal courts but those decisions were reversed in the circuit courts of appeal and certiorari was denied by the Supreme Court. In the end, those challenges were unsuccessful; they were failed attempts to turn out a principle of law of ancient standing.

Thus, the current state of the law is that contractual self-help repossession without notice, hearing, and judgment is permitted for automobiles and for other chattels that can be repossessed without breach of peace; whether prejudgment repossession is permitted as a creditor remedy, where a house must be entered to recover the merchandise, depends upon the extent to which the repossession process is overseen by a judge, rather than a court functionary.

In its current state, the law of creditor remedies seems to be nearly consistent with contractarian principles. Monies may be lent to finance the purchase of automobiles and lenders and borrowers may freely

---

[5]416 U.S. 600 (1974).
[6]Id. at 616.

engage to permit repossession, without notice, hearing and judgment, if the buyer defaults. Lenders can be made more secure in the recovery of their loans and borrowers can have more favorable borrowing terms in other respects precisely because they have consented to an arrangement that increases the security of the creditor's assets.

There may or may not be freedom to engage in similar contracts for the financed purchase of merchandise that will be located in houses or in other enclosed spaces. This depends upon the closeness with which judges oversee the repossession of such merchandise. The closer the oversight, the less secure are the creditor's assets and the more severe are the constraints on the freedom of sellers and buyers of such merchandise to undertake contracts that jointly serve their purposes.

The Reasoning of the Courts

Where prejudgment creditor remedies have been struck down, the courts' rationale has taken a somewhat class-angled ideological perspective. In *Sniadach*, Justice Douglas wrote that a "prejudgment garnishment . . . may as a practical matter drive a wage-earning family to the wall." He also wrote:

> A procedural rule that may satisfy due process for attachments in general . . . does not necessarily satisfy procedural due process in every case. . . . *We deal here with wages*—a specialized type of property presenting distinct problems in our economic system.[7]

Douglas then quoted, with apparent approval, Congressman Sullivan (chairman of the House Subcommittee on Consumer Affairs), who said in congressional debate:

> In a vast number of cases the debt is a fraudulent one, saddled on a poor ignorant person who is trapped in an easy credit nightmare, in which he is charged double for something he could not pay for even if the proper price was called for, and then hounded into giving up his pound of flesh, and being fired besides.[8]

It is not at all clear why the rule of law should not be applied uniformly to *all* who appear before the courts. Justice Douglas thought uniform application of the law was inappropriate. Wages—the payment for labor services—were, he wrote, "a specialized type of property presenting distinct problems." A rule that satisfies due process for attachments "in general" (say, of physical possessions or of bank

---

[7]395 U.S. at 340; emphasis added.
[8]Id. at 341. Quoted from 114 Cong. Rec. 1832.

340

deposits) may not do so for attachments of wages. Prejudgment attachment might be acceptable for other assets, but not for wages. He does not say with clarity why they are to be distinguished, except that he says the garnishment of wages may "drive a wage-earning family to the wall" and, by inference, that wage-earners are poor and ignorant and are objects of fraud who are easily enticed to take on an excess of debt for the acquisition of possessions for which they will pay prices that are excessively high.

Families that derive their sustenance from annuities or from rent, dividend, or interest earnings and that live beyond their means may also, of course, be driven to the wall by the attachment of their assets. Wage-earners are not necessarily poorer nor more ignorant of their prospects and their options than are earners of other kinds of income streams; and, if they were, it is not clear that wage-earners are made better-off by a differentiated rule of law, applying only to them and not to others, that informs prospective creditors that their capital is put at higher risk, if they lend to wage-earners. Nor is it clear that the poor are more commonly trapped in "easy credit nightmare[s]" than those of higher incomes. Justice Douglas surely did not know how aversion to risk is distributed in society; if he did, he did not tell us. If higher prices are charged to the poor who finance the purchase of possessions, may it not be because creditors are covering themselves against the risk of default? If creditors could not acquire this cover, perhaps they would not deal. Is the condition of the poor improved, if they cannot acquire assets to which they aspire because the law does not permit them to compensate creditors for the risk of nonpayment of debt?

In *Fuentes*, Justice Stewart sought to distinguish the Court's decision from that in *D. H. Overmyer Co. v. Frick Co.*[9] In *Overmyer*, the Court declared that a contractual waiver of due process rights was "voluntarily, intelligently, and knowingly" made.[10] Justice Stewart, in *Fuentes*, reasoned that this was because

> the contract . . . was negotiated between *two corporations*; the waiver provision was specifically bargained for and drafted by their lawyers in the process of these negotiations. . . . It was not a case of unequal bargaining power. . . . The . . . agreement . . . was not a contract of adhesion.
>
> The facts [in *Fuentes*] are a far cry from those of *Overmyer*. There was no bargaining over contractual terms between the parties who, in any event, *were far from equal in bargaining power*. The pur-

[9]405 U.S. 174 (1972).
[10]Id. at 187.

ported waiver provision was a printed part of a form sales contract and a necessary condition of the sale.[11]

The point was pursued by Justice Stewart in his dissent in *Mitchell*, where he wrote that, absent procedural arrangements prescribed by *Fuentes*, consumers were "defenseless."[12] Justice Stewart was apparently unable to understand the power of the market to compel contracts of adhesion to take forms that would be found by both buyers and sellers to be not obnoxious nor did he understand that buyers have the power to refuse to consummate transactions that do not improve their circumstances.

In *Watson v. Branch County Bank*,[13] the Federal District Court for the Western District of Michigan wrote, in a class action suit in which the district court held that self-help repossession of automobiles was unconstitutional:

> The automobile financier is typically either a large financial institution or is backed by such an institution. Financiers have overwhelming bargaining power and expertise and automobile financing contracts are typically contracts of adhesion. Consumers have no power to insist that printed contracts be changed. . . . Debtors as a practical matter have no legal remedy for abuses. The brutal consequences of the exercise of this uncontrolled self-interested private power are illustrated by. . . . The cognizable interests of the corporate creditors in repossessing automobiles without resort to legal process are *de minimis*. . . . The corporate defendants have no human rights or values at stake here, merely profits. . . .
>
> It is also important that the contracts in this case are contracts of adhesion. There is a great disparity of bargaining power, and the debtors apparently received nothing additional for the contractual self-help repossession clauses. . . . This the constitution does not permit. Liberty of waiver, like liberty of contract begins with equality of position between the parties. . . .
>
> The coercive nature of the unilateral conditions and requirements imposed upon purchasers of ordinary necessities of life in modern circumstances cannot be considered voluntary, understanding waivers of constitutional rights.[14]

A similar rationale appears in the opinion of the Federal District Court for the Southern District of California in *Adams v. Egley*.[15]

[11]407 U.S. at 95; emphasis added.

[12]416 U.S. at 635 (Stewart, J., dissenting).

[13]380 F. Supp. 945 (1974). Reversed without published opinion by the Sixth Circuit Court of Appeals, 21 May 1975.

[14]380 F. Supp. at 945.

[15]338 F. Supp. 614 (1972). Reversed by the Ninth Circuit Court of Appeals in Adams v. Southern California National Bank, 492 F.2d 324 (1973); certiorari denied 419 U.S. 1006 (1974).

Adams borrowed $1000 from a bank, executing a promissory note, and signed a security agreement giving the bank a security interest in three vehicles. The security agreement said in part: "Upon the occurrence of . . . default, the Secured Party is entitled to take possession of the vehicle. . . ."[16] Adams defaulted in his payments and the bank employed a licensed repossessor to take the vehicles. Adams challenged the self-help repossession on grounds that the repossession involved sufficient state action, under the California Commercial Code, to establish a federal cause of action and that, since summary prejudgment had occurred, his procedural due process rights had been violated.

The district court held for Adams and wrote, in part:

> While a signed contract may represent an effective waiver where the contracting parties are of equal bargaining power, it is clearly not so in all cases, particularly those involving so-called "adhesion contracts," in which the terms are specified by the seller or lender. As noted by the Supreme Court of California in *Blair v. Pitchess* [5 Cal. 3d 258 (1971)]: "The weaker party, in need of goods or services, is frequently not in a position to shop around for better terms, either because the author of the standard contract has a monopoly . . . or because all competitors use the same clauses. His contractual intention is but a subjection more or less voluntarily to terms dictated by the stronger party. . . ."
>
> . . . If the policy underlying the decision in *Sniadach* is to provide some extra modicum of legal protection to those who live on the lower economic margins of our society, it would be illogical for the courts to be dissuaded from applying that policy by the presence of standard-form contracts which often operate most harshly on the poor. . . .
>
> Where . . . the parties are both commercial entities, the bargaining power is to some extent equalized, and the purported waiver of the constitutional right to prior notice and hearing may indeed be effective. However, the California repossession statute presently under consideration is not limited to secured transactions between parties of equal bargaining power. . . .
>
> In light of *Sniadach*, then, the statutes providing for summary repossession and sale must be held unconstitutional.[17]

Standard Form Credit Contracts

Contracts of adhesion—that is to say, standard form contracts— also have been subject to review and have been attacked in the

[16]338 F. Supp. at 616.
[17]338 F. Supp. at 620–22.

administrative agencies, as well as by some judges. In 1975, the Federal Trade Commission (FTC) initiated a proceeding on credit practices that examined contracts of adhesion as a prelude to the possible adoption of a trade regulation rule. Hearings were held in four cities during 1977–78. In 1980, the FTC issued a staff report, concluding that there is market imperfection in the consumer credit market and that this imperfection derives, in part, from "the use, by creditors, of standard form instruments which contain complex conditions which are not the subject of arms-length bargaining at the point of sale."[18]

According to the FTC report, "The adhesive nature of consumer credit contracts has long been recognized." Following Ehrenzweig, the report defined adhesion contracts as "Agreements in which one party's participation consists in his mere 'adherence,' unwilling and often unknowing, to a document drafted unilaterally and insisted upon by what is usually a powerful enterprise."[19] The report then noted that "The essence of an adhesive transaction is the weaker party's lack of alternatives to accepting the contract exactly in the form in which it is presented."[20]

The FTC's staff recommended that the FTC adopt a rule that would prohibit borrowers and lenders from agreeing to credit contracts that included a number of different kinds of creditor remedies that appear often in standard form contracts. In March 1984, the FTC adopted a rule forbidding some creditor remedies; the rule was to be made effective in March 1985.[21]

The Court decisions and the FTC's record in the credit practices rule case are of a piece when they deal with standard form contracts and they both come to incorrect judgments because they examine market phenomena only superficially.

Justice Stewart wrote in *Fuentes* that the parties to the contract were not equal in bargaining power because prejudgment repossession was permitted by a provision of a (standard) form contract. In his dissent in *Mitchell,* he wrote that consumers were defenseless without procedural due process and neutral judgment. In *Watson,* the Michigan district court said that financiers have overwhelming bargaining power, that consumers may not have printed contracts

---

[18]Federal Trade Commission, Bureau of Consumer Protection, *Credit Practices,* Staff Report and Recommendation on Proposed Trade Regulation Rule, Washington, D.C., August 1980, p. 33.

[19]Ibid. For original source, see Albert A. Ehrenzweig, "Adhesion Contracts in the Conflict of Law," *Columbia Law Review* (1953): 1072.

[20]*Credit Practices,* p. 34.

[21]49 Fed. Reg. 7740 (1984).

changed, and that debtors had no legal remedy for abuses. Private power (of the creditors), the Michigan court said, was self-interested and uncontrolled and the exercise of this power had brutal consequences. In cases of contracts of adhesion, it went on to say, there is great disparity in bargaining power and consumers "received nothing additional for the contractual self-help repossession clauses." The conditions imposed upon buyers who sign adhesive contracts are, the court wrote, coercive and not voluntary and the conditions are unilaterally imposed by lenders upon borrowers.

The California District Court wrote in *Adams* that the terms of standard form contracts were dictated by the stronger party—the creditor; the borrower is not able to "shop around" because all use the same clauses; standard form contracts operate harshly upon the poor; and, where standard form contracts are used, there is not equal bargaining power.

The record of the FTC case on credit practices is replete with similar testimony and findings. Standard form contracts in the credit market are said to be "prepared for creditors" and "drawn almost entirely from the creditor's standpoint"; the clauses dealing with creditor remedies must be accepted "as is" and may not be altered; the contracts are uniform among competitive creditors; there is an absence of "arms-length bargaining" over creditor remedy terms of the contracts; and borrowers do not understand the standard form contracts they sign.

It is therefore not surprising to find the 1980 FTC staff report concluding: There is market failure in the credit market; a "free market cannot establish equity in consumer transactions" (quoting William Ballenger, Michigan Department of Licensing and Regulation); and current creditor remedies are "a product of market imperfection or imbalance of market power."[22]

The notion that standard form contracts are instruments of exploitation of debtors is based on a fundamental misunderstanding of the processes of competitive markets. There are many sellers in the credit market. There are many sellers of commodities on installment payment terms and many lenders who make loan funds available on the condition that security be provided to diminish the risk of creditor loss when default occurs. Entry into the market and exit from it is not difficult. The credit market is clearly competitive and a price-theoretic expectation is that the rate of return on investment in the market is normal and that exploitation—for which the existence of monopoly is a necessary condition—does not exist in it.

[22]Federal Trade Commission, *Credit Practices*, p. 68.

It is widely recognized that standard form credit contracts are used because the law of contracts is complex and only specialized legal practitioners have sufficient knowledge to draft the contracts in forms that the courts will enforce. If each contract were separately drawn, transaction costs would be immense; the use of the standard form, once it is drafted, reduces those costs virtually to zero. The diminution of transaction costs explains not only the existence and ubiquitous use of the standard form but also the great reluctance to alter its phrasing in separate individual transactions. Far from exhibiting market imperfection, therefore, the use of contracts of adhesion and the refusal to make changes in those contracts shows the market to be working well. The absence of negotiation for each credit transaction forestalls, for the community, the employment of large quantities of real resources that have alternative valuable social uses.

What of the terms of those contracts? Can they be expected to be drawn to favor the interests of creditors over debtors? Is there an absence of bargaining over contract terms? Is there "inequality of bargaining power" between participants in credit transactions? Do debtors get nothing in return for putting their assets at risk of prejudgment seizure by their creditors, if they should fail to make timely repayment of their debt?

The creditor remedy clauses of contracts of adhesion in credit markets are not randomly drawn. They are limited by two sets of constraints. First, they must be consistent with the rule of law. That is to say, they may require no more than the courts find acceptable in the enforcement of contracts. If they go further than this, they are superfluous. Second, they may not extend beyond limits that are defined by competition in the credit market; creditor remedies, when taken in conjunction with other credit contract clauses, may permit no more than a normal rate of return on investment. If creditor remedies go beyond those limits, the competition of new entrants can be expected, in time, to press them back to the parametric constraints that are appropriate to a normal return on investment.

Thus, though bargaining may not occur in the "negotiation" of individual credit contracts, where a standard form is used, a more cosmic form of bargaining does, in fact, occur. In this cosmic market negotiating process, creditors are not more powerful than debtors. Each of the sides of the market has its influence upon the negotiated outcome. Contract terms are the product of *both* "blades of the scissors," with demand-side and supply-side phenomena both playing out their market roles. Borrowers on the demand side of the credit market cannot extract terms that will yield less than normal rates of return; if they insist, creditors are unwilling to lend. Creditors on the supply side of the market cannot extract terms that will yield more than normal rates of return; if they do, new entrants, in competition, will offer loans on terms that are less burdensome upon borrowers. Even if entry into the credit market were so costly that incumbents on the selling side of the market were able to include remedial clauses in their standard contracts that produced for them a monopoly rent, monopoly lenders would still need to be concerned that the terms were not so onerous that they greatly reduced the willingness of borrowers to borrow. In addition, borrowers have the ultimate power of refusing to participate in ventures offered to them. They cannot be compelled to borrow on terms they find obnoxious. The power of decision lies with them.

Thus, when one thinks about the elementary characteristics of the competitive market process, it can be seen that there *is* bargaining in credit contracting and that the parties are not unequal in bargaining power.

Nor is it correct, as the Michigan court said in *Watson,* that debtors who agree to self-help repossession clauses in the contracts they sign "receive nothing additional for it." Contracts consist of baskets of properties. The aggregates of baskets produce normal investment yields. Let one component be enlarged and the forces of competition will compel another to shrink. If a lender's risk of the loss of his assets is diminished because a borrower has consented that, if he is delinquent in repayment, the collateral may be repossessed without notice, hearing, and neutral judgment, then competition will compel that the commodity be sold at a lower price or that financing terms be more attractive than would be true if the lender's risk were larger. Or, in some other components of the contract than these, the terms will be made more attractive for the borrower; in competitive markets, in the long run, the lender cannot have a higher rate of investment return than is earned in alternative investment lines.

It is clear, in the end, that the circumstances surrounding the use of contracts of adhesion in the market for credit do not make an acceptable case for the intervention of either the courts or the administrative agencies of government in the foreclosure of options for creditor remedies to which lenders and borrowers may voluntarily agree.

Courts have sought to impose constraints upon creditor remedies on grounds that exhibit preferential regard for those of lower-class origin and status, a lack of trust in the capacity of wage-earners and the poor to know and to serve their own self-interest, an unwillingness to permit individuals to make uncoerced exchange arrangements, and a failure to understand the behavioral adjustments that occur in markets that are free of constraints and in those where constraints are imposed.

Expected Market Effects of Proposed Changes

The creditor-remedy rules the courts have sought to define could be expected to have perverse effects. Rules thought to enlarge the opportunities of consumers and the poor, in fact, would impose additional costs on them. The courts have not seen this because they do not understand how markets work.

Let us suppose that in every case of alleged default—those now covered by methods of self-help repossession and those covered by writs of replevin and sequestration—the law required for repossession (1) notice to defaulters that repossession is intended, and (2) opportunity and time for the preparation of defenses, a hearing, and judgment by a neutral person showing why repossession is warranted. Let us also suppose that such a procedural rule cannot be contractually waived. What does price theory tell us would be the consequences that can be predicted, if this were the rule of law?

Under such a set of assumptions, it is likely that the consequences would be as follows:

- Real social costs would be incurred in executing judgment. Resources employed in the giving of notice, the conduct of hearings, the preparation of claims and defenses and in their delivery, and in the consideration of judgment would be lost by society to the alternative uses to which they could be put.
- The rate of physical depreciation of the social stock of capital would be increased. Automobiles, appliances, and other equipment that are collateral for loans or that otherwise secure transactions would be treated with more abuse and more imprudence in the period between notice of intended repossession and actual repossession than they would be if notice were not given and if there were no lag between the creditors' decisions to repossess and the time they take actual possession.
- More real resources would be devoted by creditors to the screening of applicants for credit to more certainly distinguish between those who will be and those who will not be probabilistic defaulters. Incremental resources consumed in the measurement of creditworthness would constitute a social opportunity cost in that they would not be available for alternative socially valuable uses.
- Some who would have passed muster for the extension of credit under less intensive credit evaluational procedures would be excluded for they would be found to offer excessive risk of default.

Those excluded would include those with volatile earnings: such as the young, the elderly, the handicapped, and the infirm. Some of them would now be deprived of borrowing opportunities they would otherwise have.

- There would be an increase in the cost of doing lending business. There would be some combination of more intensive screening of applicants for credit, increased costs of recovery of collateral, and increased risk that loans cannot be covered by repossessd merchandise. There would be, therefore, an increase in financing charges. If financing charges are uniformly applied to all borrowers, this would imply a wealth transfer from probabilistic non-defaulters to probabilistic defaulters.
- There would be a revision of lending practices to diminish the incidence of default. These revisions would include enlarging the magnitude of "down payments" and reducing the fraction of the price of merchandise that can be paid for over time; reducing the period of time in which loans must be completely paid off; and increasing the quantity of life insurance and health insurance that borrowers are required to purchase as a condition for securing loans. These changes would tend to exclude from the borrowing queue those for whom the probability of default is relatively high.
- The prices of commodities purchased for payment over time would rise relative to the prices of commodities paid for "in cash." The new price ratio, however, may not be consistent with the community's time-preference function.

It can be seen, therefore, that the application of a procedural due-process rule requiring notice, hearing, defenses, and neutral judgment for the recovery of merchandise from defaulters in secured transactions would impose costs upon society and have distributional effects that are adverse for the most disadvantaged and vulnerable segments of the community's population.

Conclusion

From the foregoing analysis, it is evident that what was intended by some judges to serve consumers and the poor actually would tend to do them harm—that is to say, judges intent on doing good would be seen as doing harm. A clearly superior alternative to judicial intervention would be a rule permitting free and unconstrained contracts by contractors who are not subject to coercive, deceptive, or fraudulent practices, with courts enforcing contracts by procedures that are contractually defined.

One could expect different procedural forms to evolve with different commodity prices that would express different degrees of risk and security of lenders. Commodity prices would then be lower for those who accept prejudgment repossession procedures—and higher for those who prefer procedures that require notice, hearing, and neutral judgment before repossession. Buyers would then choose the alternative that maximizes utility for them.

Contractarian arrangements would produce allocational and distributional effects that are preferable to the effects generated by judges seeking to do justice.

COMMENT

CONTRACTUAL REMEDIES AND THE NORMATIVE ACCEPTABILITY OF STATE-IMPOSED COERCION

Charles J. Goetz

A commentator on Professor Rottenberg's views about judicial treatment of creditor remedies has difficulty in knowing whether (1) to express fundamental agreement, objecting only that its new insights[1] are "less than meets the eye"; or (2) to complain that Rottenberg ignores a tough and provocative underlying issue while (3) straining to picture the courts as even sillier than they sometimes really are. Since there arguably is truth in each of these positions (which, after all, are not actually inconsistent), this comment will attempt to expand on all three of those themes.

The instrumentalist view of contract law, to which I am personally sympathetic, sees contracts as mechanisms for achieving mutually advantageous shifts in the allocation of rights and resources. "Executory" contracts involve only a promise of some future performance and these agreements—as Rottenberg emphasizes—critically depend on the state's coercive power to ensure that the promisee will honor his obligation. In this context, an individual's ability to subject himself to potential coercion by the state actually enlarges freedom in a highly relevant sense. Exchanges that would not otherwise be "reliable" enough to occur now become practical and trading opportunities expand. When a contractual party voluntarily embraces these

---

The author is Joseph M. Hartfield Professor of Law at the University of Virginia.

[1]As one might imagine, the cases and underlying issues discussed by Simon Rottenberg have not gone unnoticed by other commentators, some of whom have explicitly considered essentially the same economic efficiency implications. Early examples of this literature include Robert E. Scott, "Constitutional Regulation of Provisional Creditor Remedies: The Cost of Procedural Due Process," *Virginia Law Review* 61 (1973): 807–67; Robert W. Johnson, "Denial of Self-Help Repossession: An Economic Analysis," *Southern California Law Review* 47 (1973): 82–115; Edward A. Dauer and Thomas K. Gilhool, "The Economics of Constitutionalized Repossession," *Southern California Law Review* 47 (1973): 116–50; Robert W. Johnson, "A Response to Dauer and Gilhool: A Defense of Self-Help Repossession," *Southern California Law Review* 47 (1973): 151–64.

new opportunities, fully aware that the state will hold both parties to the performance of their freely exchanged obligations, a strong *prima facie* argument supports the inference of welfare-enhancement.[2]

From this perspective, remedies represent state-supplied means to ends that are generally desirable from the standpoint both of the parties themselves and usually also of the rest of society. But it seems to be well settled that society will not lend its enforcement power to certain classes of individual agreements that it finds obnoxious. Indeed, in the subset of cases where society does object to the ends served by certain agreements, it commonly withholds its facilitating power, designating such contracts unenforceable as "contrary to public policy."[3] The creditor rights decisions do not seem to fit this category where the state refuses enforcement because it might object to the substantive aims of the contracts—in these cases, the transfer of mundane products such as automobiles, consumer appliances, etc. Nor do the courts treat the cases in question within the framework of the more orthodox, albeit debatable, doctrine of "unconscionability" infecting the bargaining process that led to the formation of the contract.

Rottenberg quite properly asks why a court should withhold a fairly bargained-for remedy constructed by the marketplace to facilitate a special contractual goal that is not itself the subject of any objection. What is going on here? Rottenberg's own answer seems to be that there is a muddle-headed judicial activist attempt to benefit certain parties through a result-oriented concoction of special rules. As he points out, among the many objections is the classical one of throwing out the baby with the bathwater. The prospective effect of non-enforcement will not even aid the intended beneficiaries and, indeed, will deprive them of what were, on balance, beneficial trading opportunities.

There is little to quibble about in this basic message, one generally congenial to me. I am, indeed, elsewhere on record as attacking judicial limitations of remedies in contexts where trading gains to the parties are sacrificed without any identifiable counterbalancing gain.[4] Nonetheless, an alternative reading of this same line of cases

---

[2]The text is careful to couch this as a presumption only, since there are many qualifications to this result. Centering on systematic gaps in information, defects in the bargaining process, etc., these exceptions to the general thesis are well-known and need not be dealt with explicitly here.

[3]See *Restatement, Contracts*, 2d, §8.

[4]See especially, Charles J. Goetz and Robert E. Scott, "Liquidated Damages, Penalties and the Just Compensation Principle," *Columbia Law Review* 77 (1977): 554–94 (arguing against judicial invalidation of bargained-for liquidated damages clauses).

surfaces both a lurking problem and a defense that the courts have not been as muddle-headed as it first seems.

The *reductio ad absurdum* is a time-honored method of argumentation whose application here may be provocative even if, by definition, exaggerated in tone. Accordingly, a strong, blunt statement of the Rottenberg thesis might be that the state has an obligation to enforce *any* fairly bargained-for remedy necessary to facilitate any legitimate contractual goal. The consequences of *not* doing so, the argument runs, would be both the opportunity costs of foregone contractual gains and the excess resource costs of less efficient alternative remedies.

The thriving industry of illegal "loan sharking" provides empirical evidence that the state in fact fails to facilitate many contracts regarded as mutually beneficial by the parties involved. One aspect of illegal loan sharking depends on the refusal of the state to enforce interest rates arbitrarily adjudged to be "usurious." Even more important for our present discussion, however, is the availability to the creditor of potent extra-legal enforcement mechanisms that may extend to physical violence to the debtor's person and his possessions. From the strict economic perspective, each of these black-market transactions can claim the same presumption of mutual advantage as loans negotiated in the legal marketplace. In fact, the evidence of revealed choice shows that the "advantages" of the illegal market predominate over the legal market for hordes of people, notwithstanding the efforts of the state to stamp out such transactions through criminal and civil sanctions.

A rigidly single-minded economic analysis might urge the state to draw several inferences from the continuing robustness of the loan shark market. One is that, for many parties, the existing system of legal remedies is not as economically efficient as the extra-legal ones. A second, corollary inference is that the unavailability of the equivalents of the black market remedies in legal credit markets obstructs many mutually beneficial trades. The third possible inference, arguably following from the first two, is that legitimate market remedies ought to be expanded to include more and closer equivalents of some of the stronger illegal remedies. One suspects that many people will regard the first two inferences as entirely plausible and nevertheless balk at accepting the final policy conclusion, perhaps without being able to articulate exactly why.

It is unnecessary to overplay the role of the pixy by inviting the reader to dwell on the notion of a judicially enforced contractual "late payment penalty" calling for a broken finger per week or a Shylockian pound of flesh. Such blatantly outrageous examples are designed only to establish the existence of a polar extreme of repugnant or "unpalatable" penalties and enforcement processes that society is unlikely to impose through official participation, no matter what the prospective efficiency advantages to the affected parties. Various explanations for this exist. One is that my sense of squeamishness may make me reluctant to be co-opted, through the state as my representative, into sanctioning *judicially administered*[5] enforcement devices that, after all, benefit classes of transactions in which I am unlikely to engage. Another possibility is that, although I might myself derive transactional advantage from such rules, I accord even greater benefit to the maintenance of certain principles, values, or mere "appearances" regarding official process. In this vein, there is a traditional saying about not wishing to "soil the judicial ermine" through involvement in certain matters.

By conceding the notion of a polar extreme of state-action remedies that are beyond the pale, one necessarily confronts the spectrum between these and "ordinary" acceptable remedies and procedures. At some point along the continuum, a genuine balancing of desiderata is required: Tradeoffs between the character of the enforcement process itself and the results from the process become relevant. Traditionally, lawyers have perhaps overemphasized the former, sometimes speaking of process values as though they need not be weighed against variations in results, whether economic or otherwise. But perhaps economists too quickly assume that process values, as encapsulated in some state institution, such as the adjudication of contracts, are not also economic values that must be weighed against values produced in the market. Lawyers and economists may systematically err in different directions because each tends to be ignorant of, even scornful of, those implications of the problems traditionally addressed through the expertise of the other.

In sum, Rottenberg begs potentially important questions: Can there be a legitimate tension between process values and transaction values, even in commercial law? Is that what was troubling some courts?

The history of the creditor rights cases is, in any event, susceptible of a more optimistic reading than Rottenberg's, which tends to focus on a few early and arguably extreme cases in the relevant series. Those of us who place at least some stock in the quasi-Darwinian production of common sense by common law courts are cheered by

---

[5]Significantly, the courts took a much more laissez-faire attitude toward so-called self-help repossession without the assistance of state action. See Adams v. Southern California First National Bank, 492 F.2d 324 (9th Cir. 1973), cert. den'd. 419 U.S 1006 (1974); Flagg Bros., Inc. v. Brooks, 436 U.S. 149 (1978).

the thought that the courts, after considering a series of these cases, may ultimately have gotten it "about right" and improved on the original no-right-to-hearing situation.

It is tempting in reading these cases to jump to the conclusion that the debtor is always unjustified in resisting repossession and that, therefore, any delay in repossession is an unwarranted failure to enforce the creditor's legitimate property rights. In fact, however, some fraction of the cases (including the leading *Fuentes* case[6] discussed by Rottenberg) involve debtors whose failure to pay money due is predicated on an alleged prior failure by the creditor to perform some duty owed under the contract. In sum, since it may be debatable as to which party breached the contract and whether the nonpayment is justified, an optimal contract requires *both* parties to protect themselves against unjust assertion of possession by the other.

Consider the possibility of three kinds of contracts, varying in their modes of protection. Under Type A, creditor repossession is permitted without a hearing and an unjustified repossession can be contested by the debtor only at the final adjudication. Under Type B contracts, repossession still does not require a prior hearing, but a prompt post-repossession hearing may be demanded by the debtor. With Type C contracts, a pre-repossession hearing is required. Type C is the focus of Rottenberg's criticism, Type A was the original law, and Type B is approximately the present law.[7]

Which of these three forms is the most economically "efficient" type of contract? Obviously, they represent a spectrum of shifting degrees of relative debtor/creditor advantage. But economic theory suggests that, if the terms are known in advance, the debtor would have to "pay" for the more advantageous B and C forms with counterbalancing concessions, such as higher price, in order to secure the acquiescence of the seller. Conversely, the seller can presumably achieve his maximally protective Type A contract only by foregoing the inducements that buyers might offer to secure a B or C agreement. While space does not permit a detailed analysis here, I suggest that Type B is optimal. Briefly, Type B improves on A by protecting legitimate debtor counterclaims in the small fraction of cases where they can plausibly be asserted, while also avoiding Type C's high repossession costs and incentives for debtors unjustly to retain property through procedural delay.

---

[6]Fuentes v. Shevin, 407 U.S. 67 (1972) at 70–71.

[7]See, for example, Mitchell v. W. T. Grant, 416 U.S. 600 (1974). The Court upheld a Louisiana statute authorizing seizure without a hearing, but required that the debtor have an opportunity promptly after the attachment to contest its validity. Id. at 609–10.

If Type B were optimal, would the market produce this as the dominant form? Probably not. A little bit of reflection reveals that the state is a necessary "silent signatory" to agreements that attempt to rearrange adjudicatory procedures. It is much easier for a debtor to contract away his pre-repossession hearing than for the creditor to contract into an obligation for the state to provide a prompt post-repossession hearing on the debtor's request. Thus, one interpretation of the history that alarms Rottenberg is that courts viscerally sensed the suboptimality of the extreme Type A, overreacted with Type C mandates, then readjusted to the perfectly defensible and arguably welfare-enhancing environment of the "compromise" Type B. And, as a bonus, Type B satisfies the traditional view of procedural protections when the power of the state is invoked.

My comments then can be summed up as follows. First, I whole-heartedly agree that courts should, as a general rule, enforce fairly bargained for remedies. There is little new in this proposition, however, and Rottenberg does not come to grips with the more original and intriguing question whether process values may qualify the general rule of enforcement-provision in some limiting cases. Finally, the account of judicial activity given strikes me as unnecessarily alarmist, failing to acknowledge that the system did, after all, produce a reasonably happy ending.

16

PUBLIC USE: A VANISHING LIMITATION ON GOVERNMENTALTAKINGS

Ellen Frankel Paul

I. Introduction

On May 30, 1984, the Supreme Court of the United States decided a case that all but buried the public use restraint on the government's power to take private property. In *Hawaii Housing Authority v. Midkiff* [1] a unanimous Court condoned the taking of property by the state's housing authority from large landowners to be resold to lease-holders under the provisions of the Hawaii Land Reform Act of 1967. Justice O'Connor, writing the decision for her colleagues, concluded that nothing in the public use clause of the Fifth Amendment, as made applicable to the states through the Fourteenth Amendment, barred such a transfer.

What is ominous about the Court's failure to discover a consti-tutional impropriety in this eminent domain procedure is that from its inception, the public use proviso has been understood to be a barrier to governmental transfers of property from one owner to another, unless a clear, pressing public use can be discerned. In this instance, however, the Hawaii legislature used merely its desire to reduce the concentration of ownership in the state as a justification for the taking of property from one set of owners to be resold to another set.

What this case seemingly solidifies is a trend discernible in some state courts in recent years—a trend aided in no small part by a case, *Berman v. Parker,* [2] that the Supreme Court decided in 1954. This trend has been to neutralize the public use constraint on the govern-ment's exercise of its eminent domain power. The portion of the Fifth Amendment that reads, "nor shall private property be taken for public use without just compensation," is not a grant of power to

---

The author is Research Director and Professor of Political Science at the Social Philosophy and Policy Center, Bowling Green State University.
[1]467 U.S. 229 (1984).
[2]348 U.S. 26 (1954).

government; rather it is a limitation—indeed, two limitations—placed upon the power of eminent domain, a power that everyone at the time of the drafting of the Bill of Rights considered an inherent attribute of government. Following the logic of the Fifth Amendment, government can take property only if it adheres to two restrictions. First, the taking has to be for a public use; consequently a taking that simply takes property from one owner and sells it or distributes it to another private owner would clearly fall afoul of this public use proviso. Second, the divested property owner must be paid "just compensation."

The just compensation restraint on governmental takings has not proven entirely unproblematical. Property owners subject to eminent domain proceedings often complain that such ancillary losses as moving expenses and loss of business goodwill go uncompensated under the "fair market value" standard employed in such proceedings. When compared to the evisceration of the public use restraint, however, the just compensation portion of the Fifth Amendment at least is still fairly well intact.

The remainder of this paper reviews the historical development of judicial interpretation of the public use proviso. Section II traces this development up through *Berman v. Parker*, a decision that significantly reversed the earlier limitations placed on governmental takings. Section III examines two state court decisions—*City of Oakland v. Oakland Raiders* and *Poletown Neighborhood Council v. City of Detroit*—that figured prominently in the saga of the courts' apparent indifference to the explicit language of the Fifth Amendment's taking clause.[3] In Section IV we consider the most recent development, *Hawaii v. Midkiff*. Finally, Section V offers some concluding remarks concerning the implications of the *Hawaii* decision.

II. *Berman v. Parker* Cripples Public Use

With one mighty obfuscation Justice Douglas, in a 1954 decision that managed to mangle the law almost beyond redemption, dealt a devastating blow to the public use limitation upon what government could constitutionally take. Prior to Douglas's coup de grace in *Berman v. Parker*, "public use" had been interpreted as placing at least some limitations upon governmental confiscations. One of the most hallowed of these limitations, adverted to by a plethora of courts, was the stricture that one could not use the power of eminent domain to transfer property from one private individual to another for principally private, profit-making purposes.

[3]183 Cal. Rptr. 673, 646 P. 2d 835 (1982); 304 N.W. 2d 455 (Mich.) (1981).

Berman v. Parker eroded this limitation, as it decreed that urban renewal—even with the sale of property for development to private contractors—constituted a "public use," or in Douglas's much looser reformation of the Fifth Amendment, a "public purpose."

Even before Douglas's evisceration of the public use constraint, it had not proven much of a barrier to takings by government, or for that matter to takings by private businesses invested with the power of eminent domain as a delegation from some government. There were numerous instances in various states in which eminent domain was permitted even for transfers between private individuals, usually because such activities had been going on since colonial times, or because they were perceived as serving some desirable public end in furthering the development of the country. Examples of such transactions that transferred property from one private individual to another include the colonial Mill Acts, which carried over after the American Revolution; the practice in certain states of granting eminent domain powers to landlocked owners to take land for access roads; and such other uses as irrigation, drainage, reclamation of wetlands, mining operations, lumbering, and clearing a disputed title.[4]

These exceptions resulted more from the habits and accretions of history than from any consensus among early jurists that private takings in general were permissible. Rather, what judges found odious about transfers from one private individual to another was the injustice involved in government taking one party's property at the government's own pleasure and without any constraints and then giving it to another private party for that party's profit. This judicial distaste can be seen most vividly in a passage from Justice Chase's decision in *Calder v. Bull*, decided in 1798. Regarding laws that forcibly transfer property from one individual to another, Justice Chase remarked: "[I]t is against all reason and justice, for a people to intrust a legislature with such powers; and therefore, it cannot be presumed that they have done it."[5]

Justices still imbued with natural law conceptions of property instinctively recoiled against such transfers. The Supreme Court, however, displayed great deference to the determination by state

[4]Philip Nichols, *The Law of Eminent Domain*, 3d ed., edited by Julius L. Sackman (New York: Matthew Bender, 1980), § 7.62, from which this list is compiled. Nichols states (§ 7.61) that the taking of property for a factory from an unwilling, selfish owner, even if it would benefit the whole community, would be inadmissible. Nichols says that the public mind would instinctively revolt at any attempt to take such land by eminent domain.

[5]Calder v. Bull, 3 Da. 386, 388 (1798).

courts that a particular use constituted a public use, in that the Court never invalidated a single such determination. This deference, as we shall see, extended also to congressional acts, with the Court deferring with increasing subservience to legislative determinations of public use.[6]

By the time the Supreme Court became actively involved in the public use issue, around the turn of the 20th century, two different approaches—one narrow and one broad—had been developed by the state courts. The narrow approach greatly limited governmental adventurism in the field of takings. It limited "public use" to "use by the public," meaning that even when private companies had been delegated the power of eminent domain, their projects had to be open to the public and the public was entitled to use the property by right. The broad approach was much more flexible and expansible, as it defined "public use" by such nebulous terms as "public advantage," "public purpose," "public benefit," and "public welfare." The broad approach, therefore, transformed the eminent domain power by making it as extensive as the taxing or police powers of government.

While indecisive in choosing between these two approaches in its early adjudication, the Supreme Court by the 1920s had opted for the broader, more permissive approach. A parallel movement in the state courts transpired in the late 1930s, when federal housing subsidies for states condemning slums were widely upheld, after an initial false start when a federal court declared that the federal government could not take property for such purpose in its own name.

What has transpired in recent decades, in addition to the adoption of the broader view of public use as being "public advantage," is the Supreme Court's growing reluctance to interfere once Congress has determined that a taking is for a public use. While such a determination in earlier years was not considered conclusive and judicial review consequently was appropriate, the modern tendency has been to consider such questions almost untouchable by the courts. The slight leeway left open by the earlier cases has been effectively closed in later cases.

In *United States v. Gettysburg Electric Railway Co.* (1896),[7] for example, the Supreme Court allowed that a congressional act authorizing condemnation for the preservation of the Gettysburg battlefield

---

[6]The Court's last invalidation on the grounds of failure to satisfy the public use proviso occurred in 1937. See Thompson v. Consolidated Gas Util. Corp., 300 U.S. 55 (1937), in which the Court affirmed a district court decree enjoining the enforcement of a gas proration order of the Railroad Commission of Texas.

[7]160 U.S. 668 (1896).

was an appropriation for a "public use." Justice Peckham argued that "when the legislature has declared the use or purpose to be a public one, its judgment will be respected by the courts unless the use be palpably without reasonable foundation."[8] He went on to express the Court's well-worn doctrine of obeisance to congressional pronouncements:

> In examining an act of Congress it has been frequently said that every intendment is in favor of its constitutionality. Such act is presumed to be valid unless its invalidity is plain and apparent; no presumption of invalidity can be indulged in; it must be shown clearly and unmistakably. This rule has been stated and followed by this court from the foundation of the government.[9]

Thus even though the Court could focus here on no distinct constitutional provision that would grant the federal government the power to take property for monuments, it deduced such power from other provisions, by judicial inference from the power to declare war and raise taxes. Even this loose standard of review for palpable unreasonableness would undergo further emasculation.[10]

In *United States ex rel. TVA v. Welch* (1946),[11] Justice Black went a long way toward removing the Court from being the final arbiter over the question of public use. By an act of Congress the Tennessee Valley Authority (TVA) had been given the authority to condemn all property it deemed "necessary for carrying out its purpose" in constructing the Fontana Dam project. Construction of the dam had created a reservoir that swept away a highway that formed the only reasonable access to the plaintiffs' private property, which was sandwiched between the reservoir and a national park. Instead of constructing a new highway, which it deemed too expensive, the TVA decided to acquire the private land and add it to the national park. The six landowners complained that in taking their property, the TVA had acted beyond the authority conferred upon it by Congress. In deciding against the landowners, the Court's majority displayed the utmost deference to congressional and administrative authority. Justice Black wrote: "We think it is the function of Congress to decide what type of taking is for a public use and that the agency authorized to do the taking may do so to the full extent of its statutory authority."

[8]Id. at 680.
[9]Id.
[10]However, the Court would still insist for a while that the ultimate decision regarding what constitutes a "public use" is a judicial question. See Cincinnati v. Vester, 218 U.S. 439, 446 (1930).
[11]327 U.S. 546 (1946).

Finally, dredging up a long-dormant standard that Justice Holmes had enunciated in 1925, when Congress had spoken on the subject of public use, Black declared, "Its decision is entitled to deference until it is shown to involve an impossibility."[12] Exactly what the Court meant by an "impossibility" remains a mystery to this day. What is clear from Black's declaration, though, is that even the cursory standard of review for palpable unreasonableness found in *Gettysburg Electric Railway* had been jettisoned.

These cases set the stage for Justice Douglas to hobble the public use limitation as a restraint upon governmental condemnation. In *Berman v. Parker,* the Court was called upon to determine the constitutionality of a congressional act granting to the District of Columbia the power to acquire through condemnation tracts of land for redevelopment in blighted areas. Lands acquired could be leased or sold to private developers willing to make improvements consonant with a comprehensive general plan drawn up by the D.C. Redevelopment Land Agency. The appellants owned a department store in one of the blighted areas, but the store itself was not in disrepair. They claimed that the condemnation of their property for urban redevelopment constituted a violation of due process and a taking under the Fifth Amendment. Particularly objectionable to them was the feature of the law that might permit their property to be transferred to another private party for its own private gain.

In a decision remarkable for the ease with which it confused the central issues, Douglas and his colleagues concluded that the appellants' "innocuous and unoffending" property could be taken for this larger "public purpose" of remediating urban blight. What should have been clear to Justice Douglas was that the case before him dealt with the federal government's power of eminent domain as exercised by delegation to an agency in the District of Columbia. The issues, then, were whether the use of this power as it affected this particular instance of the taking of an unoffending department store ran afoul of the Fifth Amendment, and whether the act itself was constitutional. What Douglas discerned instead, remarkably, was a case dealing with the federal government's police powers over the District of Columbia.

This inexplicable confusion opened the floodgates for expanding the takings power of government. Why is this so? The police power is another power by which the states control property. Unlike the power of eminent domain, it does not involve confiscation, and consequently no compensation is paid to property owners when use of

[12]Id. at 552.

their property is limited under an exercise of the state's police power. The police power, rather, is a regulatory device by which states place constraints upon the use of private property for the purpose of protecting the "health, safety, morals, and general welfare" of the public. The police power is presumed by virtually all commentators to be an inherent attribute of sovereignty. It is hedged in not by any explicit constitutional restrictions—contrary to the case in eminent domain— but rather by a high court decision that warned that a too-zealous application of the police power will be invalidated because its purpose constitutionally can be achieved only through an exercise of eminent domain, with its attendant compensation. Traditionally, too, an exercise of the police power has been limited by a requirement that the regulation must serve a "public purpose." This conveniently elastic phrase makes possible a wide range of state regulatory behavior, from minimum wage laws, maximum hour legislation, and price fixing to health and safety laws, as long as they serve some rather ill-defined notion of the "public purpose."

"Public purpose" had been considered a more expansive term than "public use," so that what Douglas accomplished by his confusion of the police power with eminent domain in *Berman v. Parker* was the substitution of the more permissive and elastic criterion of the police power's "public purpose" for "public use" in interpreting the eminent domain clause. "Public use" as a constraint on governmental seizures suffered a severe blow at the hands of Douglas's witting, or unwitting, confusion.

With Douglas's opinion in *Berman v. Parker* judicial deference to legislative judgments of public purpose or public use was virtually complete:

> Subject to specific constitutional limitations, when the legislature has spoken, the public interest has been declared in terms well-nigh conclusive. In such cases the legislature, not the judiciary, is the main guardian of the public needs to be served by social legislation. . . . [T]his principle admits of no exception merely because the power of eminent domain is involved. The role of the judiciary in determining whether that power is being exercised for a public purpose is an extremely narrow one.[13]

If the legislature is "well-nigh" the final arbiter of "public need," who will protect private rights? The Court apparently lost sight of one of the principal purposes behind the Fifth Amendment's property clauses: to protect private property owners by limiting governmental confiscations of property to those instances in which an over-

---

[13]Berman v. Parker at 32.

riding public necessity made the taking necessary. This is the whole point behind the public use proviso.

As Douglas's opinion unfolds, protections for property rights fade. In one enormously influential passage (destined to be quoted in countless state and federal court decisions on the limits of both the power of eminent domain and the police power, which is not surprising considering that Douglas had so hopelessly confused the standards of the two powers), rhetoric waxed victorious over constitutional limitation. As Douglas wrote:

> We do not sit to determine whether a particular housing project is or is not desirable. The concept of the public welfare is broad and inclusive. The values it represents are spiritual as well as physical, aesthetic as well as monetary. It is within the power of the legislature to determine that the community should be beautiful as well as healthy, spacious as well as clean, well-balanced as well as carefully patrolled. ... If those who govern the District of Columbia decide that the Nation's Capital should be beautiful as well as sanitary, there is nothing in the Fifth Amendment that stands in the way.[14]

Judges at all levels of our judicial system are enamored of this passage, for it serves as a convenient peg upon which to hang decisions condoning a wide array of imaginative legislative interferences with private property, putatively in the "public interest."

Berman v. Parker is without doubt the leading case in loosening constitutional restrictions on both the taking of property under the power of eminent domain and the regulation of it under the police power. Lamentably for those who hold the view that the Constitution had as one of its principal purposes the protection of property rights, *Hawaii v. Midkiff* took up where *Berman v. Parker* left off. The Burger court would prove no less hospitable to governmental takings than Justice Douglas.

III. Two State Courts Take *Berman v. Parker* to its Limit

Recently courts in Michigan and California have seized upon the high court's reasoning in *Berman v. Parker* and have driven more nails into the coffin of the public use proviso. This trend has led to bizarre consequences, particularly in California, where the Supreme Court of California has declared it permissible for a city to take a football franchise to prevent a team from leaving the city.

---

[14]Id. at 33.

In the spring of 1980 the city of Detroit was faced with a virtual ultimatum from General Motors (GM): either come up with clean title to approximately 500 acres for a new Cadillac plant or GM would close its old plant and move its operations to a more hospitable Sunbelt locale. Hard pressed by economic reversals already, the city acceded. An old Dodge plant site would be combined with the homes of 1,362 residents of Hamtramck ("Poletown" to its residents) to form the desired parcel. Acquisition costs would range in the $200 millions, but GM would pay only $8 million to the city, and also would receive tax concessions. Supporters of the project claimed that eventually 6,000 jobs would be saved.

Skeptics pointed to the heavy-handedness exhibited by GM. Michigan Supreme Court Justice Ryan, who would eventually dissent from the opinion of his peers upholding the actions of Detroit and its Economic Development Corporation in *Poletown v. City of Detroit*, a case brought by 10 disgruntled Poletowners, had this to say:

> The evidence then is that what General Motors wanted, General Motors got. The corporation conceived the project, determined the cost, allocated the financial burden, selected the site, established the mode of financing, imposed specific deadlines for clearance of the property and taking title, and even demanded 12 years of tax concessions.[15]

As the majority of the Michigan Supreme Court viewed the issue in the case, it came down to the following consideration: Did the use of eminent domain here constitute a taking of private property *for private use*, thereby contravening the Michigan state constitution, which, like that of the United States, bars taking property "for public use without just compensation"? The state legislature, in its Economic Development Corporations Act of 1974, had granted to municipalities the use of the power of eminent domain to provide industrial and commercial sites to assist "industrial and commercial enterprise in locating, purchasing, constructing, reconstructing, modernizing, improving, maintaining, repairing, furnishing, equipping, and expanding in this state and its municipalities" to prevent and alleviate conditions of unemployment. The act declares that the functions delegated to municipalities under the act constitute an essential "public purpose." However, the Michigan Supreme Court queried: Is it legitimate for a municipality, under this act, to condemn private property to be transferred to another private party to build a plant that would add jobs and taxes to the economy?

[15]Poletown Neighborhood Council v. City of Detroit at 470.

What the Poletowners objected to was not the declaration by the legislature that programs to alleviate unemployment and promote industry constitute essential "public purposes" but rather the constitutionality of using the power of eminent domain to condemn one person's property and then convey it to another private entity, ostensibly to bolster the economy. They contended that there is a distinction in the law between "public use" and mere "public purpose," the former being a much more limiting notion, limiting the exercise of eminent domain to instances in which there will be a direct public use of the property taken, or at the very least a sense in which the pubic is the direct beneficiary of the taking. In this instance, they argued, there was only an incidental benefit to the public from the taking, with the principal beneficiary being none other than GM in its profit-making capacity, a decidedly "private use."

Detroit and its Economic Development Corporation disputed the Poletowners' contention that the GM taking was not a constitutionally legitimate public use. Rather, the city pled, the taking of this land to create an industrial site that would be used to combat unemployment and fiscal distress, constituted a "controlling public purpose." The fact that the land once acquired would be transferred to a private manufacturer did not defeat the predominant "public purpose" embodied in the taking.

In its *per curiam* decision the court summarily dismissed the argument of the Poletowners that a legal distinction exists between "public use" and "public purpose." Both terms, the court concluded, were used interchangeably and were synonyms for "public benefit." Therefore the sole issue remaining was whether this condemnation amounted to a taking for private use, thus being constitutionally prohibited, or was primarily for public benefit and only incidentally, or secondarily, for private profit, and thus was constitutionally permissible. In other words, was the condemnation primarily for public or private use?

The court paid great deference to the judgment of the state legislature. It noted that the legislature had determined that government actions of this type serve a public purpose and therefore that the "Court's role after such a determination is made is limited." The determination of what "public purpose" encompasses is a legislative function, subject to judicial review, but usually not reversible "except in instances where such determination is palpable and manifestly arbitrary and incorrect." As has become habitual in these cases, the court invoked the Supreme Court's decision in *Berman v. Parker* for good measure: When the legislature speaks, the public interest has been declared in terms "well-nigh conclusive."

The Michigan Supreme Court concluded that in this case clear benefits would accrue to the municipality in the form of alleviating unemployment and revitalizing the city, while a private benefit would accrue to GM only as an "incident thereto." The court's parting note was a homily to ad hoc decision making; it cautioned that the court's decision may not necessarily be the same in other cases where the public benefit may not be so clear and significant.

Two justices dissented from the majority's decision. Both disparaged the notion that courts ought to pay great deference to legislatures in the determination on public use. Justice Fitzgerald wrote: "If a legislative declaration on the question of public use were conclusive, citizens could be subjected to the most outrageous confiscation of property for the benefit of other private interests without redress." Both justices viewed the Poletown taking as one inspired by GM's desire for private gain, with only incidental benefit to the public. For them, clearly, the public use restriction had been transgressed.

The case of the Oakland Raiders is even more ominous. When the Oakland Raiders deserted their fans for the greener pastures of Los Angeles, thereby diminishing Oakland's municipal treasury, the city fathers, having exhausted all other remedies to retain the team, tried a novel ploy. Why not seize the team under Oakland's power of eminent domain? The California Supreme Court approved this approach by permitting the city of Oakland to pursue its case in a trial court.

Justice Richardson, writing for the majority, focused on two principal issues: first, whether intangible property (here, a football franchise and all of the property rights attendant upon that ownership) can be taken under eminent domain, and second, whether the public use constraint upon the condemnation power precludes an action of this type. The city contended that what it sought to condemn was "property," and hence subject to established eminent domain law, and that the validity of its public use contention must be determined by a court after a full trial adducing all the relevant facts. The Raiders argued that, on the contrary, eminent domain does not permit the taking of "intangible property" unrelated to realty, thereby precluding the taking of their football franchise, a "network of intangible contractual rights." On the second point, the Raiders denied, as a matter of law, that the taking could be for a "public use."

On the first issue the court concluded that intangible property is just as subject to confiscation as real or personal property. Franchises, material men's liens, contracts, bus systems (including routes and operating systems), and private utilities have all been taken by various organs of government and the takings have been upheld by the courts. Furthermore, Richardson could discern no constitutional or statutory barrier to the taking of such intangible property. Thus, despite the court's inability to discover any precedent for the taking of a football franchise, it concluded that sufficient precedent existed for the taking of other intangible property, and therefore no bar to this taking could be discerned on this ground.

The public use issue resolved itself in a manner remarkable only to those ignorant of the evisceration of the public use constraint in recent years. After rehearsing the refrain that public use is a use that concerns the whole community or promotes the general interest, but that it is "not essential that the entire community, or even any considerable portion thereof, shall directly enjoy or participate in an improvement," the court grudgingly acknowledged that no case anywhere has ever held that a municipality can acquire and operate a football team. Nevertheless Justice Richardson found sufficient analogy in other recreational purposes pursued by governments and upheld by courts to conclude that the "operation of a sports franchise may well be an appropriate municipal function." If government can acquire a baseball field in order to construct recreational facilities, employ eminent domain to take land for a county fair or to build an opera house, or take land for parking facilities at a stadium, why not this, the court wondered.

The ensuing passage in Justice Richardson's decision dramatically underscores my fear that the public use constraint as currently understood is nearly bankrupt. "A public use defies absolute definition," Richardson proceeds, quoting an earlier case, "for it changes with varying conditions of society . . . changing conceptions of the scope and functions of government." His next claim is even more troubling:

> While it is readily apparent that the power of eminent domain formerly may have been exercised only to serve traditional and limited public purposes, such as the construction and maintenance of streets, highways and parks, these limitations were not imposed by either constitutional or statutory fiat. Times change.[16]

What this implies is that once the conventional notions of judges change concerning the proper limits of government, constitutional provisions can be simply read into oblivion.

One member of the court, Chief Justice Rose Bird, entertained serious reservations about the wisdom of Oakland's action and the possible future ramifications of any holding that an organ of government has the power to take an ongoing business to prevent it from

[16]City of Oakland v. Oakland Raiders at 680.

leaving a locality. What particularly troubled her was not only the novelty of the court's interpretation of eminent domain principles but the potentiality for abuse of such a boundless power as the court propounded. If the city of Oakland were allowed to take the Oakland Raiders, then where could the line be drawn in the future? Thus,

> if a rock concert impresario, after some years of producing concerts in a municipal stadium, decides to move his production to another city, may the city condemn his business, including his contracts with the rock stars, in order to keep the concerts at the stadium? If a small business that rents a store-front on land originally taken by the city for a redevelopment project decides to move to another city in order to expand, may the city take the business and force it to stay at its original location? May a city condemn *any* business that decides to seek greener pastures elsewhere under the unlimited interpretation of eminent domain law that the majority appear to approve?[17]

These two cases proved providential, for the Supreme Court, in very short order, would put its seal of approval upon this trend toward reading the public use proviso out of the Bill of Rights.

IV. *Berman v. Parker* Comes to Fruition

The Hawaii Land Reform Act of 1967 sought to address the problem of a perceived shortage of fee simple residential land in the islands, with an attendant "artificial inflation of residential land values." The state legislature viewed the land pattern as imposing "financially disadvantageous" terms, restricting the freedom of those who wished to fully enjoy the land, and favoring the few landowners over the many.[18] The solution reached was ambitious. Homeowners who currently leased their land could invoke the aid of the Hawaii Housing Authority to take the land by eminent domain and then repurchase it at "fair market value" from the authority. When challenged by a large landholding trust, this taking provision was found not violative of the public use restriction of the Fifth Amendment by the United States District Court for the District of Hawaii. The United States Court of Appeals for the Ninth Circuit found otherwise, with the two-judge majority concluding that, as one of them wrote, "In my view, the Hawaii statute accomplishes . . . [an] invalid result, for if it does not constitute a transfer for the private use of another, that term can have no meaning."[19]

---

[17]Id. at 683, Justice Bird, dissenting, and concurring opinion.

[18]Hawaii Revised Statute, §§ 516–83.

[19]Midkiff v. Tom, 702 F. 2d 788, 805 (1983), Justice Poole's concurring opinion.

The case eventually found its way to the Supreme Court. Justice O'Connor, writing for a unanimous Court, began her analysis by rehearsing the Hawaii legislature's finding that as a heritage from Hawaii's early monarchial days of feudal land tenure, an oligopolistic pattern of landownership persisted in the islands. While the state and the federal government owned 49 percent of Hawaii's land, 47 percent was in the hands of a mere 72 private landowners. The eminent domain solution was adopted by the legislature, in preference to an alternative scheme that would have required landowners to sell to their lessees, because the landowners were leery of the federal tax consequences of outright sale. Indeed, the landowners maintained that these tax liabilities were the primary reason for their choice to lease instead of sell their land in the first place.

Berman v. Parker, not surprisingly, served as the starting point for O'Connor's analysis of whether the act violated the Fifth and Fourteenth amendments by falling afoul of the public use requirement. Here *Berman*'s confusion over police power versus eminent domain power, as I previously discussed, came to full fruition. In finding that no transgression of the public use proviso was triggered by the act, the Court's decision relied heavily upon that confusion. The Court's decision quoted extensively from Justice Douglas's remarks, particularly those equating an eminent domain case with "traditionally . . . a police power" issue and concluding that "Once the object is within the authority of Congress, the right to realize it through the exercise of eminent domain is clear." Deference to legislative judgments is also endorsed, in keeping with *Berman*.

The critical passage in the Court's decision, with its elliptical language but clearly discernible intent, is worth quoting in full:

> The "public use" requirement is thus coterminous with the scope of a sovereign's police power. There is, of course, a role for courts to play in reviewing a legislature's judgment of what constitutes a public use, even when the eminent domain power is equated with the police power. But the Court in *Berman* made clear that it is "an extremely narrow" one.[20]

The first sentence of this passage is perplexing. How can a limitation (that is, the public use requirement) be coterminous with a state's power to regulate (that is, the police power)? The remainder of the passage, however, makes the Court's meaning unmistakable. What the Court now contends is that the eminent domain power is as broad as the police power—that whatever legislatures can regulate, they can also take. This makes explicit what is still only implied

[20]Hawaii v. Midkiff at 240.

in *Berman*. Why is this so significant? Because if the police power is almost unlimited in its purview (as indeed it has been since the Court abandoned substantive due process in the late 1930s), then so is eminent domain. This, in effect, reads the public use clause as a limitation on government takings out of the Fifth Amendment. Following this reasoning, if a legislature determines that a public purpose is served by taking one individual's property and giving it to another, one would imagine that only the most blatant seizures, clothed in no public purpose language, would fail the Court's test. If the Court refuses to pierce the veil of an act's justificatory language and examine the substance of its public use claim, then the clear language of the Fifth Amendment means nothing. It is just such a strict scrutiny that the United States Court of Appeals for the Ninth Circuit was willing to undertake, and the Supreme Court was not. Their diametrically opposed conclusions, then, should come as no surprise.

The criticism of appeals court Justice Alarcon of the district court's analysis is just as pertinent a challenge to the subsequent reasoning of the high court:

> To hold ... that the public use limitation is subsumed under a "police power/due process analysis" ... would be to ignore the explicit language of the constitution and to disregard the fifth amendment protections granted to citizens of the states under the fourteenth amendment.[21]

By employing the much looser police power/due process test, under which an act need only be "rationally related to a conceivable public purpose," the Supreme Court had no difficulty upholding the Hawaii Land Reform Act. If regulating oligopolies is a legitimate exercise of the police power, and if willing buyers are unable to buy lots at "fair prices," then the Hawaii legislature's solution is a "comprehensive and rational approach to identifying and correcting market failure."[22] Whether the scheme holds out any likelihood of achieving its stated goals is not for the court to decide, said Justice O'Connor, repeating a refrain heard continuously since the late 1930s.

The reason why anyone other than a lawyer should care about *Hawaii v. Midkiff* is that by effectively neutralizing the public use limitation on government takings, the Supreme Court has opened

---

[21]Midkiff v. Tom at 799.

[22]Hawaii v. Midkiff at 242. But is this a case of market failure? As Justice O'Connor herself pointed out earlier, landowners had been dissuaded from selling their land because of government policy; that is, punitive federal tax liabilities. This hardly constitutes market failure, but rather suggests government failure.

the floodgates. Following this decision, would it be a legitimate exercise of eminent domain for a state to declare that it is a public purpose for tenants to own their apartments and then to condemn apartment houses and resell the units to their tenants? Evidently it would be legitimate, given suitable public purpose verbiage in the appropriate legislative act. Why not take a football franchise away from an owner who wants to move the team and transfer the team to a new owner?

And why should landowners lease their land when doing so could subject them to a forced sale to their tenants? This question should have given the Court pause, as it did one member of the appeals court. During the last 50 years, however, the Supreme Court has steadfastly refused to examine the cogency of legislative schemes. Now, in *Hawaii v. Midkiff*, the Court has extended its extremely loose standard of review of economic regulation under the due process clause to eminent domain proceedings. The Court has done so despite the explicit language of the Fifth Amendment: no "taking" without a public use. The modern Court has been leery of anything that may suggest the activist measures of the old Court of the early part of this century, a Court that struck down many regulatory measures as violations of the due process clause of the Fifth and Fourteenth amendments. Even if one endorses such judicial quiescence on property rights issues, which I do not, the eminent domain cases are different than due process adjudication. This is precisely because the takings clause of the Fifth Amendment is explicit in imposing limitations on takings, whereas the due process clause is much more nebulous, hence subject to judicial fads. The takings clause of the Fifth Amendment should not be so casually read out of the Constitution.

V. Conclusion

Will *Hawaii v. Midkiff* be another *Berman v. Parker* in the sense that the latter case has had such far-reaching effects in weakening constitutional protection for property rights? My expectation is that it probably will. An early harbinger comes from the California Supreme Court. In *Nash v. City of Santa Monica*, decided in October 1984, that court rejected the challenge to a rent control ordinance raised by a landlord. Nash objected to a portion of that ordinance which prohibits the removal of rental units from the market by demolition. He raised due process objections after the rent control board had denied him permission to demolish his building. His contention was that there must be a limit on the state's power to compel an individual to pursue a business against his will.

In rejecting Nash's contention, the court's majority opined that even if the rent control ordinance constrained the landlord's options—so that he only could escape his landlordly obligations by selling his property—he was no worse off than the landowners in *Hawaii v. Midkiff*. If it is permissible for a state to compel a sale of property from one private party to another, then what is wrong with constraining a landlord's options for the use of his property?

Just like *Berman*, *Hawaii v. Midkiff* seems to be spawning progeny in areas of the law beyond eminent domain, for this plaintiff raised due process, not a takings complaint. This does not bode well for the protection of property rights in the future.

INDEX OF CASES

General Index

Abolitionism, 140, 145–46
Abortion, 186, 211, 260, 266, 272
Ackerman, B. A., 225, 242–43
Administrative agencies. *See* Regulatory agencies
Administrative law, 228, 242
Administrative Procedures Act, 265
Adverse possession, 69
Advertising, 284–85
"Affirmative jurisprudence," 16–17
Agresto, John, 135n68
Alarcon, Ninth Cir. J., 371
Alchian, Armen A., 72n111, 79n140, 84n157
Alien and sedition laws, 114
Alienation, restraints on, 74
American Medical Association (AMA), 283, 285
American Revolution, 359
Anarchism, 192–93, 195
Ancillary Restraints Doctrine, 157
Anderson, Martin, 277
Annuity payments, 79–80
Anti-Federalists, 124
Antitrust law, 22, 71–74, 284; dual enforcement of, 295–97, 305; economic impact of, 73, 80, 176, 286, 292–98, 309–15; government economic regulation analogy, 164–67; interest group theory of government, 294–95; per se rules, 71, 73, 164, 253–54; and property rights, 157–63, 310–12; and public choice, 289–307; and public interest theory, 289, 302, 304–5; purpose of, 291–92; rule of reason, 72–73, 165; state-action immunity from, 101. *See also* Federal Trade Commission
Apportionment, 98
Aranson, Peter, 18, 47–110
Areeda, Philip, 304, 307
Aristotle, 184, 251
Armentano, D.T., 309, 312, 315
Arrow, Kenneth J., 226–27, 228
Asch, P., 292–93, 299
Assembly, freedom of, 125
Association, freedom of, 332–33

Assumption of risk, 235–36, 240

Bailyn, Bernard, 129n54, 190n32
Bain, J., 291, 299
Bandow, Doug, 21, 257–58
Bank secrecy, 321
Barber, Sotirios, 128
Barnett, Randy E., 20, 205–24
Base-point pricing, 73
Bastiat, Frederic, 5–6, 25–26
Bator, Paul, 189–90
Baxter, William F., 294, 299, 302, 306
Beale, Joseph H., 235, 243
"Beneficial use" theory, 67
Bentham, Jeremy, 227, 243
Berger, Raoul, 118, 187n16, 257, 277
Berlin, Isaiah, 193n39
Bernholz, Peter, 181
Bicameralism, 105
Bickel, Alexander, 120–21
Bill of Rights, xiv, xvi, 114, 122, 125–26, 137, 222; incorporation doctrine, 187; penumbras, 132. *See also specific amendments and clauses*
Bills of attainder, 123, 222
Bingham, John, 19, 137–38, 143–44, 145, 150
Bird, Rose, 273, 368–69
Black, Hugo L., 137, 168, 260, 361–62
Blackmun, Harry, 52n25
Blackstone, William, 129, 138–39, 141–42, 150
Boaz, David, 28
Bohlen, Francis, 236, 243
Boland, John C., 323n21, 324n23
Bork, Robert H., xix, 14, 26, 112–13, 115, 118, 120–21, 124, 126–27, 131–33, 134, 188n25, 291, 299, 312, 315
Bowles, Roger A., 247
Brandeis, Louis, 72n108
Brennan, William, xi–xiii, xvi–xix, 15–16, 66
Brozen, Yale, 309, 315

379

About the Editors

James A. Dorn received his Ph.D. in Economics from the University of Virginia. He is Editor of the *Cato Journal* and Associate Professor of Economics at Towson State University. He is also a Research Fellow of the Institute for Humane Studies at George Mason University and a member of the White House Commission on Presidential Scholars.

Henry G. Manne received his J.D. from the University of Chicago Law School and his J.S.D. from Yale Law School. He is Dean of the School of Law and Director of the Law and Economics Center at George Mason University. His popular economics institutes for law professors and federal judges have sparked widespread interest in the economic analysis of the law. Dean Manne has written or edited ten books and more than eighty articles.